Boom and Bust Again

*Policy Challenges for
a Commodity-Based Economy*

Edited by David L. Ryan

The University of Alberta Press

Published by
The University of Alberta Press
Ring House 2
Edmonton, Alberta, Canada T6G 2E1
www.uap.ualberta.ca

LIBRARY AND ARCHIVES CANADA CATALOGUING IN PUBLICATION

    Boom and bust again : policy challenges for a commodity-
based economy / David L. Ryan, editor.

Includes bibliographical references and index.
Issued in print and electronic formats.
ISBN 978-0-88864-628-6 (pbk.).— ISBN 978-0-88864-689-7 (pdf)

    1. Business cycles. 2. Business cycles—Alberta.
I. Ryan, David Leslie, 1954–, editor of compilation

HB3755.B66 2013   338.5'42   C2013-903355-6
                                                  C2013-903357-2

First edition, first printing, 2013.
Printed and bound in Canada by Friesens, Altona, Manitoba.
Copyediting and proofreading by Joanne Muzak.
Indexing by Adrian Mather.

The University of Alberta Press is committed to protecting our natural
environment. As part of our efforts, this book is printed on Enviro Paper: it
contains 100% post-consumer recycled fibres and is acid- and chlorine-free.

The University of Alberta Press gratefully acknowledges the support received
for its publishing program from The Canada Council for the Arts. The
University of Alberta Press also gratefully acknowledges the financial support
of the Government of Canada through the Canada Book Fund (CBF) and the
Government of Alberta through the Alberta Multimedia Development Fund
(AMDF) for its publishing activities.

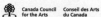

Canada   Canada Council Conseil des Arts   Alberta
                      for the Arts   du Canada   Government

To Bradford G. Reid, colleague, mentor, and friend.

Contents

Acknowledgements

1 Introduction   1
David L. Ryan

2 Bradford Reid   15
In Memoriam
David L. Ryan

3 Is There a Commodity Curse?   23
Lessons from the Past
John D. Murray

4 Three Strikes and You're Out?   39
The Inevitability of Resources Busts and its Challenges
for Alberta's Policy Makers
J.C. Herbert Emery and Ronald Kneebone

5 Output Instability in Resource-Based
and Diversified Economies   59
Alberta and Ontario
Bev Dahlby, Kathleen Macaspac, and Melville McMillan

6 I've Heard That Song Before   105
Harry James on Boom, Bust, and Diversification
Edward J. Chambers, Jason Brisbois, and Nicholas Emter

7 When Worlds Collide   133
Alberta Economic Diversification and Global Warming
Roger Gibbins

8   Savings of Non-renewable Resource Revenue   151
Why is it so Difficult? A Survey of Leaders' Opinions
Robert L. Ascah

9   Searching for Ropes and a Mast   199
How to Develop a Long-Term Plan for Alberta's Fiscal Future
Colin Busby

10   Government Revenue Volatility in Alberta   225
Stuart Landon and Constance Smith

11   Booms, Busts, and Gambling   267
Can Gaming Revenues Reduce Budget Volatility?
Brad R. Humphreys and Victor A. Matheson

12   Expenditure Management in Alberta   285
In Search of Stability
Al O'Brien

13   Alberta's Health Spending Challenge   301
Inter and Intraprovincial Differences in Health Expenditure
Stephen Duckett, Gordon Kramer, and Liesje Sarnecki

14   Bradford Reid's Mission   335
*The Practice and Promotion of Evidence-Based
Decision Making*
Alice O. Nakamura

Contributors   349

Index   355

Acknowledgements

An edited volume, such as this, relies crucially on the participation, patience, responsiveness, and goodwill of all the authors whose contributions are included. These were clearly abundant. Comments provided by anonymous reviewers of an earlier version helped improve exposition and organization. Still, a volume such as this would never see the light of day without comprehensive and effective copyediting, which was provided by Joanne Muzak. The result has been considerably improved by her often subtle modifications and/or suggestions.

Financial support that contributed to the publication of this volume, from the Institute for Public Economics, EPCOR Utilities Inc., and Alberta Treasury Board and Finance, is also gratefully acknowledged.

Introduction

David L. Ryan

Alberta is a province that is blessed with an abundance of non-renewable natural resources, including oil and natural gas. As world prices for these and other commodities, including agricultural commodities, fluctuate, Alberta's economy experiences a rollercoaster ride, with booms and subsequent busts. In the boom times, government revenues rise, employment conditions tighten, and both private and government spending generally tend to increase, often exacerbating labour market tightness and contributing to higher price inflation. The bust periods are often accompanied by various forms of belt-tightening, including government spending cutbacks, and in some cases salary rollbacks and various other austerity-type measures. When the boom of the 1980s ended and the subsequent bust set in, a common sight around Alberta was vehicle bumper stickers that (to put it politely) read, "Oh Lord, please grant us another boom. We

promise not to waste it all again." Clearly someone was listening
to at least the first part of this pleading: Alberta did experience
another boom, this time in the 2000s. Unfortunately, it appears
that not so much attention was paid to the second part, so that
what, to many, seems to be the inevitable bust followed. So far,
an equivalent set of bumper stickers has not resurfaced.

In fact, Alberta's economy had been characterized by boom-
and-bust cycles long before the discovery of vast deposits of
non-renewable resources; one of the first bust periods has been
identified with the collapse of agricultural prices in the 1930s.
For many observers, the major Alberta boom remains the period
associated with what were then peak oil prices in the 1980s,
with the subsequent bust being identified with the collapse of
those same oil prices in the mid-1980s. As the Alberta economy
accelerated in the 2000s, with the exploitation of vast oilsands
deposits, the question of whether it would be possible to some-
how try to manage the economy, to smooth the peaks and the
troughs, began to surface, although, in fact, discussion on this
very point had begun even as the bust of the mid-1980s set in.

Against this background, and as the latest bust set in, the
Institute for Public Economics, located in the Department of
Economics at the University of Alberta, decided in 2009 to hold
a conference to explore a wide range of issues associated with
the historical phenomenon of periods of boom and bust in the
Alberta economy, with a view also to their applicability in other
commodity-based economies. Such issues include diversification strategies, savings policy, energy and the environment, and
the challenges faced by government policy makers. The conference, with the same title as this volume, was held in May 2010
in Edmonton, Alberta, and was very well-attended by a mix of
politicians, government officials, business leaders, faculty, and
students. Papers were written for and presented at the conference by academics and non-academics, all with an interest in
policy analysis. The purpose of this volume is to provide much
of the material that was presented at that conference and thereby
to make it accessible to an even wider audience. Unfortunately,
not all authors who contributed and presented papers at the
conference were able to provide their papers for inclusion in

this volume, and it is not possible to reflect the input here that was provided directly by the discussants of each paper or that arose from the general discussion following each presentation. Nevertheless, 12 of the 15 main papers that were presented at the conference, as subsequently updated by their authors, are included here, so this volume represents the material that was presented, analyzed, and discussed.

The conference was held to honour the memory of Bradford Reid, a professor in the Department of Economics at the University of Alberta since 1981, and former director of the Institute for Public Economics, who died in 2009 after a lengthy battle with cancer. Several of the papers that are included here make reference to Brad and his contributions to the field of macroeconomics, particularly relating to fiscal policy and public debt management. A brief summary of Brad's research and research interests, as well as a listing of his publications, is provided in Chapter 2 of this volume. Brad's research on issues such as the size of government, the level of government spending, and the implications of alternative methods of financing such spending—including the extent to which different methods have differing effects on the economy—was and remains of relevance to everyone whose livelihood is affected by the upswings and downswings of the provincial economy and the nature and extent of governmental responses to these changes.

OVERVIEW OF CHAPTERS

The conference itself was organized around several themes, and the papers are included here in an order that at least roughly corresponds with those themes. The first paper, in Chapter 3, by John Murray, is based on an evening address at the conference that provides a general background to the boom and bust theme. Murray suggests that, while it is not likely to be possible to eliminate boom-and-bust cycles, there are lessons to be learned from past experience that can be used to dampen the effects of these cycles. He begins by placing Canada and Alberta in a wider global context, showing how they differ from other advanced

economies and other provinces respectively. He argues that
Canada and other commodity-based economies are subject to
serious economic challenges that are primarily linked to extreme
volatility in commodity prices. Although there is evidence
of long-run mean reversion in the average real price of most
commodities, often the price movements last long enough to convince investors and governments that this is no longer the case,
and various initiatives are undertaken as a result, often leading
to difficult corrections once conditions change. Policy makers
need to avoid making the situation worse and, in particular, to
learn from past mistakes. Murray identifies, among broader
policy lessons, the need for fiscal authorities to avoid behaving in
a procyclical manner as well as the need for the maintenance of
a disciplined monetary policy and structural reform. In Murray's
view, a comparison of the 1970s and 2000s suggests that we have
made encouraging steps in the right direction.

In Chapter 4, J.C. Herbert Emery and Ronald Kneebone provide some historical context for the booms and busts that have
been experienced in Alberta. Using a model based on economic
foundations, they show that resource booms cannot be the basis
of sustained rates of economic growth. Indeed, consistent with
the model, data show that Alberta's economic prosperity has only
ever temporarily grown relative to other provinces. However,
Emery and Kneebone argue that Alberta's governments have
adopted unsustainable fiscal policies based on a mistaken understanding of the implications of energy price booms. Rather than
recognizing the limited benefits of an economic boom built on
higher energy prices, and structuring a fiscal regime where the
large resource rents associated with a boom would be saved, successive Alberta governments have based Alberta's economic
success on a highly unlikely assumption of ever increasing
energy prices. As a result, Alberta continues to rely extensively
on volatile revenue to fund basic public services including health,
education, and social welfare.

The next two contributions deal with the theory and practice of economic growth and diversification. In Chapter 5, Bev
Dahlby, Kathleen Macaspac, and Melville McMillan address
issues concerning the economic instability of Alberta, due to

its reliance on natural resources, and whether economic diversification would be likely to reduce this instability. The authors
compare the economic stability of Alberta, a province particularly prone to resource-based instability, with Ontario, a province
generally considered to be well-diversified and relatively stable.
Interestingly, they find that by most measures, the degree of
instability of the Alberta economy has diminished over the past
15 to 20 years, so that the most recent energy boom had relatively
less impact than the previous one. In addition, they find some
indications that economic instability in Ontario has increased.
Using a portfolio variance model to examine the structural
sources of output instability, and a volatility index to calculate the
contribution of changes in the industrial mix to volatility for the
period 1984–2003, they find evidence of a strong positive relationship between resource-based specialization and changes in
output volatility in Alberta. Since the early 1990s, there has been
a steady decline in the size of the volatility index that parallels
a decline in the relative size of the oil and gas sector. In contrast, Ontario experienced a rise in the volatility index that can
be traced largely to the relatively high volatility of its two largest
sectors, manufacturing and finance. As a result, measures of economic instability in Alberta and Ontario have tended to converge
over the period to 2003, so that Ontario's industrial mix does not
appear to provide the stability that it once did and the resource
dependence of the Alberta economy appears to be diminishing
along with economic instability.

Chapter 6 by Edward Chambers, Jason Brisbois, and
Nicholas Emter addresses the meaning of diversification in
a non-renewable resource-based economy. Beginning with
some historical background, the authors provide an overview
of the policies and actions of successive Alberta governments
since 1970 in pursuing economic development and greater
diversification. Next, the authors examine how Australia and
Malaysia—other commodity-producing jurisdictions with
highly specialized economies—have pursued further development through diversification. They argue that the key for
jurisdictions that have been most successful in diversification
and development efforts is the consistent application of strategies

over prolonged periods. Turning to Alberta, the authors apply a portfolio analysis to quarterly employment data since 1976, using changes in Alberta risk–reward ratios—employment stability relative to employment growth—as evidence of diversification. Their results provide strong evidence of a more diversified Alberta economy over the past four decades, in terms of a reduction in this risk–reward ratio. However, when they view diversification in a more comprehensive framework, where measures of economic performance including output, income, and labour productivity are considered, the picture is not so clear.

Roger Gibbins, in Chapter 7, also considers the issue of diversification of the economy, but from a somewhat different perspective. Based on the commonly expressed viewpoint that Alberta needs to both lessen its dependence on natural resources and their inherently volatile markets and reduce its carbon footprint in an era of concerns with global warming, and the belief that these goals can best be achieved through greater economic diversification, he asks what it is we should be doing if we were to (further) diversify. Based on Canada's (and, in particular, Alberta's) comparative advantage continuing to lie with natural resources, but with pressure from global warming concerns also continuing, Gibbins considers a variety of proactive strategic options that might be adopted. These range from investing in the building blocks of a knowledge economy to leading a new energy economy, moving up the value chain, and market diversification. While all these strategies have some potential, the author argues that they all point to significant obstacles, and none build upon Alberta's existing competitive advantages that stem from a resource-based, trade-dependent economy. An alternative that he recommends is to do better what we already do well, that is, conventional resource extraction in a way that meets policy expectations in a carbon-constrained world. Such a strategy would, he points out, require saving a greater part of today's resource wealth in order to build a foundation for future prosperity through very substantial public investments.

The two subsequent chapters are concerned with saving for the future. In Chapter 8, Robert Ascah asks why saving for the future is such a difficult task. Using information gleaned from budgets and other government documents, as well as from interviews with leaders in government—elected officials and senior non-elected officials—as well as party officials and business leaders, Ascah presents a wonderful history of expenditures and net financial assets in Alberta since 1945, overlaying each with details of the government that was in power at the time and their policies. He identifies five phases in Alberta's savings/debt repayment story: debt pay-down between 1945 and 1971; buildup and home bias between 1972 and 1986; decline in savings/increase in debt between 1986 and 1993; debt pay-down from 1995 to 2004; and, finally, situational savings starting in 2005, which is a period that includes substantial endowment investments. The interviews, which were designed to provide qualitative information concerning difficulties inherent in saving resource revenue, identify such issues as volatility of resource revenue, intergovernmental relations, and public pressure on governments, as well as difficulties communicating abstract concepts to the public, and political philosophy. The chapter concludes with recommendations concerning how the missteps of history, and in particular Alberta's apparent inability to prevent the deterioration of fiscal strength, might be avoided in the future. In this regard, the author floats some interesting ideas pertaining to consideration of term limits for government leaders, or possible legislation, enacted via a referendum of Alberta citizens, that would bind politicians' hands to a decision rule that they could not readily change except through recourse to a subsequent referendum.

In Chapter 9, Colin Busby focuses on the need to save resource revenues in order to ensure intergenerational equity, that is, to maintain the benefits of a finite resource bounty for future generations. Since non-renewable resources are finite, extracting and selling them for cash represents a conversion from physical to financial wealth. Therefore, Busby argues, natural resource revenues should be managed as assets, and not treated as annual income. In addition, dependence on resource revenues entrenches unsustainable spending levels. The author focuses on the primary non-resource deficit, the difference between non-resource revenues and primary program expenditures, which is a key indicator of long-run fiscal sustainability as its negative value represents the annual drawdown on resource wealth needed to bring the budget back to balance. Busby recommends that the level of this deficit should be determined to achieve an outcome that is equitable across generations, in other words, so that each generation has the same annual spending, in today's dollars, from resource wealth. This outcome, he argues, might best be achieved by specifying a constant annual amount per capita. The basic assumptions underlying such a plan are spelled out, and sensitivity of the results to variations in these assumptions is examined. The need for a plan to adjust to such a regime is identified, along with options for providing flexibility by revisiting the plan periodically. Various implementation challenges are also discussed.

Stuart Landon and Constance Smith's work in Chapter 10 is the first of two chapters that focus on the revenue side of the equation. The Alberta government is heavily exposed to energy price volatility as it relies to a great extent on revenue derived from the production of oil and natural gas. Energy prices change substantially and unpredictably, causing large and uncertain movements in revenues, and adjusting to these movements typically involves economic, social, and political costs. The authors demonstrate that Alberta government revenues are considerably more volatile than the revenues of other provinces, but that Alberta's own-source revenues excluding royalty payments are of similar size and volatility as in other provinces. In their chapter, the authors assess several methods for reducing the volatility of revenues. An often-suggested method, tax base diversification (for example, use of a retail sales tax), is shown to have a minor effect on overall revenue volatility because Alberta's royalty revenues are such a large share of total own-source revenues. An alternative method, revenue smoothing using futures and options markets, can be expensive, is associated with significant political risks, and cannot eliminate all revenue volatility. Further, the Canadian dollar tends to appreciate when energy prices rise and depreciate when energy prices fall, so exchange rate movements have smoothed Alberta government revenues, although not by a large amount. A simulation by Landon and Smith using Alberta data shows that, in contrast, a revenue savings fund could significantly reduce revenue volatility. This type of fund leads to greater revenue stability because the revenue it contributes to the budget in any particular year is based on revenues *averaged* over prior years. Revenue uncertainty is also reduced with a savings fund since future revenue depends on known past contributions.

Brad Humphreys and Victor Matheson take a different approach to the revenue question in Chapter 11 by considering the role of revenues from gambling as an alternative source of government revenues that may have some potential to reduce overall revenue volatility. The authors begin by providing a brief history of legal gambling in Canada and the United States and summarize the advantages and drawbacks of legal gambling as a source of government tax revenue. Using data from Canadian provinces as well as US states and jurisdictions from 1989 to 2009, the contributions that gambling revenues make to state and provincial tax receipts are documented. The authors use the relationship between the return on an individual stock—which they take to be the percentage change in a jurisdiction's revenues from a particular revenue source—to the total return in a portfolio—the percentage change in that jurisdiction's total own-source revenues—to investigate the extent to which variation in gambling revenues contributes to the volatility of tax revenues over time. Their estimates reveal wide variation across provinces and states in terms of the variability over time in different sources of revenue, but while income taxes, general sales taxes, and general property taxes tend to exhibit positive co-movements with total own-source revenues, a different result is found for some other revenue sources, including remitted gaming profits. Specifically, in six of ten provinces, but not including Alberta, revenues from gaming increase when total own-source revenues decrease, so that gaming revenues contribute to stability in total own-source revenues over time. However, remitted gaming profits represent only a small fraction of own-source revenues, so that the extent to which revenues from this source can offset variation over time in own-source revenues, particularly in Alberta, is quite limited.

In Chapter 12, Al O'Brien writes about the search for stability concerning expenditure management in Alberta. In this first of two chapters concerned with expenditures, O'Brien considers the variety of policy measures and fiscal frameworks that have been adopted in Alberta over the past 35 years. These include savings rules, the Heritage Savings Trust Fund, legislated spending limits, revenue budgeting, deficit and debt repayment rules, and the establishment of a stabilization fund, a capital fund, and various research endowments. The author describes the extent of the success that each of these measures achieved in stabilizing provincial spending and also considers whether expenditure stabilization is either feasible or desirable for Alberta. O'Brien concludes that the most important rule in governing Alberta's spending patterns is that "revenue creates spending"; legislated fiscal rules are no panacea for addressing fiscal challenges inherent in a resource-dependent economy, with both political leadership and public consensus being critical to success in meeting these challenges. He views a stable and sustainable tax structure and greater stability in capital planning and investment as key components of a long-term sustainable fiscal policy that recognizes the finite nature of Alberta's resource wealth. However, the lessons from past experience suggest that this cannot be achieved simply by passing legislation to enforce savings or budgetary rules—it needs the understanding and support of the public and key stakeholders, which in turn requires simple and open communication of public policy issues and options. In particular, O'Brien argues that consistent treatment of capital spending, depreciation, and operating surpluses or deficits in the province's budgets and financial reports would make a significant contribution to the simplicity and transparency of provincial fiscal planning and expenditure management, and that the distinctions between "revenues for fiscal plan purposes" and "revenues for financial statement purposes" and between "liabilities for fiscal planning purposes" and liabilities in general need to be eliminated.

While few might dispute O'Brien's observation that "revenue creates spending," particularly in the Alberta context, it is much more difficult to figure out in practical terms exactly what to do about it. It is all very well to recommend savings funds and better capital planning and investment, as several authors have done, in order to potentially soften or smooth out at least some aspects of the boom-and-bust cycles. However, implementing such recommendations will typically involve reducing spending below what many (but not all) regard as the unsustainable levels that it attains during boom periods when revenues are flowing more freely. And even if the specific recommendations do not involve decreasing such spending outright, but "merely" slowing its rate of increase, this will still typically involve a loss of services that may have been provided as a result of the increased funding, services that may now be viewed as "crucial" and that require ever increasing funds just so they can be maintained. A particular example of this is spending on health care.

It seems that almost everybody knows, either directly or anecdotally, about someone who seems to be waiting an unreasonably long time in a queue for some health care related procedure. Given this, it is reasonable to ask how a government could possibly consider spending less on health care simply to alleviate some of the perceived concerns with boom-and-bust cycles. To even start to address this question is akin to walking through a minefield, as some topics, and spending areas, seem virtually untouchable. Yet, with the majority of Alberta government expenditures being allocated to key areas like health and education, these types of questions need to be addressed if any serious attempt is to be made to start saving more as a means of addressing some of the boom and bust associated problems. In particular, one of the key questions that need to be asked is whether we are getting a good "bang for the buck" for spending in these areas. If not, then perhaps there is more scope for reducing spending (but possibly spending smarter) in these apparently untouchable areas than has previously been recognized.

With this in mind, the second chapter that focuses on expenditure, Chapter 13 by Stephen Duckett, Gordon Kramer, and Liesje Sarnecki, deals specifically with Alberta's health expenditures, comparing their levels and growth in specific areas with health outcomes and comparable expenditures in other provinces, and examining differences in these expenditures within

Alberta. Standardizing for certain exogenous factors by focusing on real per capita expenditures adjusted for age and gender differences, the authors examine trends in expenditures on hospitals, other institutions, capital expenditures, physician expenditure, and public health expenditure. While health expenditure has been increasing in all Canadian provinces between 1996 and 2008, over this period Alberta's total health expenditure per capita increased from a level roughly similar to other Canadian provinces to a level that identifies it as a high-spending outlier. However, the extent of this increase differs across different types of expenditures—Alberta's spending choices resulted in substantial increases in expenditure in some areas (for example, hospitals) but lower rates of growth or even disinvestment in others (for example, other institutions such as seniors' accommodation). The authors examine the impact of these higher relative expenditures on activity, to try to disentangle the effects of increased volume of services and higher unit costs, and on access and quality, in an attempt to determine if Alberta's higher spending is associated with improvements in either of these dimensions of health care. To the extent it can be measured, the authors find that Alberta's higher level of spending was associated with higher utilization, higher unit prices, and higher factor prices. But the benefit of the higher spending did not translate into better relative performance on access measures (such as waiting times). Comparative performance on quality measures was mixed.

These findings of course only pertain to health care spending, and there are many other areas where the potential for spending cuts might be investigated. But such investigations require information, as do any subsequent recommendations for and implementations of specific actions. Particularly in terms of the latter, as several authors here point out, one of the requirements is an effective communication strategy, a strategy that is convincing to the public and key stakeholders in terms of public policy issues and options. Of course, such communication also relies crucially on the availability of information. This brings us to the final chapter in this volume, Chapter 14 by Alice Nakamura, which provides a summary of the preceding chapters in the context of the more general issue of evidence-based decision making. Specifically, she notes that the various authors' contributions advance evidence-based decision making in one or both of two ways: as additions to the policy-relevant empirical economics literature for Canada, or as helpful contributions to the cause of improving the data available for policy-relevant research and decision making in Canada. Nakamura then asks why evidence-based decision making does not appear to be more the norm in Canadian public affairs, speculating that this may in part be due to limited availability of suitable statistical evidence. Focusing on the post-conference issue concerning Statistics Canada and the abolition of the mandatory long-form census in Canada, Nakamura identifies the urgent need for reforms to protect the information that Canadians need in order to be able to practice evidence-based decision making. Protecting the data sources Canada has had, she argues, is an important component of helping to ensure a bright future for evidence-based decision making in Canada.

Taken together, the chapters in this volume collectively contribute to analysis, understanding, and policy prescriptions associated with the boom and bust phenomenon that is frequently observed in commodity-based economies. Written primarily in the context of Alberta, but with the general focus being much broader, they address the nature of the economy's dependence on the resource sector, the past and expected continuing volatility of natural resource prices, issues related to diversification of the economy, and challenges associated with limiting spending increases and generating savings in such an environment. It would be overly brave to claim that the solutions to the attendant problems of boom-and-bust economies are provided here. In any event, many aspects of the recommendations that are made may be judged to be politically unappealing. But even if they are cast in such a light, there is surely something to be said for knowledge of not just how the boom-and-bust problems arose and why they may continue to arise, but also of the mistakes, sometimes exacerbating ones, that have been made in response to various booms and busts in the past. In addition to contributing such knowledge, the work in this volume also suggests how these mistakes might be avoided and how boom-and-bust issues might be effectively addressed on an ongoing basis.

Bradford Reid

In Memoriam

David L. Ryan

This volume and the conference on which it was based honour the memory of Bradford Reid, associate professor of economics, former chair of the Department of Economics at the University of Alberta, and former director of the Institute for Public Economics, who died in January 2009 after a long and courageous battle with cancer.

It may seem at first surprising that anything with the title "Boom and Bust Again: Policy Challenges for a Commodity-Based Economy" would be the vehicle used to honour Brad's memory. To understand its appropriateness, it is necessary to know a little about Brad. This short note provides a summary of Brad's career in economics, then gives some additional background on Brad and his economic interests, and finally explains why this volume is an appropriate tribute to him.

Born in Saskatchewan, Brad obtained a bachelor of commerce from the University of Saskatchewan prior to completing a master's degree in economics at the University of Alberta in 1977. After obtaining a PHD in economics from the University of Toronto, he returned to a teaching position in the Department of Economics at the University of Alberta in 1981 and remained there throughout his academic career. Brad taught macro-economics, as well as monetary theory. In more recent years, he created and taught a popular course on the economics of professional sport. Brad was a superb teacher, but also a demanding one, as many students—especially those who thought that any course with the words "sports economics" in its title must be a soft option—discovered.

Brad's research focused predominantly on macroeconomics and public economics, and he published in several edited volumes as well as articles in a wide variety of international journals, including *Journal of Macroeconomics, Journal of Monetary Economics, The Review of Economics and Statistics, Economic Inquiry, Canadian Journal of Economics,* and *Public Choice.* Brad was particularly interested in issues concerned with the size of government, the level of government spending, and the implications of alternative methods of financing such spending, including the extent to which different methods have differing effects on the economy.

In addition to his excellence in research and teaching, Brad devoted much of his time to professional and administrative activities. As well as roles as chair of the department from 1999 to 2004, and associate chair from 1993 to 1997, Brad also supervised many MA and PHD students, acted as a referee for a number of prestigious journals, was associate editor of *Canadian Public Policy* from 1986 to 1990, and was very active in the Institute for Public Economics, including a term as director between 2003 and 2006. He also served for one year as president of the University of Alberta's Faculty Club.

Brad's medical issues surfaced in early 2006, and he spent much of his remaining time on medical and, subsequently, disability leaves. Regrettably, this prevented many students from experiencing his booming lectures (there was no provision for dozing off in Brad's classes), his subtle sense of humour, but more importantly, his passion for ensuring that students (and colleagues!) understood the forces and particularly the incentives that underlie economic decisions. Brad retained his good spirits and interest in public affairs through most of this period, and he shared his insights on a wide variety of topics at periodic off-campus lunches with some of his colleagues.

As a macroeconomist who had spent many years teaching and writing about how and why Keynesian-type solutions were unlikely to work effectively and who believed very strongly in the power of market forces, Brad was more than a little bemused by the recent rush by governments to apparently, and in his words, forget all the lessons that had been learned in this field in the past 20 years, and attempt to spend their way out of the current recession. It is only fitting, therefore, that this volume is dedicated to the memory of Brad and his many contributions.

Although Brad was a macroeconomist, his interests were much too extensive to be summarized so easily. As I've mentioned earlier, he also researched and taught in the fields of monetary economics and public economics. While Brad's interests and contributions in these three fields in themselves might be enough to explain the link between Brad and the topic of this volume, a very brief and selective look at his publications, which are listed at the end of this note, is even more informative.

In 1977, Brad, then an MA student in the Department of Economics at the University of Alberta, wrote his MA thesis (back in the days when MA students in economics wrote theses) on "Aircraft Noise and Residential Property Values," specifically examining the case of the municipal airport in Edmonton. By the time part of this work was published in the journal *Land Economics* (McMillan, Norrie, and Reid 1980), Brad had moved on to his PHD thesis, "Government Debts and Economic Activity: Empirical Evidence on the Ricardian Equivalence Hypothesis," which he completed at the University of Toronto in 1983. To use Brad's words, this hypothesis "maintains that when individual economic agents correctly anticipate and capitalize the future tax liabilities associated with the issuance of government debt then deficit financing is equivalent to tax financing and substitution between these two revenue-generating instruments may have no impact on the level or composition of aggregate demand"

(Reid 1983). Brad subsequently published several papers concerning empirical evaluation of aspects of the Ricardian equivalence hypothesis, particularly the strict debt neutrality hypothesis that holds that current deficits have little or no effect on current consumption decisions, so that government decisions of whether to finance their expenditures through taxation or deficits will have equivalent aggregate impacts. It is obviously exceptionally unfair to quote selectively from a body of work like this, produced over many years, using different methodologies and data sets, without putting the quotes in their proper context, and obviously without the ability to offer the author an opportunity to provide what would have no doubt been a measured and quite clear response. However, some very brief excerpts from his papers on this topic (with emphasis added) may help explain a little about Brad and how he was a true academic, one who would let the data tell the story it had to tell, rather than selectively choosing results that supported a particular position he might have wished to advance.

> The empirical evidence generated in this paper [involving separating permanent and transitory income flows] *rejects* the strict debt neutrality proposition of the Ricardian Equivalence Hypothesis (Reid 1985a, 475).
>
> The empirical evidence generated by this investigation [involving tests of Granger causality between the stock of money and the flow of income] *does not support* the strict debt neutrality position [of the Ricardian Equivalence Hypothesis] (Reid 1985b, 321).
>
> The evidence generated by this analysis [pooling data for different provinces] *does not support* the strict neutrality proposition [of the Ricardian Equivalence Hypothesis] (Reid 1989, 121).
>
> The empirical results we obtain [from an examination of the relationship between the term structure of asset returns and macroeconomic policy variables] *are consistent with* the debt neutrality proposition of the Ricardian Equivalence Hypothesis (Boothe and Reid 1989, 65).

Many people have heard stories about putting two economists in a room and obtaining three divergent opinions. As the above quotes show, in some cases varying opinions on the same topic can be obtained from just one economist. Non-economists might argue that this shows why economics and/or economists in general are not useful or perhaps are not to be trusted, but most economists would point out the opposite. The field of economics is about understanding the forces that underlie economic decisions and actions, not about pushing a particular ideology, and the more you learn and understand about a topic, the better able you are to analyze it, determine the likely implications of certain actions, and reach conclusions. Brad was a master of this approach. He was interested in many, and perhaps even almost all, questions in economics (including some questions that non-economists might argue lie well outside the realm of economics), and rather than push a particular viewpoint, he sought ways to investigate these issues by assembling and analyzing appropriate data using various economic models. Many of his publications, listed at the end of this article, reflect these widespread interests.

Yet, the titles of his publications alone are insufficient to reveal the wide extent of Brad's interests and intuition, which in many cases, due to his general reluctance to seek the spotlight, was only evident to those who came to know Brad very well, or in some cases, to students in some of his classes. Brad had an incredible ability to apply economic analysis to almost any problem, and he had outstanding economic intuition. As I think most economists would agree (and that's a brave statement in itself), probably the two key concepts to understanding economic problems are opportunity costs (what you give up when you take a particular action) and incentive-induced behaviour, or more specifically, the (usually unintended) incentives implicit in particular actions, and the behaviour that these are likely to induce. Brad was keenly interested in these aspects of economic behaviour, and he had the ability to seemingly instantly determine these components of almost any suggested action, although in reality his observations were based on a good deal of thought and economic analysis and intuition. As a result, he tended to have very strong views, but also exceptionally well-argued views, on such issues as (to name just a few) the use of public funds to construct downtown sports arenas, the provision of expensive public transit (especially LRT), public versus private provision of health services, increasing spending on health, the so-called P3 development model (public–private partnerships), determination of electoral boundaries, and, perhaps of most relevance here, appropriate levels of government spending and methods of raising revenue in a resource-based economy.

To return to the theme of this book, it seems appropriate to consider some quotes selected from the conclusion of Brad's article with André Plourde on the topic of natural resource revenues and the Alberta budget (Plourde and Reid 2002).

> Since the late 1980s...natural resource revenues are less important as a share of total provincial government revenues, and thus as a vehicle for financing expenditures (22).
>
> Recent budgetary experience generates some concern regarding the viability of the government's current budgeting rules (22).
>
> There is some reason to be concerned that program expenditure growth coupled with the reductions in personal income taxes may have created a situation where the antideficit rule is no longer sustainable during an economic downturn or a significant resource price decline (23).
>
> Apart from...short-run budgeting considerations, there are reasons for concern about the ability to generate fiscal surpluses in the medium to long run (23).

And finally,

> These potential developments...generate concerns regarding the ability of Alberta's non-renewable natural resource sector to continue to provide revenues large enough to sustain the kinds of large budgetary surpluses that have been realized in the recent past (23).

Quotes like these, from 2002, with the experience of previous boom-and-bust cycles behind us, and with the latest boom well under way, certainly appear to provide an appropriate backdrop to and indeed motivation for the subject matter of this volume.

Brad's research on issues concerned with the size of government, the level of government spending, and the implications of alternative methods of financing such spending—including the extent to which different methods have differing effects on the economy—was and remains of relevance to everyone whose livelihood is affected by the upswings and downswings of the provincial economy and the nature and extent of governmental responses to these changes. I think he would have been greatly interested in the presentations and discussions that took place over the one and a half days of the conference and that are preserved in this volume. It is to our detriment that he could not have added what would have been informed and incisive commentary.

Publications by Bradford G. Reid

Boothe, Paul M., and Bradford G. Reid. 1986. "The Market Value and Maturity Structure of Government of Canada Debt, 1967–83." *Canadian Journal of Economics* 19 (3): 443–68.

———. 1989. "Asset Returns and Government Budgets in a Small Open Economy." *Journal of Monetary Economics* 23: 65–77.

———. 1992. "Debt Management Objectives for a Small Open Economy." *Journal of Money, Credit, and Banking* 24 (1): 43–60.

———. 1993. "An Overview of Canadian Fiscal Federalism: Current issues and Prospects for Reform." Information Bulletin #19. Edmonton: Western Centre for Economic Research, University of Alberta.

———. 1998a. "Credibility, Flexibility and Risk: Designing Balanced Budget Rules." *Policy Options* 19 (1): 16–18.

———. 1998b. "Fiscal Prudence and Federal Budgeting in the Medium Term." In *Fiscal Targets and Economic Growth*, edited by T. Courchene and T. Wilson, 240–65. Kingston, ON: John Deutsch Institute for the Study of Economic Policy.

———. 2001. Introduction to *Deficit Reduction in the Far West: The Great Experiment*, edited by Paul M. Boothe and Bradford G. Reid, vii–xiii. Edmonton: University of Alberta Press.

———, eds. 2001. *Deficit Reduction in the Far West: The Great Experiment*. Edmonton: University of Alberta Press.

Landon, Stuart K., and Bradford G. Reid. 1990. "Government Deficits and Money Growth." *Review of Economics and Statistics* 72 (3): 382–89.

———. 2005. "The Impact of the Centralization of Revenues and Expenditures on Growth, Regional Inequality and Inequality." Working Paper 2005(4), Institute of Intergovernmental Relations, Queen's University.

Lucas, Robert F., and Bradford G. Reid. 1991. "The Choice of Efficient Monetary Arrangements in the Post Meech Lake Era." *Canadian Public Policy* 17 (4): 417–33.

McMillan, Melville, Kenneth Norrie, and Bradford G. Reid. 1994. "Canada and Quebec in a New World: The PQ's Economic Proposals." *Constitutional Forum* 6 (1): 11–18.

McMillan, Melville L., Bradford G. Reid, and David W. Gillen. 1980. "An Extension of the Hedonic Approach for Estimating the Value of Quiet." *Land Economics* 56 (3): 315–28.

- Plourde, André, and Bradford G. Reid. 2002. "Natural Resource Revenues and the Alberta Budget." In *Alberta's Volatile Government Revenues: Policies for the Long Run*, edited by L.S. Wilson, 3–24. Edmonton: Institute for Public Economics, University of Alberta.

Reid, Bradford G. 1977. "Aircraft Noise and Residential Property Values: Hedonic Estimates of the Costs of Aircraft Noise in the City of Edmonton." MA thesis, Department of Economics, University of Alberta.

———. 1982. "The Effect of the Changing Size and Composition of Government Purchases on Potential Output: A Comment." *Review of Economics and Statistics* 64 (3): 525–27.

———. 1983. "Government Deficits and Economic Activity: Empirical Evidence on the Ricardian Equivalence Hypothesis." PHD diss., Department of Economics, University of Toronto.

———. 1985a. "Aggregate Consumption and Deficit Financing: An Attempt to Separate Permanent from Transitory Effects." *Economic Inquiry* 23: 475–86.

———. 1985b. "Government Debt, National Income and Causality." *Applied Economics* 17 (2): 321–30.

———. 1989. "Government Budgets and Aggregate Consumption: Cross-Sectional Evidence from Canadian Provincial Data." *Journal of Macroeconomics* 11 (1): 121–32.

———. 1998. "Endogenous Elections, Electoral Budget Cycles and Canadian Provincial Governments." *Public Choice* 97: 35–48.

———. 2001. "Provincial Fiscal Positions: A Historical Perspective." In *Deficit Reduction in the Far West: The Great Experiment*, edited by Paul M. Boothe and Bradford G. Reid, 89–109. Edmonton: University of Alberta Press.

———. 2003. "Fiscal Management and Stabilization Policy in Federal Systems: The Experience of Argentina and Mexico." In *Fiscal Relations in Federal Countries: Four Essays*, edited by Paul M. Boothe, 41–51. Ottawa: Forum of Federations.

Reid, Bradford, and Tracy Snoddon. 1992. "Redistribution under Alternative Constitutional Arrangements for Canada." In *Alberta and the Economics of Constitutional Change*, edited by Paul M. Boothe, 65–105. Edmonton: University of Alberta Press.

Is There a Commodity Curse?

Lessons from the Past

John D. Murray

INTRODUCTION

As the title of the collection suggests, we have seen many boom-and-bust cycles in the commodity sector. This raises one obvious and central question: How can we avoid them in the future? More specifically, how can Canada and Alberta get out of this seemingly endless cycle of feast or famine? The answer, regrettably, is that it isn't possible to eliminate the cycle entirely. The best that we can hope to do is to dampen its effects by learning from past experience. History, it has been said, is a good teacher, but policy makers are not always good students. In what follows, I review some of this history, in the context of the importance of natural resources to the Canadian economy and the evolution of commodity prices, and present a few thoughts on how we, as policy makers, might make better use of these sometimes painful lessons.

ALBERTA AND CANADA ARE DIFFERENT
FROM THE REST

Canada's economy is different from most other advanced economies. Primary commodities—resources—account for a much
larger share of our national gross domestic product (GDP). The
estimated size of the sector varies according to how it is defined,
but using a reasonably conservative approach, and based on
Statistics Canada data, one finds that resource production represents about 10% of Canada's GDP, 5% of total employment, and
45% of export sales. The share of resource production in US GDP,
by comparison, is only 5%. Canada is a large net exporter of raw
materials, unlike the United States, which is a large net importer.
In this respect, the United States is similar to most other
advanced economies. On the other hand, as Figure 3.1 shows,
countries such as Canada, Australia, and Norway (not shown),
are the exceptions.

Alberta is also different when compared with most—but
not all—of the nine other provinces in Canada. In 2006, the
last year for which Statistics Canada has comparable figures,
resources accounted for roughly 32% of Alberta's GDP. This was
lower than the figure for Newfoundland and Labrador (at 40%)
and only slightly higher than that for Saskatchewan (at 29%). But
as Figure 3.2 shows, it was far above that of the other provinces.
In British Columbia, for example, natural resources accounted
for less than 10% of GDP, while in Ontario—not surprisingly—
it was barely 2%. The bottom line, simply stated, is that Canada
is different, and Alberta is more different still, from many of its
counterparts.

SPECIAL CHALLENGES OF
A COMMODITY-BASED ECONOMY

Canada's natural resources are a tremendous gift. They have
brought us enormous material benefits—higher incomes and
greater economic security than in many other countries. Most
other countries would gladly trade places with us, should we ever

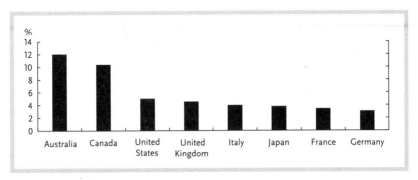

FIGURE 3.1 Natural Resources as a Percentage of GDP

Source: World Bank World Development Indicators

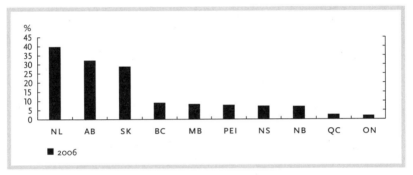

FIGURE 3.2 Natural Resources as a Percentage of Provincial GDP

Source: Statistics Canada

grow tired of our rich resource endowment. Indeed, there are probably several provinces that would gladly trade places with Alberta.

This isn't to say that being a commodity-based economy is problem free. In fact, this collection is largely about the problems or, more positively, the challenges that our dependence on commodities sometimes creates. Some economists have gone so far as to say that there is a "commodity curse."[1] They suggest that rich resource endowments are actually inimical to economic development. Comparing the experiences of a large set of countries, they observe that commodity-based economies tend, on average, to have slightly lower growth rates, as well as lower income levels, than their resource-poor counterparts (see Figure 3.3).

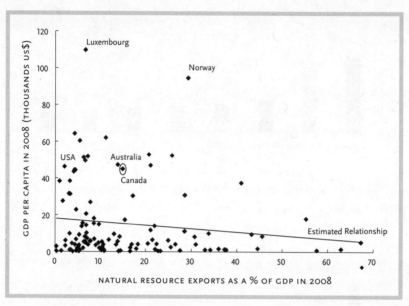

FIGURE 3.3 Is There a Commodity Curse?

Source: World Bank

Before becoming overly concerned or taking strong objection to this claim, I should add that the statistical relationship shown in Figure 3.3 is rather weak and is dominated by the results for a large number of developing countries, for which the conservatorship of their resources has proven to be more of a challenge. The evidence for advanced resource-producing countries, such as Canada, is typically much more positive. Once again, Canada is an exception.

The reasons that have been put forward by way of explaining the so-called commodity curse have both a political and an economic dimension. Researchers have found that many countries with rich resource endowments suffer from weak governance and a democratic deficit. The governments are often despotic, and the countries prone to armed conflict and civil unrest. Property rights aren't respected, and institutional arrangements are weak.

This, obviously, is not an accurate characterization of countries like Canada, Australia, New Zealand, and Norway. Nevertheless, Canada and all other commodity-based countries are subject to serious *economic* challenges, linked primarily to the extreme volatility of commodity prices.

THE LONG AND SHORT OF PRICE VOLATILITY

Some countries are large enough commodity producers (or consumers) that their actions can materially influence global commodity prices. Saudi Arabia might be an example. But these are certainly the exception. For the most part, commodity producers are price takers. They sell a fairly homogeneous product in a highly competitive market, and their actions have little effect on the price that they receive.

Unfortunately, for countries like Canada and provinces like Alberta, these prices are typically volatile and highly uncertain. This volatility is caused, in large part, by the unusual nature of the short-run demand and supply curves associated with most commodity markets. The products that commodity-based economies sell typically have extremely low short-run demand elasticities (i.e., demand is not very responsive to price changes). Supply is similarly inelastic, since it often takes time to bring new production online if prices suddenly rise, or to reduce production if prices suddenly drop.[2] Any move in either of these curves, therefore, is likely to lead to outsized changes in global prices.

As shown in Figure 3.4, this erratic behaviour is evident in the movement of most commodity prices through time. Commodity prices are typically much more volatile than those of other goods or services—and one of the most volatile commodity prices of all is that of oil (Figure 3.5). This is bad news for energy producers, and clearly complicates the task of planning and investment. As Figure 3.6 indicates, oil and natural gas (energy) now account for the majority of Canada's commodity production.

Another important feature worth noting is that the long-run demand and supply elasticities for most commodities are typically much higher. If commodity prices remain high, consumers find ways to economize on their use, or find substitute products. New supplies also gradually come online. All of these factors

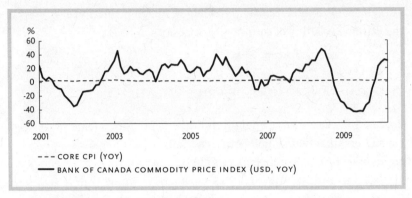

FIGURE 3.4 Commodity Price Volatility

Source: Bank of Canada, Statistics Canada

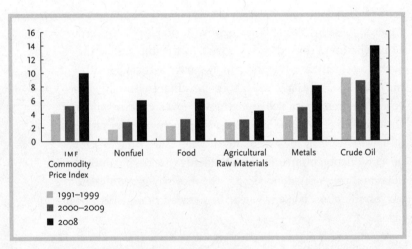

FIGURE 3.5 Commodity Real Price Volatility

Source: IMF
Note: Volatility is calculated using the standard deviation of monthly changes in real commodity price indices (deflated by the US consumer price index)

work to push prices lower. In this sense, there is a self-correcting mechanism at play. Indeed, over the very long run—and here, I am referring to decades—the average real price of most commodities has been surprisingly stable (Coletti 1992–93). Figures 3.7 and 3.8 illustrate this phenomenon with oil and food prices. Economists refer to this as "mean reversion." If we knew that this sawtooth pattern would always be repeated—short-run spikes

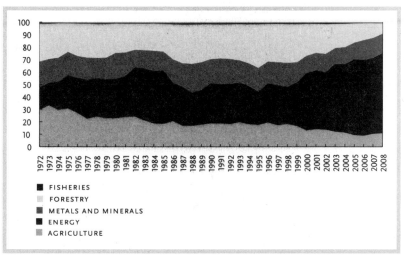

100
90
80
70
60
50
40
30
20
10
0

1972 1973 1974 1975 1976 1977 1978 1979 1980 1981 1982 1983 1984 1985 1986 1987 1988 1989 1990 1991 1992 1993 1994 1995 1996 1997 1998 1999 2000 2001 2002 2003 2004 2005 2006 2007 2008

■ FISHERIES
▩ FORESTRY
■ METALS AND MINERALS
■ ENERGY
▩ AGRICULTURE

FIGURE 3.6 The Changing Composition of Canadian Commodity Production

Source: Bank of Canada

followed by an overshoot on the down side and an eventual return to the long-run mean—it would save a lot of unnecessary cost and disappointment.

But hope springs eternal, and many of the price movements last just long enough to convince investors and governments that "this time it is different." And·there is always a chance that some day it *will* be different. In the intervening period, long-range investments may have been set in train, new facilities built, and workers relocated—all initiatives that have to be reversed once prices correct. This is not always a problem, however. If prices stay high (or low) for a sufficiently long time, these reallocations of capital and labour could well be warranted and yield valuable returns, even if prices eventually revert to trend.

The trouble is that businesses, households, and policy makers often get caught out. They overreact and have diffi- culty engineering a smooth course correction once conditions change. The inherent difficulty associated with predicting how long a boom (or bust) might last, and how high (or low) prices might go, makes the process extremely risky. Critics worry that a commodity-based economy will constantly find itself in

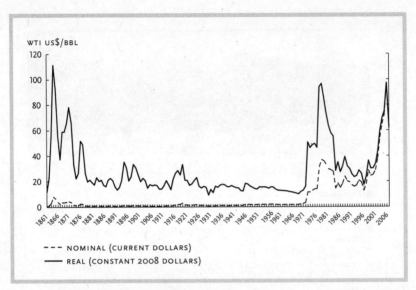

FIGURE 3.7 Nominal and Real Oil Prices

Source: British Petroleum

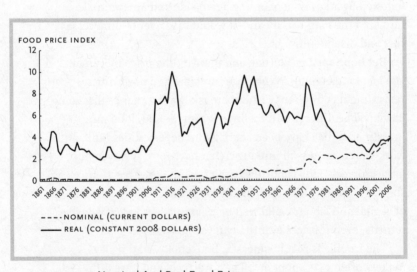

FIGURE 3.8 Nominal And Real Food Prices

Source: Bank of Canada

motion, never quite settling down. When this constant churning is combined with volatile price changes, the ongoing costs and probability of a significant miscalculation can be high.

THE POLICY MAKER'S HIPPOCRATIC OATH: FIRST, DO NO HARM

One of the most important things that policy makers can do is to avoid making the situation worse. Canada's experience during the 1970s provides helpful lessons in this regard. Although every boom and bust is in some way unique, there is sufficient commonality across commodity cycles, which means that this period is still instructive.

Fiscal authorities in the 1970s assumed that the commodity boom would last forever, or at least for a very long time. They believed that the elevated revenues that they were suddenly receiving in the form of higher royalties and tax receipts would continue to grow. New, ambitious government programs were launched, which exacerbated the dramatic economic upturn that was already in progress, and nothing was saved for a rainy day.

Monetary authorities at the time didn't have the benefit of a policy framework anchored on an explicit inflation target. They also underestimated the effect that the run-up in commodity prices would have on demand conditions, and they compounded the errors by overestimating the supply potential of the economy. More specifically, they failed to appreciate the serious negative effects that higher commodity prices—principally, energy prices—would have on the economy's production capacity. The generalized price increases that were subsequently observed across the economy were at first dismissed as one-off effects that would soon pass out of the inflation numbers.

The exchange rate appreciation that was triggered by the improvement in Canada's terms of trade over this period, which would have helped contain inflationary pressures, was actively resisted for fear of what it might do to other sectors of the economy and employment. The result, when commodity prices subsequently collapsed, was a continuing spiral of rising government deficits and double-digit inflation, both of which took many years to resolve. The ultimate cost in terms of lost output and employment was enormous.

WHAT CAN POLICY MAKERS DO TO IMPROVE THE SITUATION?

Now, let me turn from Canada's experiences in the 1970s to some of the broader policy lessons that can be drawn. Policy makers can learn from past mistakes and help to ensure better outcomes in three important ways. First, fiscal authorities should avoid behaving in a procyclical manner, exaggerating the boom with aggressive increases in spending and stimulative tax reductions. Additional infrastructure may be needed to support private investment in certain areas, but by strengthening their fiscal positions in good times, governments can help to relieve inflationary pressures and smooth consumption. This is the motivation for Alberta's Sustainability Fund and the Heritage Savings Trust Fund. Fiscal strengthening can also help to relieve upward pressure on the exchange rate.

The second way in which authorities can help is by maintaining a disciplined monetary policy. Monetary authorities must stay focused on their primary mission of preserving price stability, helping businesses and households to see through the cycle, and promoting better decision making by keeping inflation low, stable, and predictable. This is what Canada's monetary policy framework now provides: greater focus, greater accountability, and greater discipline. The two key elements of our current framework are, first, an explicit monetary policy goal—the 2% target for inflation—and, second, a flexible exchange rate.

Canada's flexible exchange rate gives the Bank of Canada the monetary policy independence that is required to successfully pursue and attain its inflation objective. The flexible exchange rate also serves as an automatic buffer, helping to cushion the economy and dissipate the effects of the commodity shock. Trying to resist these exchange rate movements typically imposes even greater costs on the economy, since the underlying pressures don't disappear; they simply manifest themselves in other ways. These take the form of much higher wages and domestic prices in the case of a commodity price boom and, ultimately, lower employment and output. Necessary adjustment is delayed and leads to a more exaggerated cycle in the overall economy.

Another important lesson that has been learned relates to the production capacity of the economy. The Bank of Canada is now more sensitive to the negative supply effects that are associated with large relative price movements and the economic restructuring that follows, adjusting its estimates of potential output appropriately to avoid inadvertently overstimulating the economy.

The third and final way that governments can help the economy to cope with commodity cycles is through structural reform. In normal times, the Canadian economy generally performs quite well, but it is still subject to unhelpful frictions and barriers. These affect the resilience of the economy and its ability to weather shocks, making it difficult to reallocate resources in a flexible, efficient manner. Canada has made good progress over the past three decades in allowing goods and services to move more easily. Further efforts to reduce interprovincial trade barriers would be welcome, for instance, extending the excellent Trade, Investment and Labour Mobility Agreement (TILMA) and the New West Partnership initiatives.

Governments, of course, are not the only ones responsible for ensuring a well-functioning economy. They are not even the most important players. That role rests with the private sector, which must take responsibility for its actions, looking through the boom–bust cycles and curbing any excessive exuberance or pessimism.

HOW HAVE WE BEEN DOING LATELY?

The first decade of the twenty-first century has been extraordinary in many ways and, if nothing else, has provided a useful check on whether the prescriptions that I have just described are being applied. A supercycle in commodity prices, followed by the biggest financial crisis of the postwar period, represents a significant stress test.[3] Fortunately, the preliminary results are encouraging.

The 1970s and the 2000s differ in significant ways. The boom–bust experience in the 1970s was triggered by an unprecedented supply shock and exacerbated by overly stimulative fiscal and monetary policies. Interest rates had to be boosted to over 20% in the early 1980s and combined with aggressive budget tightening in the early 1990s to bring the macroeconomy under control. In contrast, the boom portion of the commodity cycle from roughly 2006–2008 was the result of increased demand for commodities—much of it coming from Asia. It was also fuelled by excessive leverage and elevated asset prices in financial markets. Commodity prices collapsed when the asset bubble burst, and policy makers had to move with unprecedented speed and co-operation to deal with the fallout.

Unlike the situation in the 1970s, consumer price index (CPI) inflation through the past five years has remained relatively stable, as Figure 3.9 shows, despite the size of the shocks that hit the economy during the recent global economic crisis. Inflation expectations also remained well anchored during the crisis, and, as a result, the Bank of Canada was able to ease monetary policy aggressively without losing the confidence of private agents. The ultimate costs of the crisis in terms of unemployment and lost output, although serious and painful, were nevertheless smaller than many had feared.

The Bank's measure of core inflation, CPIX, proved to be an invaluable tool in this regard. CPIX strips away eight of the most volatile components—including several commodity prices—in the total consumer price index, giving the Bank, as well as businesses and households, a more reliable measure of how strong or weak underlying inflation pressures might be.

The flexible exchange rate has also been allowed to do its job over this period. Although some of the short-term movements in the exchange rate may have been excessive, such as the run-up to US$1.10 in November 2007, on balance Canada's flexible exchange rate has helped to cushion the economy on the way up and on the way down—an appreciation followed by a depreciation. Fiscal authorities at the federal and provincial levels also

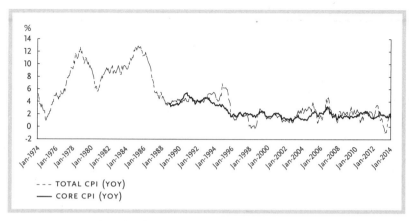

FIGURE 3.9 Core and Total Inflation

Source: Statistics Canada

acted responsibly in the years preceding the "bust" of late 2008 and early 2009, taking some of the edge off the boom and leaving adequate fiscal headroom when extra stimulus was required. Encouraging steps, as noted earlier, have also been made with regard to structural reforms, although much more still needs to be done in this area.

CONCLUSION: WHERE ARE COMMODITY PRICES HEADED NOW?

So, where might things be going now, as we look ahead towards the middle of the decade? I'd like to end the chapter by saying a few words about the near-term behaviour of commodity prices and the projection that the Bank released as part of its April 2010 *Monetary Policy Report.*

Before discussing our commodity price projections, I must admit that we, at the Bank of Canada, regularly make use of some simplifying assumptions. Absent a more reliable guide, we typically base our projections for many commodities on the prices embedded in futures curves.[4] This is particularly true for oil and natural gas. We realize that these curves are not a very reliable forecasting tool. But we, and other forecasters, have yet to find a better alternative. The curves do provide a measure of what knowledgeable agents are expecting and are willing to put their money on. Every institution and investor that tries to anticipate commodity price developments experiences similar challenges. Commodity prices, as noted earlier, are inherently volatile and difficult to predict.

You might ask, then, what are the futures curves and the Bank projecting now? In its April 2010 *Monetary Policy Report*, the Bank left its base-case projections for 2010–2012 commodity prices largely unchanged from what it had projected in the January 2010 *Monetary Policy Report*. Oil and natural gas prices, as judged by the profiles of the futures curves for these commodities, are projected to rise quite modestly over this same period, while non-energy prices are projected to increase by a cumulative 30%. These increases are driven by the strengthening global recovery, most notably in China and other Asian emerging-market economies (EMES). Indeed, as Figure 3.10 shows, most of the upward pressure on commodity prices since the early 2000s has come from the EMES. These economies are expected to keep growing, barring any unforeseen shock. Does this mean another commodity supercycle?

It is tempting to look at recent developments and extrapolate into the future. China and India alone account for more than 40% of the world's population. If these two economies continue to grow at annual rates of 8% to 10%, as they have, more or less, over the 2005 to 2010 period, they will soon overtake even the largest advanced economies, and their prospective demand for commodities could be enormous. Couple this with the fact that many of the world's resources are non-renewable or are in limited supply, and you have a recipe for something that's surely breathtaking. It's enough to make us all Malthusians.

Before we race to this conclusion, however, we need to remember the problems that have arisen in the past when we assumed that commodity prices would rise continuously, or at least would stabilize at a much higher level. It's always tempting to think that the next commodity cycle will be different. Where have we heard that before? The scenario that I have just outlined is not implausible. That is what makes it so seductive. I can't say

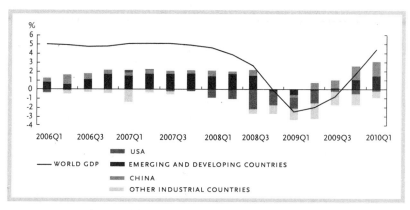

FIGURE 3.10 Growth in World GDP and Contribution to Global Growth of Oil Demand

Source: IMF

definitely that commodity prices won't rise to unprecedented levels, but if history is any guide, continuous rapid upward movement in real (inflation-adjusted) prices—oil or otherwise—is unlikely, as is a large permanent increase in the real price level. History suggests, therefore, that we should proceed with caution and, to use a rather corny commodity cliché, not count our chickens before they hatch.

In closing, let me mention our new Bank of Canada commodity price index (BCPI). This is a chain Fisher price index of the spot or transaction US dollar prices of 24 commodities produced in Canada and sold in world markets, with weights updated on an annual basis using recent commodity production data.[5] As such, the BCPI is a noteworthy addition to the suite of publicly available price information because, as we've just discussed, the price of commodities in Canada has important implications for the economy, and the interpretation of developments in commodity markets is important to the conduct of monetary policy. Clearly, we need to have available the most accurate, representative, and flexible measure of movements in overall commodity prices possible. This new BCPI, which incorporates a new methodology, is designed to fulfill these objectives. Values of this new index are now published regularly in the Bank of Canada's monthly "Banking and Financial Statistics" publication.

Notes

1. For a detailed discussion of six channels through which natural resource endowments may have negative effects on a country's economic performance, thereby creating such a curse, see Frankel (2010).
2. Some commodities are also subject to frequent supply disruptions that accentuate price volatility.
3. See Erten and Ocampo (2012) for a discussion of supercycles in commodity prices, including identification of the associated time periods.
4. See Alquist and Kilian (2010).
5. For more details, see Kolet and Macdonald (2010).

References

Alquist, Ron, and Lutz Kilian. 2010. "What Do We Learn from the Price of Crude Oil Futures?" *Journal of Applied Econometrics* 25 (4): 539–73.

Bank of Canada. 2010. *Monetary Policy Report*. April.

Coletti, Don. 1992–93. "The Long-run Behaviour of Key Canadian Non-energy Commodity Prices: 1900 to 1991." *Bank of Canada Review* Winter: 47–56.

Erten, Bilge, and José Antonio Ocampo. 2012. "Super-Cycles of Commodity Prices since the Mid-Nineteenth Century." DESA Working Paper No. 110, United Nations Department of Economic and Social Affairs, February.

Frankel, Jeffrey A. 2010. "The Natural Resource Curse: A Survey." Faculty Research Working Paper Series, Harvard Kennedy School, Cambridge, MA, February.

Kolet, Ilan, and Ryan Macdonald. 2010. "The Fisher BCPI: The Bank of Canada's New Commodity Price Index." Bank of Canada Discussion Paper No. 2010-6.

Three Strikes and You're Out?

The Inevitability of Resources Busts and its Challenges for Alberta's Policy Makers

J.C. Herbert Emery and Ronald Kneebone

INTRODUCTION

In fall 2008, Alberta experienced its third bust in the oil and gas sector since 1945. Apart from Ernest Manning's era (1943–1968), in each of the booms that preceded the busts, Albertans chose to view boom conditions as permanently higher growth paths resulting in unsustainable budget choices. When the bust occurred, there was a perception that the bust conditions were products of adverse price shocks, in the absence of which the economy would have continued to grow rapidly.

Was this a sensible belief? Were it not for bad luck would the Alberta economy have continued along the fast growth paths experienced during booms? Have the fiscal choices made by the government of Alberta been derailed by bad luck in the form of resource busts or by poor planning in the form of mismanaging the risk of an uncertain future?

In their critique and extension of the "staples" view of resource-based development, Chambers and Gordon (1966) demonstrated that for a small open economy like Alberta, natural resource exports cannot be the source of sustained increases in per capita incomes. In the long run, dependence on natural resource exports results in a larger, but not necessarily richer, economy and population. The only contribution to the economy of the natural resource is the rents accruing to "land" or the natural resource base. Importantly, this is true even if natural resources prices do not fall. This result, plus the observation that resource price busts inevitably follow price booms, is what has caused economists to be persistent in their attempts to persuade governments to adopt fiscal approaches that encourage public saving and discourage an overdependence on what is inevitably an unreliable source of revenue. Yet, this advice has not been heeded. If it had, the large resource rents associated with a boom would have been saved to ensure a reliable stream of income for the future, low and constant tax rates, and public expenditures free from the danger of a boom-and-bust cycle in public finances.

Our goal in this chapter is first to present the case, built on the foundation of an economic model, that resource booms cannot be the basis of sustained high rates of economic growth. We then turn to the data to show that, consistent with the model, Alberta's economic prosperity has only ever temporarily grown relative to that in other provinces. Examining the government's finances since it gained access to resource revenues, we show how a mistaken understanding of the implications of energy price booms has encouraged the government of Alberta to adopt unsustainable fiscal policies. We conclude that the government has failed to learn from previous episodes of boom and bust and so continues even today to engage in a high-risk strategy of basing Alberta's economic success on a highly unlikely assumption of ever increasing energy prices.

THE OIL PRICE BOOM OF THE 1970S AND
THE AFTERMATH

Mansell (1997) notes that the petroleum boom of the 1970s was not seen as a transitory, short-lived boom that would be followed by an inevitable bust, but as a permanently higher growth path for the Alberta economy. In hindsight, an obvious question is how, in a cyclical industry like oil and gas, did a boom in oil prices between 1973 and 1985 come to be treated as a permanent state of affairs? Perhaps more perplexing, after experiencing the bust following that boom, how did it again come to be treated as a permanent state of affairs during the energy boom of 2000 to 2009?

Although the full extent of the price collapse in 1986 may not have been predictable, oil prices were never expected to continue rising at the rapid pace of the late 1970s. Doern and Toner (1985) argue that there were clear signs as early as 1981 that prices were not going to keep rising. Laxer (1983) argues that it was clear to many by 1982 that there was a glut in world oil supply and that oil prices were falling. Yet, as Mansell notes, many forecasters continued, despite these signals, to predict large oil price increases for the long term. And when the international price of oil (West Texas Intermediate) did collapse from US$31 in November 1985 to less than US$13 per barrel in March 1986, many were uncertain if this price collapse signalled a permanent state of affairs or just a temporarily low price.

In the short run, the Alberta government and many Albertans apparently believed that oil prices would rebound, following a "hockey stick" pattern—remaining flat for a while but then turning up. Mansell describes the Alberta government's short-run response to the downturn as one where it continued to spend, hoping that the resulting economic growth and a rebound in oil prices would solve the growing deficit problem. The longer-term difficulty for the province was that lower oil prices looked as if they would continue and would thus require dramatic changes for Alberta. Forecasts were also emerging that Alberta's economy would continue to decline if oil prices remained low. For example, it was forecast in 1987 that oil imports would displace Alberta oil from the Ontario market by 1995, which might lead to calls for resurrecting the 1961 National Oil Policy that "gave" the Ontario oil market to Alberta producers (Waverman 1987). Thus, after 12 years of high and generally rising prices of oil, the only obvious permanent change in Alberta's economy by 1986 was that it was larger, but only because it had a larger population than before the oil price boom. As we show later in this chapter, after the collapse of oil prices in 1986, average incomes for Albertans had fallen back to the Canadian average.

Only after a long period of uncertainty over whether high oil prices would return did Albertans finally came to grips with the reality that high oil prices after 1973 were a transitory boom and that the good times might not return. The best expression of that realization came in 1993 with the appearance of Premier Ralph Klein elected on a platform of draconian cuts to public spending in order to return to balanced provincial budgets.

During the energy price boom experienced between 2000 and 2009, there was a return to the belief that the strong growth of the Alberta economy was not a transitory boom (Harrington 2006). As we describe in a later section, over this period, the budgeting choices of the government also reflected this expectation of the persistence of the boom conditions—an expectation that seems to have survived even the dramatic fall in energy prices in 2009. The 2009 and 2010 Alberta budgets avoided serious spending cuts, added $2 billion to the budget for health care, and cut health care premiums, liquor taxes, and other revenues, suggesting the Stelmach government is expecting the slowdown related to energy prices to be transitory—a repeat of previous behaviour that caused us to wonder if it would be déjà vu all over again (Emery and Kneebone 2009). Only in the 2012 budget did the government start to muse about the possibility of there being a need for spending cuts or tax increases—musing that did not, however, translate into budgetary actions.

Can oil and gas exploitation cause sustained income growth in Alberta? If so, under what conditions? As discussed above, there has been a confusion of the importance of two aspects of energy prices: the level and the growth rate. One view holds that the boom conditions need never end if energy prices remain "high." The other view maintains that boom conditions can only be sustained with sustained growth in energy prices. We show below that strong economic growth is associated with *growth* in energy prices and is not correlated with the *level* of energy prices in the long run.

Chambers and Gordon (1966) devised a simple, yet elegant, model of the Canadian economy to demonstrate why natural resource exports in periods of resource booms cannot be a source of sustained growth in per capita GDP. Boyce and Emery (2011) augment the Chambers and Gordon model to allow for technical progress in the resource sector and to account for the influence of an exhaustible natural resource stock (a.k.a. oil and natural gas). Their extension of Chambers and Gordon demonstrates that in the absence of energy price growth, and/or technical progress in the extraction of natural resources, growth rates of per capita income will be slower than in non-resource economies.

The mechanism that is behind this strong conclusion is the high elasticity of factor supply in a small open economy, in other words, the free flow of labour and financial capital into and out of the economy.[1] For Alberta, the high rates of capital and labour inflows in response to increases in oil and natural gas prices are indicative of the factor price arbitrage process that in the long-run returns Alberta per capita incomes back to where they were before the resource boom occurred. In the Chambers and Gordon model, the only long-run effects of a resource boom are high "land rents" (incomes to the fixed factor) and a larger economy. Other than the natural resource rents, the long-run effect of the resource boom is a larger economy, as measured by GDP, but not necessarily a richer economy as measured by per capita GDP. The slower growth of the resource-abundant economy modelled by Boyce and Emery (2011) reflects the declining rents to the owner of the natural resource due to resource depletion from production.

J.C. Herbert Emery and Ronald Kneebone   43

The simplest illustration of the dynamics of a resource boom can be seen from Chambers and Gordon's (1966) model. Chambers and Gordon consider a small open economy where producers are price takers on world markets and where free capital mobility ensures that the ratio of capital to labour in the small open economy adjusts so that the owners of capital earn the world rate of return. Since the capital stock adjusts to the quantity of labour to hold the capital to labour ratio fixed, it is sufficient to consider production only in terms of the labour input.

There are two sectors in the basic Chambers and Gordon model, wheat (resources) and gadgets (manufacturing).[2] When considering the Alberta economy, we could consider the resource sector as being located in Alberta and the gadget sector representing non-resource production in the "rest of Canada." Chambers and Gordon assume that "gadgets" are produced with only labour (L) according to constant returns to scale, and constant marginal product of labour. The resource sector produces its output with labour and a "land" factor (e.g., energy reserves) that is fixed in supply. The fixed supply of land results in a diminishing marginal product of labour. With perfectly competitive factor markets, each factor of production is paid the value of its marginal product (output price times the marginal product of labour). Increases in output prices will shift the demand for labour in the sector. Because the marginal product of labour in the gadget sector is constant, the demand for labour in the gadget sector is perfectly elastic. So long as labour is mobile between the resource and gadget sector, the gadget sector sets the wage for the economy. Workers move between sectors until at the margin the last worker hired in each sector is paid the same wage.

This equilibrium is depicted in Figure 4.1A where W_o is the economy-wide wage, D_r is the demand for labour in the resource sector and L_r is the level of employment in the resource sector. The return to land (land rents) is the value of labour employed in the resource sector that is in excess of the wage, as represented by the shaded area.

Figure 4.1B shows the effect of a higher price of the resource sector's output in the short and long run. As depicted, the higher resource price shifts the demand for labour in that sector to the

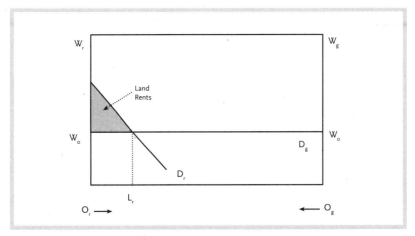

FIGURE 4.1A Illustration of the Chambers and Gordon Two-Sector Model

Notes: The horizontal axis represents the total supply of labour $L=L_r+L_g$ in the economy. The left axis measures the wage paid in the resource sector and the right axis measures the wage paid in the gadget sector. Equilibrium is where the demand for labour curves intersect. In equilibrium the wage W_o is paid in both sectors; L_r workers are employed in the resource sector and $L-L_r$ workers are employed in the gadget sector. The highlighted area under the labour demand curve in the resource sector represents the income to the fixed factor land.

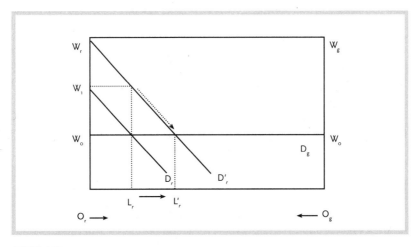

FIGURE 4.1B

Notes: When the resource price increases, demand for labour shifts to the right. In the short-run, the allocation of labour between sectors is fixed resulting in an increase in the wage paid in the resource sector to W_r. In response to the higher wage labour moves from gadgets to the resource sector until the wage is again W_o in both sectors. In the long run, the resource sector is larger, land rents are higher but there is no growth in per capita income.

right from D_r to D'. In the short run, with the allocation of labour between the two sectors temporarily fixed, the wage paid in the resource sector rises to W_1 and so per capita incomes rise. In the long run, workers in the gadget sector migrate to the resource sector in response to the higher wage, and migration continues until employment in the resource sector increases to L'_r and the real wage in both sectors is once again W_0. Thus per capita income has returned to what it was prior to the boom. The total return to land had now increased to an amount measured by the area under the curve D'_r and above W_0. The only lasting effect of the boom is an increase in the total and the per capita share of the return to land.

This simple illustration highlights why a high price level for the output of the resource sector cannot result in sustained growth of per capita incomes. The resource boom in the long run raises the income of the fixed factor, land, and increases the size of the resource economy by increasing its population. But, other than the per capita land rents, incomes in the resource sector are not higher because of the boom.[3]

The main message of these models for policy makers is that, while falling resource prices will obviously cause a resource bust, even with permanently higher resource prices, the effects of resource booms on economic prosperity—as measured by per capita incomes—are transitory. Only an increased return to land is a long-lasting result of the boom.[4] There are only two forces that can sustain a resource boom: permanent growth in the resource price and technical progress in the resource sector. But, even resource price growth and technical progress must be strong enough to offset the negative growth influences of resource depletion. In the absence of those two economic forces, resource booms inevitably bust, even if resource prices do not fall. Finally, the only other way to convert transitory benefits of the resource boom into permanent income benefits for the resource economy is to follow the "Hartwick Rule" and save the resource rents to invest in financial assets that will yield a permanent source of income for the resource economy.

Does this simple two-sector model provide a reasonable representation of the Alberta economy? The simplest way to consider

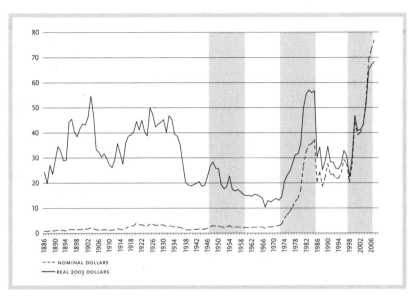

FIGURE 4.2 Alberta's Three Oil Price Booms: Nominal and Real (2003$) Price of Oil, Edmonton Par, 1886–2007

this question is to recognize that, if the model is correct, then per capita incomes in Alberta should have a tendency to revert to the Canadian average income over the long run (or at least a long run ratio). This prediction is stronger for labour incomes than for GDP since the rents to the fixed factor, the resource or land, can result in persistent changes in the ratio of Alberta GDP to Canadian GDP.

Figure 4.2 shows the nominal and constant dollar oil prices in Canada from 1886 to 2006, along with frames showing Alberta's three oil booms. The first was the Manning boom (1947–1960); the second was the Lougheed–OPEC boom (1973–1986); and the third the most recent Klein/Stelmach boom (1998–2008). Figure 4.3 shows the ratio of Alberta personal incomes to Canadian personal incomes. Personal income is dominated by labour market earnings. In Figure 4.3, the reversion of Alberta average income to the national average is clear after the first two booms. The reversion is not apparent yet in the most recent boom because, over the sample period depicted in the figure, oil prices were increasing throughout. Now that oil prices

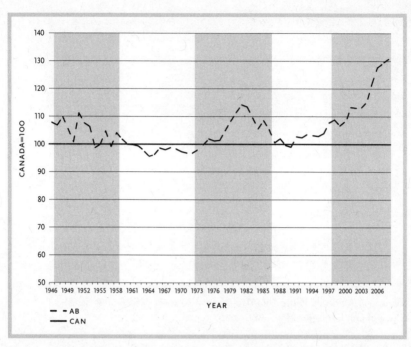

FIGURE 4.3 Personal Income Per Capita Relative to the Canadian Average, 1946–2008

Source: CANSIM, Table 3840013

have stabilized somewhat, we expect the reversion of Alberta incomes to the national average to become apparent.

This simple model of the Alberta resource boom has several implications for framing policy discussions. First, one could argue that growth in total GDP, rather than per capita GDP, increases the tax base for the Alberta government, which enriches the public sector. It must be recognized, however, that GDP growth also slows down as the resource economy returns to equilibrium. Second, it is not clear that higher GDP due to a larger population in the resource-based economy is a net gain. Increases in population not only increase the tax base, but also as we have seen in Alberta, increase demand for government goods, services, and investment in public infrastructure (schools, hospitals, roads, etc.). Only if the increase in population results in scale economies in public service delivery can there be a gain for

Alberta. On the other hand, if the population growth results in congestion in the use of services, service delivery costs could rise by more than tax revenues.

A second key policy implication is that because the only source of increased incomes in the resource boom is the income of the fixed factor land/resource base, public policy should focus on capturing a share of those rents. For rents capitalized in real estate prices, property taxes would be the appropriate tax base to consider. For the resource base, the government needs to consider how much rent to collect through the upfront sale of mineral rights and how much rent to collect through production royalties and other taxes on producers. Note that attempts by the Crown owner of the resource to collect a higher share of royalties will result in less activity in the resource sector and reduce the size of the Alberta economy. Note also that the standard of living of Albertans is largely unaffected because per capita GDP growth would not be affected.

THE APPROPRIATE PUBLIC POLICY RESPONSE TO TEMPORARY BOOMS

We noted earlier that economists have been persistent in their attempts to enlighten government to the policy choices consistent with best outcomes given the inevitability of the resources busts that follow booms. What advice have they provided? Economists have suggested that governments that enjoy substantial revenues from the exploitation of non-renewable resources should strive to do three key things: (1) collect a share of the increased return to land; (2) avoid relying on unstable revenue to finance long-term commitments to key public policies; and (3) hold on to the share of the increased return to land. How has the government of Alberta done with respect to these three pieces of advice?

With respect to the first issue—collecting a share of the increased return to land—the government of Alberta has done well. Early on, the provincial government established a regulatory regime that provides it with royalties based on the revenue earned by private firms on the sale of non-renewable energy

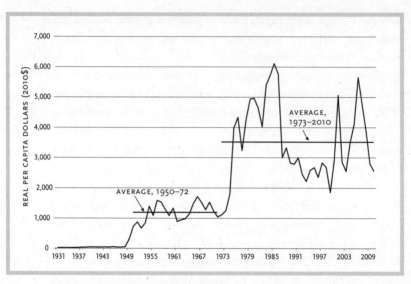

FIGURE 4.4 Resource Revenue, 1931–2010

resources. The government does not maintain an equity stake in any firms involved in the exploitation of non-renewable resources; its income is due solely to the collection of royalties and from the sale of leases that entitle private firms to explore and produce those resources. When all is said and done, the regulatory and royalty regime in Alberta is generally considered to strike an appropriate balance between encouraging private sector efficiency and ensuring the owners of the resource—the citizens of Alberta through their provincial government—a reasonable share of the value of the resource.

Figure 4.4 measures, in real per capita dollars, the amount of revenue accruing to the government of Alberta as a result of the exploitation of non-renewable resource revenues since 1931, when Alberta first gained control of resource revenues from the federal government.[5] After establishing a royalty regime capable of yielding an average of $1,200 per person (2010 dollars) to provincial revenues, the combination of OPEC and a renegotiation of royalty rates in the early years of the Lougheed government increased Alberta's share of the increased return to the land. Since 1973, this share has averaged $3,500 per person. The volatility of this

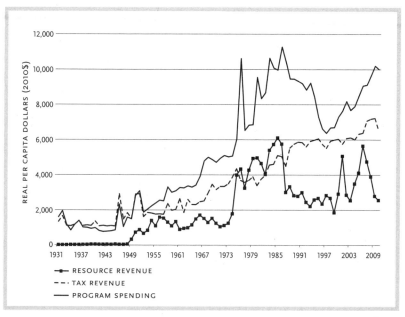

FIGURE 4.5 Program Spending, Tax Revenue, and Resource Revenue, 1931–2010

revenue is clear from Figure 4.4 and corresponds to the boom-and-bust cycle in energy prices described earlier.

With respect to satisfying the second key recommendation—avoid relying on unstable revenues to finance long-term commitments to key public policies—the government of Alberta has been considerably less successful. Figure 4.5 superimposes data pertaining to provincial government program spending and tax revenue on the information from Figure 4.4.[6] Figure 4.5 tells an interesting story. It shows that in the years prior to 1947, when resource revenue started to become a noticeable share of total revenue, program spending and tax revenue were of near identical amounts and fluctuated together. Thus, balanced budgets were the norm and increases in spending were funded with increases in taxes. There was, in other words, a clear "tax price" associated with changes in spending; during this period, if citizens of Alberta desired new government spending, they would need to pay the price in terms of higher taxes.

Not long after 1947, this close connection was broken. By the early 1950s, what we call a "budget gap" opened between spending and tax revenue. From that point forward, although the tax price of government spending would increase more or less steadily, spending itself would take on boom-and-bust characteristics. A close inspection of Figure 4.5 shows that dramatic changes in resource revenue were almost without exception followed in close order by equally dramatic changes in program spending in the same direction. Thus, following the OPEC price shocks of the early and late 1970s, program spending spiked upward in the years immediately following. The dramatic fall in resource revenues in 1986 was similarly followed, in the succeeding year or two, by cuts to program spending. It is noteworthy that the response of program spending to falls in resource revenues tended to be considerably smaller than the response of spending to increases in resource revenues.[7]

The one exception to the close connection between resource revenues and program spending was the dramatic cut to spending in the mid-1990s without any associated change in resource revenues. This period is associated with the efforts of then newly elected Premier Ralph Klein to reduce spending in conformity with an election promise to balance the provincial budget. We will return to a discussion of this period shortly.

Figure 4.6 presents similar information to Figure 4.5 but does so using the idea of the "budget gap," which was raised earlier. The size of the budget gap—defined as the difference between total spending and tax revenue—measures the amount of resource revenue required to balance the provincial budget. Here we see a very close connection between resource revenues and the size of the budget gap, and thus the extent of the government's dependence on resource revenues. Changes in resource revenues almost invariably resulted in changes in the budget gap. As the previous figure shows, most of the adjustment to the budget gap came in the form of adjustments to program spending, both up and down. The one exception to this close relationship was, again, the mid-1990s when Klein imposed significant cuts to spending and the budget gap without there being much change in resource revenue. The close connection was, however, soon re-established

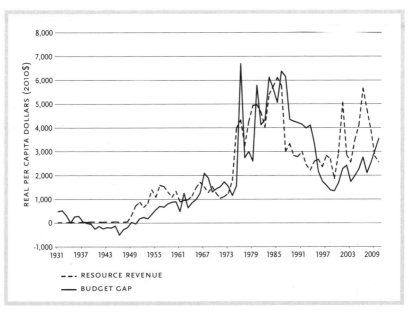

FIGURE 4.6 The Budget Gap and Resource Revenues, 1931–2010

as the growth in resource revenue since 1998 has been associated with a corresponding increase in spending.

The Klein era is interesting not only because it is an aberration but also because it is an era of fiscal feats that presented unique opportunities. Klein's first term as premier was notable for a drastic reduction in provincial government spending. The origin of these cuts—introduced beginning in 1993—was the collapse of oil prices in 1986.[8] Resource revenues in fiscal year 1987 were just 38% of what they were a year earlier. Despite ending an earlier commitment to save some fraction of non-renewable resource revenues and the investment income earned on earlier savings, the budget plunged into deficit in 1986 and would remain in deficit for the next nine fiscal years. During those nine years, to the end of fiscal year 1994, the provincial government moved from a net asset position of $12,600 million in 1985 to a net debt position of $8,400 million by the end of fiscal year 1994. Budget deficits over this period averaged over $2,000 million per year, an amount equal to about 16% of program spending. Concern over these persistent deficits and the resulting accumulation of debt provided the focus of the election campaign in the summer of 1993. Premier Klein was elected to a majority government on a platform of a 20% cut to program spending. The first budget of the new government called for not only a deep but also a speedily implemented 20% cut in spending to be completed by the end of fiscal year 1996.

The effect of these drastic cuts is shown in Figure 4.6 by the dramatic reduction in the size of the fiscal gap after 1993. By 1999 the fiscal gap, at just over $1,300 per person, was back to what it had been prior to the OPEC price shocks and well below the average level of real per capita resource revenues for the post-1972 period. The result was large budget surpluses and, in short order, the elimination of net debt.

This effort afforded the provincial government the opportunity to reinstitute an approach not seen since the early 1950s: the imposition of a tax price on new spending, which required tax revenue to increase with any new spending. Such a policy would involve maintaining a constant budget gap and, except for possibly extraordinary falls in energy prices, annual budget surpluses. Such a policy would ensure a commitment to long-term saving, and, perhaps most importantly, it would establish a funding foundation for spending on health and education based not on volatile and uncertain energy prices, but on taxation of incomes and consumption.

Unfortunately, this brief period of fiscal rectitude was just that—brief. As Figure 4.6 shows, when resource revenues began to climb after 1999, so too did the size of the budget gap. A combination of increases in real per capita spending and cuts to tax rates once again had the budget gap chasing increases in resource revenues, so that by 2009, just as resource revenues collapsed, the provincial government had erased the efforts of the first Klein government and had re-established the budget gap at the level it was in 1993. The opportunity afforded by the drastic cuts of the first Klein government to impose discipline on government spending and to free decisions about spending on health and education from the vicissitudes of energy revenues was, by 2009, totally undone.

With respect to satisfying the third and last key recommendation—to hold on to the owner's share of the increase return

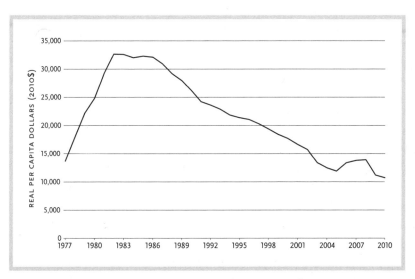

FIGURE 4.7 Alberta Heritage Savings Trust Fund Equity, Fiscal Years 1977–2010

to land resulting from energy price booms—the government of Alberta has again been considerably less than successful. After establishing the Alberta Heritage Savings Trust Fund (AHSTF) in 1976, then Premier Peter Lougheed committed the provincial government to saving 30% of resource royalties in that fund. What's more, the fund would retain 100% of the investment income earned on it. The negative effects of the National Energy Program (1981) and the 1982 recession combined to cause the government to choose between its commitment to saving and its commitment to maintaining spending. It chose the latter, and as a result in 1982 the government diverted all of the investment income earned by the AHSTF to general revenues and reduced the percentage of resource revenue deposited in the AHSTF from 30% to 15%. Following the collapse of energy prices in 1986, the commitment to saving some fraction of non-renewable resource revenues was completely abandoned. After 1988 all resource revenue would now enter general revenues, as would all investment income earned on the now moribund AHSTF.

Figure 4.7 measures from inception to March 2010, the value of the AHSTF in real per capita dollars.[9] Despite an effort beginning in 2005 to "inflation-proof" the AHSTF with annual contributions (an effort that has proved to be spotty), the AHSTF at the end of fiscal year 2010 was worth less in real per capita terms than it was upon inception over 30 years ago.

What was the purpose of these three pieces of advice that economists have persistently put forward to the provincial government? The purpose was to structure a fiscal regime where the large resource rents associated with a boom would be saved. This would have had a number of beneficial effects: It would have ensured a reliable stream of revenue in the form of the investment income earned by a growing savings fund; it would have forced the imposition of a positive tax price on new spending and so forced voters to examine the trade-off between higher taxes and higher levels of public services; and it would have freed public expenditures on health and education from relying on unpredictable energy revenues. In short, the purpose of this advice was to prevent the inevitable boom-and-bust nature of the Alberta economy from affecting public finances and so the levels of taxation suffered by, and public services enjoyed by, all Albertans.

CONCLUSION

We have, in this chapter, presented the case, built on the foundation of an economic model, that resource booms cannot be the basis of sustained high rates of economic growth. Consistent with the Chambers and Gordon model, our examination of the data shows that Alberta's economic prosperity has only ever temporarily grown relative to that in other provinces. Examining the government's finances since it gained access to resource revenues, we show how a mistaken understanding of the implications of energy price booms has encouraged the government of Alberta to adopt unsustainable fiscal policies.

Successive provincial governments—and the voters who elect them—have failed to appreciate the limited benefits of an economic boom built on higher energy prices. As a consequence, throughout the province's history, the provincial government—with the support of voters—has engaged in a high-risk strategy of basing Alberta's economic success on a highly unlikely assumption of ever increasing energy prices. The result is seen today in the form of a high level of dependence on volatile revenues to fund such basic public services as health care, education, and social transfers.

Notes

1. The free flows of labour and capital are well known to Albertans. Booms are associated with a significant increase in in-migration of people, and, as the provincial government has discovered recently in response to adjustments to the royalty regime, financial capital reacts quickly and strongly to perceived changes in the investment climate.
2. They also have a version of the model with a non-tradable, or "haircut," sector.
3. Boyce and Emery (2011) extend this model and show that adding consideration of resource depletion, the size of the resource economy and the land rents are also not sustainable as the demand for labour in the resource sector shifts back to the left over time.
4. But even here, with resource depletion resource rents are also dissipating, so all increases in incomes are transitory. With bad institutions, corruption, rent-seeking or poor resource management, resource rents can also be dissipated, resulting in lower income levels than otherwise.
5. Data for Figures 4.4, 4.5, and 4.6 are from two sources. Boothe (1995) provides data on provincial government finances from 1905 to 1991. This source provides the data we use here for the years 1931–1982 inclusive. Data for the years 1983–2010 are from budget papers of the government of Alberta (various years). In our figures, "resource revenue" is defined as the sum of "total resource rents" and "resource investment income" in Boothe and the sum of "natural resource revenue" and "investment income" in budget papers. In both cases, "resource revenue" is meant to measure the revenue gained through the collection of royalties and leases and the income earned on previously saved resource revenues.
6. In the data from Boothe (1995) the measure of "tax revenue" is defined as the difference between total revenue and total resource rents plus resource investment income. In data from Alberta budgets, the measure of "tax revenue" is the difference between total revenue, on the one hand, and natural resource revenue plus investment income on the other. In both cases, "tax revenue" is a measure of the revenue provided to the government by the application of tax rates on personal and corporate incomes, taxes on consumption, and federal government transfers. In both sources, "program spending" is the difference between total expenditures and debt servicing costs.
7. Kneebone and McKenzie (2000) provide and discuss empirical evidence of this behaviour.

8. The Canadian dollar price of a barrel of oil delivered to Edmonton (Alberta) fell from an average of $37.28 in 1985 to $20.49 in 1986 (calculated using data reported in Natural Resources Canada [2002]).

9. Nominal dollar values of the AHSTF is from Alberta Heritage Savings Trust Fund, Annual Report, 2009–10. Data is presented according to fiscal years. We denote 2010 as representing the value of the fund as of the end of March 31, 2010. Real per capita values are calculated using data on Alberta's population and the all-items CPI for Alberta. Sources for these data are Statistics Canada's CANSIM database, data series v15 and v41692327 respectively.

References

Boothe, Paul. 1995. *The Growth of Government Spending in Alberta*, Canadian Tax Paper 100, Canadian Tax Foundation.

Boyce, John R., and J.C. Herbert Emery. 2011. "Is a Negative Correlation Between Resource Abundance and Growth Sufficient Evidence that there is a 'Resource Curse'?" *Resources Policy* 36 (1): 1–13.

Chambers, Edward J., and Donald F. Gordon. 1966. "Primary Products and Economic Growth: An Empirical Measurement." *Journal of Political Economy* 74: 315–332.

Doern, G. Bruce, and Glen Toner. 1985. *The Politics of Energy: The Development and Implementation of the NEP*. Toronto: Methuen Publications.

Emery, J.C. Herbert, and Ronald D. Kneebone. 2009. "Will it be Déjà vu All Over Again?" SPP Briefing Papers 2 (1). University of Calgary, School of Public Policy, April.

Harrington, Carol. 2006. "To Boom or Not to Boom." *Calgary Inc.*, January/ February, 33–44.

Kneebone, Ronald, and Kenneth McKenzie. 2000. "A Case of Institutional Endogeneity? A Case Study of the Budgetary Reforms of the Government of Alberta, Canada." In *Institutions, Politics and Fiscal Policy*, edited by R. Strauch and J. von Hagen, 235–61. Boston: Kluwer Academic Publishers.

Laxer, James. 1983. *Oil and Gas: Ottawa, the Provinces and the Petroleum Industry*. Toronto: James Lorimer and Company.

Mansell, Robert L. 1997. "Fiscal Restructuring in Alberta: An Overview." In *A Government Reinvented: A Study of Alberta's Deficit Elimination Program*, edited by Christopher J. Bruce, Ronald D. Kneebone, and Kenneth J. McKenzie, 16–73. Toronto: Oxford University Press.

Waverman, Leonard. 1987. "The Impact of $(US)15 Oil: Good News and/or Bad News." *Canadian Public Policy* 13 (1): 1–8.

Output Instability
in Resource-Based and
Diversified Economies
Alberta and Ontario

Bev Dahlby, Kathleen Macaspac, and Melville McMillan

INTRODUCTION

Policies that promote economic diversification have received wide
public approval because they are perceived to contribute to economic stability and security. In resource-dependent regions, it is
generally believed that diversifying the economy would make the
region less sensitive to the boom-and-bust cycle brought about by
external volatilities. Economic diversification is also regarded as
a means of securing long-term economic growth in the event of
structural changes, such as the decline of the region's resource
base. On the other hand, some contend that diversification
policies are a costly and unnecessary form of government intervention. Critics of diversification policies argue that economic
agents can manage the adverse effects of economic volatility
through adjustment mechanisms, such as interregional migration and consumption smoothing. They also argue that the

government can mitigate the undesirable impact of specialization through sound fiscal policies and the provision of social safety nets to individuals. The perceived relationship between economic diversification and stability has been the rationale behind the development of volatility indicators as "performance measures" for provinces, especially for western Canada.

The objective of this chapter is twofold. First, we examine and compare the economic stability of Alberta, a province particularly prone to resource-based instability, with that of Ontario, a province considered to be well-diversified and relatively stable. Second, we examine the contributions of changes in the industrial mix to economic volatility using a portfolio variance framework.

The chapter is organized as follows. The next section discusses the empirical and theoretical issues surrounding the relationship between economic diversity and stability. The third section provides a review of how instability has been defined and measured in the literature, with a focus on the portfolio variance approach. In the fourth section, we calculate and compare regional economic instability (REI) indices based on various economic indicators for Alberta and Ontario. In addition, we examine how changes in the industrial structure over time have had an impact on regional economic instability in the two provinces by deriving the contribution of changes in the industrial mix to the volatility (CIMV) index. The fifth section gives a brief summary of the key findings and offers some concluding remarks.

THE LINK BETWEEN DIVERSITY AND STABILITY

The widely held belief that diversity promotes economic stability has been the basis for policies that promote economic diversification, even though it has been conventional to argue that there exists an inherent trade-off between growth and stability. The theory of comparative advantage implies that growth is derived from specialization. However, specialization increases the vulnerability of a region to idiosyncratic risk.[1] Hence, economic diversification is seen as a means of spreading risks across sectors in the region, thereby leading to greater economic stability.

In resource-abundant regions, such as those in western Canada, resource-based specialization has been the cornerstone of economic growth and development, but at the same time is also believed to be the main source of economic volatility.

To examine the link between diversity and stability, it is useful to start off by looking at the relationship between specialization, growth, and instability in the context of a small open economy. According to staple and export-based theories, exogenous demand plays a major role in regional economic growth, and this in turn is driven by its price or demand in the world market. An increase in the world price of, or demand for, a region's primary export creates an incentive for its producers to boost production, thereby raising the sector's demand for factor inputs. In a small open economy, the higher demand for the resource commodity causes labour and capital to move into the region. In addition, the expansion of the resource sector also generates direct and indirect impacts on the rest of the economy. First, the growth of the resource sector increases the demand for its inputs (backward linkage) as well as raising supply to local industries for which its product is an input (forward linkage). Second, the government experiences an increase in revenues from the resource sector arising from higher royalties and corporate income tax revenues. This, in turn, feeds through to other sectors in the economy, such as higher spending on infrastructure or education, which creates another round of effects. Third, higher employment in the region raises overall regional income and leads to further increases in aggregate demand through greater consumer spending and higher personal income tax revenues.

Although resource-based specialization acts as a stimulus to economic growth, it certainly has many drawbacks, as illustrated by the experience of western Canada in the early 1990s and in underdeveloped economies (for instance, Ghana and Nigeria). First, it is argued that the world prices of primary products fluctuate considerably, making export earnings highly volatile and an unreliable source of growth for the regional economy (Gillis et al. 1996). The interindustry linkages have the reverse impact during a contraction in the resource sector arising from highly volatile or declining prices. Furthermore, the impact of demand shocks on regional output also affects the price of factor inputs. In the case of a rapidly expanding resource sector, these supply-side effects can be highly destabilizing, a phenomenon coined by economists as the "Dutch Disease." For example, the rapid expansion of the resource sector bids up wages in the region in order to attract labour into the sector. The upward pressure on costs, combined with slow short-run adjustment in the labour supply, hurts other industries that have not experienced higher prices for their goods or services, thereby reducing their competitiveness.

Although the supposition that diversification leads to greater stability is somewhat compelling, there have been numerous criticisms of this hypothesized relationship on both empirical and theoretical grounds. On the empirical front, there is inconclusive evidence on whether diversity promotes stability and growth. While there are several explanations offered by scholars for this empirical puzzle, the most prevalent is that most measures of diversity are theoretically or empirically flawed (see Kort 1981; Malizia and Ke 1993; Siegel, Johnson, and Alwang 1995a; and Wagner and Deller 1998). This lack of consensus among scholars on the most appropriate measure(s) of diversity is due to the fact that the concept is used in a wide range of disciplines, such as industrial organization, regional economics, and finance. Hence, the concept of diversity is developed within the different theoretical frameworks of each discipline, leading to different approaches to its measurement. Meanwhile, some suggest that other factors such as the use of small sample sizes, exclusion of control variables in the analysis, and flawed regression techniques account for the lack of empirical substantiation on this relationship (Kort 1981; Smith and Gibson 1987; and Malizia and Ke 1993).[2]

With regard to the theoretical issues, there has been a lot of discussion on the possibility of simultaneously pursuing economic stability and growth through diversification (see Kort 1991; and Siegel, Johnson, and Alwang 1995a). Some have tried to reconcile this trade-off by placing the concepts of growth and stability into perspective. Wagner and Deller (1998, 542) claim that the "simultaneous pursuit of growth and stability is not contradictory when viewed in terms of the short-run and long-run." In the short-run, regional planners develop policies aimed at promoting growth of industries where the region has comparative advantage. Over time, however, greater diversity in the economic structure is needed for the region to achieve stability. Wagner and Deller (1998, 542) thus view diversification as the "long-run envelope of the region's short-run efforts in promoting growth."

Parallel to this argument is the longstanding hypothesis that economies become more diversified as they become more developed. Studies that have examined the economic history of rich countries such as Canada have traced their development to resource-based specialization, and this continues to hold true for developing economies (Innis 1920). This historical trend suggests that specialization is a precursor of diversification and long-run stability and that diversification naturally evolves at different points on the development path. In addition, there is cross-country evidence that sectoral concentration follows a U-shaped pattern in relation to a nation's income level (Imbs and Wacziarg 2003).[3] At first, economies diversify at early stages of development, but then start to specialize again at some later point in the development process. The turning point is such that, for most Organisation for Economic Co-operation and Development (OECD) countries, higher income levels are associated with more specialization. However, such findings may not hold at the regional level given that external economies that induce industrial localization and specialization are stronger at the regional than country level.

THE CONCEPT AND MEASUREMENT OF STABILITY AND DIVERSIFICATION

Economic Instability

Malizia and Ke (1993, 222) define (economic) stability as the "absence of variation in economic activity over time." Based on that definition, which we utilize here, economic instability pertains to fluctuations in economic activity.

Although there is no consensus on the best measure of instability, there is at least some consistency in how it has been measured in the literature. Most studies employ a variance-based statistic wherein the main difference lies in the method employed to calculate the benchmark against which deviations are measured. This study employs the following measure of the regional economic instability (REI) index used by Postner and Wesa (1985) and Mansell and Percy (1990):[4]

1.
$$REI = \left[\frac{\sum_{t=1}^{T}\left(e_t - \hat{e}_t\right)^2}{\left(T-3\right)\overline{e}^2} \right]^{1/2}$$

where e_t is the actual value of the economic variable of interest (e.g., output) in year t, $\overline{e}$ is the mean over the selected period, T is the number of observation periods, and $\hat{e}_t$ is the predicted value of the variable based on a non-linear (quadratic) time trend, defined by:

2. $\hat{e}_t = \hat{\beta}_0 + \hat{\beta}_1\left(t\right) + \hat{\beta}_2\left(t^2\right)$

By subtracting the estimated trend value from the actual (e.g., output) series, we are isolating the instability element from the trend component of the series.[5] This de-trending procedure has been used in the literature especially when analyzing the relationship between economic instability and other variables using regression analysis. The deviations from the trend are squared and summed to calculate the variance, which, in turn, is divided by the mean (squared) to standardize for size of region so as to facilitate meaningful interregional comparisons. We then take the square root of the resulting term to generate a standard deviation-based measure of instability. Note that since the REI index is based on squared deviations, proportionally greater weight is attached to larger deviations. Loosely speaking, the REI index is a measure of the fluctuations in a variable (e.g., output) around its trend values relative to its average value, and a higher index implies greater instability, and vice versa.

As discussed in Section 2, the conventional belief that resource-dependent economies are more unstable has its roots in both theory as well as the historical experience of some regional and underdeveloped economies. Mansell and Percy (1990) validate this empirically for western Canada by calculating the REI index using data on population, GDP, and personal income over the period 1961–1985. They found that the western provinces were among the most unstable provinces in Canada with respect to these variables, with Alberta emerging as the most volatile province. They also found Alberta to exhibit the greatest employment variability among all provinces in Canada during the same period, to a degree that is considerably higher than Texas and Oklahoma, two US states that have a similar economic base. Much of the same picture emerges from the study of Postner and Wesa (1985) using data on employment levels from 1970 to 1983. Their results show that the western provinces (particularly Alberta) had greater employment instability compared to the central provinces, particularly Ontario.

The Portfolio Variance Approach

Diversity measures can be broadly classified into four classes:[6] entropy or equiproportional, type-of-industry, portfolio variance, and the input–output model. The first two are traditional measures used in the regional economics literature and ascribe instability to either having an unequal distribution of economic activity (e.g., output) among sectors or specialization in inherently unstable sectors. One of the major limitations of these measures is that they are one-dimensional in their approach to measuring instability. More specifically, these measures only look at the instability of individual sectors (own-sector instability) without taking into account their relationship to other sectors in the region (cross-sectoral instability). This shortcoming has led to the development of measures that take into account the importance of interindustry relationships, one of which is the portfolio variance approach.

The portfolio variance framework was originally developed in finance by Markowitz (1959) and later applied in the regional economics literature by Conroy (1975) and Brown and Pheasant (1985). This chapter uses the portfolio variance framework to decompose aggregate volatility into own-sectoral and cross-sectoral components. The variance in aggregate output, or the portfolio variance (V), is defined as:

$$3. \quad V = \sum_{i=1}^{N} w_i^2 V\left(X_i\right) + \sum_{i=1}^{N} \sum_{j=1, j \neq i}^{N} w_i w_j Cov(X_i, X_j)$$

where w_i is the share of sector i in total provincial GDP and is calculated by dividing the average GDP in sector i $(\bar{X}_i)$ by the average of the total provincial GDP during the selected period, $V(X_i)$ is the variance of GDP in sector i, $Cov(X_i, X_j)$ is the covariance of GDP between sector i and sector j, and N is the number of industries in the region. Furthermore, $V(X_i)$ and $Cov(X_i, X_j)$ are calculated as follows:

$$4. \quad V\left(X_i\right) = \left[\frac{\sum_{t=1}^{T}\left(X_{it} - \hat{X}_{it}\right)^2}{(T-3)} \right]$$

$$5. \quad Cov(X_i, X_j) = \left[\frac{\sum_{t=1}^{T}\left(X_{it} - \hat{X}_{it}\right)\left(X_{jt} - \hat{X}_{jt}\right)}{(T-3)} \right]$$

where X_{it} is the actual GDP level in industry i at time t and $\hat{X}_{it}$ is the predicted GDP level in industry i at time t based on a non-linear (quadratic) time trend as in equation (2). Note that similar to the REI index, we measure output volatility in terms of the deviation of the actual level of output from its trend.

There are several studies in Canada that have used the portfolio variance approach to measure the relative sectoral employment instability of the western provinces compared to other regions. Postner and Wesa (1985), for instance, used this to show the industrial disaggregation of the province-wide REI measures based on employment. They found a remarkable pattern of similarity across western and central provinces. In almost all provinces they found that the construction and primary sectors (which include forestry and mining) displayed the highest employment variability among the eight industries used in their analysis, while transportation, communication and utilities, trade, and finance were the least unstable sectors. Manufacturing, on the other hand, ranked somewhere in the middle of the instability rankings among industries. A disaggregation of the manufacturing sector also revealed some similarities across provinces, especially among western provinces, including the relative instability of primary manufacturing sectors (such as wood, petroleum, and coal products) compared to other manufacturing subsectors.

Chambers (1999) also employed the portfolio variance approach to study changes in employment volatility over time in Alberta, British Columbia, and Saskatchewan. In his study, he utilized quarterly percent changes in employment from 1976 to 1998 to calculate the three provinces' employment variances for two subperiods: the first period (Q1 of 1976 to Q4 of 1987) and the second period (Q1 of 1988 until Q2 of 1998). Similar to previous studies, he found the three provinces to be more unstable than the national average in the first period, with Alberta recording the highest level of employment instability. In the second period, however, Alberta experienced both a relative and absolute decline in employment variability, resulting in the province becoming the least unstable in terms of employment. An industrial disaggregation of the province-wide variances also revealed that the relative stability of Alberta was due to the significant reduction in the variances of the majority of industries. In addition, Alberta's manufacturing, construction, finance, and services sectors became more stable in the second period than in the other two western provinces.

Although the portfolio variance is a very useful indicator of which sectors in the region contribute to economic instability, there are several criticisms of its applicability in regional economic analysis. Unlike the equiproportional and type-of-industry measures, the portfolio method is a variance-based measure of diversity; that is, a lower variance is believed to indicate a more diversified and more stable economy and vice versa. Therefore, the portfolio variance approach should not be used to test the relationship between diversity and stability since the latter is also measured in terms of variance.[7] It is also argued that there are fundamental differences between an individual's financial portfolio and a regional economy. Unlike in a financial portfolio, the addition of a new sector often requires significantly large costs and its effects are often lagged (Siegel, Johnson, and Alwang 1995a). Moreover, due to differences in comparative advantage, there are benefits to having a certain industry vary by region (Sherwood-Call 1990). Finally, the portfolio variance approach does not capture the dynamics behind interindustry relationships. More specifically, the covariance term only indicates the direction and degree in which two sectors move together, but offers no further insight on how these two industries may be linked (Wagner 2000).

Before concluding this section, it is important to also discuss an interesting application of the portfolio variance framework to the study of diversification policies. Gilchrist and St. Louis (1991) pioneered the idea of integrating the concept of risk-return trade-off into input–output (I–O) models in Canada. Using 1979 input–output tables for Saskatchewan, they assessed three alternative strategies for diversification. First, they developed a model of an open regional economy wherein the level of sectoral activity is assumed to be determined by the allocation of labour among sectors. Second, they assumed that the regional economy is subject to (sector-specific) productivity and price shocks. Third, these shocks determine the expected level and variance of regional income via their effects on the value-added output in the sector. Regional planners can adopt policies to try to improve a region's welfare by reallocating labour among various sectors, where welfare is assumed to be increasing in expected regional income and decreasing in the variance of regional income. This redeployment of labour is what the authors defined as diversification. They restricted their analysis to three forms of diversification strategies: (1) targeted sectoral development, wherein labour is drawn evenly from the remaining sectors in the economy and moved into the targeted sector; (2) reduced sectoral dependency, wherein diversification is aimed at releasing labour from an unstable sector (such as primary industries) to be absorbed by another (relatively more stable) sector; and (3) regional self-sufficiency, wherein labour is directed away from specialized export sectors and towards import competing industries.

The results were quite revealing. First, Gilchrist and St. Louis (1991) developed an "efficiency frontier," which showed the best possible combinations of the expected level and the variance of regional income (risk-return combinations) for Saskatchewan. Based on the sectoral labour allocation observed in 1979, they found Saskatchewan to be considerably below the frontier, indicating that there is room for welfare improvement. Second, they found agriculture to be a relatively risky sector that yielded below average returns. This supports the recurring policy theme in Saskatchewan that moving away from agriculture is an effective diversification strategy. Third, they found that most manufacturing sectors are more stable but have lower returns, while other resource-based industries (such as mining) offer higher returns at the expense of greater instability. Their results confirm the conventional wisdom that expanding the manufacturing sector is stabilizing. However, Saskatchewan has tended to specialize in natural resources, as these sectors yield higher per capita income. Finally, their results indicate that self-sufficiency is not an appropriate strategy for Saskatchewan since they find trade to be significantly important to living standards.

The Contribution of Changes in the Industrial Mix to Volatility

In addition to looking at cross-sectoral volatility, the portfolio variance approach also provides a framework for analyzing how changes in the region's economic structure can affect (i.e., increase or decrease) the aggregate regional variance. Rewriting equation (3), since $V(X_i) = Cov(X_i, X_i)$, the variance in output of a province can be expressed as:

3A.
$$V = \sum_{i=1}^{N} \sum_{j=1}^{N} w_i w_j Cov(X_i, X_j)$$

Any change in the variance due to changes in the province's industrial mix can be approximated using a second order Taylor series approximation as:

6. $$\Delta V = \sum_{i=1}^{n} \frac{\partial V}{\partial w_i} \Delta w_i + \frac{1}{2} \sum_{i=1}^{n} \frac{\partial^2 V}{\partial w_i^2} \left(\Delta w_i\right)^2$$

where:

7. $$\frac{\partial V}{\partial w_i} = \sum_{j=1}^{n} 2 w_j Cov\left(X_i, X_j\right)$$

and

8. $$\frac{\partial^2 V}{\partial w_i^2} = 2V\left(X_i\right)$$

Therefore, we will define the CIMV (Contribution of Changes in Industrial Mix to Volatility) index as the approximate percentage change in the variance of output due to a change in the province's industrial mix, or:

9. $$CIMV = \frac{\Delta V}{V} 100 = \frac{1}{V}\left[\sum_{i=1}^{N}\sum_{j=1}^{N} 2 w_j Cov(X_i, X_j)\Delta w_i + \sum_{i=1}^{N} V\left(X_i\right)\left(\Delta w_i\right)^2 \right] 100$$

The CIMV index shows how changes in the industrial structure (i.e., the sectoral shares in provincial GDP) over time have contributed to changes in provincial output instability.

Note that there are two components to the CIMV index. The first component depends on the covariances of the sectors' output fluctuations, while the second component depends on the variances of the sectors' outputs. The expansion of any sector will then give rise to a covariance effect and a variance effect. It will be useful to measure these effects for a one percentage point increase in the output share of any sector. The covariance effect (CE) for sector i will be given by:

10. $$CE_i = \frac{1}{V}\left[\sum_{j=1}^{N} 2w_j Cov\left(X_i, X_j\right)\right], \quad j \neq i$$

and the variance effect (VE) for sector i will be given by:

11. $$VE_i = \frac{\left(0.01 + 2w_i\right)V\left(X_i\right)}{V}$$

While VE_i is always positive, the CE_i can be positive or negative. The covariance effect can reduce the volatility of total output if the fluctuations in the output of sector i are negatively correlated with a weighted average of the output fluctuations in other sectors, where the weights are the output shares of the other sectors. The expansion of an industry with a negative covariance effect would reduce the volatility of the economy if it is not more than offset by its variance effect. However, since most private sector activities are affected by the same common shocks, such as interest rate increases, or are linked through provision or purchase of intermediate inputs, such as the manufacturing sector providing drilling rigs and pipe to the oil and gas sector, the covariance effect for most sectors will be positive. In the next section, we use the CIMV index and the decomposition into a covariance effect and variance effect to examine how changes in the industrial structure in Alberta have affected the volatility of total output in the province.

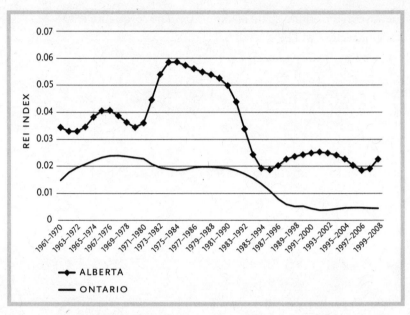

FIGURE 5.1 Regional Economic Instability Indices for Population: Alberta and Ontario

EMPIRICAL ANALYSIS

The Relative Instability of Alberta and Ontario

Using data on levels of population, employment, per capita real GDP, per capita real personal income, and per capita real consumption, we calculate the REI indices, using equation (1), for Alberta and Ontario. We also find it insightful to examine the REI index values from nominal per capita GDP and nominal per capita personal income. Rather than calculating individual REI values for comparison, we calculate a series of REI indices for each economic variable so as to observe the trends in the REI indices as well as to be able to compare levels. Most of our data extend from 1961 to 2008.[8] While we estimate the trend values, using equation (2), over the full period, we calculate the REI indices for a sequence of 10-year periods. That is, for example, we determine the REI for 1961–1970, for 1962–1971, 1963–1972, etc.

		1961–70 to 1999–2008*	1961–70 to 1984–93	1961–70 to 198X–†	1985–94 to 1999–2008	198X–9X to 1999–2008‡
Population	AB	0.0352	0.0434		0.0221	
	ON	0.0146	0.0200		0.0059	
Employment (1966–2009)	AB	0.0684	0.0863	0.0939	0.0473	0.0470
	ON	0.0392	0.0336	0.0309	0.0459	0.0462
GDP real pc	AB	0.0565	0.0739	0.0788	0.0313	0.0329
	ON	0.0458	0.0366	0.0333	0.0591	0.0590
Personal Income real pc	AB	0.0785	0.0800	0.0851	0.0760	0.0708
	ON	0.0373	0.0397	0.0305	0.0462	0.0451
Consumption real pc	AB	0.0548	0.0601	0.0652	0.0464	0.0439
	ON	0.0416	0.0432	0.0434	0.0390	0.0397
GDP nominal pc	AB	0.2115	0.2558		0.1408	
	ON	0.0951	0.1248		0.0474	
Personal Income nominal pc	AB	0.1367	0.1695	0.1569	0.0841	0.0851
	ON	0.1107	0.1426	0.1379	0.0597	0.0415

TABLE 5.1 Average REI Indices for Economic Indicators over Various Years

* Except for Employment, which is for 1966 to 2009.
† Period varies by variable unless ending at 1984–93. End points are 1981–90 for Employment, 1980–89 for real GDP, 1981–90 for real Personal Income, 1980–89 for real Consumption, and 1988–97 for nominal Personal Income.
‡ Period varies by variable unless 1985–94 is the starting point; 1982–91 for Employment, 1981–90 for real GDP, 1982–91 for real Personal Income, 1981–90 for real Consumption, and 1989–98 for nominal Personal Income.

up to the final 10-year period, 1999–2008. This procedure provides a series of 39 REI values for the sequence of 39 ten-year periods available between 1961 and 2008. Thus, we can observe the trend in the REI index and compare the trends in Alberta and Ontario as well as the levels of the REI indices. We plot those trends in figures, and discuss the results below.

Our REI index values for population are uniformly larger for Alberta than for Ontario (Figure 5.1), a result that is consistent with Mansell and Percy (1990). For the 39 ten-year periods between 1961 and 2008, the average REI index was 0.0352 for Alberta and 0.0146 for Ontario (Table 5.1). The largest differences between the two series reflect the rapid population growth in Alberta from the early 1970s to the early 1980s and suggest that associated interregional migration flows into the province

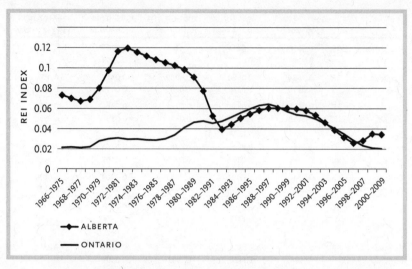

FIGURE 5.2 Regional Economic Instability Indices for Employment: Alberta and Ontario

are highly sensitive to economic conditions in Alberta relative to those in other provinces. Both Alberta and Ontario show reduced instability since the mid-1980s.

Figure 5.2 shows the REI indices for employment. The REI values for Alberta were much larger than those for Ontario until the early to mid-1980s, but since then the two have been at similar levels and followed parallel paths. The Alberta boom that ended in 2008 is reflected in only a slight deviation in the most recent Alberta REIs from those of Ontario. Figures 5.3 and 5.4 show the actual and the estimated trend employment in Alberta and Ontario. Alberta's employment fluctuates around the trend line more so than does Ontario's. Alberta experienced rapid employment growth in the 1970s but slipped back during the early 1980s. Ontario had a noticeable blip in employment in the late 1980s. Employment in both provinces, but more so in Ontario, suffered setbacks in the 1990s as indicated by the trend paths. Alberta employment was notably above trend in 2007 and 2008 but moved back toward the trend line in 2009 while Ontario's slipped slightly below. These figures illustrate the patterns leading to the REI index values for employment.

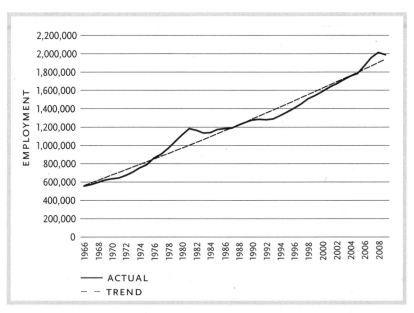

FIGURE 5.3 Alberta Employment: Actual and Trend Estimate

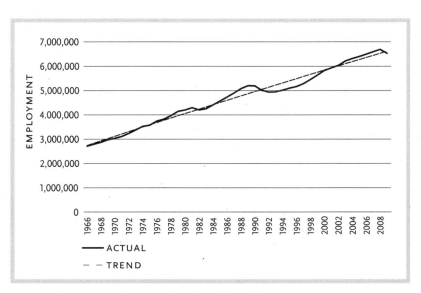

FIGURE 5.4 Ontario Employment: Actual and Trend Estimate

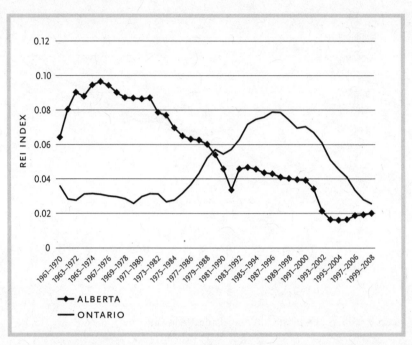

FIGURE 5.5 Regional Economic Instability Indices for Per Capita Real GDP: Alberta and Ontario

Particularly striking are the contrasting trends in the REI indices of real per capita GDP. Those are shown in Figure 5.5. Other than for the decades up to the mid-1970s, economic instability has been almost steadily and substantially declining in Alberta. Through the 1970s, the REI value was about 0.09, but the values for the most recent data (notably for the years 2002 to 2008) are about 0.02. That represents a decline to one-quarter of the levels in the 1970s. Meanwhile, the instability of real per capita GDP in Ontario increased sharply during the late 1980s and the 1990s, declining only notably in the past decade.

The differences in the stability of the two provinces are demonstrated in Figures 5.6 and 5.7. Figure 5.6 shows that real per capita GDP in Alberta deviated most substantially from the trend between 1970 and 1983. In Ontario, however, the greatest fluctuations about the trend occurred from 1985 to 2000. The energy boom (and bust) of the 1970s and early 1980s resulted in instability in Alberta that far exceeded that of the most recent boom (and

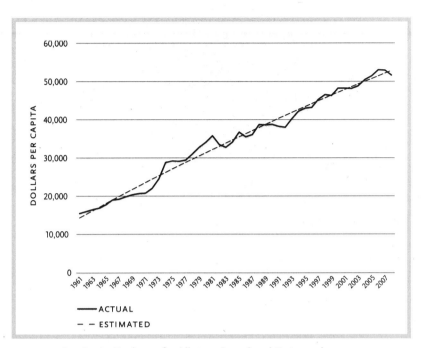

FIGURE 5.6 Per Capita Real GDP for Alberta: Actual and Estimated

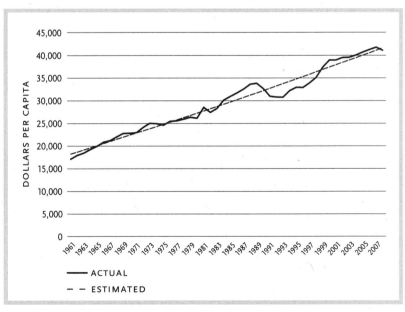

FIGURE 5.7 Per Capita Real GDP for Ontario: Actual and Estimated

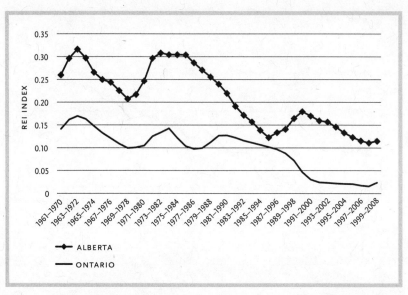

FIGURE 5.8 Regional Economic Instability Indices for Nominal Per Capita GDP: Alberta and Ontario

bust). Economic stability in Alberta began with a period of relatively stable, and relatively low, energy prices. The earlier energy boom seems to have had only a modest effect on the stability of the Ontario economy, but Ontario was greatly affected by the economic doldrums of the 1990s. While the REI values of the two provinces are currently close to one another, it will be interesting to see whether the post-2008 crisis causes the two to diverge.[9]

The REI indices for nominal per capita GDP show a rather different pattern (Figure 5.8). For the nominal measure, the instability index values for Alberta are consistently greater than those in Ontario.[10] The averages over the full period are 0.2115 and 0.0951 respectively. Both schedules, however, have a declining trend—Alberta moving from an average of 0.256 until 1984–1993 to 0.141 thereafter, while, for Ontario, the averages for those periods move from 0.125 to 0.0474. Declining inflation rates throughout much of this period may contribute to the reduced instability measures over the full period. However, there is more. Comparing the REI patterns of nominal and real per capita GDPS in each province suggests that price (presumably

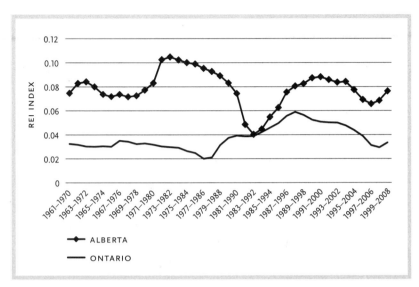

FIGURE 5.9 Regional Economic Instability Indices for Per Capita Real Personal Income: Alberta and Ontario

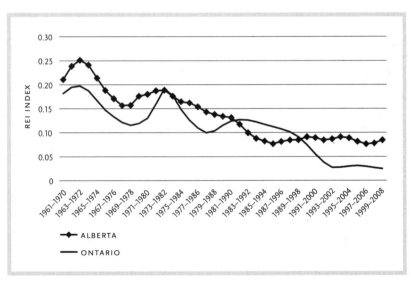

FIGURE 5.10 Regional Economic Instability Indices for Per Capita Nominal Personal Income: Alberta and Ontario

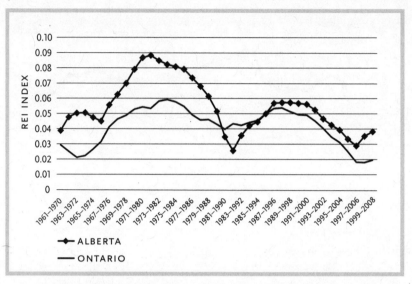

FIGURE 5.11 Regional Economic Instability Indices for Per Capita Real Consumption: Alberta and Ontario

primarily energy price) instability continues to contribute substantially to economic instability in Alberta, but the instability in Ontario is primarily associated with fluctuations in real output per capita. To illustrate, post-1985, the average REI values for nominal and real per capita GDP in Ontario are quite similar (0.0474 and 0.0591) but, for Alberta, the difference remains relatively large (0.1408 versus 0.0313).

Real personal income is less stable in Alberta than in Ontario (Figure 5.9). In fact, for only two or three of the 10-year periods are the numbers comparable. Over the full study period, the average REI index for Alberta was 0.0785, more than twice the 0.0373 value for Ontario. Interestingly, however, is that real personal income became more unstable in Ontario after 1980 though still less so than in Alberta. REI values for nominal personal income per capita in the two provinces are shown in Figure 5.10.[11]

Although real income has been consistently more unstable in Alberta, real per capita consumption variability has not been much different in the two provinces except for during Alberta's boom in the 1970s (Figure 5.11). In fact, since the mid-1980s, the two REI indices have similar values (averaging 0.0439 in Alberta and 0.0397 in Ontario, Table 5.1) and have followed similar paths.

The figures suggest that there was a transition in the early 1980s where the REI indices tended to diminish in Alberta and the trend lines for Alberta and Ontario tended to move closer together. That is, differences in the economic instability of Alberta and Ontario, while still present, tended to decline. Though already noted, this pattern is most evident in the data presented in Table 5.1. There we separate the decade sequences from 1961 to 2008 into two periods—from 1961–1970 to 1984–1993 and from 1985–1994 to 1999–2008—using the end of 1984 and the beginning of 1985 as the separation point. The mean REI index values for each of our economic indicators are calculated for the two periods. In the case of Alberta, the mean REI value for all indicators is smaller in the second period than in the first. On average, the later values are 58.3% of those of the earlier period— implying about a 40% average reduction in the instability measures in Alberta. Among the real measures (i.e., population, employment, real per capita GDP, personal income, and consumption), the reductions are largest for population, employment, and real per capita GDP. The change for real per capita income is the smallest. In Ontario's case, the mean REI values actually increase in the second period for employment, real per capita GDP, and real per capita personal income. For the most recent period, the mean REI values for employment and real per capita GDP in Ontario are actually larger than those in Alberta. If we set the break point separating the two periods to be where the decade REI values of Alberta and Ontario are closest for the particular series (rather than always at 1984–1993 decade), the differences in the means between the two periods simply reinforce our results.

To summarize, the Alberta economy has become more stable, while, by many indicators, the Ontario economy has become less stable. It appears that the diversity offered by the Ontario economy has not provided or does not provide as much protection against economic instability as it once did, and the natural resource sector in Alberta has not had the destabilizing influence that it had in the 1970s and early 1980s.

Macaspac (2007) studied output instability in western Canada. While she calculated only a single REI index value for the 1981–2006 period, those were calculated for all provinces. Her results are consistent with those reported here for Alberta and Ontario. She found that the western provinces exhibited greater relative stability than generally perceived and, based on nominal data, showed absolute and relative improvement in their stability over time. In addition, she found that Ontario, a province that has traditionally been regarded as a more stable and a more diversified economy with a strong manufacturing base, exhibits greater instability. An interesting feature of her results is that an interprovincial comparison reveals that for the five real indicators (i.e., population, employment, and real per capita GDP, personal income, and consumption) the provinces with the largest REI index values for 1981–2006 (i.e., those with REI measures ranked first second or third largest) were Newfoundland and Labrador (five times), Ontario (four times), British Columbia (three), Nova Scotia (two) and Saskatchewan (one). Not only did Alberta not rank in the top three, it ranked below the Canadian average in three instances. It appears here too, that economic diversity does not guarantee economic stability. Interesting to note, however, is the high rank of Newfoundland and Labrador—a small province experiencing a resource-driven boom during part of that period.

Sources of Output Instability: The Portfolio Variance Framework

Using equations (4) and (5), we calculate the variance–covariance matrices for Alberta and Ontario using data on real GDP by industry (in constant 1997 prices) for the period 1984–2003. A change in Statistics Canada data prevented us from extending the period analyzed.[12]

Our results, which are presented in Tables 5.2 and 5.3, show that the resource sectors are among the most volatile sectors in Alberta. Looking at the industry variances (which are the diagonal elements in the variance–covariance matrices) we find that Alberta's oil and gas (OAG) sector has the highest variance in terms of output. This is followed by manufacturing (MAN) and construction (CON). High output volatility in these sectors is amplified by their substantial shares in the Alberta economy. During the period 1984–2003, oil and gas, manufacturing, and construction sectors accounted for an average of 18%, 9%, and 7% of total provincial output, respectively.

Now that we have identified the most volatile sectors in Alberta, it is interesting to see how these highly volatile sectors may be linked (positively or negatively) to the remaining industries. Our results show that output fluctuations in Alberta's oil and gas sector move in opposite direction to most industries, as shown by the relatively high number of industries with negative covariances (14 out of the total 21 industries), thereby reducing aggregate output instability. However, the oil and gas sector has a very large positive covariance with manufacturing. This significant positive linkage between the two sectors is not surprising given the province's orientation towards resource-based manufacturing industries. One puzzling result, however, is the negative covariance between oil and gas and construction. In contrast to the oil and gas sector, output fluctuations in manufacturing and construction move in tandem with most industries (as well as with each other). This, combined with their relatively high volatility and large shares in total provincial output, adds to Alberta's overall output instability.

We now turn our attention to Ontario, which has been traditionally regarded as one of the most diversified and stable provinces in Canada. Our results show that the manufacturing sector is the main source of Ontario's aggregate output instability both in terms of own-sectoral and cross-sectoral volatility (as shown by the positive, and in many instances large, covariances with 16 out of the total 21 industries). Construction and finance also exhibit high output volatility. These three sectors represent almost half of Ontario's total provincial output (with manufacturing, finance, and construction representing an average of 22%, 21%, and 6%, respectively, of aggregate output during the period under observation), so volatility in these industries should account for a substantial share of Ontario's overall output volatility. Moreover, the manufacturing and finance sectors display

	CAP	FOR	SAA	OAG	MIN	SAM	UTL	CON	MAN	WHL	RET
CAP	**75.33**	-0.41	-0.63	102.04	1.57	26.47	-3.90	16.22	37.52	-12.15	-7.25
FOR	-0.41	**0.38**	0.00	-5.27	0.13	1.53	-0.08	-1.02	0.29	0.31	0.17
SAA	-0.63	0.00	**0.16**	-8.42	0.17	-2.13	-0.25	0.83	-3.03	1.36	1.19
OAG	102.04	-5.27	-8.42	**892.49**	-15.78	85.39	20.16	-97.29	131.14	-119.37	-83.09
MIN	1.57	0.13	0.17	-15.78	**3.28**	-6.43	-4.18	3.49	-2.43	2.63	4.10
SAM	26.47	1.53	-2.13	85.39	-6.43	**113.85**	20.55	63.97	141.83	14.25	-14.73
UTL	-3.90	-0.08	-0.25	20.16	-4.18	20.55	**16.03**	26.22	35.63	3.05	3.53
CON	16.22	-1.02	0.83	-97.29	3.49	63.97	26.22	**203.61**	174.21	51.14	43.07
MAN	37.52	0.29	-3.03	131.14	-2.43	141.83	35.63	174.21	**284.16**	26.64	-7.64
WHL	-12.15	0.31	1.36	-119.37	2.63	14.25	3.05	51.14	26.64	**65.64**	20.85
RET	-7.25	0.17	1.19	-83.09	4.10	-14.73	3.53	43.07	-7.64	20.85	**34.30**
TRA	27.52	-1.06	-1.82	151.52	0.90	43.30	10.75	57.00	110.59	-4.02	-6.05
INF	-0.58	-0.13	0.46	-23.64	1.02	-4.24	1.48	19.11	4.94	5.45	7.67
FIN	-8.15	0.35	-1.14	14.56	0.10	27.54	8.78	46.42	65.33	7.53	6.03
PRO	14.18	-0.82	0.10	-0.71	3.15	21.64	9.13	84.10	79.06	13.31	17.32
ADM	2.32	0.48	0.16	-20.18	0.29	2.30	1.81	12.59	6.39	5.25	5.39
EDU	0.74	-0.18	0.96	-58.42	4.04	-14.07	-0.54	28.70	-1.49	10.89	17.17
HC	-29.71	0.91	1.97	-158.35	0.03	-34.88	-11.24	-34.09	-92.82	17.88	11.66
ART	-0.84	0.25	0.09	-5.73	0.00	0.45	-0.24	-2.66	-3.38	3.96	0.72
ACC	-0.96	-0.06	-0.19	0.20	-0.08	12.38	5.74	32.32	33.29	5.69	5.88
OTH	-8.09	0.03	0.65	-41.20	-0.52	-4.44	0.06	6.36	-11.55	11.12	6.39
GOV	-13.48	0.21	1.35	-85.57	-0.06	-23.91	-6.40	-15.16	-52.62	4.39	5.24

TABLE 5.2 Variance–Covariance Matrix for Alberta: Based on Real GDP, 1984–2003

Note: Variances and covariances are divided by 1,000 for ease of presentation.
Legend: CAP=Crop and Animal Production, FOR=Forestry and logging; SAA=Support activities for agriculture and forestry, OAG=Oil and Gas, MIN=Mining, SAM=Support activities for mining and oil and gas, UTL=Utilities, CON=Construction, MAN=Manufacturing, WHL=Wholesale Trade, RET=Retail trade, TRA=Transportation and warehousing (excl. postal services and transit & ground passenger), INF=Information and cultural industries (excl. broadcasting & telecom), FIN=Finance, PRO=Professional, scientific, and technical services, ADM=Administrative and support, EDU=Education, HC=Health care and social assistance, ART=Arts, entertainment, and recreation, ACC=Accommodation and food services, OTH=Other services (except public administration), GOV=Public Administration.

	TRA	INF	FIN	PRO	ADM	EDU	HC	ART	ACC	OTH	GOV
CAP	27.52	-0.58	-8.15	14.18	2.32	0.74	-29.71	-0.84	-0.96	-8.09	-13.48
FOR	-1.06	-0.13	0.35	-0.82	0.48	-0.18	0.91	0.25	-0.06	0.03	0.21
SAA	-1.82	0.46	-1.14	0.10	0.16	0.96	1.97	0.09	-0.19	0.65	1.35
OAG	151.52	-23.64	14.56	-0.71	-20.18	-58.42	-158.35	-5.73	0.20	-41.20	-85.57
MIN	0.90	1.02	0.10	3.15	0.29	4.04	0.03	0.00	-0.08	-0.52	-0.06
SAM	43.30	-4.24	27.54	21.64	2.30	-14.07	-34.88	0.45	12.38	-4.44	-23.91
UTL	10.75	1.48	8.78	9.13	1.81	-0.54	-11.24	-0.24	5.74	0.06	-6.40
CON	57.00	19.11	46.42	84.10	12.59	28.70	-34.09	-2.66	32.32	6.36	-15.16
MAN	110.59	4.94	65.33	79.06	6.39	-1.49	-92.82	-3.38	33.29	-11.55	-52.62
WHL	-4.02	5.45	7.53	13.31	5.25	10.89	17.88	3.96	5.69	11.12	4.39
RET	-6.05	7.67	6.03	17.32	5.39	17.17	11.66	0.72	5.88	6.39	5.24
TRA	**63.03**	1.62	24.17	34.72	-0.09	0.16	-53.77	-2.75	12.71	-9.67	-28.71
INF	1.62	**3.61**	1.14	7.96	1.89	5.43	0.88	-0.19	3.02	2.00	2.01
FIN	24.17	1.14	**41.09**	20.44	2.00	-1.00	-19.80	-1.87	11.03	-0.98	-10.63
PRO	34.72	7.96	20.44	**44.75**	3.04	12.87	-25.24	-2.24	13.01	-0.20	-11.24
ADM	-0.09	1.89	2.00	3.04	**3.21**	2.17	0.54	0.82	2.57	1.03	-0.42
EDU	0.16	5.43	-1.00	12.87	2.17	**16.59**	4.72	-0.84	2.38	1.89	4.49
HC	-53.77	0.88	-19.80	-25.24	0.54	4.72	**58.47**	2.32	-8.75	12.92	31.26
ART	-2.75	-0.19	-1.87	-2.24	0.82	-0.84	2.32	**1.08**	-0.38	0.73	-0.06
ACC	12.71	3.02	11.03	13.01	2.57	2.38	-8.75	-0.38	**7.04**	0.41	-4.88
OTH	-9.67	2.00	-0.98	-0.20	1.03	1.89	12.92	0.73	0.41	**5.26**	7.68
GOV	-28.71	2.01	-10.63	-11.24	-0.42	4.49	31.26	-0.06	-4.88	7.68	**21.21**

	CAP	FOR	SAA	OAG	MIN	SAM	UTL	CON	MAN	WHL	RET
CAP	**44.0**	-1.0	-0.1	-0.2	-20.9	0.6	2.0	-160.5	314.2	-10.7	-0.3
FOR	-1.0	**7.6**	0.7	-0.2	6.6	2.1	5.7	113.8	288.9	71.9	66.2
SAA	-0.1	0.7	**0.3**	0.0	1.9	0.0	-0.9	22.5	25.7	12.0	9.0
OAG	-0.2	-0.2	0.0	**0.1**	-0.4	-0.3	0.6	-4.9	-11.2	-3.2	-2.4
MIN	-20.9	6.6	1.9	-0.4	**43.8**	4.3	-18.7	422.2	143.1	171.0	103.0
SAM	0.6	2.1	0.0	-0.3	4.3	**3.2**	3.5	45.5	135.6	22.6	23.1
UTL	2.0	5.7	-0.9	0.6	-18.7	3.5	**145.4**	-209.5	158.6	-92.6	-17.8
CON	-160.5	113.8	22.5	-4.9	422.2	45.5	-209.5	**5371.8**	2908.6	2321.6	1524.3
MAN	314.2	288.9	25.7	-11.2	143.1	135.6	158.6	2908.6	**16803.7**	2652.0	2841.1
WHL	-10.7	71.9	12.0	-3.2	171.0	22.6	-92.6	2321.6	2652.0	**1215.3**	844.3
RET	-0.3	66.2	9.0	-2.4	103.0	23.1	-17.8	1524.3	2841.1	844.3	**784.5**
TRA	32.8	29.0	3.5	-1.2	31.7	17.1	-13.4	511.3	1686.9	341.6	321.9
INF	-20.1	38.3	6.7	-1.0	98.4	15.5	-38.5	1286.3	1493.6	624.6	474.9
FIN	-159.8	92.6	16.7	-4.3	287.3	29.0	-80.1	3471.1	2522.7	1515.3	1081.5
PRO	0.8	72.7	12.1	-5.9	174.6	32.0	-86.0	2211.0	3134.7	1164.4	896.1
ADM	-6.5	23.8	4.4	-0.7	74.8	11.1	-36.2	954.1	961.9	455.1	317.7
EDU	-23.6	-2.8	1.0	0.8	12.3	-7.4	-3.8	94.0	-431.5	11.1	-22.5
HC	-70.7	7.1	4.9	2.5	74.8	-10.4	-24.4	797.7	-808.8	248.5	85.5
ART	-15.6	10.3	1.8	0.1	32.3	4.3	-1.8	388.5	238.5	168.9	106.5
ACC	8.0	36.0	6.7	-1.5	90.7	17.4	-74.6	1139.6	1831.2	604.7	484.7
OTH	-16.5	19.4	4.4	0.3	51.4	5.5	-10.9	621.3	693.4	296.4	230.1
GOV	-57.6	-12.6	1.2	3.9	20.1	-17.0	7.4	89.2	-1381.4	-90.6	-173.3

TABLE 5.3 Variance–Covariance Matrix for Ontario: Based on Real GDP, 1984–2003

Note: Variances and covariances are divided by 1,000 for ease of presentation.
Legend: CAP=Crop and Animal Production, FOR=Forestry and logging; SAA=Support activities for agriculture and forestry, OAG=Oil and Gas, MIN=Mining, SAM=Support activities for mining and oil and gas, UTL=Utilities, CON=Construction, MAN=Manufacturing, WHL=Wholesale Trade, RET=Retail trade, TRA=Transportation and warehousing (excl. postal services and transit & ground passenger), INF=Information and cultural industries (excl. broadcasting & telecom), FIN=Finance, PRO=Professional, scientific, and technical services, ADM=Administrative and support, EDU=Education, HC=Health care and social assistance, ART=Arts, entertainment, and recreation, ACC=Accommodation and food services, OTH=Other services (except public administration), GOV=Public Administration.

	TRA	INF	FIN	PRO	ADM	EDU	HC	ART	ACC	OTH	GOV
CAP	32.8	-20.1	-159.8	0.8	-6.5	-23.6	-70.7	-15.6	8.0	-16.5	-57.6
FOR	29.0	38.3	92.6	72.7	23.8	-2.8	7.1	10.3	36.0	19.4	-12.6
SAA	3.5	6.7	16.7	12.1	4.4	1.0	4.9	1.8	6.7	4.4	1.2
OAG	-1.2	-1.0	-4.3	-5.9	-0.7	0.8	2.5	0.1	-1.5	0.3	3.9
MIN	31.7	98.4	287.3	174.6	74.8	12.3	74.8	32.3	90.7	51.4	20.1
SAM	17.1	15.5	29.0	32.0	11.1	-7.4	-10.4	4.3	17.4	5.5	-17.0
UTL	-13.4	-38.5	-80.1	-86.0	-36.2	-3.8	-24.4	-1.8	-74.6	-10.9	7.4
CON	511.3	1286.3	3471.1	2211.0	954.1	94.0	797.7	388.5	1139.6	621.3	89.2
MAN	1686.9	1493.6	2522.7	3134.7	961.9	-431.5	-808.8	238.5	1831.2	693.4	-1381.4
WHL	341.6	624.6	1515.3	1164.4	455.1	11.1	248.5	168.9	604.7	296.4	-90.6
RET	321.9	474.9	1081.5	896.1	317.7	-22.5	85.5	106.5	484.7	230.1	-173.3
TRA	**207.0**	196.1	337.7	385.4	138.2	-53.0	-51.1	39.2	242.2	90.0	-141.1
INF	196.1	**359.8**	881.3	624.8	256.8	6.6	141.5	96.0	347.2	181.3	-36.3
FIN	337.7	881.3	**2729.7**	1579.4	604.3	120.2	553.4	256.9	756.7	460.5	64.3
PRO	385.4	624.8	1579.4	**1341.5**	452.2	-15.1	155.2	153.0	661.4	291.3	-187.2
ADM	138.2	256.8	604.3	452.2	**199.6**	0.6	106.5	70.3	255.5	124.5	-17.6
EDU	-53.0	6.6	120.2	-15.1	0.6	**48.3**	99.6	8.3	-22.9	18.1	83.3
HC	-51.1	141.5	553.4	155.2	106.5	99.6	**375.9**	74.6	62.3	112.2	262.2
ART	39.2	96.0	256.9	153.0	70.3	8.3	74.6	**35.8**	80.4	52.5	28.1
ACC	242.2	347.2	756.7	661.4	255.5	-22.9	62.3	80.4	**395.1**	167.6	-101.2
OTH	90.0	181.3	460.5	291.3	124.5	18.1	112.2	52.5	167.6	**108.2**	24.3
GOV	-141.1	-36.3	64.3	-187.2	-17.6	83.3	262.2	28.1	-101.2	24.3	**293.6**

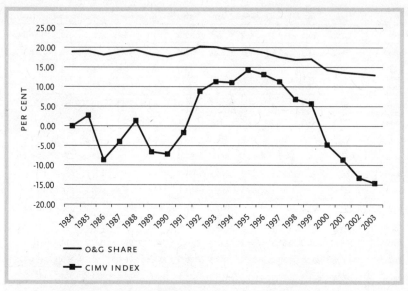

FIGURE 5.12 The CIMV Index and Output Share of the Oil and Gas Sector in the Alberta Economy, 1984–2003

significantly large, and mostly positive, covariances with most sectors in the province.

The CIMV Index

For a small open economy such as Alberta, economic instability can increase either because the world economy becomes more volatile or because the economy becomes more reliant on industries that are more prone to shocks or are more highly correlated with the shocks to each other. To measure the contribution of the change in industrial structure to aggregate output instability, we derived the Contribution of Changes in Industrial Mix to Volatility, or CIMV, Index in equation (9). This index represents the approximate percentage change in the variance of output due to changes in the province's industrial mix. We calculate the CIMV Index for Alberta and Ontario using the output-based variance–covariance matrices calculated earlier.

Figure 5.12 and Table 5.4 show the CIMV index for output for Alberta for the period 1984–2003. In these calculations, 1984 is

Year	Province	
	Alberta	Ontario
1985	2.68	2.38
1986	-8.62	1.27
1987	-3.97	0.45
1988	1.34	2.64
1989	-6.63	2.28
1990	-7.2	-1.85
1991	-1.66	-7.62
1992	8.84	-6.1
1993	11.27	-3.87
1994	11.09	0.32
1995	14.28	3.74
1996	13.14	5.4
1997	11.3	7.37
1998	6.79	10.06
1999	5.66	11.8
2000	-4.79	17.43
2001	-8.62	11.37
2002	-13.26	11.95
2003	-14.61	10.54

TABLE 5.4 CIMV Index (in percentage): Alberta and Ontario, Based on Variance–Covariance Matrix of Real GDP by Industry (Base Year 1984)

the base year, and the index indicates how changes in the output shares of the 22 industrial sectors since 1984 have affected the variance of output in Alberta, assuming that the variances and covariances of the outputs of the individual sectors have remained constant over time. Figure 5.12 shows that changes in Alberta's industrial mix led to an increase in output volatility starting in the early 1990s. However, in the years following 1995, changes in the industrial mix have steadily reduced the variance of total output. The CIMV index indicates that the change in the industrial mix in Alberta between 1984 and 2003 reduced the variance of output by 14.6%.

Which industries contributed to this reduction in output volatility? An obvious candidate is the oil and gas sector in Alberta.[13] Figure 5.12 shows that the output share of the oil and gas sector

	Alberta 1984–1990	1991–1996	1997–2003	Alberta Change 1984–2003	Ontario 1984–1990	1991–1996	1997–2003	Ontario Change 1984–2003
CAP	2.44%	2.87%	2.36%	0.20	1.08%	0.99%	0.94%	-0.40
FOR	0.15%	0.22%	0.26%	0.18	0.42%	0.24%	0.24%	-0.27
SAA	0.22%	0.17%	0.13%	-0.08	0.08%	0.08%	0.06%	-0.03
OAG	18.62%	19.40%	15.11%	-5.94	0.04%	0.03%	0.01%	-0.03
MIN	0.22%	0.42%	0.48%	0.42	1.18%	0.98%	0.74%	-0.63
SAM	2.44%	2.28%	2.51%	-0.30	0.10%	0.05%	0.06%	-0.07
UTL	3.04%	2.90%	2.46%	-0.54	3.60%	3.44%	2.68%	-1.71
CON	7.49%	6.26%	7.93%	0.22	6.72%	5.30%	4.97%	-0.96
MAN	7.79%	9.16%	10.74%	3.19	21.98%	21.11%	22.65%	-0.72
WHL	4.05%	4.48%	5.33%	2.58	4.60%	5.58%	6.78%	3.64
RET	4.95%	4.36%	4.85%	0.36	5.43%	4.99%	5.27%	-0.14
TRA	3.76%	4.44%	5.01%	1.14	2.94%	2.99%	2.99%	-0.04
INF	1.13%	0.77%	0.85%	-0.45	1.90%	1.50%	1.69%	0.01
FIN	15.96%	16.21%	16.96%	1.27	19.28%	21.86%	22.23%	4.04
PRO	3.13%	3.27%	4.78%	1.82	3.39%	3.67%	5.04%	2.30
ADM	1.53%	1.65%	1.81%	0.56	1.87%	2.15%	2.44%	1.03
EDU	5.18%	4.29%	4.07%	-1.30	6.16%	5.95%	4.69%	-2.39
HC	5.62%	5.51%	4.32%	-0.82	6.52%	6.80%	5.73%	-0.96
ART	0.90%	0.82%	0.67%	-0.20	1.08%	1.05%	0.96%	-0.08
ACC	2.91%	2.65%	2.64%	-0.50	2.77%	2.30%	2.26%	-0.70
OTH	2.47%	2.40%	2.27%	-0.07	2.66%	2.51%	2.33%	-0.36
GOV	6.00%	5.48%	4.44%	-1.74	6.20%	6.45%	5.25%	-1.52

TABLE 5.5 Mean Output Shares by Sector and Change: Alberta and Ontario

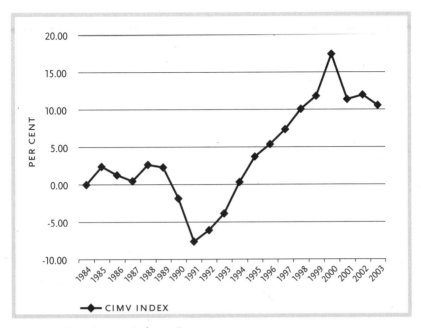

FIGURE 5.13 Ontario CIMV Index, 1984–2003

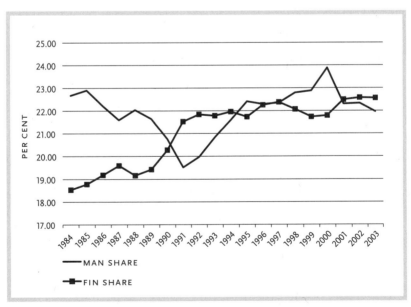

FIGURE 5.14 Output Shares of Manufacturing and Finance in the Ontario Economy, 1984–2003

Contribution to the Change in Volatility Through a One Percentage Point Increase in the Sector's Output Share

	Covariance Effect	Variance Effect	Total Effect
CAP	1.005	0.114	1.119
FOR	-0.044	0.000	-0.044
SAA	-0.084	0.000	-0.084
OAG	-0.355	8.023	7.669
MIN	-0.115	0.001	-0.113
SAM	1.873	0.165	2.038
UTL	0.543	0.026	0.570
CON	0.966	0.785	1.751
MAN	2.664	1.372	4.036
WHL	-0.493	0.167	-0.326
RET	-0.405	0.089	-0.316
TRA	2.169	0.153	2.323
INF	-0.033	0.003	-0.030
FIN	0.686	0.344	1.030
PRO	0.988	0.094	1.082
ADM	-0.036	0.003	-0.032
EDU	-0.315	0.041	-0.274
HC	-2.186	0.163	-2.023
ART	-0.086	0.001	-0.085
ACC	0.435	0.011	0.446
OTH	-0.335	0.008	-0.327
GOV	-1.153	0.061	-1.092

TABLE 5.6 Percentage Increase in the Variance of Total Output from a One Percentage Point Increase in the Output Share of Each Sector

steadily decreased from around 20% in the early 1990s to about 13% in 2003, and the trend in its output share mirrors the trend in the CIMV index.[14] As shown in Table 5.5, the combined increase in the output shares of the manufacturing, wholesale, finance, and professional services sectors in Alberta between 1984 and 2003 was larger than the decline in the output share of the oil and gas sector. In contrast to Alberta, the change in Ontario's industrial mix led to an upward trend in its CIMV index starting in the early 1990s, as depicted in Figure 5.13 (and Table 5.4). By 2000, changes in Ontario's industrial mix had increased

Contribution to the Change in Volatility Through a One Percentage Point Increase in the Sector's Output Share

	Covariance Effect	Variance Effect	Total Effect
CAP	0.018	0.001	0.019
FOR	0.117	0.000	0.117
SAA	0.015	0.000	0.015
OAG	-0.004	0.000	-0.004
MIN	0.172	0.001	0.173
SAM	0.048	0.000	0.048
UTL	-0.010	0.006	-0.004
CON	2.077	0.376	2.453
MAN	1.288	4.272	5.560
WHL	1.347	0.085	1.432
RET	1.201	0.051	1.252
TRA	0.592	0.008	0.600
INF	0.798	0.009	0.807
FIN	1.215	0.667	1.882
PRO	1.488	0.069	1.557
ADM	0.541	0.006	0.547
EDU	-0.063	0.003	-0.060
HC	0.043	0.029	0.072
ART	0.186	0.001	0.187
ACC	0.829	0.013	0.842
OTH	0.394	0.004	0.398
GOV	-0.331	0.021	-0.309

TABLE 5.7 Percentage Increase in the Variance of Total Output from a One Percentage Point Increase in the Output Share of each Sector

the variance of total output by 17.4%. As shown in Figure 5.14, manufacturing's share in Ontario has fluctuated, while there has been a steady increase in the output share of finance, which, as our analysis below indicates, contributes to an increase in volatility.[15] By the end of the period, changes in the industrial mix in Ontario had increased the variance of total output by 10.5%.

Further insights into the effects of changes in the industrial composition on volatility of total output can be obtained by computing the percentage changes in volatility due to covariance and variance effects from a one percentage point increase in a sector's output share of the total economy.[16] Positive values in the column labelled "covariance effect" in Tables 5.6 and 5.7 mean that the expansion of the sector tends to increase the volatility of total output because that sector's output is on average positively correlated with output fluctuations in other sectors of the economy. Negative values indicate that an expansion of the sector tends to reduce volatility of total output because its output fluctuations are negatively correlated with those in other sectors. The values in the column titled "variance effect" show how a one percentage point expansion in the sector's share of output increases the variance of total output because of its own volatility. The sum of the covariance and variance effects shows the total impact on the CIMV Index of a one percentage point increase in the output share of the sector.

For example, a one percentage point increase in the output share of the agriculture sector (CAP) in Alberta would increase volatility indirectly by 1.005% because its output fluctuations are positively correlated with other sectors, and increase total output volatility by 0.114% directly because of its own volatility. As a result, volatility of total output would increase by 1.119% if the output share of the agricultural sector increased by one percentage point. Note that a one percentage point increase in the output share of agriculture in 1984 was equivalent to a 40% increase in its total output.

Table 5.6 indicates that expansion in the agriculture, support activities for mining and oil and gas, utilities, construction, manufacturing, transportation, finance, professional services, and accommodation and food sectors in Alberta are associated with increased volatility through their linkages with other sectors, and that this is especially true of the manufacturing and transportation sectors. The oil and gas sector has a negative covariance effect. (This result is very surprising and further analysis will be required to understand the reasons for it.) The other sectors with relatively large negative covariance effects are wholesale, retail, health care, and public administration.

The oil and gas sector has by far the largest variance effect, and it also has the largest total effect. Manufacturing also has a large total effect, indicating that a general expansion in the present manufacturing sector in Alberta would not reduce the volatility of total output. Construction and transportation also have large positive total effects. Only health care, and to a lesser extent public administration (GOV), has a large negative total effect, indicating that an expansion of these sector produce the largest reduction in the variance of total output.

The changes in the sectors' output shares between 1984 and 2003 shown in Table 5.5, combined with the sectors' contributions to volatility shown in the last column in Table 5.6, help to explain why the changes in the industrial mix in Alberta reduced output variance by 14.6%. The share of the oil and gas sector declined by 5.94 percentage points, and a one percentage point change in the share of output for this sector contributes much more to total output volatility than does any other sector. The sectors that expanded the most in Alberta between 1984 and 2003—manufacturing, wholesale, finance, and professional services—contributed to volatility, but were less volatile than the oil and gas sector. (Indeed the increase in the relative size of the wholesale sector actually contributed to a reduction in volatility.) Thus, the reduction in the output share of the oil and gas sector was primarily responsible for the decline in the CIMV index in Alberta. The sectors that expanded were not low volatility sectors, but they contributed less to volatility than the oil and gas sector.

For Ontario, construction has the largest positive covariance effect, followed by the professional services, wholesale, manufacturing, finance, and retail sectors, all of which have positive covariance effects exceeding 1.0 (see Table 5.7). The only sector with a relatively large negative covariance effect in Ontario is public administration (at -0.331). Manufacturing has the largest variance effect. Otherwise, only those for finance and construction are notable. Manufacturing also has the largest total effect. The other sectors with large positive total effects in Ontario are construction, finance, and professional services.

The 10.5% increase in the CIMV index in Ontario between 1984 and 2003 was primarily caused by the expansion of the finance, wholesale, and professional services sectors, all of which are relatively large contributors to output volatility, as shown in the last column in Table 5.7. The decline in the output share of the manufacturing sector reduced total output volatility, but its output share declined by only a modest amount and not enough to offset the increase in volatility caused by the expansion in finance, wholesale, and professional services. Some have suggested that NAFTA and trade liberalization have been responsible for the increased volatility of the Ontario economy, but our analysis suggests that the expansion of the finance, wholesale, and professional sectors contributed to the increased volatility of total output in Ontario and that trade liberalization, which primarily affected the manufacturing sector in Ontario, was, unless it augmented fluctuations in manufacturing output, not directly responsible for the increase in volatility of the Ontario economy through expansion of the manufacturing sector's relative size.

There are some interesting differences between the total effects found in Alberta and Ontario in these two tables. First, the total effects are almost all positive in Ontario (for 18 of 22 sectors) while in Alberta there is a more even split with 10 positive and 12 negative. Thus, in Alberta, more sectors have a relatively large negative, and stabilizing, covariance effect. Second, although there are 10 sectors across the two provinces having a positive total effect exceeding 1.0%, only four of them are common to both Alberta and Ontario (manufacturing, construction, finance, and professional). That is, the sectors contributing to instability are for the most part different. The two sectors with negative impacts exceeding 1.0 are both in Alberta (health and public administration). Third, the average positive total effect is notably larger in Alberta than in Ontario (2.206 versus 0.998). The average negative total effect is also larger in Alberta than in Ontario but the difference is less (-0.395 versus -0.094). Fourth, the sector that has the largest positive total effect is larger in Alberta (oil and gas at 7.669) than in Ontario (manufacturing at 5.560). Thus, while there are fewer sectors in the Alberta economy where relative expansion tends to increase variance or instability, the impact on variance of a given change in those sectors is greater and contributes to the greater volatility remaining in the Alberta economy.

CONCLUSION

This chapter examines and compares the economic stability of Alberta, a province particularly prone to resource-based instability, with that in Ontario, a province considered to be well-diversified and relatively stable. Using data on population, employment, per capita gross domestic product (GDP), per capita personal income, and per capita consumption, we calculate regional economic instability (REI) indices for the two provinces and examine and compare levels and trends from 1961 to 2008. One result is that most measures indicate that the degree of instability of the Alberta economy has diminished over the past 15 to 20 years. In Ontario, however, these measures have, for the most part, increased or remained the same. Thus, instability indicators in the two provinces have tended to converge, although those in Alberta still tend to exceed somewhat those in Ontario.

Next, we employ the portfolio variance model to examine the structural sources of output instability in Alberta and Ontario. In contrast to previous papers that used data on employment or income, we use data on real output by industry to calculate the variance–covariance matrices for the two provinces. Similar to past findings, we find that the resource sector (oil and gas) is the primary source of Alberta's output instability. While we do not find output fluctuations in this sector to be procyclical with most industries, we find that they have a significantly large covariance with manufacturing, an industry that is also a highly volatile Alberta industry in terms of output. Furthermore, we find the manufacturing sector also displays extensive linkages to most industries. These findings, combined with the significant size of the manufacturing sector, mean that output fluctuations in this sector have a vast effect on aggregate output instability. In Ontario, manufacturing is the dominant source of instability. Also, this sector is positively (procyclically) linked with most other sectors of the economy, a considerable number of which are themselves relatively large and intertwined (particularly finance but also professional, construction, and wholesale and retail trade).

Finally, we derive and calculate the contribution of changes in the industrial mix to volatility (i.e., the CIMV index) based on output for the period 1984–2003. Our results suggest that there is a strong positive relationship between resource-based specialization and changes in output volatility in Alberta. That is, the steady decline in the relative size of the oil and gas sector starting in the early 1990s has been accompanied by a steady decline in the CIMV Index.[17] This trend is in contrast to Ontario—a province that is traditionally regarded as stable because of its diversified economy—which experienced a rise in the CIMV index. Using the portfolio variance model, we find that Ontario's aggregate output instability can be traced largely to the relatively high volatility of its two largest sectors—manufacturing and finance—as well as these sectors' substantial linkages to many industries. It appears that Ontario's industrial mix has not provided or does not provide as much protection against economic instability as it once did, while the economic instability associated with the more natural resource-based economy of Alberta has diminished since the 1970s and early 1980s. Reasons for these trends may be based, in Alberta's case, in part on the increasing size and the broader economic opportunities that scale (coming from considerably expanded population, employment, and GDP) provides. Ontario, meanwhile, has become more exposed to the international economy (and so somewhat more like Alberta in that regard) with free trade agreements, expanded international trade, and a fluctuating Canadian dollar. Ontario, it appears, was also more severely impacted by the recession in the 1990s.

Authors' Note

This chapter is a revision and extension of Kathleen Macaspac's MA research paper, submitted to the Faculty of Graduate Studies, University of Alberta, in September 2007. Unlike Macaspac's paper, this chapter focuses the analysis on fewer, only two, provinces (Alberta and Ontario) but in more detail. The views expressed in this chapter are those of the authors and should not be attributed to their employers. The authors thank S. Francisco and N. Razavilar for their valuable research assistance.

Notes

1. Idiosyncratic (or non-systematic) risk is a terminology used in finance that refers to the risk that affects a particular asset or firm. This type of risk can be eliminated or reduced by portfolio diversification. This is in contrast to market (or systematic) risk, which has to do with general market conditions that are common to all assets or firms (Bodie, Kane, and Marcus 1995).

2. See Dissart (2003) for a comprehensive summary of empirical studies done on regional economic instability and diversity.

3. In the working version of their paper (Imbs and Wacziarg 2000), the authors propose a model predicting this non-monotonic relationship through the interaction between rising productivity levels and falling transport costs. According to their model, an increase in the relative productivity of a country increases the range of commodities produced locally. On the other hand, demand externalities make it optimal for firms to cluster and localize, resulting in falling transport costs. These two forces compete along the development path and the outcome is based on which force dominates the other.

4. This REI index was introduced by Conroy (1975) and used in US studies on diversity and instability. The benchmark $ê_t$ can be calculated using values based on linear, quadratic, or log linear time trends. Others also employ moving average or historical values. See Mansell and Percy (1990) for other differences among various measures of economic instability.

5. In the economics literature, economic instability has four components: trend, cyclical, seasonal, and random. Trend corresponds to movements that are relatively stable and depicts the general direction over a long period of time. Cyclical changes (or business cycles), on the other hand, are defined as alternating sequences of contraction and expansion in the economy and recur at certain intervals of variable length. The main difference between the trend and cycle is that the trend corresponds to a period that is longer than that of cycle. Seasonal fluctuations are repetitive and systematic movements in the economy and are tied to particular seasons. Random refers to variations in the economy attributable to random or unpredictable shocks.

6. See Wagner and Deller (1998), Wagner (2000), and Siegel, Johnson, and Alwang (1995a) for a complete review and critique of diversity measures available in the literature.

7. This may explain why in studies that have examined different diversity measures, the portfolio variance emerged as the best diversity measure in explaining cross-sectional differences in instability.

8. For employment, the data extend from 1966 to 2009.

9. Both provinces have suffered economic shocks that will increase their REIs somewhat but two additional years of data are insufficient to discern a pattern. Even with the upheaval, a significant reversal is unexpected.

10. Our quadratic in time equations for the estimation of nominal per capita GDP do not predict well, and the REI values are sensitive to the resulting errors. We believe this problem is largely the product of relatively high inflation rates in the early years and relatively low rates in the later years. Consequently, for each province, we merged two trend estimates to generate the predicted values and the consistent REI indices reported.

11. The REI values for nominal personal income per capita in the two provinces are of similar magnitudes and follow roughly comparable paths (Figure 5.10). They are large in the early years and trend downwards over time with those for Alberta only deviating notably from and stabilizing above those for Ontario during the latter periods. Again, declining inflation during much of the period analyzed may contribute to the rather parallel paths. Comparison of the nominal and real REI values shows that the bulk of the instability in nominal incomes is due to price changes and not due to real income changes. For example, the mean REI value for nominal per capita income in Ontario over the 1961–2008 series is 0.1107 while the mean for the real index is only 0.0373 (Table 5.1).

12. Data collection and indexing were changed. The latest consistent series is only available from 1997 to 2008.

13. Percentage shares and percentage point changes in the output shares by industry in Alberta from 1984 to 2003 are shown in Table 5.5. Oil and gas declined 5.94%. Manufacturing, however, increased 3.19%.

14. Analysis of an unofficial series for Alberta over the years 1990 to 2008 yields a CIMV index with a similar pattern and its downward trend continues after 2003.

15. See Table 5.5 for changes in the shares of industries during this period.

16. To illustrate, a sector representing 5% of the economy would be increased to 6%. A one percentage point increase for each sector means that the impact of the change in each sector is of the same magnitude relative to the total economy but will vary in relative magnitudes among the sectors. The one percentage point change is relatively larger for a sector comprising 5% of total output than for a sector comprising 10% of total output. Note too that no adjustment is made for other sectors shrinking, in aggregate, by 1%.

17. There was an earlier decline in the industry share from the late 1970s into the early 1980s.

References

Acemoglu, Daron, and Fabrizio Zilibotti. 1997. "Was Prometheus Unbound by Chance? Risk, Diversification, and Growth." *Journal of Political Economy* 105 (4): 709–51.

Armstrong, Harvey W., and Jim Taylor. 2000. *Regional Economics and Policy.* 3rd ed. Oxford: Blackwell Publishers Inc.

Attaran, Mohsen. 1987. "Industrial Diversity and Economic Performance in US Areas." *Annals of Regional Science* 20: 44–54.

Bahl, Roy W., Robert Firestine, and Donald Phares. 1971. "Industrial Diversity in Urban Areas: Alternative Measures and Intermetropolitan Comparisons." *Economic Geography* 47 (3): 414–25.

Berry, Brian J.L., and Paul J. Schwind. 1969. "Information and Entropy in Migrant Flows." *Geographical Analysis* 1: 5–14.

Bodie, Zvi, Alex Kane, and Alan J. Marcus. 1995. *Essentials of Investments*. 2nd ed. Boston: Richard D. Irwin.

Brewer, H.L. 1985. "Measures of Diversification: Predictors of Regional Economic Instability." *Journal of Regional Science* 25 (3): 463–70.

Brewer, H.L., and Ronald L. Moomaw. 1985. "A Note on Population Size, Industrial Diversification, and Regional Economic Instability." *Urban Studies* 22 (4): 349–54.

Brown, Deborah J., and Jim Pheasant. 1985. "A Sharpe Portfolio Approach to Regional Economic Analysis." *Journal of Regional Science* 25 (1): 51–62.

Chambers, Edward. 1999. "Employment Variability in Three Western Provinces: Is there More Stability?" Information Bulletin #53. Edmonton: Western Centre for Economic Research, University of Alberta.

Clemente, Frank, and Richard B. Sturgis. 1971. "Population Size and Industrial Diversification." *Urban Studies* 8 (1): 65–68.

Conroy, Michael E. 1975. "The Concept and Measurement of Regional Industrial Diversification." *Southern Economic Journal* 41 (3): 492–505.

Crowley, Ronald W. 1973. "Reflections and Further Evidence on Population Size and Industrial Diversification." *Urban Studies* 10 (1): 91–94.

Cutler, Addison T., and James E. Hansz. 1971. "Sensitivity of Cities to Economic Fluctuations." *Growth and Change* 2 (1): 23–28.

Dissart, Jean-Christophe. 2003. "Regional Economic Diversity and Regional Economic Stability: Research Results and Agenda." *International Regional Science Review* 26 (4): 423–46.

Garrison, Charles B., and Albert S. Paulson. 1973. "An Entropy Measure of the Geographic Concentration of Economic Activity." *Economic Geography* 49 (4): 319–24.

Gilchrist, Donald A., and Larry V. St. Louis. 1991. "Directions for Diversification with an Application to Saskatchewan." *Journal of Regional Science* 31 (3): 273–89.

Gillis, M., D.H. Perkins, M. Roemer, and D.R. Snodgrass. 1996. *Economics of Development*. 4th ed. New York: W.W. Norton and Company.

Henderson, J. Vernon. 1983. "Industrial Bases and City Sizes." *American Economic Review*, Papers and Proceedings 73 (2): 164–68.

Hoover, Elgar M. 1971. *Introduction to Regional Economics*. 1st ed. New York: Alfred A. Knopf.

Houston, David B. 1967. "The Shift and Share Analysis of Regional Growth: A Critique." *Southern Economic Journal* 33 (4): 577–81.

Imbs, Jean, and Romain Wacziarg. 2000. "Stages of Diversification." Working Paper No. 2642, Centre for Economic Policy Research, London, UK.

———. 2003. "Stages of Diversification." *American Economic Review* 93 (1): 63–86.

Innis, Harold A. 1920. *The Fur Trade in Canada.* New Haven, CT: Yale University Press.

Jackson, Randall W. 1984. "An Evaluation of Alternative Measures of Regional Industrial Diversification." *Regional Studies* 18 (2): 103–12.

Kort, John R. 1981. "Regional Economic Instability and Industrial Diversification in the US" *Land Economics* 57 (4): 596–608.

Macaspac, Kathleen D. 2007. "The Measurement of Output Instability in Western Canada." MA Research Project, Department of Economics, University of Alberta.

Malizia, Emil E., and Shanzi Ke. 1993. "The Influence of Economic Diversity on Unemployment and Stability." *Journal of Regional Science* 33 (2): 221–35.

Mansell, Robert L., and Michael B. Percy. 1990. *Strength in Adversity: A Study of the Alberta Economy.* Edmonton: University of Alberta Press.

Markowitz, Harry M. 1959. *Portfolio Selection: Efficient Diversification of Investment.* New Haven, CT: Yale University Press.

Medvedkov, Yu V. 1970. "Entropy: An Assessment of Potentials in Geography." *Economic Geography* 46 (Supplement: Proceedings. International Geographical Union. Commission on Quantitative Methods): 306–16.

Postner, Harry H. and Lesle M. Wesa. 1985. "Employment Instability in Western Canada: A Diversification Analysis of the Manufacturing and Other Sectors." Discussion Paper No. 275, Economic Council of Canada, Ottawa.

Rodgers, Allan. 1957. "Some Aspects of Industrial Diversification in the United States." *Economic Geography* 33 (1): 16–30.

Saint-Paul, Gilles. 1992. "Technological Choice, Financial Markets and Economic Development." *European Economic Review* 36 (4): 763–81.

Shaffer, Ron. 1989. *Community Economics: Economic Structure and Change in Smaller Communities.* Ames: Iowa State University Press.

Shear, James A. 1965. "A General Measure of Diversity." *Professional Geographer* 17 (1): 14–17.

Sherwood-Call, Carolyn. 1990. "Assessing Regional Economic Stability: A Portfolio Approach." *Economic Review,* Federal Reserve Bank of San Francisco (Winter), 17–26.

Siegel, Paul B., Thomas G. Johnson, and Jeffery Alwang. 1995. "Regional Economic Diversity and Diversification." *Growth and Change* 26 (2): 261–84.

Smith, Stephen M., and Cossette M. Gibson. 1987. "Economic Diversification and Employment Stability in Non-metropolitan Counties." Staff Paper No. 137, Department of Agricultural Economics and Rural Sociology, Pennsylvania State University.

Thompson, Wilbur R. 1965. *A Preface to Urban Economics.* Baltimore: Johns Hopkins University Press.

Vining, Rutledge. 1946. "The Region as a Concept in Business-Cycle Analysis." *Econometrica* 14 (3): 201–18.

Wagner, John E. 2000. "Regional Economic Diversity: Action, Concept, or State of Confusion." *The Journal of Regional Analysis and Policy* 30 (2): 1–21.

Wagner, John E., and Steven C. Deller. 1998. "Measuring the Effects of Economic Diversity on Growth and Stability." *Land Economics* 74 (4): 541–60.

Wasylenko, Michael J., and Rodney A. Erickson. 1978. "On Measuring Economic Diversification: Comment." *Land Economics* 54(1): 106–10.

Wundt, Bruce D., and Linda R. Martin. 1993. "Minimizing Employment Instability: A Model of Industrial Expansion with Input-Output Considerations." *Regional Science Perspectives* 23 (1): 81–93.

Data Appendix: Definitions of Variables and Data Sources

- CPI—Consumer Price Index, all-items using 2001 basket content. Base year: 1992=100. Source: Statistics Canada (CANSIM, Table 326-0002).
- Employment—number of persons who worked for pay or profit (full-time and part-time). Source: Statistics Canada (CANSIM, Labour Force Survey, Table 282-0008 for 1981–2006 and Provincial Economic Accounts, Table 384-0035 for 1966–1980).
- Nominal Consumption—Personal Expenditure on Goods and Services in current prices. Source: Provincial Economic Accounts, Statistics Canada (CANSIM, Table 384-0015 for 1961–1980 and Table 384-0002 for 1981–2006).
- Nominal GDP—Gross Domestic Product in current prices. Source: Provincial Economic Accounts, Statistics Canada (CANSIM, Table 384-0015 for 1961–1980 and Table 384-0002 for 1981–2006).
- Per Capita—Calculated by dividing a variable by population.
- Personal Income—Personal income in current prices. Source: Provincial Economic Accounts, Statistics Canada (CANSIM, Table 384-0035 for 1961–1980 and Table 384-0013 for 1981–2006).
- Population—Source: Statistics Canada (CANSIM, Table 051-0001).
- Real Consumption—Personal Expenditure on Goods and Services in chained 1997 prices. Source: Provincial Economic Accounts, Statistics Canada (CANSIM, Table 384-0002).
- Real GDP by industry—Gross Domestic Product at basic prices, by North American Industry Classification System (NAICS) in 1997 constant dollars. Source: Statistics Canada (CANSIM, Table 379-0025).
- Real GDP—Gross Domestic Product in chained 1997 prices. Source: Provincial Economic Accounts, Statistics Canada (CANSIM, Table 384-0002).
- Real Personal Income—Calculated by dividing Personal Income by CPI times 100.

I've Heard That Song Before

*Harry James on Boom, Bust,
and Diversification*

Edward J. Chambers, Jason Brisbois, and Nicholas Emter

INTRODUCTION

Diversification rhetoric has been part of western Canadian discourse in much of the twentieth century, intensifying during periods of economic stress—"bust"—during the 1920s and 1930s, the late 1950s and early 1960s, and the 1980s, but less direct and more nuanced in tone during relatively good economic times. Those in western Canada saw themselves as producers and shippers of commodities into national or foreign markets and therefore subject not only to large price fluctuations, but also to the vagaries of international trade policy. Uncertainty about access to foreign markets went hand in hand with what was perceived as domestic policies that raised costs and inhibited opportunities both as producers and consumers.

General outlines of diversification are found in a number of sources (Conroy 1975; Siegel, Johnson, and Alwang 1995;

Wagner 2000). The concept has special application in an economy like that of Alberta where the proceeds from the extraction of non-renewable resources do not make the economy wealthier. Exploitation erodes the asset base. To use a simple analogy, the wealth of the household does not increase when it liquidates the home; to maintain wealth, cash proceeds must be applied to acquire alternative assets. Similarly, the province's challenge—regrettably one it has not always met—is to use the economic rents received from resource exploitation to maintain, even enhance, the asset base of the economy. Interest group pressure to spend the entire proceeds now, will, as we know, be very strong, testing the will of political leadership to protect the interests of future generations. An approach that respects these interests assures the transfer of non-renewable resource assets into alternatives—financial assets, human capital, and physical assets—effectively diversifying the wealth portfolio of the economy. Put otherwise, with appropriate policies the wealth portfolio of the province becomes more diversified.

More generally, diversification is a dynamic evolving process, one in which the economy transitions toward an optimal combination of aggregate and per capita growth characterized by structural change that moderates the impact of cyclical or other instabilities. Diversification may, then, be related to both growth rates and their path. For a jurisdiction with a core economy of non-renewable resources, price bubble boom conditions can generate, for a time, very high growth rates. However, these economies have a high risk–reward ratio, so that when the bubble abates, the growth will lapse. Such economies are volatile, and diversification in economic structure is seen as a means of moderating volatility.

To a provincial resource-driven economy, high volatility is a non-trivial issue. High volatility imposes costs. In the public sector, one of the disadvantages is its effect on revenue flows. A tax structure heavily dependent on resource rents, one in which these are absorbed into general revenues without provision for offsetting asset acquisition, is unstable. There is abundant evidence that instability in revenue flows ties into public expenditures, inducing a form of outlay feast or famine that exacerbates the effects of the business cycle. In the private sector, high volatility adds to the fragility and complexity of managing human resources, planning capital expenditures, forecasting other input requirements, and projecting housing demands. For the household, a "boom–bust" environment can contribute to social breakdown. General recognition of the costs of volatility and the desire to moderate them speak to the sustained search for policies and actions that promote growth within a stable framework, prompting the use of incentives to change the industrial composition of a provincial economy.

In this chapter, we consider first some historical background on diversification with particular reference to Alberta. The chapter then proceeds to look at how other jurisdictions with highly specialized economies have pursued further development through diversification. The latter part of the chapter brings Alberta into focus through a standard portfolio analysis evaluating changes in employment stability relative to employment growth over the past four decades. Results are set against a backdrop that contrasts some key economic variables during the recent commodity price bubble with earlier periods. The chapter closes with a consideration of the policy issues involved.

ALBERTA'S DIVERSIFICATION AND DEVELOPMENT POLICIES SINCE 1970

This section provides an overview of the Alberta government's policies for economic development and diversification since the early 1970s. The purpose is neither to evaluate the success of individual policies nor to draw direct links to the results presented in the analytical section of this chapter. Rather, the purpose is to show how the policies evolved, to discuss the cumulative result of the policies in terms of today's economic environment, and to comment on how future progress can be achieved.

In 1971, Albertans elected a Progress Conservative government that ran on a platform entitled "New Directions for the Seventies." The platform included what was billed as Alberta's first industrial strategy, designed to support a province in transition. The strategy is best described by paraphrasing then Premier Peter Lougheed's elaboration of the strategy in the Alberta legislature, as recorded in *Alberta Hansard*, October 1974.

> As a province in transition, we should diversify and become less dependent upon unprocessed resources, particularly non-renewable resources....We have four supplementary goals; to spread the growth across the province...to strengthen small and locally controlled businesses...to upgrade the skills of our citizens to create higher productivity...and to capitalize upon our natural advantages such as food-growing potential and the assured supply of petrochemical feedstock.

The ensuing decade saw increased government involvement and investment in the economy, some of which was designed to create the infrastructure necessary to facilitate diversification, and some of which was designed to ease the strain of an overheated economy. These strategies were made possible by the high revenues generated by extensive activity in the oil and gas sectors. Notable examples of government investment in private businesses and Crown enterprises included Pacific Western Airlines, the Alberta Energy Company, Prince Rupert Terminal, Alberta Opportunity Company, Agriculture Development Corporation, Alberta Home Mortgage Corporation, and various investments made through the Heritage Savings Trust Fund, including the purchase of one thousand grain hopper cars. Despite realizing significant losses in some of the government-funded ventures, the strategy persisted until the early 1980s.

The global recession of 1982, with six consecutive quarters of decreasing Gross National Product (GNP) had dire consequences for Alberta. Albertans realized that continuous economic growth was not guaranteed and adjustments were necessary. The Alberta Budget Address in March 1984 stated: "1984 will be a year of economic recovery....However, it will be a year of recovery, not a return to the boom period of 1979–1981....The fact is that Alberta is in transition from a period of super-heated artificially high growth to one of more normal, sustainable growth."

As the premier noted in the legislature on October 19, 1983, "We came to the conclusion...that it was an appropriate time for us to reassess Alberta's economic strategy." Requests for submissions were made to many organizations and associations for their views on Alberta's industrial strategy. The result was the white paper entitled "Proposals for an Industrial and Science Strategy for Albertans 1985 to 1990," which was released in 1984. The paper, at over one hundred pages, provided a comprehensive assessment of Alberta's past economic policies and potential for future opportunities. But in essence, the paper was designed to explore the question, "how involved should government be in the economy?" This is demonstrated by the policy options presented in the paper, which asked, should the government:

- Remain active and supportive of the Alberta economy or concentrate on encouraging a good climate for private investment?
- Defer royalties on oilsands projects so that construction will proceed now and jobs will be created, or impose immediate royalties and risk projects not proceeding?
- Select specific sectors or areas for special support?
- Use tax incentives, subsidies or grants to encourage economic activity?
- Press universities and other educational entities to prioritize job-directed versus general education?
- Play a role in the international marketing of Alberta's products and services?

The paper also contained a detailed proposal to facilitate the commercialization of technology in Alberta—a topic that resurfaced later.

Public reaction to the paper was intense, and dozens of organizations contributed submissions expressing views on the appropriate degree of government economic intervention. But in the latter years of Premier Lougheed's administration and throughout Premier Don Getty's administration, the predominant issue was coping with increasing deficits and the economic downturns of the late 1980s and early 1990s. Development and diversification strategy took a back seat to other issues, and the white paper never resulted in a formal economic strategy.

When Premier Ralph Klein assumed office in 1992, he pledged to turn the economy around after a hard recessionary period. In 1993, he released the document "Seizing Opportunity: Alberta's New Economic Development Strategy." It was based in part on the results of several consultation exercises, such as "Toward 2000 Together," "Creating Tomorrow," "Vision 2000," and the "Premier's Council on Science and Technology." The document set out the new role for government in the economy based on creating a climate conducive to investment and job creation through low taxes and skills development and an improved regulatory environment. It was clear that Albertans had expressed their thoughts on the white paper policy options by participating in the consultations.

"Seizing Opportunity" announced that direct assistance to business would be reduced or eliminated and any efforts toward development or diversification would be based on building on existing strengths in the agriculture and food sector, tourism, petroleum products, forestry, small business, and high technology infrastructure. The government would facilitate private sector investment in the emerging industries of construction and engineering; environmental products and services; communication and information technologies; telecommunications and electronics; aerospace and advanced materials; health services and biotechnology; and transportation. The document's conclusion stated, "We now have a map to guide Alberta's economic development and diversification."

Part of Premier Klein's strategy was creating the Alberta Economic Development Authority (AEDA) in 1994. AEDA consists of volunteers representing businesses, governments, local economic development authorities, labour, and post-secondary institutions. AEDA's mandate is to develop strategies and make recommendations to government to remove barriers to economic growth and expand investment, business opportunities, and jobs for Albertans. Soon after it was created, AEDA released its own economic vision entitled "A New Economic Strategy for

Albertans: Building on the Alberta Advantage," which reaffirmed the direction provided in the "Seizing Opportunity" document.

In the fall of 1997, the government held a growth summit that engaged Albertans in a province-wide discussion about priorities for action. At the same time, the Alberta Science and Research Authority developed "Securing Tomorrow's Prosperity: Sustaining the Alberta Advantage," an innovation strategy designed to expand Alberta's knowledge-based economy. It repeated the commitments from the earlier documents regarding building a skilled workforce, creating a competitive business climate through low taxes, streamlining regulation, and creating more infrastructure, as well as making a commitment to building Alberta's innovation system and increasing research and development. It also pledged to assist the growth of a restated set of value-added sectors, which included energy technologies and services, value-added energy products, agri-food, building and wood products, tourism, information and communications technologies, health and bio-industries, and environmental technologies and services.

In 1998, "Get Ready Alberta: Strengthening the Alberta Advantage" was released. The document stated, "the Government of Alberta is proud to present to Albertans this new economic strategy...the strategy builds on the province's strengths and sets bold targets for moving forward." The document recommitted to the objectives of the preceding documents, and set 2005 targets of job creation, university enrolment, and a provincial technology network.

In 2005, AEDA and the provincial government released a 2005 update to "Securing Tomorrow's Prosperity: Sustaining the Alberta Advantage." The document repeated the earlier commitments, but set the stage for more cultivation of non-energy value-added sectors by defining outcome measures of sector performance to be achieved by 2013.

When Premier Ed Stelmach assumed office in 2006, it became clear that Alberta's competitive advantage was slipping. Other jurisdictions had made their tax rates more competitive; the overheated economy was driving the cost of labour and materials to unacceptable levels; infrastructure was insufficient to support the high level of growth; and power rates (historically one of Alberta's greatest competitive strengths) were no longer competitive. In addition, Alberta's productivity performance was stagnating.

In response, the government created Productivity Alberta, with a mandate to improve Alberta's performance. Premier Stelmach also renewed the focus on technology commercialization, releasing "Alberta's Action Plan: Bringing Technology to Market" which announced initiatives such as a science and research experimental development tax credit, a $100 million Alberta Enterprise Corporation to participate in venture capital funding, and innovation vouchers to assist firms in accessing support for specific technologies. And in July 2009, the Premier's Council for Economic Strategy was created to help give a broad, external perspective on what Alberta needs to do to secure the province's long-term prosperity. The council will provide guidance on actions the Alberta government can take to best position the province for the next 30 years.

Early in 2010, the government introduced the Alberta Competitiveness Act, which authorizes the creation of a body that will develop initiatives to increase competitiveness, develop performance benchmarks for competitiveness, encourage innovation and technology adoption, and create effective regulatory systems.

As demonstrated above, the Alberta government has taken an active role in cultivating economic development and diversification over the past 30 years. But it is clear that the approach has not been consistent. At various periods, the strategy has been highly interventionist, laissez-faire, or focused on improving the business climate while assisting selected sectors. It is also clear that the economic cycle has repeated itself, and the 1984 budget statement that "Alberta is in transition from a period of super-heated artificially high growth to one of more normal, sustainable growth" was true only temporarily. The fact is that boom and bust has become an old, familiar score, and little progress has been made at smoothing the cycles.

But as the analytical section of this chapter demonstrates, using employment data as a measure, the Alberta economy has become more diversified over the last 10 years. So what can be done to improve Alberta's diversification performance further and create a more stable economy? The answer most likely lies in consistency. Jurisdictions that have been most successful in diversification and development efforts have employed a variety of strategies, but the common denominator has been the consistent application of the strategies over prolonged periods.

If Alberta is to enhance its competitive position and improve its diversification performance, the current government and future governments must be less willing to change horses in midstream. Consistency must be brought to bear, both in terms of identifying priority issues and in the selection of target sectors for development, the latter of which has been the subject of continuous redefinition since 1970. As the number of economic players in Alberta expands, with the activity of the provincial government's Department of Finance and Enterprise being supplemented by the Alberta Innovates–Technology Futures provincial corporation, the Alberta Economic Development Authority, and the Premier's Council for Economic Strategy, time will tell if the necessary degree of policy consistency can be achieved.

STRATEGIES FROM OTHER JURISDICTIONS

The pursuit of economic diversification with the goal of stable economic development and growth, whether through micro or macroeconomic policies, is not constrained to Alberta. Many other countries in various stages of development have made economic diversification an explicit goal of the government. Various means have been attempted to achieve this end, some more successful than others. What follows is a summary of actions taken by two other jurisdictions similar to Alberta—Australia and Malaysia—in their attempts to diversify, and the resulting economic impacts.

Australia

Australia, like Canada, is a nation blessed with rich endowments of natural resources. Traditionally, resource-based industries have produced roughly 80% of Australia's exports. With a heavy dependence on these industries, the Australian economy has been subject to periods of high volatility.

In the 1960s, strong worldwide economic growth, driven by a commodities boom, was mirrored in Australia, whose economy grew at an average annual rate of 5.3% over the decade. During this period, the unemployment rate averaged less than 2% while inflation averaged 2.5% per annum. Unfortunately, such economic conditions fostered policy complacency. The Australian economy remained overly regulated and was dependent on a few key industries. It was characterized by not only cyclical volatility, but a "clear structural break" and "structural deterioration" in the 1970s, which was initially instigated by the first of two oil price shocks. Over this decade, the average annual growth rate of GDP fell to 3.2%, whereas the coefficient of variation (a measure of volatility) jumped to 2.1 from 1.5 the decade before. Inflation rose to an average of 10.6% per annum and the unemployment rate began to rise precipitously.

By the early 1980s, due in part to economic recession, the unemployment rate was over 10% and inflation still raged, albeit to a lesser extent than in the previous decade. After falling to roughly 6% by the end of the decade, the unemployment rate again rose to over 10% as a result of the recession in the early 1990s. Inflation fell to an average annual rate of 2.3% in the 1990s, while growth averaged 3.6% per annum. Unemployment was below 7% by the end of the decade. Most significantly, however, the coefficient of variation dropped to 0.8, an obvious sign that the Australian economy had become more diversified.

This diversification is evident in Australia's industrial composition. The sectoral share of agriculture fell from almost 10% to 3%, while the share for manufacturing fell from nearly one-quarter of the economy to roughly an eighth over the 40-year period from 1960 to 2000. During this time, the contribution of other sectors increased, reaching almost 80% by 2000.

Most structural change occurred during the 1970s and to a lesser extent in the 1980s. The key questions of interest are what structural reform policies were implemented by the Australian government, and did these actions diversify the economy?

The Australian government started its path to structural reform in the 1970s through reforms to international trade policy, which at the time was heavily protectionist. Reductions in the effective rate of tariff protection on all products, other than motor vehicles and their parts, textiles, clothing, and footwear, were introduced and sustained over the period 1970–2000. Turning the focus to the export sector, the Export Market Development Grant Acts of 1974 provided government assistance in the development of export markets, providing up to 50% reimbursement of the costs incurred in establishing these markets. In 1975, the Export Finance and Insurance Corporation was established to provide insurance against political risk to exporters. From 1970 to 2000, trade as a share of GDP rose from approximately 28% to 42%. A 25% across the board tariff cut, implemented by the Whitlam government, heavily impacted the agriculture, mining, and manufacturing sectors of the economy, but was not accompanied by reforms to enhance the competitiveness of the product market or flexibility of factor markets. These reforms would not be made until the early 1980s.

In the mid-1980s, the government's reorientation of the domestic economy continued to rest upon export-oriented policies and liberalization. Key reforms were the reduction of high tariffs and other protective barriers, deregulating the financial services sector, reducing the number of trade unions, and privatization of utilities, most notably electricity. The exchange rate was allowed to float by the end of 1983 and capital controls were relaxed. The non-traded goods sector was also targeted in the 1980s, specifically the transportation, communication, and the aforementioned utilities sectors. Education, training, and labour market imperfections were also given priority. Notably, there has been "little backsliding" on reform, even in the face of adverse economic conditions and political opposition.

Furthermore, in 1995, the government instituted a National Competition Policy to complement its sectoral approach to microeconomic reform, with the goal of providing a compre-hensive framework for reform in all areas of the economy. The combination of these policies has resulted in Australia having the lowest barriers to trade and investment of all the OECD coun-tries, as well as becoming one of the most competitive and liberal domestic OECD economies. However, the macroeconomic effects of Australia's program of structural reform were not soon evi-dent, especially during the recessions of the early 1980s and 1990s. Such measures, nonetheless, are accredited with at least partially spurring the 43 quarters of uninterrupted expansion preceding and up to March 21, 2001. Recently, energy has been a principal driver of growth, and, in 2002, a new and unique market in renewable energy was implemented. The Australian government has also promoted the nation as an "information economy," and, in 2000, it introduced a new tax system designed to dually raise government revenue and stimulate growth in the services and high technology sectors.

In sum, Australia, through reduced trade barriers; the pro-motion of exports; labour, capital, and financial market reforms; and microeconomic sector targeting, hastened the country's shift, over the period 1960–2000, from a resource-dominated economy to one characterized by a relatively more diversified eco-nomic base. However, since 2009, with the rise of China with its demand for commodities and energy, and the resulting commod-ities boom, regressive signs are apparent. The manufacturing sector has declined further, and its exports have been outpaced by those of the mineral/oil sector. Mineral and fuel exports still account for roughly 41% of merchandise exports. Investment has been primarily in the mineral/oil sector, particularly coal, oil, and gas, which has adversely impacted other sectors of the economy. Employment has also been displaced towards extraction indus-tries. The lack of clear and effective taxation policies on extraction industries and a fund by which to collect and spend resource rev-enues, such as in Norway and Alaska, is also an issue.

Clearly, during "boom" periods, diversification and its tell-tale signs are less apparent than in periods of "bust," wherein the need to diversify again becomes apparent. It appears that break-ing this cycle of "feast and famine" is of critical importance, but requires a forward thinking, long-term outlook that is likely to result in a contemporaneous welfare loss. Resource endowments, in this light, can be both a curse and a gift.

Malaysia

Malaysia, a federation of 13 states, gained independence from the British Empire in 1957. Well-endowed with natural resources, it is the world's largest producer of natural rubber, tin, and palm oil. Malaysia is also a net exporter of oil and liquefied natural gas. The legislative power of the Malay states is limited, but, as is the case in Canada, the states control the development of natural resources.

Following independence, the Malaysian economy grew rapidly for two decades with average annual GDP growth of 6% in the 1960s and 7.8% in the 1970s. Inflation was relatively low in the 1960s (1%) but jumped in the 1970s and 1980s.

Pre-1970s, however, the Malay economy was highly vulnerable to commodity price fluctuations due to its heavy dependence on a limited number of resources, primarily rubber and tin, which accounted for almost 80% of gross export earnings from 1951 to 1969. From 1956 to 1960, 23.3% of GDP and 63.3% of gross exports were generated from rubber. In 1957, this industry employed 28.9% of the labour force. Over this period, the average annual fluctuation in the price of rubber (rubber revenue) was 11.9% (12.6%), with a maximum of 21.1% (30.5%). In light of this, the Malaysian government implemented a series of five-year plans with the aim of promoting industrial development and increasing the range of agricultural products that the country produced. Budgeting, both on the revenue and expenditure sides, was utilized as an effective tool in the transformation of the economy. Initially, development policy took the form of import-substitution industrialization, promoted through protective measures, and then shifted to export promotion and heavy industrialization, often fostered through the use of subsidies.

In regard to the revenue side of the government budget, fiscal policy has been used extensively to promote the development of the manufacturing sector. Both incentives and tariff protection for certain industries were utilized, along with various forms of tax relief for the manufacturing and agriculture sectors, as well as human resources, R&D, exports, and technology adoption. Between 1971 and 1981, 2,177 projects that qualified for tax incentives were approved by the Malaysian Industrial Development Authority. In 1979 and 1980, the total proposed capital investment of 994 approved projects was aided by incentives totalling US$2.9 billion.

On the expenditure side, the government created Malaysian Industrial Development Finance Ltd. (MIDF) in 1960 in order to provide medium- and short-term loans and equity capital to industries, an area in which the banks were of little assistance. By 1971, annual loans issued by MIDF totalled US$12 million, or almost 80% of total financing made available to industrial enterprises, which were primarily start-ups and entrepreneurial business. By 1982, 2,388 loans had been issued, with an accumulated value of US$471 million. Furthermore, MIDF also opened industrial estates to provide factory buildings to small- and medium-sized enterprises (SMES). From 1964 to 1982, Malaysian Industrial Estates Ltd. completed 556 factories, distributed among 42 projects, and dispersed across 20 locations in the country. Some 385 industrial projects were created, with capital investment of US$45 million, employing 31,000 Malaysians.

The government also provided grant assistance to selected crops, which helped foster the growth of the palm oil and cocoa industries. Export duties on crude palm oil attracted investment in refining capacity. Between 1970 and 1980, value-added in the agriculture sector jumped from 9% to 25%, while its export value rose from under US$40 million to US$500 million. The total contribution of agriculture over this period fell from 32% to 22%, and the country is no longer dependent on rubber. Rubber's share of commodity exports fell from 53% in 1961 to 25% in 1981. Manufacturing flourished over this period, increasing its share of GDP from 8.5% to 20.5%. In 1994, the shares of agriculture and manufactures in exports were 14% and 78%, down from 66% and up from 8.5%, respectively, in 1960. By 1995, the shares of agriculture and manufacturing in GDP fell and rose to 14% and 33%, respectively.

The implementation of Program and Performance Budgeting in 1969 is often credited as an important factor behind Malaysia's success in that it made budget documents more relevant; the treasury became more development oriented; budget dialogue became more meaningful; and a foundation for good management was established. Furthermore, rents in Malaysia have been allocated in ways that have encouraged investment in productive activities. Rather than being used for simple investment or employment generation, rents have been used for the development of domestic production capacity. The Petroleum Development Act of 1974 allowed the government to capture most of the resource rents from oil development. It also gave the federal government control over petroleum, unlike other resources, as well as the Crown corporation Petronas, which is widely considered to be a well-run company with a good international credit rating. The logging industry in Malaysia is another story. Poorly regulated, loggers are not taxed sufficiently to cover the real cost of deforestation and the industry seeks to maximize short-term profits rather than long-term returns.

In sum, budgeting, and both import-substitution based and export-oriented industrialization have been used as effective tools in aiding economic diversification efforts in Malaysia. Fiscal incentives for manufacturing and funding support for industrial and agricultural development have helped wean the economy from its heavy dependence on a few commodities, particularly tin and rubber. As a result, the standard of living in the country has increased dramatically, and Malaysia is often touted as one of the success stories of East Asia.

EVIDENCE OF DIVERSIFICATION IN ALBERTA

Let us turn to evidence on economic diversification in Alberta. Generally, in diversification studies, interest centres on the composition and performance of a key macro variable such as output or employment. This requires a choice in terms of how to address the evidence, since there is no universally accepted method of measuring diversification. A widely-used method such as shift-share analysis emphasizes composition by taking two points in time, calculating the changes in structure that have taken place between them, and segmenting out national or industry-wide sources of change from those attributable to "local" factors. A location quotient approach again takes two points in time and looks for a trend toward reduced variance—more equal weighting—in the components of the aggregate variable.

However, static measures like these do not get to the core of diversification: reduction of volatility in the economy and a possible trade-off with growth rates. In contrast, portfolio analysis, adapted from the finance literature, focuses on growth, the stability of that growth, and covariance between components of the macro variable. The estimates are calculated from time series data, implying that portfolio analysis is dynamic rather than static. A diversified investment portfolio spreads risk among various asset holdings. Effective diversification is assessed by the volatility of the portfolio. In applying the model to an economy, the industry composition of the macro variable makes up the portfolio, with "return" measured by the macro variable growth rate and "risk" measured by the variance and covariance of portfolio components. Applied over time, this will identify if stability has increased, decreased, or remained unchanged as the economy evolves both absolutely and in relation to the aggregate measure. The questions are: (1) Has there been a change in the absolute level of volatility? (2) If so, how is volatility related to the rate of change in aggregate employment?

Attractive though the method may be, it is important to recognize key differences between a real sector portfolio model and its financial counterpart. Carolyn Sherwood-Call (1990) and others (Brown and Pheasant 1985; Board and Sutcliffe 1991) have conveyed these differences. Primarily, natural endowments yield different comparative advantages, and that does much to determine a real sector portfolio. These endowments impose constraints on the extent that regions can—perhaps even should—experience a realignment of their real sector. Provinces run with what they have at their core. The question becomes one of the extent to which those comparative advantages can be leveraged and diffused—through entrepreneurial initiative, skill transfer and the like—into productive activity in other industrial sectors.

Then there is flexibility. An investor can immediately alter the asset mix of a portfolio with the execution of a buy or sell order. The pursuit of risk-altering change in a real sector portfolio has no market equivalent to the market for financial assets. The markets through which real sector change—whatever the means—may accrue, is very imperfect, and sought after adjustments are orders of magnitude away from the instantaneous adjustments possible in financial markets.

A third point is that returns to financial assets are independent of portfolio ownership. A share of IBM generates the same net income whether the owner resides in Brazil or Austria. However, growth performance and the volatility of a given sector are not independent of geography. Hence, there is a spatially specific component to real sector performance in the return and volatility of any component of the portfolio.

With these caveats in mind, the real sector portfolio selected is Alberta employment from the monthly Canadian Labour Force Survey (LFS). The data include both employees and the self-employed of both sexes, 15 years of age and older. As shown in Table 6.1, the employment portfolio includes 16 components, five in the goods and 11 in the services sector. Use of this data set has both advantages and disadvantages. Advantages include the welfare implications of employment as well as the fact that the data are both intra-annual and comprehensive. A disadvantage is the sampling error in the sector data. Monthly data were seasonally adjusted, quarterly averaged, logarithmically differenced, and converted to annualized rates of change. Using a quarterly average moderates the effects of random influences on the data. Results have been estimated for three eras: 1976–1987; 1987–1996; and 1997–2009. The "return" in each era is the growth rate in employment; the "risk" is the sum of variance and covariance in the 16 sector components.

A close look at this real sector portfolio highlights another important difference from financial assets that affects interpretation of whatever results are generated. The individual

Goods Sector	Services Sector
• Agriculture	• Trade (including wholesale and retail)
• Forestry, Fishing, Mining (including oil and gas)	• Transportation and Warehousing
• Utilities	• Finance, Insurance, and Real Estate
• Construction	• Business, Building, and Support Services
• Manufacturing	• Professional, Scientific, and Technical
	• Educational Services
	• Health and Social Assistance
	• Information, Culture, and Recreation
	• Accommodation and Food Services
	• Other Services (including personal services)
	• Public Administration

TABLE 6.1 Employment Subsectors

components already contain a degree of diversification. It is as if each is made up of a conglomerate whose activity is diverse. Alternatively, one can think of a portfolio being made up of sectors having activity subsets with minimal overlap. For example, agriculture consists of not only grain but also livestock operations together with cultivation of specialty crops; manufacturing is both durable and non-durable and in Alberta is not dominated by any particular industrial sector; information demand functions bear little relation to those confronting either cultural activities or recreation; forestry activities are remote from oil and gas exploration; and there is a mix of skills in the professional and technical component. As the underlying subsets of activities in each of the components evolve there will be an anticipated effect on variances.

To reiterate, weighted component variances and covariances add up to total variance and determine the volatility of the portfolio. Weights used in this analysis are the average shares of total employment accounted for by each sector in each era. Other things equal, the larger is the weighted variance in the respective sectors, the higher is aggregate employment volatility. The second component of total variance is the weighted covariance—the interdependence between the respective sectors. Should employment in sectors move in the same direction—the case of positive covariance—the net result is increased total variance and magnified volatility in the economy. Should employment changes move in opposite directions—the case of negative covariance—the net effect is to reduce total variance and to moderate volatility. In sum, lower levels of variance and greater negative covariance mean reduced volatility in the regional employment portfolio. To simplify, in the case where employment consists of two sectors:

$$VP = w_1^2 V_1 + w_2^2 V_2 + 2 w_1 w_2 Cov_{12}$$

where VP is portfolio variance, V_1 and V_2 are the variances, w_1 and w_2 are the respective weights in total employment, where $w_1 > 0$, $w_2 > 0$, and $w_1 + w_2 = 1$, and Cov_{12} is the covariance. Thus, portfolio variance depends on the size of V_1 relative to V_2, the size of w_1 relative to w_2, and the nature of the covariance.

More generally:

$$VP = \sum_i \sum_j w_i w_j V_{ij}$$

where V_{ij} denotes the variance $(i = j)$ or the covariance $(i \neq j)$ for each employment sector or pair of employment sectors, and w_i and w_j are the industry weights based on the provincial composition of employment.

Readings of employment variability from the portfolio model can be taken as a proxy for the state of diversification in each selected era. Further, the model allows assessment of each sector's contribution to total volatility.

To begin, for each era, absolute volatility results and volatility relative to the rate of employment growth, based on estimates derived from quarterly log differences in the respective employment sectors, are converted to annual percent changes. In performing these calculations, all quarters within an era have been included with no exceptions for recessionary periods. The results, shown in Table 6.2, indicate a striking reduction in total variance and a decline of well over one-half in employment variability relative to employment growth from the level of the first era. That indicates, at the very least, a strong reading on a key symptom of diversification—more stability in the employment portfolio.

	1976/2–1987/1	1987/2–1996/4	1997/1–2009/4
(1) Total variance*	22.94	5.27	6.84
(2) Employment†	3.12	1.56	2.76
(3) Ratio (1)/(2)	7.35	3.38	2.48

TABLE 6.2 Total Variance Relative to Employment Growth,
Selected Periods, 1976Q2 to 2009Q4 (annualized % change)

Source: Basic employment data from Table 2820011, CANSIM II
* Derived from quarter over quarter percent changes in the 16 LFS components of employment
converted to annual rates.
† Derived from quarterly changes in aggregate LFS employment converted to annual rates.

To examine the elements of this change more closely, Table 6.3 reports the distribution of total variance between the goods and the service sectors of the economy.[1] Here, a number of results stand out. First, variance in the goods sector is disproportionately large and in the service sector disproportionately low compared to respective employment shares. This is a result consistent with many studies that emphasize the stabilizing role of the service sector, including the fact that the latter contains publicly funded employment. Second, over time, there are substantial declines in both the goods and the service sector total variance, most notably in the goods sector, much of it associated with declines in the variance of each component. Several things seem to have brought this about. These include the fact, previously emphasized, that the coverage of components is very broad—such as mining, forestry, and fishing and also manufacturing—so that changes supportive of stability through a broadening and deepening of activity occurred within them. Probably, too, the very high annual rates of growth in self-employment helped in the second era. Third, in the service sector covariance sums are consistently negative, while in the two more recent eras the goods covariance approached neutrality (zero) in contrast to the positive covariance in the earliest period. For the entire 16 components of employment in the first era, those with negative covariance had a weight of 0.38 in the portfolio; in the second era this had increased to 0.66, and in the most recent period to 0.76; those with negative covariance in the second era remained in that category in the most recent period.

| | 1976/2–1987/1 | | 1987/2–1996/4 | | 1997/1–2009/4 | |
	Goods	Services	Goods	Services	Goods	Services
Total variance*	13.84	9.10	1.93	3.34	3.81	3.03
Variance	10.45	10.95	1.66	5.02	3.74	8.44
Covariance	3.39	-1.85	0.28	-1.68	0.07	-5.40
Share of Total Variance	0.60	0.40	0.37	0.63	0.56	0.44
Share of Total Employment	0.32	0.68	0.28	0.72	0.28	0.72

TABLE 6.3 Variance and Covariance in the Goods and Service Sectors, Selected Periods, 1976Q2 to 2009Q4 (annualized % change)

Source: Basic employment data from Matrix 2820011, CANSIM II
* Derived from quarter over quarter percent changes in the 16 LFS components of employment converted to annual rates.

A legitimate question is whether Alberta's experience is similar to other provinces, specifically British Columbia and Saskatchewan—two jurisdictions with a history of boom–bust. A similar analysis applied to these provinces finds that Alberta has, over this period, the best record in moving from high to low risk–reward ratios and in reducing absolute levels of total variance. It can also be said that Alberta, more so than the other two provinces, enunciated and pursued diversification as a clear policy priority.[2]

A commodity-based terms of trade boom occurred in Alberta prior to the 2008–2009 recession, which is often compared to the earlier boom periods, most notably the late 1970s through 1981. Given the strength of the recent expansion, one might have expected, based on the 1981–1984 downturn, that the recent "bust" would have generated more severe consequences than the current evidence indicates. The portfolio analysis helps us understand why, in finding that Alberta has changed pretty dramatically over the last four decades; should this evolution continue, it is unlikely that the province can be characterized nationally and globally as a classic "boom–bust" economy. Surely that is good news. We want to turn now to some not so good news.

DIVERSIFICATION AND ECONOMIC PERFORMANCE

While the portfolio model suggests a strong presence of diversification measured by reduced risk–reward employment ratios, this transition is not a panacea. How is employment growth in a more diversified economy related to national job growth, and what about absolute and relative levels of GDP growth and productivity improvements? A look at these metrics provides a more comprehensive framework within which to set diversification. To do this we consider two periods, 1987–1996 and 1997–2009.

During 1987–1996, the Alberta economy was relatively free of positive or negative energy price shocks and of any upward price trend, in marked contrast to the 1997–2009 years. For example, during 1997–2009, unit prices rose at an annual rate of 13%, the standard deviation of the annual price of crude per barrel was 10 times its magnitude in 1987–1996, and the standard deviation in the price of natural gas was nine times greater. It is to be expected that absence of bubbles in the earlier period and their presence in the later period would appear in the terms of trade—the ratio of export to import prices—and indeed they do. The standard deviation in the terms of trade rose by a factor of 8.0 in the later period, compared with 2.5 in British Columbia and 1.7 in Ontario. In the later years of the second period (2003–2007), Alberta's terms of trade bubble resulted in provincial GDI (Gross Domestic Income) exceeding GDP by an average of 15%. Within the more diversified economy, the "boom" conditions of these years were, in reality, terms of trade froth.

Consideration of highly aggregative data reveals how the Alberta economy, displaying more of the characteristics of diversification, fared in the two eras and compared to the national economy.

First, consider the annual rate of growth (%) in total hours of employment, as shown in Table 6.4. While the growth rate in actual employment hours in Alberta is substantially above the national rate in both periods, it is in the 1987–1996 period that the relative performance was more notable. Much of the Alberta increase in the early period is accounted for by the increase in self-employment; this rose at a rate of 5.55% in the service sector

	Alberta Hours Growth	Canada Hours Growth	Ratio Alberta/Canada
1987–1996	1.6	0.5	3.2
1997–2009	2.8	1.7	1.6

TABLE 6.4 Alberta and Canada Employment Hours Growth Rates, 1987–1996 and 1997–2009

	Alberta GDP Growth	Canada GDP Growth	Ratio Alberta/Canada
1987–1996	3.2	1.7	1.9
1997–2008	3.6	3.0	1.2

TABLE 6.5 Alberta and Canada GDP Growth Rates, 1987–1996 and 1997–2008

Source: GDP from CANSIM, Table 3840002. Growth estimated from a fitted log linear trend.

	Alberta GDI Growth	Canada GDI Growth	Ratio Alberta/Canada
1987–1996	3.1	1.6	1.9
1997–2008	6.6	3.5	1.9

TABLE 6.6 Alberta and Canada GDI Growth Rates, 1987–1996 and 1997–2008

Source: GDP, export and import price data from CANSIM II, Tables 3840002 and 3840036. Growth estimated from fitted log linear trend.

and 2.63% in the goods sector, or well above double the rates of the later era.

Second, consider GDP, shown in Table 6.5. Alberta outperforms Canada in both periods but most strongly in the earlier period; despite the apparent provincial boom in the later period, growth then was only modestly better than the national rate. In fact, on that evidence it is reasonable to conclude there was no Alberta boom.

Third, comparing the information in Table 6.5 with GDI values in Table 6.6 reveals that, while there is little difference between GDP and GDI in the first period, in the second period Alberta GDI increased at an astonishing 6.6% annual rate.

Therein lies the recent Alberta "boom": one entirely attributable to the terms of trade effect. From the point of view of households and other spending units in an economy, it is the purchasing power of income that is more significant than measures of output. If there is a difference in the price levels of what one sells abroad and what one buys abroad, then there is an impact on income. If the average prices at which exports sell exceed the average prices that residents must pay for imports, then there is a gain in real income in the sense that the purchasing power of the export bundle is greater than it was before. In contrast, if the opposite is true, then the purchasing power equivalent of exports is less and real income is diminished. In many jurisdictions the terms of trade effect is of little consequence because of a high degree of price homogeneity between their exports and imports. However, in the case of Alberta, the dominant fossil fuel export displays high price volatility compared with import products. The result is substantial swings in the terms of trade and consequent impacts on real income, so that the terms of trade is a main avenue through which commodity price booms and busts work their way into the economy.

Of the possible ways in which a province can take advantage of terms of trade effects, several stand out in this case. First is capital formation, with investment in non-residential structures and in machinery and equipment increasing at respective annual rates of 6.3% and 11.1%. Second is housing, where the annual growth rate for 1997 to 2007 (omitting the 2008 housing downturn) was 5.3%. Third is government capital formation and current expenditures, which grew at annual rates of 11.4% and 4.9%, respectively. All these rates are far in excess of Alberta's GDP growth of 3.6%. The result is private sector investment in non-residential structures and in machinery and equipment that averaged 24.3% of GDP in 1997–2008, which, by way of comparison, was 2.3 times the GDP share in Ontario, 2.1 times that in British Columbia, and 1.9 times the national share. Alberta's share of this spending in 1997–2008 at 24.3% compares with a share of 14.4% in 1987–1996.

No one would deny that advances in productivity rather than ephemeral movements in the terms of trade—over which the province has no say—are the foundation of improved living standards. It is recognized that the key to advances in

	Alberta	Canada	Ratio Alberta/Canada
1987–1996	1.6	1.2	1.3
1997–2008	0.8	1.3	0.6

TABLE **6.7** Alberta and Canada Labour Productivity Rates, 1987–1996 and 1997–2008

Source: GDP and actual hour data from CANSIM, Tables 3840002 and 2820028. Growth in productivity estimated from a fitted log linear trend.

productivity is business capital spending with special emphasis on machinery and equipment in which imbedded new technology is linked to improved labour performance.[3] Labour productivity in Alberta compared to national values for the two eras is shown in Table 6.7.

These contrasting results, attributable in the second period entirely to the dismal negative performance of the goods sector, are the worst of any province in the country. They run in the face of conventional wisdom and are hard to rationalize—not only did the rate of productivity advance decelerate drastically from 1987 to 1996, but it did so in the face of extremely high rates of capital spending, the highest of any province, far exceeding the national and approaching rates of capital formation in China. The explanation frequently proffered is transitioning from conventional oil and gas to the higher cost oilsands extraction. Comparisons may be drawn with other energy producing provinces, Saskatchewan and Newfoundland, where productivity grew at respective rates of 2.1% and 4.5%.[4] In Alberta, business capital spending (2002 dollars) excluding housing totalled $475 billion, or approximately $270,000 per employed person. No matter what rationalization may be suggested, that such a large capital infusion should produce such meagre social returns raises serious questions that lead to doubts about both market efficacies and policy direction.[5]

It might be argued that oilsands development represents "diversification" in the source of fossil fuel energy supply and in the opportunity for downstream, value-added upgrading links. However, though there may be diversification in supply, the ensuing product becomes part of the broad stream that accommodates the demand function for fossil fuel. This suggests increased specialization rather than diversification. There are other qualifications. Diversification usually considers sector growth that, for example, broadens the range of activities in the economy as a growth increment rather than a replacement of one activity by another. The oilsands are a replacement for conventional oil and a high cost one at that. Yet, there is an important lesson pertinent to diversification in all this. It reiterates that whatever the policy, its impact should not detract from activities with competitive cost structures by direct and sustained support through incentives for those whose costs are non-competitive.

CONCLUSION

To state that diversification is a policy objective means acceptance of an anticipated change in the underlying structure of the economy. However, this is not to say that the process should be state-directed. Alberta possesses certain necessary capacities, including abundant entrepreneurship, an educated and well-trained labour force, pools of capital, and a reasonably good transport and communications infrastructure. To secure diversification, the private sector does not need government direction but it does need the "right" set of incentives. Key is the absence of a sustained price bubble so that returns from the resource sector retreat into line with opportunity earnings.

In the Alberta case, the fossil fuel price bubble is the issue at hand. No one knows if price signals will be more, less, or equally strong compared to the past; international market conditions having nothing to do with Alberta will dictate that. Viewed from this perspective, diversification in a regional economy is hostage to unit price. Seen from another perspective, a key determinant of the fossil fuel unit price is the set of user preferences for that as opposed to competing sources of energy. Scientific evidence about the carbon footprint of fossil fuels alters user behaviour and affects preferences for more environmentally benign sources of energy, including solar, wind, and biomass, at a pace very much determined by technology. The pace at which these cut into the market share of fossil fuels will be determined by technology's impact on production costs and capital expenditures to increase their capacity. Also, consider that if a fossil fuel price bubble should occur in this context, one very different from historical experience, the likely effect would be to further accelerate the rate of technological change in alternative sources. These are all elements that combine to reinforce the uncertainty about a large and sustained future price bubble. That in itself should be supportive of diversification.

For a province recognized nationally and internationally as a leader in fossil fuel production, transformative thinking is extremely difficult. There is denial about the science of climate change; there are extrapolations of future energy demand and continued faith in the dominant position of fossil fuels; and there is acceptance that boom and bust is simply an industry attribute. This prevailing wisdom that is present throughout much of the economy obfuscates the diversification process.

Authors' Note

The authors would like to acknowledge the helpful contributions from Al Craig and Duane Pyear.

Notes

1. Results for each of the 16 sectors are available from the authors.
2. The detailed results for Saskatchewan and British Columbia are available from the authors.
3. See the study by Macdonald (2008).
4. We have used for our comparisons annual GDP (2002 chained $) divided by total actual hours worked as an approximation of labour productivity. A more desirable measure would be a measure of multifactor productivity for which national but not provincial data are available. Note that our estimate of Alberta labour productivity over 1997–2008 of 0.8% annually is above the Statistics Canada published estimate of 0.6%. On this see, Statistics Canada, *The Daily*, January 10, 2010.
5. A more complete comparison would look at Alberta productivity during the 1976–1986 period when the last terms of trade bubble and ensuing bust occurred. Actual hours increased during this period at an annual rate of 2.7%, which is comparable to 1997–2008. Regrettably, provincial real GDP estimates prior to 1981 are, in our judgement, shaky, and we have avoided any estimation.

References

Alberta. 1987. "Alberta's Diversification and Economic Development Policies and Programs." Edmonton: Government of Alberta, July.

———. 1994. "White Paper: Proposals for an Industrial and Science Strategy for Alberta, 1985 to 1990." Edmonton: Government of Alberta, July.

Board, John, and Charles Sutcliffe. 1991. "Risk and Income Trade-offs in Regional Policy: A Portfolio Theoretic Approach." *Journal of Regional Science* 31 (2): 191–210.

Brown, Deborah J., and Jim Pheasant. 1985. "A Sharpe Portfolio Approach to Regional Economic Analysis." *Journal of Regional Science* 25 (1): 51–63.

Canada. 1987. *A Framework for Diversification in Western Canada.* Ottawa: Department of Supply and Services.

Conroy, Michael E. 1975. "The Concept and Measurement of Regional Economic Diversification." *Southern Economic Journal* 41 (3): 492–505.

Economic Council of Canada. 1984. *Western Transition.* Ottawa: Department of Supply and Services.

Gruben, William C., and Keith R. Phillips. 1989. "Diversifying Texas: Recent History and Prospects." *Economic Review*, Federal Reserve Bank of Dallas, July.

Macdonald, Ryan. 2008. "The Resource Boom: Impacts on Provincial Purchasing Power." Statistics Canada Cat. No. 11-624-M-No. 021, Ottawa.

Sherwood-Call, Carolyn. 1990. "Assessing Regional Economic Stability: A Portfolio Approach." *Economic Review*, Federal Reserve Bank of San Francisco (Winter), 17–26.

Siegel, Paul B., Timothy C. Johnson, and Jeffrey Alwang. 1995. "Regional Economic Diversity and Diversification." *Growth and Change* 26 (2): 261–84.

Statistics Canada, Labour Force Survey.

Wagner, John E. 2000. "Regional Economic Diversity: Action, Concept, or State of Confusion." *The Journal of Regional Analysis and Policy* 30 (2): 1–22.

When Worlds Collide

Alberta Economic Diversification and Global Warming

Roger Gibbins

INTRODUCTION

The onset of global warming, and even more so the onset of
provincial, national, and international *policies* to combat greenhouse gas (GHG) emissions, pose a very significant challenge to
Alberta's resource-based economy.[1] This challenge takes on even
more weight when we realize that it reinforces those who argue
that we should/must lessen the province's economic dependence
on natural resources and their inherently volatile continental
and global markets. Indeed, the argument is often made that the
road to sustainable economic prosperity for Albertans is paved
by the conversion to an urban, knowledge-based economy where
resource industries play a declining role in both the provincial
economy and government revenues. In this sense, the necessity
to respond to the policy challenge of global warming provides
the opportunity to do what we should already be doing, and that

is weaning ourselves off the teat of natural resources. To shame-lessly mix metaphors, from the lemon of global warming we can make the lemonade of a more diversified twenty-first-century economy.

There is, then, an appealing convergence between policy responses to global warming and the longstanding quest for the Holy Grail of greater economic diversification. By pursuing diversification we might also reduce Alberta's carbon footprint, thereby killing two proverbial birds—but not ducks!—with one stone.[2] Global warming will force us to choose the policy path of economic diversification and finally abandon the easy path of resource dependency. Thus, the worlds of Alberta's resource-based economy and global warming may collide with positive effect. *Or not.*

HEWERS OF WOOD, DRAWERS OF WATER

This argument fits neatly within a broader Canadian economic development strategy dating back to Sir John A. Macdonald and the National Policy. In 1879, the minister of finance in Macdonald's Conservative government declared that "the time has arrived when we are to decide if we will simply be hewers of wood and drawers of water." In the political culture of the late nineteenth century, the hewing and drawing description was heavy with religious portent, for as the Bible intoned (Joshua 9:23), "Now therefore, you are cursed, and you shall never cease being slaves, both hewers of wood and drawers of water for the house of my God." Clearly, being a hewer or a drawer was not a good thing!

The minister answered his own question by imposing a 30% tariff wall on imports, a wall designed to build manufactur-ing industries in Canada by protecting those industries from American competition. And, by and large, the National Policy was successful in laying the foundation for the modern manu-facturing economy that came into full bloom following the end of the Second World War. Now admittedly, that foundation was primarily laid in central Canada where the great bulk of the

Canadian population lived, domestic markets were strong, and access to American and European markets was easiest. As western Canadian settlement took off in the decades following 1879, the National Policy brought few benefits and at least the perception of substantial costs to the region, particularly with respect to tariffs that made the importation of American farm machinery prohibitively expensive.³ For western Canadians, the National Policy did not seem to be national at all. Thus if we paint with an exceptionally broad brush, it can be argued that while Ontario and Quebec shed the biblical injunction, western Canadians continued to be hewers and drawers, albeit from a much broader resource base that spread beyond grains and timber to include coal, natural gas, oil, potash, and uranium. The modern industrial economy found its home in central Canada, and western Canadians sat unhappily on the sidelines of that industrial economy.

But what about more recent times? The collapse and then partial rebound of commodity markets during the 2008 to 2010 period demonstrate what can happen to hewers and drawers, in terms of volatility in revenues and incomes, in a turbulent global economy. However, we are also seeing unrelenting international pressure on Canada's manufacturing industries. Indeed, it might be argued that in the years to come, resource prices will remain strong in the face of strong global demand while the competitive pressure on the manufacturing sector will only increase. In short, the western Canadian hewers and drawers may not be cursed in the foreseeable future, whereas those associated with traditional manufacturing interests in central Canada may begin to wonder at their biblical fate.

None of this is to suggest that Sir John A. got it wrong in 1879; I would argue that for his time he got it right, and that as a consequence Canadians enjoyed more than a century of quite remarkable prosperity. However, the world has changed, as worlds do, and it is less clear today that the path to sustainable economic prosperity leads through the conventional manufacturing sector. For example, the auto industry, which used to be our industrial flagship, is now taking on water as its sails fray under international fire. Maybe, just maybe, it is time for the western Canadian hewers and drawers to have their day in the sun. Maybe the west's resource-based economy will be better able to weather the global economic storms that lie ahead than will manufacturing industries facing intensifying competition from the same developing world that will provide the market demand for western Canadian resources.[4] We will prosper by producing what global markets want to buy, and they may well have a stronger appetite for our natural resources than for our manufactured goods.

However, what do we do if Canada's comparative advantage in the years to come lies with natural resources *and* the pressure from global warming policy continues and even intensifies? How do we survive and prosper if the very resources we hew and draw are portrayed as an obstacle in the battle to reduce GHG emissions?[5] Are there economic development strategies that can square this circle, providing sustainable prosperity to resource-based economies in a carbon-constrained world?

HEWERS AND DRAWERS IN A CARBON-CONSTRAINED WORLD

Converting to a low carbon economy is particularly challenging for a provincial economy that heavily relies on hydrocarbon exports.[6] While one could certainly envision a future where Alberta communities cover their energy needs through greater conservation, better urban planning and building design, and a mix of renewable and low carbon energy sources—wind, solar, geothermal, biomass, and even nuclear—none of these are exportable forms of energy. Alberta is not going to export wind power to Montana, where there is lots of wind and no people; this would be the twenty-first-century equivalent of carrying coals to Newcastle. Nor will we export solar power to California, or geothermal power anywhere; renewable energy tends to be locally distributed and not exportable over the distances that Alberta producers face. An Alberta economy without hydrocarbon exports would therefore be very different, for green exports will not replace conventional energy exports. Alberta's economy would undoubtedly be greener but also much smaller and less capable of supporting the present array of public services and perhaps even the present population. If we are resolutely embarked upon a path towards a low carbon economy, with a much greater focus on renewal energy sources, locally distributed power and reduced energy consumption, then Alberta's future could be in peril.

What, then, would be an appropriate strategic response to this dilemma? Let's begin with the "Hail Mary" option, hoping that concern over global warming turns out to be akin to Y2K and H1N1, a temporary scare that soon evaporates. In other words, maybe the challenge of a resource-based economy competing in a carbon-constrained world will just go away. Realistically, however, even if we put the scientific evidence on climate change and global warming aside, there is too much investment momentum towards a low carbon economy, too many scientists, environmental NGOs, and entrepreneurs, both private and public, with their shoulders to the wheel for the movement towards a low carbon economy, or at least a lower-carbon economy, to stop. This train has left the station.

A more realistic version of the Hail Mary strategy would be to assume that continental and global demand for hydrocarbons will remain strong despite policy initiatives to address global warming, and that when economic push comes to environmental shove, voters at home and in our markets will be more concerned about energy security than about global warming. At the very least, their enthusiasm for policies to address global warming will be tempered by economic concerns. A variant of this is to assume that our energy mix will change going forward, as it will, that renewables will play a larger and larger role in that mix, but that the pace of change to our patterns of production and consumption will be slow. This is sort of like saying, "yes, a low carbon economy is coming, but by the time it gets here I'll be dead" (as will most of today's electorate).

The problem with all of these strategies, loosely defined, is that they are not ones over which Albertans have any influence, much less control. The fate of global warming—the most pressing issue of the twenty-first century or scientific hype?—is certainly not up to us to determine. Albertans will also contribute little to the pace of technological change, and we will not be in a position to affect global demand for our products; we are price takers and not price setters. These strategies all imply a passive "wait and see" with a significant risk of adverse outcomes and with little appeal to Albertans desperate to find a sense of direction for Alberta's future. In fact, they are not options at all in that they are beyond our control, they are not choices that *we* can make. It is more useful, therefore, to turn to strategic options that are more proactive in nature, things that we can do rather than waiting passively for the world to unfold.

OPTION 1: RICHARD FLORIDA'S KNOWLEDGE ECONOMY

It is tempting to conclude that resource-based economies are in a state of inevitable and even rapid decline, with or without the policy challenges emerging from global warming. There is a great temptation to believe that Macdonald's National Policy was right, although perhaps the path forward is with the knowledge-based economy rather than with an industrial, manufacturing economy. When the future is seen in this way, then a sensible economic diversification strategy would focus on public investment in the building blocks of the knowledge economy—on advanced education and training, on research, development and commercialization, on design and engineering skills. Here the blueprint is provided by Richard Florida's (2002; 2008) strategy for attracting and retaining the new creative class. His magnets are vibrant urban communities, a focus on the arts, diversity, world-class universities, trendy restaurants, and great public spaces. In other words, bail on the resource-based economy as quickly as possible, and catch up with a knowledge-based global economy that is moving on. Hewers and drawers, begone!

Certainly this option would solve the challenge that global warming policies pose for Alberta as we would begin to exit from resource production. It is also very alluring to think that Alberta could transform itself into the new Silicon Valley, Singapore, or Barcelona, or perhaps even the new Florence.[7] If you close your eyes for just a moment, you can picture the Smart Cars drifting silently down leafy boulevards lined by outdoor cafés and coffee shops with free Internet access. However, every other city, state, and country seems to be embarked towards the same destination. We may attempt to compete within the Richard Florida paradigm by encouraging rich urban environments with lots of museums, educational institutions, and fashionable restaurants, but why should our success be any better than the success of Hong Kong, Florida's Pittsburgh (which he left), or Sydney? Why should generic economic models work any better here than they will in hundreds, thousands of other communities around the world? For instance, we may and indeed should try to develop world-class educational institutions, but we are joining a very long queue; no one neglects post-secondary education as an essential economic development tool. The brutal reality is that for none of the Florida magnets do we have any natural competitive advantage, and, in fact, as January in Edmonton or Calgary will demonstrate, we may have inherent disadvantages; imagine the Smart Cars embedded in snow drifts as café patrons on Calgary Trail or Macleod Trail huddle inside, car dealerships on either side. Will our cities be more powerful magnets for creative human capital than London, Paris, or New York? Perhaps, but likely not.[8]

It should also be noted that public policy may have limited capacity to realize Florida's vision, and we are, after all, talking about public policy when we talk about economic diversification. There are things we can do with public investment, including better urban transit and greater connectivity to international airports. We can increase funding for the arts, and we can invest more heavily in public spaces, education, immigration, and security. But with other aspects of the Florida model we get into areas of questionable policy leverage; imagine, for a moment, a Government of Alberta Department of Trendy Restaurants and Exciting Gallery Openings. Moreover, we would be investing heavily in W.P. Kinsella's *Field of Dreams* strategy of building an attractive urban environment and hoping they—the internationally mobile creative class—will come, when there is a good chance that they will head for other more established environments with warmer weather and a good beach.

While we do not want to do anything to make the province *less* attractive to the creative class, it would be foolish to exaggerate what we might be able to do *through public policy intervention* to attract the creative class.[9] We might become the new Florence or the new Barcelona, but we might also become just another photocopy of a master design adopted around the world, but one for which we have no competitive advantage.

OPTION 2: LEADING THE NEW ENERGY ECONOMY

Although it would be impossible for Alberta to lead the world in the new information economy writ large, it may be possible to be world-class in a small slice of that economy. Here many people make the argument that Alberta could lead the *new energy economy*, that we could be a global centre for research, development, and commercialization relating to wind power, solar, biofuels, and geothermal. The hope is that our existing expertise relating to the production of hydrocarbons could be redirected towards renewable energy sources, that we would have a head start on less energy-intensive economies. Today's weakness—our reliance on carbon fuels—could become tomorrow's strength.

Fuelling this aspiration are two assumptions: first, that we can capture some of today's conventional energy wealth to build a research infrastructure for renewables, and, second, that existing expertise can be easily redeployed, that engineers are engineers whose creativity can be channelled into renewable resources with little cost or loss in efficiency. Thus, with respect to economic diversification, we would diversify *within* the energy sector by investing heavily in renewables and by moving away from conventional hydrocarbon energy sources such as oil, coal, and the oilsands.[10] The threat of global warming and associated public policies would be turned on its head as we cash in on the opportunities generated by the new energy economy.

Here we have had some success on analogous fronts. The creation of the Alberta Heritage Foundation for Medical Research was an outstanding success in first capturing natural resource wealth and then using that wealth to build medical research capacity in Alberta that would never have developed through market forces alone. The government intervened in the economy, and did so successfully. Another example may turn out to be the provincial and federal government investment in nanotechnology—using today's resource wealth to build a new knowledge frontier unrelated to the resource fundamentals of the provincial economy. These are important successes to keep in mind.

In many ways, this is a very appealing diversification vision— we could become a world energy centre across the full range of renewable energy sources from wind and biofuels to solar and geothermal (but perhaps not tidal power). However, it is important to recognize that we would be a small player in a very large and very competitive global environment where many of our competitors have already invested heavily, have greater investment capacity, and much larger domestic markets. We have to ask whether we have any inherent competitive advantage that would dislodge the German lead in wind power, or the Spanish lead in solar, or China's likely lead across the whole energy terrain. Can a provincial economy of less than four million residents hope to compete? It seems more likely that success would only come if we picked our shots and focused exclusively on a single renewable energy source such as wind or geothermal, but even in this case success would be uncertain. Our competitors are simply too big, too well resourced, and, to put it bluntly, too competitive. Global leadership for a province with 1/1,840 of the world's population will not be easy.

None of this means, of course, that Albertans will not adopt and adapt new energy technologies, for they will. We may even be early adopters, although this is unlikely given the inertia of conventional energy. However, adopting and adapting innovations from afar is quite different from an economic diversification strategy designed to make Alberta a leader in global markets, with others adopting technologies developed here. The new energy economy jobs in Alberta may be more for solar panel installers than for solar panel designers or manufacturers.

OPTION 3: MOVING UP THE VALUE CHAIN

A common theme in discussions of economic diversification is the need to "move up the value chain," to capture for Albertans the added value that comes from processing natural resources. This theme takes many forms and is illustrated in many ways. For example, the argument is frequently made that we should not export bitumen, but instead should first upgrade the bitumen and then export higher valued petroleum products. In Saskatchewan, the debate focuses on the current export of uranium ore—would it be possible to refine the ore within Saskatchewan and also to realize opportunities for high-end products such as medical isotopes? Can the province get away from dependency on the low end of the value chain and capture some of the value-added now being captured by other countries importing Saskatchewan ore? Other illustrations include the development of a diamond processing industry in the Northwest Territories (rather than shipping the uncut diamonds to Antwerp or India) and processing BC timber into final products such as furniture before export.

Moving up the value chain has great appeal as an economic diversification strategy. It builds from our natural resource base, but brings high-end jobs presently located in our export markets back into the region. We might still be hewers and drawers, but we would be hewers and drawers of products located further up the value chain. The problem is that our current resource markets have just as much interest in retaining value-added jobs as we have in repatriating them to Alberta. If our customers are largely dependent on Canadian resources, they may have little option but to accommodate our interest in value-added exports. However, if we are in a more competitive position, market interest in our value-added products will be weak. It may be the case, for example, that excess refinery capacity on the Gulf Coast drives an American interest for bitumen imports that would not exist for upgraded petroleum products, and that, while the world faces a shortage of uranium ore, it has an abundance of refining capacity.

In the final analysis, we will succeed by producing what the world wants to buy. The bitter reality may be that the world wants our natural resources, but wants them from the bottom of the value chain. Our ability to move up the value chain will be constrained if international markets have little appetite for the value-added products we would like to produce. It should also be noted that this diversification strategy does not protect us from the onslaught of global warming policies, as we will still be immersed in the extraction of natural resources, wherein lie the demons of global warming. As attractive as it may be, "moving on up" may fail with respect to both economic diversification and meeting global warming policy challenges.

OPTION 4: MARKET DIVERSIFICATION

A slightly different option to changing what we make is to diversify the markets in which we are selling our products. More specifically, we could reduce our market dependency on the United States by opening up new markets, particularly new markets in the booming Asia-Pacific economies. This is the strategic thinking that lies behind the Asia-Pacific Gateway initiative and the related infrastructure investment in Pacific ports and rail linkages. It is also the thinking that lies behind the proposed Northern Gateway pipeline that would link Alberta hydrocarbon production to Asian markets through new port facilities in Kitimat, British Columbia.

There is no question that a broader range of export markets would reduce Alberta's vulnerability to downturns in the American economy,[11] or to border restrictions induced by the threat of terrorism or protectionist sentiment in the US Congress. It might also bring higher prices through greater competition. However, a broader range of markets *for the same suite of products* is at best a very mild form of economic diversification. Market diversification itself makes sense on many fronts, but it is not a diversification strategy if we keep producing the same things, albeit for different markets.

It should also be noted that market diversification through greater Asia-Pacific trade could lead to a *less diversified* provincial and regional economy. If our markets shift from continental markets south of the border to Asia-Pacific markets, we may encounter less interest in value-added production and more interest in unprocessed natural resources. We may sell more, but more of what we sell may come from the bottom of the natural resource value chain. This in turn would compound our challenge with global warming as we would be locked in even more to the resource intensive industries that contribute disproportionately to greenhouse gas emissions.

OPTION 5: "DANCE WITH THE ONE WHO BRUNG YA"[12]

All of the options discussed above have considerable appeal and undoubtedly some potential. However, none offer the potential of being *the* diversification strategy. Indeed, they all point to significant obstacles on the path towards greater diversification. They embrace objectives common to every political jurisdiction, such as greater value-added production, or they embrace generic models such as that offered by Richard Florida. What they do not do is build upon *existing competitive advantages* stemming from a resource-based, trade-dependent economy.

A fifth economic diversification option is to do just that, to build around rather than displace our conventional resource core. In other words, concentrate on what we do well, but do it better— do conventional resource extraction in a way that meets policy expectations in a carbon-constrained world. The strategy would be based on the cleaner/greener production of oil, gas, coal, and, yes, the oilsands. If successful, Alberta's new technological expertise could well find global markets; we could be the go-to economy for those seeking better ways of producing conventional energy resources. "Dance with the one who brung ya" by focusing on what we do best, but do it better. If Alberta is to produce a constructive global "value add," it is more likely to come through greener forms of conventional energy production than it is through breakthroughs with renewables where we face extremely tough competition.

Here an interesting model is provided by the mining industry in British Columba, which has spun off over six hundred firms dealing with mining technologies, finance, legal advice, marketing, and environmental management.[13] Although these firms are rooted in the BC mining experience, most of their work is done elsewhere in the world. They are global firms selling Canadian expertise, and in many ways the engineering, finance, legal and environmental expertise developed in the Alberta oil patch is being marketed globally in the same way.

The goal, in other words, is to move up a somewhat different value chain than that associated with upgrading petroleum resources. We could compete with the best of the world *on our own turf,* which would not be the case for a diversification strategy built around renewable energy sources. And, we would be addressing the global warming challenge by reducing the carbon footprint of conventional resource production; we would use the environmental challenges associated with resource extraction as opportunities for national and perhaps international leadership on environmental mitigation and less carbon-intensive forms of production. Although it would be tempting to focus on reducing the carbon footprint associated with not only the *production* of hydrocarbon energy resources but also their *consumption,* Alberta does not enjoy any competitive advantage in this latter case, and our small domestic market renders a leadership role unlikely. Alberta's leverage, such as it is, comes from the supply and not the demand side of the energy equation.

In short, our future prosperity may rest on our ability to build upon rather than escape from a resource-based economy. *If* we can use today's natural resource wealth to build around our core strengths, and this is a big *if,* then we may be neither cursed nor slaves. And, with luck and effective marketing, we can be seen as part of the solution to GHG emissions rather than exclusively as part of the problem.[14] We are, and will remain, an export driven economy. Our future lies in exporting cleaner forms of energy that meet new market expectations and in exporting the related technological and financial expertise. Cleaner conventional energy production is the most likely pathway to sustainable prosperity as it plays to our strengths rather than trying to shore up our weaknesses.

Underlying this option is the critically important assumption that Canadian, continental, and global demand for hydrocarbons will remain strong for decades and perhaps generations to come. An economic development strategy based on the cleaner/greener production of hydrocarbons would make no sense if the world is about to wean itself off carbon-based fuels. However, I believe, keeping in mind that I'm a political scientist and not an energy economist, that the transition to a low carbon economy will not be quick. There is too much inertia in the present energy and transportation systems, and there are too many energy demands that cannot be addressed by renewables (e.g., many forms of transportation fuels) for the transition to be quick. Our energy mix will change over time, with renewables coming to play a larger and larger role, but it will take decades to transform our energy systems and convert our existing capital stocks.[15] Therefore we have a reasonable period of time in which to monetize existing hydrocarbon resources, but in a way that is compatible with the new policy regimes associated with the reduction of GHG emissions.

None of this will be easy, but it is the strongest card we have to play. In a sense, we are what we are, and the path forward is to be better at what we do rather than embarking down a different economic trajectory altogether. We can borrow from the other diversification options sketched in above by building a knowledge-based economy, but doing so around the natural resource core. We do not want to shun manufacturing, but rather encourage manufacturing that builds from and supports the natural resources core of the regional economy, manufacturing that goes with and not against the grain of our comparative advantage on the global stage.

This would mean, however, much more than rhetoric, much more than green talk. It would mean very substantial public investments, quite likely dwarfing those associated today with carbon capture and storage. This means that an economic diversification strategy must also be a public savings and investment strategy; it means that we will have to save more of today's resource wealth in order to build the foundation for tomorrow's economic prosperity.

CONCLUSION

In the years ahead, we will see countless random acts of economic diversification as individuals set up clothing firms in Calgary and manufacturing plants in Edmonton. In an economy with little central planning and a great deal of space for firms and individuals, we will continue to muddle through as we have done in the past, with many failures and surprising pockets of success. However, the public policy question of the day is what should *governments* do, if anything, to encourage economic diversification? Here, undoubtedly, we will see a bit of everything as governments cover their bets and respond to a diverse range of economic and political demands. And yes, we will and probably should dabble in renewable energy sources, seeking ways in which the technological developments taking place elsewhere can be adapted and adopted in Alberta. But, as Brian Mulroney suggested, our primary response should be to "dance with the one who brung ya."

If we are to develop a coherent diversification strategy, the starting points are clear. First, save a greater percentage of resource wealth than we do today, resource wealth that can be used to fuel economic diversification. The pathway to success is to capture and use today's hydrocarbon wealth to secure tomorrow's hydrocarbon future. Second, focus on our competitive advantage, on what we know best and where market demand is most predictable—focus on the greener production and consumption of hydrocarbon resources. Third, plan. We will not be successful by happenstance or luck; we will not drift into where we need to be. We will succeed by design, and not by whistling in the dark, hoping external threats to our economy evaporate. Fourth, test diversification strategies against both low price and high price energy scenarios. We don't know whether tomorrow will bring a $200 or a $20 a barrel price for oil, but we do know that the different diversification strategies will play out quite differently across these two price scenarios. Fifth, test diversification strategies against national economic development strategies, and against Alberta's place within a complex federal state where many of the important policy levers rest within the hands of the federal government, and where interprovincial co-operation is increasingly essential.

Notes

1. It is difficult to tell with any certainty just how serious the global warming *policy* challenge might be for Alberta. (The impact of global warming per se on Alberta is even more difficult to predict.) Given the inconclusive outcome of the 2009 Copenhagen Conference and a great deal of policy uncertainty in the United States, policy action on global warming may be stalled. However, I am working from the premise that, over the long run, policy evolution will encourage a more carbon-constrained economy. Although the sense of urgency about global warming may have diminished, all signs continue to point to the same destination.

2. It is important to keep in mind that GHG emissions are only one aspect of a carbon footprint. In October 2010, Syncrude, one of the largest producers of crude oil from Canada's oilsands, was fined $3 million for the deaths of 1,600 ducks, in April 2008, in one of its oilsands tailings ponds in Alberta.

3. For the most part the National Policy did not discriminate against the west by design, and in 1879 there was not much of a west to discriminate against, apart from the Aboriginal population, who faced their own brand of discrimination. However, the application of the National Policy across a regionalized economy had that effect, thereby generating the strong support that western Canadians gave to the Free Trade Agreement and the North American Free Trade Agreement more than a century after the National Policy was put into place.

4. The regional imbalance and strains on fiscal federalism resulting from this scenario would be serious indeed, but cannot be adequately addressed here.

5. Not all resources in western Canada will be tarred by the global warming brush; potash is a notable exception. However, conventional and unconventional oil, coal, uranium (depending on where the environmental movement eventually comes down on nuclear power), and perhaps even natural gas are vulnerable resource sectors.

6. The same case, and to only a slightly lesser degree, could be made for Canada as a whole.
7. It is easier to apply the Florida model to Calgary and Edmonton than it is to Peace River or Medicine Hat.
8. Concern is often expressed that harsh international images of oilsands development may make Alberta's communities less attractive for a highly mobile creative class. Here the competition will come from cities like Vancouver, currently billing itself as "the greenest city in the world."
9. There may also be electoral resistance to investing heavily in what is, after all, a class-based strategy.
10. There is some confusion whether natural gas is in or out of the new energy economy.
11. Assuming, of course, that downturns in the American economy are not reflected in downturns of the global economy.
12. As former Canadian prime minister Brian Mulroney famously said in referring to the need to build on the Canada–US relationship.
13. My thanks to Jock Finlayson, executive vice-president of the Business Council of British Columbia, for bringing this illustration to my attention.
14. Others are clearly thinking along these lines. In late 2008, Alberta Energy released a provincial energy strategy with a strongly stated emphasis on environmental sustainability (see "Launching Alberta's Energy Future: Provincial Energy Strategy," http://www.energy.alberta.ca/Org/pdfs/AB_ProvincialEnergyStrategy.pdf), while the energy industry in Alberta launched a conceptually similar PR campaign under the slogan, "Alberta is Energy."
15. There is no question that my next car will be more fuel efficient, but I hope that the next car is some years away. New forms of residential construction will be more energy efficient, but we have a vast stock of existing residential supply that will not turn over quickly. Cities will become more compact and more energy efficient, but the suburban design of Calgary and Edmonton will take generations to change.

References

Florida, Richard. 2002. *The Rise of the Creative Class: And How It's Transforming Work, Leisure, Community, and Everyday Life*. New York: Basic Books.
———. 2008. *Who's Your City?: How the Creative Economy Is Making Where to Live the Most Important Decision of Your Life*. New York: Basic Books.

Savings of Non-renewable Resource Revenue

Why is it so Difficult?
A Survey of Leaders' Opinions

Robert L. Ascah

WHEREAS substantial revenues are being received by the Province from the sale of non-renewable resource revenues owned by the people of Alberta; and

WHEREAS there is a limited supply of non-renewable resources and therefore revenues from the sale of those resources will ultimately be reduced; and

WHEREAS it would be improvident to spend all such revenues as they are received; and

WHEREAS the Legislative Assembly of Alberta considers it appropriate that a substantial portion of those revenues be set aside and invested for the benefit of the people of Alberta in future years"

—Alberta Heritage Savings Trust Fund Act, Chapter 2, Statutes of Alberta, 1976

To provide prudent stewardship of the savings from Alberta's non-renewable resources by providing the greatest financial returns on those savings for current and future generations of Albertans.
—Alberta Heritage Savings Trust Fund Amendment Act, 1996, Chapter A-27.01, Statutes of Alberta, 1996

INTRODUCTION

The subject of savings of non-renewable resource revenue in Alberta has been woven into the political history of the province since at least 1947 when Leduc No. 1 came on stream. The problem of the public debt in the 1930s and the question of savings remain as challenges that continue to vex Alberta policy makers. The objective of this chapter is to investigate why, at least in the context of Alberta, it appears to be difficult to save resource revenues. In the second section, the cumulative amount of savings, as reflected in net assets (or liabilities), is compared with various measures such as program expenditures, income, and GDP, to assess the efficacy of savings over a 65-year period. In order to better understand the political economy of policy making concerning the savings of resource revenue, a brief history of savings policies in Alberta from 1945 to 2010 is provided in the third section. Qualitative background to the question of the difficulties inherent in the savings of resource revenue, based on the different perspectives of leaders in government (elected officials; senior, non-elected officials), party officials, and business leaders, is presented in the fourth section. Some general conclusions and policy recommendations are made in the final section.

HAS ALBERTA SAVED ENOUGH?[1]

One of the queries of policy analysts examining Alberta's savings history is "have we saved enough?" Figure 8.1 shows net financial assets (liabilities) and total program expenditure on a per capita basis from 1945 to 1991 in 1986 dollars. The figure illustrates a significant buildup of assets and retirement of debt through

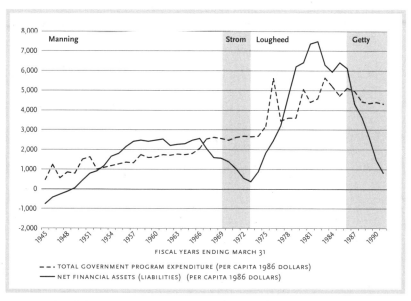

FIGURE 8.1 Total Government Program Expenditure and Net Financial Assets, 1945–1991 (Per capita 1986 dollars)

Source: Boothe (1995, 8–23)

1960 and then a flattening when net financial assets crested for a decade then began a very steep drop at the end of the Manning period and through the short-lived Strom government. Elevated spending commencing in 1965 made a tremendous difference to the financial position of the province inherited by the Lougheed government, as evidenced by the steep decline in financial assets per capita.

Figure 8.2 illustrates the spectacular impact that the discovery of oil at Leduc had on financial assets as a percentage of provincial income in the 1950s. A similar effect occurs in the 1973–1982 period; subsequent to 1973 and the OPEC embargo, a very rapid rise in financial assets occurs, which is then arrested by the oil price levelling off. However, this figure shows both the power of resource revenue on the province's fiscal fortunes and also the dangers of a buildup of fixed program costs. It reveals that while the spending coverage ratio was similar in both boom periods, financial assets as a portion of provincial income during the early 1980s peak were somewhat higher than levels

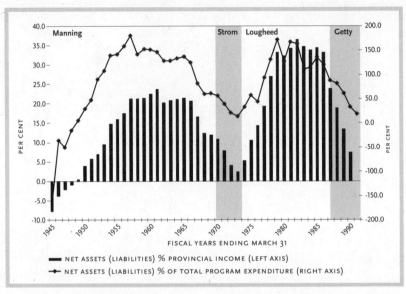

FIGURE 8.2 Total Financial Assets (Liabilities) as Percentage of Provincial Income and Total Program Expenditure, 1945–1991 (1986 dollars)

Source: Boothe (1995, 8–23)

experienced in the 1950s. If one lesson could be drawn, it is that during the late 1960s, without an explicit savings plan, a great opportunity to expand, or at least maintain the level of reserves relative to provincial income, was lost.

Figure 8.3 illustrates Alberta's net financial assets and total spending on a per capita (2002 dollars) basis from 1981 to 2010.[2] This figure reveals that total spending peaked in 1985–86, dropped steadily until 1996–97,[3] and thereafter climbed steadily through the final years of the Klein administration until 2007–08, the first fiscal year of the Stelmach government. Interestingly, the level of real (2002 dollars) per capita spending of $7,845 in 2007–08 was not much different than in the last year of the Getty administration. Figure 8.3 shows that total net assets on a per capita, constant dollar basis fell dramatically during the 1980s. Through the 2000s they have increased to a level slightly higher than in 1981, suggesting that in 2010 the province's net financial asset position is relatively sound.

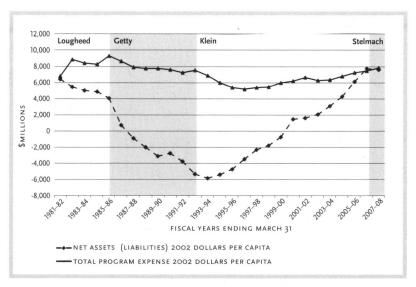

FIGURE 8.3 Net Assets (Liabilities Including Pension Liabilities) and Total Program Expense, 1981–2008 (Per capita 2002 dollars)

Source: Alberta Budget, 1998, 58; Alberta Budget, 2010, 89; CANSIM, Tables 326-0021, Consumer Price Index, All-items, 2005 basket, annual and Table 051-00011, Estimates of population, by age group and sex for July 1.

Figure 8.4 shows net assets and liabilities both as a percentage of GDP and as a percentage of total program expenditures. Net assets peaked at 19% of GDP in 1981–82, fell throughout the 1980s and early 1990s, but had grown back to 15% of GDP by 2007–08. During the first peak in 1981–82, savings represented 95% of a current year's spending; this percentage fell drastically until the mid-1990s, but had recovered by 2007–08 to represent 96.5% of fiscal 2008 spending.[4] Thus, by the end of the Klein ministry, savings as a percentage of GDP was lower than during the Lougheed period, while savings as a percentage of total program expense was virtually the same as at the previous peak. That said, the most important element in the figures is the evidence of fiscal instability.

Since the timing and duration of downturns and booms cannot be known a priori, the necessity to moderate fiscal instability through strict decision rules should be evident. Given the cutbacks that occurred in 1993–1997, and despite the savings

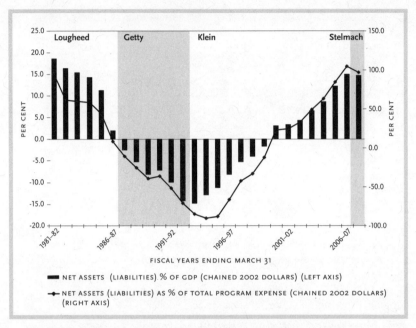

FIGURE 8.4 Net Assets (Liabilities Including Pension Liabilities) as Percentage of GDP and Total Program Expense, 1981–2008 (Chained 2002 dollars)

Source: Alberta Budget, 1998, 58; Alberta Budget, 2010, 89; CANSIM, Tables 326-002, Consumer Price Index, All-items, 2005 basket, annual and Table 384-0001, Gross domestic product (GDP), income-based, provincial economic accounts, annual.

of the late 1970s and early 1980s, one could argue that even savings at 19% of GDP, or roughly one year's spending, were insufficient in the face of a brutal resource price downturn. Thus, it is important to understand obstacles to saving resource revenue given the context of highly volatile resource revenue. So why don't we save? What gets in the way?

HISTORY OF SAVINGS

There are essentially five phases in Alberta's savings (debt repayment) story, each of which is considered in more detail below. The first phase, from 1945 to 1971, is termed "debt pay-down, experimentation, and decline." The second phase, from 1972 to

1986, is categorized by a buildup of financial assets and "home bias" and is associated with the use of savings to foster new private and public infrastructure in the province. The third phase, from 1986 to 1993, is a period of decline in Alberta's savings accounts, along with burgeoning public debt. During this time, a number of economic development investments, which some academics considered to be "forced industrialization," were written down in value. The fourth phase, debt pay-down and transformation, which consisted of paying off the debt as a form of savings, started in 1994–95 when deficits were eliminated and concluded in 2004 when the "25-year mortgage" was paid off.[5] This phase of transformation was carried out through amendments to the Alberta Heritage Savings Trust Fund Act, which not only reconfirmed the status of the fund as the primary savings vehicle but also restructured the fund into an endowment fund with assets principally invested outside the province.[6] The final phase, from 2005 to 2010, is classified as "situational savings," where large unanticipated surpluses were used to top up the Heritage Fund, to pay dividends to Albertans ("Prosperity bonus" or "Ralph bucks"), and to make a range of endowment investments (e.g., Cancer Prevention Legacy Fund).

Debt Pay-down, Experimentation, and Decline, 1945–1971

During this period, non-renewable resource revenue as a percentage of total revenue ranged from 1.4% to 47%.[7] Figure 8.5 illustrates the amount of non-renewable resource revenue received by the province of Alberta, the province's surplus or deficit position, total program spending, and the net financial assets or liabilities of the province from 1945 to 1991, all on a per capita basis (Boothe 1995, 8–23).[8] The impact of the Leduc oil discovery on the province's finances is significant. In a very short period of time, the province had accumulated financial assets of about $2,500 per capita in 1986 dollars.

One aspect that may explain why so much resource revenue is spent as opposed to saved is the accounting treatment of resource rents. Until 1972, the provincial government operated two revenue accounts—an operating and a capital account.[9] Only land

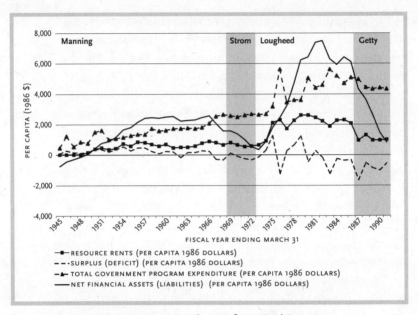

FIGURE 8.5 Resource Rent, Surplus (Deficit), Total Program Spending, and Net Financial Assets (Liabilities), 1945–1991 (Per Capita 1986 dollars)

Source: Boothe (1995, 8–23)

sales were treated as a capital item, while the abundant royalties were included in the income account. Thus, sales of assets via royalties were regarded as ordinary revenue, and this policy was inherited by the Lougheed regime. This treatment meant that all royalties flowed into the government's operating account and were used to fund services, new programs, and infrastructure, thus acclimatizing Albertans to expect excellent public services and low taxes. As can be seen by Figure 8.5, the huge increases in revenue allowed the provincial government to save, as new spending was not keeping up with revenue. However, this would change in the late 1960s.

When reviewing budget speeches from the 1950s and 1960s, there is evident tension between the pressures to spend and the recognition that resource prices fluctuated. In his March 4, 1955 budget speech, Treasurer Clarence Gerhart noted,

The Government has been criticized for accumulating surpluses while at the same time, demands for increased expenditures and the abolition of some sources of revenue have been persistent. This attitude is not new. It is evidenced by the following quotation from a budget address delivered in 1895 by Sir Vernon Harcourt—"With each year, new expenditures are demanded from all sides for every sort of thing, and at the same time these increases of expenditures are suggested, the abolition of some source of revenue is attempted." The practice persists you observe. (Government of Alberta 1955, 6)

This would become a perennial theme. In the 1962 budget, Treasurer E.W. Hinman complained,

It has been said that the worst health problems of our country are those brought on by our excesses—over-eating, over-drinking, over-playing, over-loafing, and over-worrying, chiefly about keeping up with the Joneses. I would suggest that the social, economic, and political ills of which we complain may be attributed to like causes in that we have acquired *insatiable appetites* for excesses of services, of subsidy and assistance, of security, of facilities for entertainment and leisure, and of promises and assurances, all at public expense. The symptoms of the resulting sickness of citizenship are discernable in our surrender of independence, of initiative, of reliance on reason, of dignity and in our abandonment of our willingness *to contribute as individuals to pay a fair share of the costs of the services enjoyed by society collectively* and to work for the preservation of the freedoms on which our way of life depends. (Government of Alberta 1963, 2, emphasis added)

While the control of spending was foremost in the mind of the treasurer, in any democratic society there are of course interests that continue to push for more public services. The bounty of resource revenue and rising surpluses put successive governments on the defensive. In responding to criticisms that the government was hoarding, Treasurer Gerhart also noted the "insatiable" needs of the population:

The second conclusion to which I refer and which also must now be obvious to all, is that the revenues accruing from taxation and the development of our natural resources, however buoyant, will never exceed the constant need for progressive capital development and the consistent public demands for more and better standards of social services. (Government of Alberta 1955, 29)[10]

The tension between expanding government programs and the political philosophy of a right-of-centre government was one faced by both Social Credit and Progressive Conservative governments. Without a clear policy for savings or spending, the tendency was to lower taxes and increase spending. One of the constituencies important to the Manning government was municipalities.[11] In Ernest Manning's final year as treasurer, he went to great lengths to emphasize the increasing support the government was providing to municipalities. In this budget, Manning mooted the possibility that provincial grants to municipalities could eliminate property taxes. He quickly dismissed that idea but went on to hint at what might be done with the accumulating savings.

It may be that the time is coming when the interests of responsible self-government will be better served by levelling off the measure of provincial financial aid and distributing *directly to the individual citizens of each community an equitable share of the revenues* accruing from the development of their natural resources in the form of citizen's participation dividends. Such a policy not only would enhance the financial ability of ratepayers to meet the operating costs of autonomous local government but would recognize each citizen's personal stake in the natural resources of the province and *his right to an equitable share of the benefits accruing from their orderly development*. (Government of Alberta 1954, 28, emphasis added)

While the Social Credit government did not establish an explicit savings policy for the resource revenue, in 1957 they experimented in paying dividends to individuals—perhaps harkening back to the 1935 election promise of a $25 per month "social dividend." Treasurer Hinman offered the following explanation for the payment to citizens.

> Of this [statutory] amount, $11,000,000 will be required for the distribution of a Dividend to all Canadian citizens who have resided in the Province of Alberta for five years and who have attained the age of twenty-one years. The amount of distribution will be one-third of the net royalties from Oil and Gas produced from Provincial lands in the previous fiscal year. This distribution is being made in order that Alberta residents may share personally in the prosperity resulting from the development of our Oil Industry. (Government of Alberta 1957, 22)[12]

Several things are noteworthy about this experiment. First, eligible citizens must have resided in Alberta for a minimum of five years, thus discouraging in-migration for the benefit. Second, the government used one-third of the previous year's resource revenues. Interestingly, the one-third measure is very close to the 30% rule adopted by the Lougheed government in 1976.

Another, soon to be perennial, issue was the growing dependence on resource revenue, as noted in the 1956 budget. Hinman remarked,

> The Budget I am presenting to you tonight reflects the confidence of the Government in the ability of our people to maintain our economic progress through another year. It reflects too, some measure of caution in the degree to which we feel it safe to subscribe to expenditure policies which must, by their nature, call for pyramiding costs years after year, whether or not there may be correspondingly increased revenue. (Government of Alberta 1956, 3–4)

Predicting non-renewable resource revenue introduces a high degree of uncertainty in provincial budget making. This uncertainty arises from two main factors. First, the production of oil and natural gas relied on the private sector raising capital and accepting the risks of development. This reliance on the private sector was foundational for Social Credit and, to varying degrees, the Progressive Conservatives. Second, oil price fluctuations, to the extent that royalties and lease sales were price sensitive, added another layer of uncertainty. In addition, both capital investment and oil price fluctuations were positively correlated. As Hinman noted, the worry was a buildup in the cost structure of government when resource revenues could plummet. This would become a recurrent challenge for successive governments.

Another theme in provincial budgets at that time was the aversion to debt and the goal of reducing the debt. In the 1953 budget, Manning declared that Alberta was the first province that had accumulated cash surpluses and investments in excess of its total indebtedness (Government of Alberta, March 6, 1953, 3). In his 1958 budget address, Treasurer Hinman, reiterated this aversion in the following terms:

> This budget bespeaks the resolve of the Government to stick to these economic principles by which it has been guided for twenty-six years; *that debt is to be abhorred and avoided*, that *taxation should be kept to such minimums as can be justified*, that the dignity of the individual can be assured only by insisting that the individual accept full responsibility of citizenship; that inherent in democracy is the wisdom of keeping in the hands of the people important decisions of government by de-centralization of the authority to collect and to spend, that the Government must serve the will of the people in guaranteeing the freedoms already mentioned and in attempting to make financially possible all those services physically and desirable. (Government of Alberta 1958, 28, emphasis added)

As the above quote reveals, the philosophy of low taxes is very much embedded in Alberta's fiscal history.

As Figure 8.5 illustrates, the final two terms of Social Credit (under Manning and then Strom) were characterized by spending increases, flat revenue, and a drawdown of financial assets. Budget speeches were notable in citing the dangers of overspending, but the ramp-up in spending proved the admonitions were hollow. The concept of ever-rising public services and infrastructure was well-embedded when the August 1971 election of Peter Lougheed occurred.

Buildup of Assets and Home Bias, 1972–1986

Between 1972 and 1986, non-renewable resource revenue as
a share of total revenue ranged between 25% and an astound-
ing 65% in fiscal 1979–80. As Figure 8.5 illustrates, after
the 1973 OPEC embargo, resource revenue grew prodigiously
in Lougheed's first, second, and third terms (1971–1982).
This period is also associated with rising tensions within the
Canadian federation over the question of Alberta's new wealth.
This tension, principally involving Ottawa, Ontario, and Alberta,
manifested itself in several ways. John Turner's 1974 federal
budget removed the deductibility of royalties in the corporate
income tax structure. In addition, to cushion gasoline consumers from spiking prices at the pump, oil prices were held for a
period at one-half the world price.[13] Fears were voiced by various
governments that Alberta could draw out investment and labour
from other provinces through a combination of low taxes and
high quality public services.

What to do? The establishment of the Alberta Heritage
Savings Trust Fund in 1976 was both an act of statesmanship
and astute politics. By educating Albertans that these resources
were finite and some portion needed to be saved for a time when
these resources were depleted, Alberta's Heritage Fund served
to elevate Alberta's stature and profile on the national scene. The
Alberta Heritage Savings Trust Fund Act established four com-
partments for investments: 1) the Canada Investment Division;
2) the Alberta Investment Division; 3) the Capital Projects
Division ("deemed assets"); and 4) cash and marketable securities.[14] Tables 8.1A–8.1D show the growth of the Heritage Fund
over the 1976–1987 period. These tables list the key investments
during this growth period. Of particular note was that the act
was silent on how to take money *out* of the fund. This silence
appears to be based on the expectation that resource revenue
would remain at elevated levels.[15] In this very firm commitment
to savings was a subtle trade-off: money would not be spent on
direct provincial programs,[16] thus satisfying conservative political philosophy of low taxes and small government, but the home

at March 31 ($millions)	1977	1978	1979	1980	1981	1982	1983	1984	1985	1986	1987
Canada Investment Division*											
Newfoundland	50.0		146.0	109.6	74.5	—	—	—	—	—	
Nova Scotia			98.0	147.0	108.1	75.0	—	—	—	—	—
Prince Edward Island		46.8		28.0	19.5	44.4	—	—	—	—	—
New Brunswick				110.0	74.1	—	—	—	—	—	—
Hydro Quebec			189.5		74.8	—	—	—	—	—	—
Manitoba			75.0		108.3	74.8	—	—	—	—	—

TABLE **8.1A** Heritage Fund Investments: Canada Investment Division, 1977–1987

includes loans guaranteed by these provincial governments

bias in investment policy itself was directed at meeting underlying demands for housing, new energy investment (Syncrude), and agriculture.

Several policy objectives are evident from this investment portfolio. First, the Canada Investment Division made loans available to all Canadian provinces and the federal government at interest rates equivalent to those at which Alberta could borrow. At a time of rising interest rates, for provinces with weaker credit ratings, the availability of the funds and the concessions were certainly a way of alliance building with other Canadian provinces.[17] In 1983, the province suspended loans to Canadian provinces. This decision coincided with a period of abnormally high interest rates being paid by Albertans, and public opinion quickly evolved to the view that the Alberta government should be supporting its own citizens and businesses and not providing "low interest loans" to other provinces.[18] Two other significant investments with intergovernmental aspects were the Ridley Grain Terminal in British Columbia's Prince Rupert and grain cars purchased through the Capital Projects Division (Dr. J. Peter Meekison, interview, March 15, 2010).

The Alberta Investment Division's main activity during the first decade of the fund's operation was to make available funds to rapidly growing provincial Crown corporations. These

at March 31 ($millions)	1977	1978	1979	1980	1981	1982	1983	1984	1985	1986	1987
Provincial Corporations**											
Alberta Agriculture Development Corporation			138.0	53.0	139.0	232.0	181.0	144.0	127.0	109.0	
Alberta Mortgage and Housing Corporation	227.0	122.0	210.0	210.0	435.0	800.0	700.0	220.0	100.0	185.0	188.0
Alberta Municipal Financing Corporation				175.0	450.0	382.2	664.2				
Alberta Housing Corporation	155.0	95.9	64.0	93.0	126.0	204.0	300.0	170.0			
Alberta Opportunity Company			71.5	24.5	28.0	34.0	58.0	42.0	35.0	34.0	33.0
Alberta Government Telephones				1043.0	289.7	348.5	339.4	15.0			
Alberta Heritage Foundation for Medical Research				300.0							
Alberta Heritage Scholarship Fund					100.0						

TABLE 8.1B Heritage Fund Investments: Alberta Investment Division: Provincial Corporations and Other Investments, 1977–1987

** gross issuance

large investments assisted provincial corporations in meeting their capital requirements during the economic boom. Housing shortages during the late 1970s and early 1980s caused the government to respond to the crisis through lending to individuals and developers (Jim Dinning, interview, March 23, 2010).[19] The loans to the Alberta Opportunity Company (established in 1972) and the Alberta Agricultural Development Corporation were also seen as good politics with key constituencies (small business and farmers). While these corporations could borrow with a government guarantee on the capital markets, with the fund's large

at March 31 ($Millions)	1977	1978	1979	1980	1981	1982	1983	1984	1985	1986	1987
Alberta Energy Company	75.5	0.2	0.1	0.6		0.3					
Bank of Alberta									1.6		
Bralorne Resources		5.0									
Calgary Power		19.7					0.1				
Canadian Commercial Bank						5.0	-27.7				
Cities Services Canada — #	57.1	29.9	12.9								
Gulf Canada	63.7	32.8	3.5								
Interprovincial Steel and Pipe						5.0					
Northland Bank									50.0	5.0	
Ridley Grain Ltd.							31.4	85.2	12.8	4.6	
Syncrude†	120.0	59.0	46.6	8.9	4.7	255.3	-27.7	31.2	-3.5	19.6	24.7

TABLE 8.1C Heritage Fund Investments: Alberta Investment Division: Other Investments, 1977–1987, Flows not Stock

† net of proceeds from sale of synthetic crude, etc.

and growing pool of cash and marketable securities, investing in Alberta was deemed to be a sound investment. Government and potential investors alike shared a common refrain: "What better place in the world to invest than Alberta?"

Alberta Energy Company, established in 1973 with grants of oil and natural gas rights in the Suffield and Primrose blocks, was another concrete example of province-building, as were the fund's investments in Syncrude, Gulf, and Capital Cities. These latter investments were regarded as a high-risk venture, with government involvement required to share the technological and operating risks as well as to keep the project from collapsing.

The most significant development in the early history of the Heritage Fund appeared in the March 1983 budget. The province, facing a recession, falling investment, rising unemployment,

at March 31 ($millions)	1977	1978	1979	1980	1981	1982	1983	1984	1985	1986	1987
Alberta Investment Division	1566	2276	3167	3140	4524	6335	8158	8079	8151	8177	7847
Capital Projects Division — Vencap								200	200	200	200
Energy Investment Division					25	25	25	25	24	16	9
Canada Investment Division	50	96	270	929	1492	1909	1903	1896	1870	1864	1857
Commercial Investment Division						189	199	199	201	217	233
Deposits and Marketable Securities and other assets	566	879	1013	1617	1577	1242	1112	1377	1828	2242	2599
Total Financial Assets	**2182**	**3251**	**4450**	**5686**	**7618**	**9700**	**11397**	**11776**	**12274**	**12716**	**12745**
Capital Projects Division — Deemed Assets	36	123	255	733	961	1309	1605	1935	2162	2402	2629
Total Investments	2218	3374	4705	6419	8579	11009	13002	13711	14436	15118	15374
External Investments‡	616	975	1283	2546	3069	3340	3214	3472	3899	4323	4689

TABLE 8.1D Heritage Fund Investments: Division Breakdown

‡ sum of Canada Investment Division, Energy Investment Division and Deposits and Marketable Securities
Source: Alberta Heritage Savings Trust Fund, Annual Reports, 1976–2010.

and a real estate crisis caused by high interest rates, cut the 30% resource transfer to the fund to 15%. In addition, effective the previous September, all investment income would, for 24 months, flow into the province's General Revenue Fund. Treasurer Hyndman noted,

> The central pillar of Alberta's financial management strategy is the Alberta Heritage Savings Trust Fund. It was set up in 1976 to *smooth the transition* from a situation in which government revenue is derived largely from depleting natural resources to one where

services must be financed by more conventional revenue resources like taxation. Implicit in the design of the Heritage Fund was the notion that it would be available for *a "rainy day."*

...In fact, in the near future external borrowing may well be needed to meet the capital needs of these Crown corporations. The Heritage Fund *is tied up in mortgages and committed to loans for years ahead* until repayments by homeowners and other borrowers become available in significant amounts. (Government of Alberta 1983, 12, emphasis added)

This decision had significant ramifications for the province's finances. Figure 8.6 projects the size of the fund had all the money been reinvested or if an endowment was created with a distribution rule of 5% of the principal sum of the fund.[20] This figure illustrates the dramatic differences due to investment retention and compounding investment returns. Of course, the figure does not illustrate what would have been given up in terms of infrastructure such as schools, hospitals, or various programs.

Thus, in 1983 the bloom fell off Alberta's fiscal rose. Towards the end of the Lougheed period, the picking of "winners and losers" by government emerged. While many of these investments were paid back in full, there appeared to be little in the way of coherent strategy for investment. Investments in Alberta-based financial institutions perhaps could be seen as encouraging the establishment of a regional financial services sector. However, with the exception of the Bank of Alberta (now Canadian Western Bank), the fund's involvement in two failing banks underlined the weakness of the home bias in investment policy. Investments in Bralorne Resources, Calgary Power (later TransAlta), NOVA, and TCPL also fit in with a home bias in investment strategy. In fiscal 1983–84, Vencap Equities was seeded with a $200 million loan from the Heritage Fund, demonstrating a belief that the private sector was either unable or unwilling to finance emerging businesses. This vehicle, with equity sold to the public, had a mixed history. It was eventually sold to Onex Corporation in October 1995 at a significant discount.

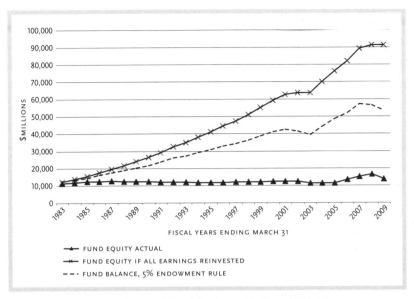

FIGURE 8.6 Heritage Fund: Actual Fund Equity vs. Projected if 1) All Income Reinvested or 2) 5% Endowment Rule, 1983–2009

Source: *Alberta Heritage Savings Trust Fund, Annual Report, 2010, 16 and author's calculations.*

Another example of home bias was the Capital Projects Division (CPD), which was created to provide infrastructure of "lasting value to the people of Alberta." With so much revenue flowing into the treasury, the CPD was designed to provide infrastructure *additional* to the basic needs of the province.[21] This division affirmed an important aspect of Alberta politics—that the money should stay inside Alberta.

Decline, 1986–1993

Between 1986 and 1993, non-renewable resource revenue as a percentage of total own-source revenue ranged between 17% and 26%. This period is described as a decline in the sense that not only was the Heritage Fund's real value eroded by inflation, but by the close of this period the province had accumulated $22.7 billion in debt to finance recurring deficits.[22]

at March 31 ($millions)	1988	1989	1990	1991	1992	1993	1994
Provincial Corporations†							
Alberta Agriculture Development Corporation	41.0	47.0		40.0	100.0		
Alberta Mortgage and Housing Corporation	155.0	76.0	78.0	99.0	87.0		
Alberta Municipal Financing Corporation						73.0	
Alberta Opportunity Company	48.0	85.0	31.5	28.0	23.0	30.0	
Small Business Term Assistance Fund	200.0						

Other Investments	1988	1989	1990	1991	1992	1993	1994
Alberta Energy Company		30.0		7.6	7.8	8.6	-183.3
Alberta-Pacific Pulp Mill Project					67.2	128.6	84.6
Bank of Alberta							
Lloydminster Bi-provincial Upgrader		2.4	27.4	109.1	82.2	-132.6	-18.7
Millar Western Pulp Ltd.	50.7	69.3			-46.1		-53.5
Northland Bank							
NOVA Corporation — debenture & common shares	150.0		24.5				
OSLO			4.0	1.8	-5.8		-4.3
Syncrude — ##	25.6	3.1	6.8	-5.2	4.5	-18.8	-158.1
TELUS common shares				1193.9			
TransCanada Pipelines					150.0		

TABLE 8.2A Alberta Investment Division Investments: Provincial Corporations and Other Investments, 1988–1994

† gross issuance

In 1986, Don Getty became premier and inherited a government spending base that was significantly above the provincial per capita average. In his first year in office, a dramatic fall in resource revenues was caused by plummeting oil prices. Coupled with the decrease in resource revenues was a traumatic decline in real estate prices that adversely impacted the government in a number of ways. First, the value of the mortgage portfolio of AMHC and the Alberta Housing Corporation declined precipitously as individuals and developers could no longer afford to pay interest, and many walked away from their homes and investments. While the fund was protected by the provincial guarantee or Crown-agent status on these debentures, the General Revenue Fund was providing assistance to the corporations to pay the Heritage Fund. Such circularity tended to damage the credibility of the fund.

at March 31 ($millions)	1988	1989	1990	1991	1992	1993	1994
Alberta Investment Division	7520	7397	6887	5875	4658	4421	3706
Capital Projects Division—Vencap	200	200	113	118	122	127	131
Energy Investment Division	1	—					
Canada Investment Division	1470	1388	1306	1189	1182	1175	1069
Commercial Investment Division	263	287	316	340	345	339	400
Deposits and Marketable Securities and other assets	3108	3140	3665	4602	5732	5889	6588
Total Financial Assets	**12562**	**12412**	**12287**	**12124**	**12039**	**11951**	**11894**
Capital Projects Division — Deemed Assets 1987	2758	2913	3047	3197	3282	3366	3437
Total Investments	15320	15325	15334	15321	15321	15317	15331
External Investments‡	4841	4815	5287	6131	7259	7403	8057

TABLE 8.2B Heritage Fund Investments: Division Breakdown

‡ *sum of Canada Investment Division, Energy Investment Division and Deposits and Marketable Securities*
Source: Alberta Heritage Savings Trust Fund, Annual Reports, 1976–2010.

Second, with the real estate crash, provincially regulated credit unions became undercapitalized, and the provincial treasury quickly organized a massive restructuring of the system.[23] A third effect was the significant decline in oil and gas investment caused by the drop in oil and gas prices. This also reduced personal and corporate income tax flows.

In terms of investment activity, as Tables 8.2A and 8.2B show, the government decided to use the Heritage Fund as a vehicle to support a nascent forestry industry, finance an upgrader in Lloydminster, and pay for planning costs for a new oilsands operation (OSLO). Several of these investments were written down. In addition to losses and write-downs in the Heritage Fund, other investments or guarantees outside the fund, such as a magnesium plant, NovAtel, and Gainers, earned the Getty government the reputation of being fiscally challenged. New loans to provincial corporations fell as demand for housing and other infrastructure dropped in the weak Alberta economy. A major initiative during this period was the privatization of Alberta Government Telephones, which resulted in the province swapping debt for equity in the new corporation. Table 8.2B also illustrates the buildup of the fund's cash and marketable securities as provincial corporation and Canada Investment Division investments matured.

By the end of this period, the public mood had shifted to the view that large government was a problem, and the 1993 election was fought on who would scale down government and restore the province's creaking finances. During this period, the rise of the Reform Party, whose main platform was fiscal conservatism and reducing the size of government, had an important influence on policy deliberations in Alberta. This was also a time when federal and provincial finances came under increasing scrutiny by investors and rating agencies (Hon. Ken Kowalski, interview, April 19, 2010).

Aversion to Debt and Transformation, 1994–2004

Between 1994 and 2004, non-renewable resource revenue as a per cent of total own-source revenue ranged between 15% and 45%. Ralph Klein's assumption of the Progressive Conservative leadership in December 1992 coincided with a historically low popularity rating for the party of about 17%. Laurence Decore, as the popular Liberal Party leader and former mayor of Edmonton, made the 1993 election a close race. Prior to calling an election, Premier Klein appointed a financial review commission that examined the province's fiscal situation. The "Williams Report" warned of the dangers of running current deficits and made a series of sweeping recommendations to address the financial crisis (Alberta Financial Review Commission 1993).[24] As an interview with a former minister of finance revealed, Alberta's finances at this time were seen to be unstable (Patricia Nelson, interview, March 22, 2010). Klein also abolished the MLA (Members of the Legislative Assembly) pension plan that was seen by the public as too generous, thus removing an emotion-laden election issue. Many observers labelled the election as involving a choice between "nasty cuts and brutal cuts." At the end of the day, the public returned the Conservatives to office with a reduced, but comfortable, majority.

The election campaign reflected the public's concerns over fiscal management. The newly elected premier had a mandate to correct the fiscal situation. In several interviews, former politicians and senior public servants noted the strong alignment in thinking between the public, the bureaucracy, and the "new" government. As such, the conditions for significantly cutting services were as ideal as could be expected for the new government. Based on the mantra of keeping taxes low ("it doesn't take any brains to raise taxes"), the government set out to control spending, acknowledging that control over revenue, particularly resource revenue, was illusory. Spending control took the form of absolute cuts to all departments, with health and education being spared somewhat. From 1993–94 to 1996–97 program spending fell from $15.1 billion to $12.7 billion. The government's credibility was enhanced by pay cuts that politicians, civil servants, health care workers, educators, and provincial corporation staff accepted, perhaps grudgingly. As many in the private sector lost jobs or were underemployed through the late 1980s and early 1990s, there was less public sympathy for the fate of government workers.

In remarkably short order, the deficit was eliminated in 1994–95, two years ahead of schedule. The government then turned to paying down the debt. A significant part of the government's communications at this time involved an emphasis on the deadweight nature of the debt's servicing costs—payments that did nothing to improve public services in Alberta. It was often said by senior government ministers that it was unfair to leave debts to our children and grandchildren (Patricia Nelson, interview). Further, as the economy improved, in part due to pro-business policies encapsulated in the "Alberta Advantage," reducing and then eliminating debt became the focus for the government. Figure 8.7 illustrates the powerful momentum of paying down debt as interest savings were liberated.

During this period a number of "trip-wires" or fences were placed around the capacity of the government to spend more than revenues could accommodate. Notable legislation included the Deficit Elimination Act, the Taxpayers Protection Act, the Fiscal Responsibility Act, and the Government Accountability Act. Consolidated financial reporting and quarterly fiscal updates were mandated. In many respects, Alberta led the way in

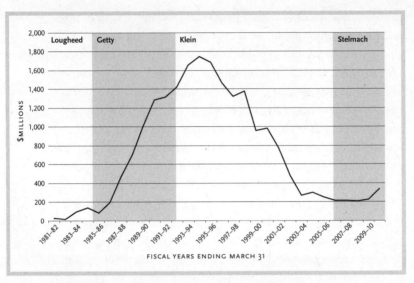

FIGURE 8.7 Debt Servicing Costs, 1981–2011 Estimates

Source: Alberta Budget, *1998, 58 and* Alberta Budget, *2010, 89.*

Canada in taming deficits, financial reporting, and performance measurement.

The new premier introduced structural changes to the budgeting system that directly involved backbench MLAs in decision making through a number of standing policy committees. These committees, chaired by a government MLA, and made up of ministers and backbenchers, reviewed budgets and business plans. In the early years, the committees and Treasury Board gained the reputation of being brutal on spending. Another facet of Klein's premiership was the tendency of consulting with the public. This was evident in a Red Deer roundtable on the budget in 1993 as well as efforts to survey Albertans on questions relating to fiscal policy.[25]

The most significant change from a savings and investment perspective occurred in 1996. In December 1994, a public consultation process on the Heritage Fund's future was launched, followed up by an all-party Review Committee. A key finding was the public's desire to retain the fund (Government of Alberta, Alberta Heritage Savings Trust Fund 1995, 5). In 1996, the government changed the mandate of the fund to "provide prudent stewardship of the savings from Alberta's non-renewable resources by providing the greatest financial returns on those savings for current and future generations of Albertans."[26] The days of direct political involvement were over as the amendments set out a 10-year period for conversion from a "home bias" fund to a professionalized, arms-length management style. An MLA oversight committee was retained while an Investment Operations Committee "involving private sector expertise" would work with Treasury. Treasurer Jim Dinning noted,

> It [the fund] can no longer be used by government for economic development or social investment purposes. The focus is on getting a solid financial return rather than using the Fund's resources as a tool for implementing government policies. We have now a distinct, arms-length relationship between the Fund and the government of the day. (Government of Alberta, Alberta Heritage Savings Trust Fund 1996, 2)

The Investment Operations Committee provided further insulation from political direction. Recognizing that the real value of the Heritage Fund had declined significantly, provision was made to inflation-proof the fund. Noteworthy was the absence of an explicit endowment rule that would have provided greater stability to the flow of funds to the General Revenue Fund as the Heritage Fund transitioned towards more equities. While inflation-proofing was a proxy for retaining the value of the fund, it was conditional on the province's overall finances.

After the 1997 election, which saw an increased number of Tories elected, a long series of large, unanticipated surpluses saw the province repay maturing debt quickly. The government built up a "debt retirement account" in the General Revenue Fund to pay off provincial debt as it came due. The unanticipated surpluses were due to rising oil and natural gas prices (as opposed to production increases) and a forecasting rule that used average prices from previous years. During this period, criticism was levelled at the government for its pessimistic resource revenue forecasts. According to two previous finance ministers, it was much easier to sell a large surplus than to be caught short and be forced to cut spending (Patricia Nelson, interview; Shirley McClellan, interview, April 6, 2010).

As non-renewable resource revenue reached $10.6 billion resulting in a $6.6 billion surplus in fiscal 2000–01, the government sought policy guidance from a Financial Management Commission chaired by David Tuer, a Calgary oil executive and former senior official in the province's energy department.[27] The commission highlighted resource revenue volatility and recommended that all non-renewable resource revenue flow to an expanded Heritage Fund, and that the fund should direct the lesser of $3.5 billion or the average of resource revenue for the previous three years to the General Revenue Fund for ordinary expenses. The commission, while praising the government for its fiscal management, was critical of the government's failure to meet commitments for capital spending. It recommended a formula to smooth out capital spending (Alberta Financial Management Commission 2002). A real concern was that the province was paying off debt rapidly but was creating a new type of debt in the form of the deferred capital maintenance—or an "infrastructure deficit." This problem led to an aggressive policy response by the government to tackle this new form of "deficit" via a multi-year Capital Plan.

The government did not accept the commission's recommendation for an expanded Heritage Fund. Rather, they established a separate Sustainability Fund in the General Revenue Fund that could address short-term revenue fluctuations.[28] The fund could not make up in-year operating shortfalls in other revenue. It could only be used to pay for emergencies and disasters, including paying for assistance under the Natural Gas Price Protection Act (Government of Alberta 2003).[29] The fund could not be drawn down below zero. Payment into the fund was the first priority for year-end surpluses until a balance of $2.5 billion was reached. In the early years of the fund, due to drought and the BSE crisis,[30] significant sums were withdrawn from the Sustainability Fund, thus reducing overall savings (Patricia Nelson, interview; Shirley McClellan, interview).

Situational Savings, 2005–2011

Between 2005 and the 2011 budget, non-renewable resource revenue as a percentage of total own-source revenue ranged between
21% and 45%. As Figure 8.8 illustrates, the provincial government moved into a net asset position in 2000–01, and over the
next five years attacked the debt sufficiently aggressively that by
fiscal 2005–06, Finance Minister Shirley McClellan was able to
proclaim that Alberta had no debt (Government of Alberta 2005,
7).[31] Over the course of the final term of Klein's premiership,
unanticipated surpluses were either spent or tucked away without any fully articulated strategy. In fiscal 2006, a $500 million
Alberta Cancer Prevention Legacy Fund was created. In 2006,
a payment of $1.4 billion from the anticipated 2005–06 surplus
was made to all Alberta residents. In fiscal years 2005–2007,
$2 billion was transferred to the Heritage Fund and another
$1 billion was allotted to a separate account in the Heritage
Fund for the Advanced Education endowment. In 2007–08,
the last fiscal year of large unanticipated surpluses, $918 mil-
lion was added to the Heritage Fund. This approach could also
be regarded as an ad hoc or "cookie jar" approach, where "special
interests" could be rewarded with one-off "investments."

As political pressure continued to build for infrastructure
to support the booming economy and rising population, the
level of capital spending grew dramatically. In fiscal 2003–04,
capital plan spending accounted for $1.7 billion, or about 7% of
total spending. By 2008–09, capital spending had climbed to
$7.6 billion, representing slightly more than 20% of provincial
spending (Figure 8.9). Institutions seeking infrastructure funds
argued that, unlike program spending, such investments would
create immediate construction employment and longer-term
economic spin-offs and social returns in the fields of education
and health. Nevertheless, the huge capital investment catch-up
drove construction costs higher in an economy arguably that was
already overheating from the huge oilsands and conventional oil
and gas investment.[32]

Since fiscal 2008, the provincial government has faced deficits, making savings policy irrelevant. The government under

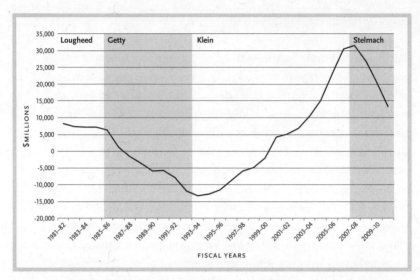

FIGURE **8.8** Total Net Assets (Net Debt) Including Pension Liabilities, 1981–2011 Estimates

Source: Alberta Budget, *1998, 58 and* Alberta Budget, *2010, 89.*

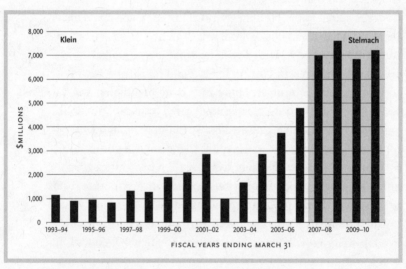

FIGURE **8.9** Capital Investment, 1993–2011 Estimates

Source: Alberta Budget, *2010, 89.*

Premier Stelmach, responding to the absence of a clear policy under the previous government, initiated an Investment and Savings review in August of 2007.[33] While the report was completed in December 2007, the findings were not released publicly until 11 months later. The press release accompanying the publication of the report tersely noted, "The Government received the report earlier this year and continues to consider its recommendations, along with information from a wide variety of sources, in the development of a new savings and investment strategy" (Government of Alberta, News Release 2008). The management of this report's release leaves one to conclude that formulating a new savings policy was not a priority for the Stelmach government, especially in the light of the huge budgetary challenge that emerged in the summer of 2008. In any event, given the 2008 global recession and the fall in natural gas prices, the matter of savings has been superseded by the goal of battling a large deficit.

PERSPECTIVES OF LEADERS

A list of the government, business, and association leaders who were interviewed for this project appears at the end of this chapter. The interviewees were not selected at random and therefore no statistical analysis has been undertaken. The purpose of the interviews was to provide qualitative background to the question of the difficulties inherent in the savings of resource revenue. The group of leaders is segmented into four categories (political, public service, business, association), representing individuals who were involved directly or indirectly in decision making, or had a financial interest in the policy decisions around taxation, regulation, investment, and spending.[34] Their collective responses are considered below in four broad categories.

Nature of Non-renewable Resource Revenue

Virtually all interviewees stressed the volatile nature of resource revenue and the virtue of saving some of this revenue. Some interviewees were asked to reflect on whether the Alberta public understood the difference between ordinary government revenue, such as taxes and user fees, and non-renewable resource revenue (or the sale of an asset and its conversion into cash or other financial assets). In the political group, the general view was that resource revenue was not widely understood by the public as being different from ordinary revenue (Jim Dinning, interview).[35] There was recognition that few Albertans understood the portion of spending that was financed by resource revenue, or the connection that resource revenue kept taxes artificially low. Several interviewees drew the distinction between the general public and a smaller group of "politically-literate" Albertans. While opinions differed, several current and former politicians spoke of the need for engaging and educating the general public, not only the smaller policy community, about the differences between the different types of revenue (Kevin Taft, Jim Dinning, and Mike Percy interviews).

From a public servant's perspective, there was broad recognition that resource revenue was different, but in concert with the political group, there was also acceptance that very few in the public understood the distinction between ordinary revenue and resource revenue. Interviews with public servants indicated that inside government, little effort was allocated to educating the public on this distinction. Several interviewees stressed the difficulties in communicating the unique nature of this revenue source.

Another theme mentioned was resource depletion, a key reason for the Heritage Fund's creation. One of the original reasons for saving was the concern in the 1970s that conventional oil production was falling. In the 1980s and 1990s natural gas production ramped up and superseded oil royalties as a driver of the provincial economy and the provincial treasury. Today, new technologies permit reserve life to be extended. Furthermore, with the improvement in oilsands extraction, reserve life is measured in decades, if not centuries.[36] As natural gas revenue displaced oil as a primary driver in revenue, and as the oilsands, with long-term reserves, began to supersede natural gas and oil as the dominant revenue source, the depletion and savings argument diminished. The complexity of Alberta's evolving petroleum resource base, when compared with other jurisdictions with more predictable depletion "curves," has undoubtedly contributed to a diminished concern about the need to save among Alberta residents.

From a business perspective, the challenges posed by a public sector with a *fixed cost* spending base that is financed, in part, by highly volatile revenue, were highlighted. Given this volatility, the view was that variable revenue should not be spent on everyday expenses but could be used for more longer-term infrastructure or endowment investments. Another element identified was the changing nature of resource exploitation: as low cost reserves were depleted, the economics of exploration and development shifted, meaning that, over time, resource rents extracted by the government would fall, as would corporate income tax. It was also noted that there was a trade-off between saving, or buildup of financial assets, and the capital infrastructure in the province—if more was saved, less infrastructure would have been available to support the Alberta economy.

Intergovernmental Relations

In reflecting on the federal–Alberta conflict, some politicians pointed to the palpable fear that Ottawa would swoop into Alberta and take money from the province. This was particularly pronounced in 1982 with the election of Gordon Kessler under the banner of the separatist Western Canada Concept party. According to one former Social Credit minister, there was fear that if Alberta didn't do something with the revenue, Ottawa would intervene and take the revenue (Robert Clark, interview, April 6, 2010). The new Heritage Fund, as a "storage place" for the large sums entering the provincial treasury, was a means of addressing criticism from the rest of the country that Alberta was getting rich on the backs of the Canadian consumer. The act of saving, as opposed to spending frivolously, demonstrated that Alberta was stewarding its resources wisely, and this was also good for Canada as a whole. The initial loans to the eastern provinces were regarded by one former treasurer as a means of protection, assisting Alberta in its intergovernmental relations, and were good business as well (Jim Dinning, interview). On the question of Ottawa actually swooping in to steal Alberta's savings, while several senior former public servants mentioned the fear of unilateral Ottawa action, there was no concrete evidence of this being planned by the federal government. Nevertheless, in political terms, a larger piggy bank, which might be targeted by outside forces, is a part of the political dynamic around savings.

In interviews with senior public servants, there was recognition that tensions within the federation played some role in the design of the savings program launched by the Lougheed government. The view was held that the Canada Investment Division was a means of building goodwill amongst other provinces (Dr. J. Peter Meekison, interview). It was noted by several public servants that alliances with Quebec, a very strong advocate of provincial rights, and Newfoundland with large, untapped, offshore energy resources, were assisted by these loans. Premier Lougheed's establishment of an intergovernmental affairs department in 1971 demonstrated a high priority in influencing the intergovernmental affairs agenda.[37]

The Heritage Fund's creation may also have been influenced by discussions around equalization. Alberta supported equalization but had concerns about the nature of the formula, in particular, the inclusion of non-renewable resource revenue. To the extent that all non-renewable resource revenue flowed into the General Revenue Fund, Ottawa and other provinces could justifiably argue that these revenues should be subject to equalization. In the end, the decision to include only 50% of non-renewable resource revenue, while Alberta was taking in 70%, could be seen as a victory of sorts.

After 1982–83, all lending through the Canada Investment Division ceased. The government decision reflected several considerations. First, with very high rates of interest being charged to Alberta farmers, businesses (through Alberta Opportunity Company and Alberta Treasury Branches, Alberta Agricultural Development Corporation) and municipalities (through Alberta

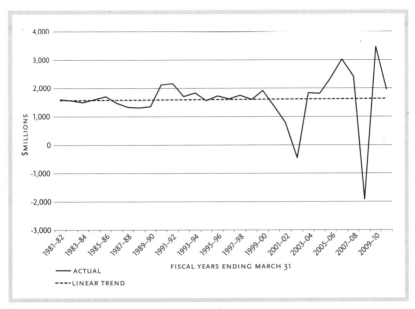

FIGURE 8.10 Investment Income, 1981–2011 Estimates

Source: Alberta Heritage Savings Trust Fund, Annual Report, 2010, 16.

Municipal Financing Corporation), loans to other provinces at below-market rates were difficult to justify (Allison O'Brien, interview). Second, the government was on the cusp of taking all income out of the fund and cutting the resource transfer into the fund by half. Third, the successful conclusion of constitutional talks that embedded provincial ownership of resources in provincial hands likely lessened the need for alliance building. Finally, the 15% statutory limit for provincial loans had almost been reached.

Economic and financial factors also were also identified as key reasons for slowing down the rate of savings. The recession in the early 1980s and the extraordinarily high interest rates were crucial background factors in the decision to suspend income transfers and reduce transfers. The financial crisis, beginning in the fall of 2007, was another example, with Heritage Fund losses having a significant impact on government finances. These losses created some negative perceptions of the Heritage Fund as a savings vehicle.[38] Figure 8.10 illustrates the higher variability of income since the endowment structure of the fund was modified to include larger investments in equities.

Constraints or Obstacles to Saving

Democratic Government—Public Opinion

One of the most commonly cited obstacles to saving was the functioning of the democratic process. Identification of this issue recurred throughout the interviews with politicians, who spoke of the demands from the public or special interests, whether they be unions, municipalities, schools, universities, or hospitals. Public servants who were interviewed acknowledged the pressure upon elected officials who were trying to do the right thing. Elections, the desirability of offering new programs to meet new needs, and building new infrastructure projects are all part of the engine of democratic decision making. As discussed below, without some externally imposed constraint, it is very difficult for elected officials to resist demands for more public spending, especially when revenue was abundant. A number of interviewees also mentioned the shorter-term time horizons of political actors that make it difficult to engage in longer-term planning. Another constraint, noted by former Premier Klein, derived from powerful public sector unions that resisted restructuring efforts.

Spending Pressures

A second, commonly cited obstacle to savings was the growth of government spending. There are a number of elements underlying this concern. First, the "infrastructure deficit" arising from the sharp capital spending reductions in the mid-1990s became the foundation for a huge catch-up in infrastructure spending. One former cabinet minister stressed both the pressures on capital spending, including the high rates of inflation, but also the ongoing commitment to budget operating funds well into the future. Emergencies such as drought and BSE were cited as examples of unexpected disasters that required increased spending to save an industry in crisis. Former politicians and senior public servants also spoke of the seemingly insatiable thirst from the public for public services (Jim Dinning, interview). These were not glib, throw-away comments; rather, they were acknowledgements of the pressures facing elected officials. Implicit and explicit in many comments is that spending is "good" and cuts to spending are "bad." One politician said that when oil prices fell in 1986, the Cabinet was reluctant to respond drastically by enacting massive cuts that would reverse decades of progress in public services and infrastructure (Hon. Ken Kowalski, interview). Another variant on this theme was the view that if governments have access to revenue, without some binding rule against spending, governments will find a path to spend. From the viewpoint of urban municipalities, it was acknowledged that competition was fierce with the oil patch when prices were high. The industry's drive to get oil out of the ground meant they would bid up labour and material costs (John McGowan, interview, April 20, 2010).

In the early 2000s, the balanced pacing of debt pay-down came to be associated with "re-investment." It was widely acknowledged by politicians and public servants that at the conclusion of the "Klein cuts," there was a growing expectation for "pay-back," or a return to more "normal" times. Several politicians also noted the demands for increased spending during a downturn as a means of smoothing the boom-and-bust cycle.

Westminster Model
In discussions with civil servants and politicians, the utility of a "trip wire" was recognized as vital in reducing demands for spending and thereby allowing larger sums of money to accumulate to reduce fiscal instability.[39] In a Westminster system of government the doctrine of parliamentary supremacy holds that succeeding legislatures can undo previously legislated decision rules. This was apparent in the 1983 budget that transferred all income from the Heritage Fund into general revenue. This was also true with annual increases in the Sustainability Fund resource revenue threshold from 2003 to 2007. A former politician (Mike Percy, interview) noted the importance of placing fences around a savings fund and protecting the savings

funds from the whims of politicians "and those who pressure politicians" (Jim Dinning, interview). Another former politician spoke of the need for a political shield to limit demands for more spending. A current politician spoke of the importance of building a consensus with the public on certain principles and processes.

Communications

Coupled with an inadequate understanding of the difference between resource revenue and ordinary revenue is the challenge of communicating an abstract concept such as provincial savings, and how such savings fit in with the big picture of the province's finances (Shirley McClellan, interview). What is the rationale to save, particularly in an economy that seems to be constantly growing, within an *apparently* stable environment with low taxes and good public services? A related challenge was communicating the nature of the "surpluses." Should these revenue windfalls be termed "surpluses" or simply the manifestation of higher petroleum prices?

In some respects, achieving savings through paying debt off in the 1990s was relatively easy to communicate. Debt was something all Albertans with mortgages or car loans could relate to. For older Albertans with firm memories of the Great Depression, the burdensome nature of debt was well understood. A former finance minister stressed the unproductive nature of debt service costs—payments that could have gone into existing or new government programs. As well, the government was able to communicate in a straightforward way about relieving the burden of debt from our children (Patricia Nelson, interview).[40]

One interviewee noted that without a clear savings strategy, decision rules are largely irrelevant. This also goes to the earlier comment that communicating a savings rationale can be difficult; especially if the strategy, the end goal, is not clear.

Uncertainty of Resource Revenue Flows

Among public servants, attention was drawn not only to the infrastructure deficit, but also to the *uncertainty* and *duration* in the unanticipated surpluses of the 2000s. In this period, it was the *price* fluctuations, and less so production fluctuations, that created uncertainty. Huge, unanticipated surpluses somewhat undermined the credibility of central agencies that had estimated revenues that, in hindsight, were too low.

Political Philosophy

Another important constraint identified by several public servants and in an article by former Deputy Treasurer A.F. Collins is the relationship between government and the private sector. Both the Manning and Lougheed governments and their successors, to varying degrees, supported a strong, free enterprise economy. While Lougheed (once termed "Peter the Red" for his overnight takeover of Pacific Western Airlines), took a pragmatic approach to investments like Syncrude and Ridley Grain, it was more in a secondary role. The Lougheed government saw public infrastructure as a foundation for building *private* wealth in the province, which could then assist in contributing to building community infrastructure in the province (Allison O'Brien, interview). The attitude did shift toward the end of the Lougheed era, where a number of economic development white papers, promoted more activist involvement in the economy in order to direct investment and enhance economic diversification.

A number of politicians identified the philosophy of low taxes and no sales tax as a specific constraint on a succession of governments. This mantra, combined with a desire not to gut spending, meant that a continuation of the savings policy initiated by Lougheed was not an option for the government. While low taxes were certainly a feature of the Social Credit government and the Lougheed government, the shifting nature of political discourse in Canada in the early 1990s with the emergence of Preston Manning's Reform Party also gave more impetus and credibility to maintaining low taxes, trimming deficits, and eschewing government spending.

"Concrete" Measures

Another obstacle to savings is the proclivity of politicians to invest in infrastructure. Manifest in the Capital Projects Division was the desire of Lougheed and his government to provide public infrastructure that would not otherwise be available without the resource-revenue bounty. With a rapidly growing population demanding housing, roads, schools, and hospitals, the Alberta Investment Division and the Capital Projects Division were able to finance further construction, thus meeting political demands from municipalities, school boards, and the general public.

These types of incentives were also present in the 2000s with the Capital Plan. Capital spending, unlike program spending, is concrete. Political leaders can point to a school, road, hospital expansion, or social housing and thereby make the role of government immediate and real. Moreover, such capital projects show that specific problems are being addressed.[41] However, more mundane capital investments, such as maintenance, arguably as important as new facilities, are less likely to receive the same political support (John McGowan, interview).

Incentives

Alberta Pride

In general, there were fewer incentives identified for savings than there were obstacles. In conversations with former public servants about the Lougheed period, it was very clear that the new premier was determined to raise the stature of Alberta in Canada. Having been through the experience of the depression, Lougheed was quite aware of the transitory nature of commodity cycles. Perceived as a province-builder, and understanding the value of the resources in Alberta, he took a number of steps to bolster the capacity of the provincial public service, specifically in treasury, as well as the new federal and intergovernmental affairs and the natural resources departments. The Heritage Fund was a concrete symbol that Alberta had arrived, and it appealed to Albertans' desires for financial security (Jim Dinning, interview). The Heritage Fund's endurance through the deficit in the 1980s and the losses in the 2000s demonstrated that the Heritage Fund had obtained almost "sacred" status in the minds of the public. Finally, Lougheed and his caucus could point with pride to the Heritage Fund for its good works—both inside and outside Alberta. The opening of new facilities, and associated employment in these facilities, was always a positive for re-election prospects.

Creating the Heritage Fund and channelling some of Alberta's oil wealth back into the rest of the country was an obvious coup for a province accused by Ontario Treasurer Frank Miller of "ripping the country apart" (quoted in Simeon 1980, 183). This re-channelling of funds demonstrated that Alberta was prepared to share its wealth, and that not all resource revenue would be squandered immediately in lowering taxes, enhancing public services, and drawing workers from other parts of the country. The Canada Investment Division was a clear example of Alberta showing leadership on the national stage.

CONCLUSIONS AND RECOMMENDATIONS

A number of conclusions can be drawn from the preceding analysis. First, the absence of a savings strategy makes it more difficult for governments to restrain spending and thereby to optimize savings for long-term fiscal stability goals. This was evident in the waning years of the Social Credit Administration and in the recent period from 2005 to 2010. Second, in the absence of a strict savings rule, the uncertainty surrounding the duration of elevated resource revenue makes it much more difficult for governments to restrain spending. Third, the longevity of a government led by one individual erodes policy innovation and fosters a climate where increased spending—or a "cheque-book" approach to governing becomes a substitute for sound fiscal policy (Shirley McClellan, interview). This is evident over the past decade under Klein, Stelmach, and now Premier Redford, where steady spending increases have depended on ever-higher levels of resource revenue and a resort to depleting existing savings. Fourth, in the Westminster system, a savings rule can easily be broken. This can be a good thing, permitting flexibility to respond to real emergencies. Yet, there is a downside too, since there is no constitutional check anchoring long-range financial planning.

Fifth, political will and commitment, in alignment with the public sector, is a powerful means for transforming the trajectory of public finances (e.g., Klein's first term). Sixth, the Alberta government's longstanding ideological commitment to a low tax system has constrained the government's capacity to save effectively in the long-term, and thus increases fiscal instability. Finally, the current fiscal and political environment is characterized by the drawdown of financial assets, situational borrowing for capital, the maintenance of a very low tax environment, and an acquiescent public. In such an environment, questions of whether and how much to save, as well as concerning the fiscal irrationality of Alberta consuming all its resource revenue, are likely to remain, unfortunately, of interest only to the policy community.

This historical review of a fundamental aspect of Alberta's democratic evolution (budgetary policy, debt and savings) suggests that, with the exception of Klein's first two ministries, the longevity of a government may lead to deterioration in fiscal strength. Such deterioration includes a reduction in net assets or rise in net debt, a fall in net assets in relation to total spending, and outsized expenditure increases relative to population growth and inflation. In contrast, new leaders and governments often capture the attention and support of the electorate with a new vision and fresh approach to government. This clearly was the case in 1971 and 1993 where the electoral turnout was higher than historical averages.[42] However, in the final campaigns under Lougheed in 1979 and 1982, the platform tended to be one of battling Ottawa rather than bold new policy initiatives. Similarly, in the later 2001 and 2004 Klein campaigns, elections tended to be votes for the status quo as opposed to a new vision for the province. After completing the mandate's vision in the first term and offering a new vision for a second term (Heritage Fund for Lougheed, and debt pay-down for Klein), it is perhaps human nature to begin to defend the status quo that was, in large part, created from policy actions of the previous six to eight years.

While the American system with its separation of powers differs markedly from our parliamentary system, perhaps it is time to experiment, either through legislation or through the constitution of political parties, with the notion that two terms under one premier is sufficient to enact a new vision for the province. Many objections of course may be offered: How to deal with minority governments? Should other offices be subject to similar limits? Should this be the determination of political parties as opposed to legislatures? In any event, the legislature can change the rules at a stroke of a pen. Furthermore, one might argue that Alberta has been well-served by long-serving premiers. Nevertheless, the potential benefits that might be expected to arise from term limits for premiers makes this an issue that is worthy of more detailed consideration.

A second policy recommendation also looks south and north (Alaska) to limit the capacity of elected officials to mortgage the Alberta economy with short-term, expedient fiscal policies. As noted above, under the Westminster model, legislative assemblies can amend or repeal fiscal rules when inconvenient circumstances arise. This raises the question of how legislators and governments can be made to be bound by certain fiscal rules that cannot be easily changed. In Alberta, there are two precedents in this regard. The Constitution of Alberta Amendment Act, 1990, which addresses Métis settlements, requires a legislative amendment and a plebiscite with settlement members to enact changes. The Constitutional Referendum Act, 1992 required a referendum before ratification of a possible change to the constitution of Canada, and the referendum was deemed to be binding on the government of Alberta (Morton 2004, 3n).

Under the Constitution Act, 1982, provinces "have complete authority to amend their constitutions as they see fit," except for the office of the lieutenant-governor (Morton 2004, 1). According to F.L. Morton, section 45 of the Constitution Act reaffirmed provinces "exclusive" jurisdiction over their respective constitutions. Thus, in terms of imposing fiscal rules that cannot be easily set aside, one possibility is to impose them in such a way that they can only be amended through resort to referenda mandated by a provincial constitution. A key element of entrenching or constitutionalizing fiscal savings rules is the conflict that arises as a result of limits on a legislature's authority that attempts to bind policy discretion of future governments. According to Morton, this "marks a departure from and modification of Dicey's classical model of parliamentary supremacy" (2004, 3). So long as the bar of the amending rule is not set significantly above the initial referendum hurdle, a provision that clearly speaks to the goals of the segregation and savings of non-renewable resource revenue could be initiated. The starting point would be with Alberta legislators engaging their citizens in a tough conversation about fiscal uncertainties and Alberta's unstable fiscal history.[43] Building a consensus would include highlighting certain uncomfortable truths, such as the fact that Alberta's health care spending is significantly higher than Alberta's take from both personal and corporate income tax. Ultimately, this exercise would result in a referendum to amend the Alberta Act to tie politicians' hands to a decision rule that could only be changed through another referendum requiring a majority or super majority (i.e., 60%) of votes, and whose outcome would be binding on the government. Thus, recourse to the simple expediency of repealing a troublesome section in a money bill would be replaced by requiring elected officials to debate and defend the rationale for a change. Protections could also be built into the Alberta Act that would require the auditor general to provide a special opinion on the fiscal position of the province leading into the referendum. Such a recommendation would require all legislators to engage the public in the debate. While Alberta has been blessed to have experienced more good than bad fiscal years, sound stewardship requires that history's lessons be understood, and its missteps not repeated.

Author's Note

The author wishes to thank David Armstrong, Linda Ascah, John Cotton, Virendra Gupta, Oryssia Lennie, J. Peter Meekison, Dale Moll, Al O'Brien, Rob Reynolds, and Will Van't Veld for their comments and suggestions on an earlier draft of this chapter. All errors of fact or interpretation are mine.

Notes

1. The data for the research consists of two discrete time series. The data set for 1945 to 1991 is derived from Boothe (1995, 8–23). Boothe uses

1986 dollars in his data. The second set of data for 1981 to 2010 is taken from Alberta Budget 2010, 89 and Alberta Budget 1998, 58.

2. Pension liabilities are deducted in the calculation of net assets.

3. Fiscal 1992–93 is an anomaly as the Klein government wrote down financial assets producing higher spending. This is a common occurrence when "new" governments take office.

4. Assets or savings is a "stock" recorded on the province's balance sheet while spending is an annual "flow" recorded on the province's statement of operations or income statement.

5. Technically, debt was still outstanding at this time but a debt retirement account was created to offset the outstanding debt.

6. Internal government discussions at the time examined the possibility of winding the fund down and using its assets to pay down some of the approximately $23 billion in outstanding debt.

7. Investment income derived from government surpluses or investment earnings of the Heritage Fund and other funds, such as the Sustainability Fund, are *not* considered as resource revenue.

8. All numbers are in 1986 dollars.

9. In 1971–72, the capital account in the balance sheet of the province was eliminated. The capital account balance sheet included advances from the federal government for roads, advances to Alberta Government Telephones. The income statement account included revenue such as land sales, highways grants from the federal government, advances and payments from the municipal loans revolving fund, and expenditures principally on highways.

10. A similar warning was issued by Treasurer Anders Aalborg in 1967: "After 20 years of uninterrupted budget surpluses Albertans have, we fear, become complacent regarding provincial finances. The greatly expanded outlays for education, health and welfare services, together with the heavy capital expenditures required for capital projects and increased assistance to municipalities, cannot be met indefinitely out of the current revenues of the Province" (Government of Alberta 1967, 6).

11. Municipal politicians are often an important source of recruitment into provincial politics and therefore a special constituency. In C.E. Gerhart's 1955 budget, a 50% share in the province's fuel tax was ceded to municipalities.

12. See An Act to Enable Citizens of Alberta to Participate Directly in the Benefits Accruing from the Development of Oil and Gas Resources in the Province, S.A., 1957, Ch. 95. MLAS were permitted to receive the dividend under the act.

13. The government of Alberta claimed that $15 billion in foregone revenue was given up by the province (Western Economic Opportunities Conference, 1973, cited in Simeon 1980, 188).

14. Alberta Heritage Savings Trust Fund Act, Chapter 2, Statutes of Alberta, 1976, section 6. The Canada Investment Division was limited to a maximum of 15% of the fund; the Alberta Investment Division had no limits, and the Capital Projects Division was capped at 20% of the fund.

15. In a paper presented in the fall of 1979, Deputy Treasurer A.F. Collins noted, "It is currently expected that the General Revenue Fund will not be in a deficit position for at least ten years. At some point, however, the AHSTF may be used to supplement other revenues to finance the operation of government" (see Collins 1980, 165).

16. With the exception of the Capital Projects Division that went through a legislative estimates process.

17. Notably, Ontario never borrowed from the fund as its borrowing costs were slightly lower than Alberta's.

18. Major interest shielding programs were a feature throughout the 1980s under Premiers Lougheed and Getty (Allison O'Brien, interview, March 9, 2010).

19. Alberta Mortgage and Housing Corporation (AMHC) and the Alberta Housing Corporation in 1981 were involved in roughly one-half of housing starts (Government of Alberta, Alberta Budget Address, April 14, 1981, 17).

20. For simplicity, the model assumes the reinvestment rate is the actual rate earned by the fund during the whole period, as opposed to returns on a theoretical asset mix.

21. The Lottery Fund, created in 1988, was also spending viewed as being additional to basic needs and was widely criticized as being a fund that was closely monitored and directed by government members.

22. In 1992, at the end of Don Getty's tenure, a Spending Control Act was belatedly legislated. The act required that spending could not increase more that 2.5% above the budgeted figure, subject to various adjustments in the forecast base (S.A. 1992, Ch. S-21.7).

23. In addition, the following provincially regulated institutions failed: Principal Group, including First Investors and Associated Investors, Heritage Savings and Trust, and North West Trust. Investors in First Investors and Associated Investors received a distribution of about $85 million, including contributions from other provinces.

24. Key recommendations in the *Report to Albertans* included: 1) develop and adopt a workable and enforceable fiscal plan first to balance revenue and spending in a way that eliminate overspending on a sustainable basis, and second, in the longer term, to generate a surplus to eliminate the net debt; 2) downsize the entire government infrastructure; and 3) develop budget estimates for revenues and expenditures on the basis of realistic and conservative assumptions (Alberta Financial Review Commission 1993, 6). It is often the case that a new government of a different political stripe calls for an external review of the government's finances after entering office. In this case, a government of the *same* political stripe brought in external advisors. The report clearly conditioned the public that drastic fiscal medicine was necessary to arrest the deteriorating financial position of the province.

25. In the spring of 1996, the government received 61,000 responses in a survey entitled "Straight Talk, Clear Choices," that found the top priority for the government was to pay down debt as fast as possible. In 1997, the government organized a growth summit that recommended

that the savings in lower debt servicing costs be applied to general government spending. In the fall of 1998, "Talk it Up–Talk it Out" garnered over 80,000 respondents re-affirming that debt pay-down was still the top priority with 51% supporting tax cuts versus 4% wanting further spending. In 2000, the government conducted a survey called "It's Your Money," asking for public feedback. This garnered 125,000 respondents who listed permanent tax cuts as their top priority. In the fall of 2004, "It's Your Future" survey received 300,000 responses with health and education being identified as clear priorities (Government of Alberta, Budget 2005, 133–38).

26. Alberta Heritage Savings Trust Fund Act, S.A. Ch. A-27.01, Preamble.

27. After 9/11, the government made intra-year fiscal adjustments to reduce spending in light of the increased uncertainty about the global economic situation. This adjustment caused concerns particularly in the construction sector.

28. Financial Statutes Amendment Act, S.A., 2003, Ch. 2. In addition to the Sustainability Fund, a Capital Account was created into which flowed excess revenue above the maximum limit of $2.5 billion for the Sustainability Fund. In 2002, Liberal MLA Ken Nicol introduced a private member's bill, Bill 208, the Fiscal Stability Fund Calculation Act, 2002 that was based on similar concerns emanating from the Financial Review Commission. The "Fiscal Stability Fund" was directed at "stabilizing the fiscal position of the Government in responding to the cyclical nature of the Alberta economy, protecting the sustainability of social programs, and improving the long-term fiscal planning framework of the Government" (Bill 208).

29. The title of this Alberta budget was *Making Alberta Even Better* (April 8, 2003).

30. BSE stands for bovine spongiform encephalopathy, commonly known as mad cow disease.

31. This Alberta budget was titled *Investing in the Next Alberta*.

32. Public–Private Partnerships or P3 were an alternative financing mechanism for capital projects whereby private firms would build roads or schools and receive a long stream of repayments, and upon maturity the government would own the asset.

33. Extensive work by the Canada West Foundation in 2005 and 2006 on an Alberta savings policy also contributed to a recognition that a savings policy was required.

34. While most participants in the research permitted attribution of comments, there were a number that did not agree to attribution. Attribution was conditional on interviewees reviewing the text of the chapter.

35. MLA Kevin Taft noted that most Albertans do not know the difference between taxes and royalties (Interview, April 14, 2010). Former MLA Mike Percy noted that Albertans don't understand the difference between a "stock" of wealth and "flow" of revenue (Interview, April 9, 2010).

36. See Scarfe and Powrie (1980, 168), who develop a simple model for
    determining the amount of annual savings of resource revenue given
    reserve depletion and the real rate of investment returns.
37. For example, in 1979, during the Western Premiers' Conference in
    Prince George, a side trip was organized to tour Prince Rupert where
    the Heritage Fund was financing a new grain terminal.
38. This point can also be made with respect to the losses in the fund in
    2002–03.
39. Bill 201, Funding Alberta's Future Act, introduced by Liberal
    Opposition leader Kevin Taft in 2007, required 30% of non-renewable
    resource revenue be placed in an Alberta Futures account. Several
    sub-funds were to be established including a Post-Secondary Education
    Fund to replace the Access to the Future Fund, a Humanities, Social
    Sciences, and Arts Endowment Fund, and an Opportunity Fund.
40. Figure 8.7 illustrates the increase and decrease in debt servicing costs
    that limited or encouraged spending on other citizen-facing activities.
41. The Klein government was heavily criticized for its slow response to
    the transportation, housing, and social problems arising from the vast
    investments taking place in the Fort McMurray region.
42. *1971: 71.9%; 1975: 59.6%; 1979: 58.1%; 1982: 66%; 1986: 47.2%; 1989:
    53.6%; 1993: 60.2%; 1997: 53.7%; 2001: 52.8%; 2004: 44.7%; 2008:
    41.3%* ("Voter Turnout in Recent Alberta Provincial Elections," 2010,
    Elections Alberta, http://www.elections.ab.ca/public%20website/927.
    htm; *Wikipedia*, s.v. "List of Alberta General Elections," last modified
    18 May 2012, http://en.wikipedia.org/wiki/List_of_Alberta_general_
    elections).
43. Alberta is the only Canadian province to default on its debt, which
    occurred in 1936.

References

Alberta Financial Management Commission. 2002. *Moving from Good to
    Great*.
Alberta Financial Review Commission. 1993. *Report to Albertans*, March.
Boothe, Paul. 1995. *The Growth of Government Spending in Alberta*. Toronto:
    Canadian Tax Foundation.
Collins, A.F. 1980. "The Alberta Heritage Savings Trust Fund: An Overview
    of Issues." Special issue, *Canadian Public Policy* 6: 158–65.
Government of Alberta, Alberta Heritage Savings Trust Fund. 1977–2010.
    Annual Reports.
Government of Alberta. 1946–2011. Annual Budget Addresses.
———. 2008. "Report Released on Alberta's Savings and Investment
    Strategy." News Release. November 19. http://alberta.ca/
    ACN/200811/24786B1AE3659-F3BF-39F1-519A63F0E373A3EE.html.

Morton, F.L. 2004. "Provincial Constitutions in Canada." Paper presented at "Federalism and Sub-national Constitutions: Design and Reform" conference, Center for the Study of State Constitutions, Rockefeller Center, Bellagio, Italy, March.

Scarfe, B.L., and T.L. Powrie. 1980. "The Optimal Savings Question: An Alberta Perspective." Special issue, *Canadian Public Policy* 6: 166–76.

Simeon, Richard. 1980. "Natural Resource Revenues and Canadian Federalism." Special issue, *Canadian Public Policy* 6: 182–91.

Interviewees

Elected and Senior Party Officials

Robert Clark—Social Credit Cabinet Minister, 1966–1971 and MLA, 1960–1981

Jim Dinning—Progressive Conservative Cabinet Minister, 1986–1997

Brian Heidecker—Progressive Conservative Party official, member of Financial Management Commission

Ralph Klein—Premier, 1992–2006

Hon. Ken Kowalski—Speaker and former Cabinet Minister, 1979–2012

Brian Mason—MLA and New Democratic Party Leader, 2000–present

Shirley McClellan—Progressive Conservative Cabinet Minister, 1987–2007

Patricia Nelson—Progressive Conservative Cabinet Minister, 1992–2004

Kevin Taft—MLA for Edmonton Riverview, 2001–2012, and former Liberal Opposition Leader

Senior Officials

Jack Davis—Deputy Minister, Executive Council, 1997–1999

G. Lynne Duncan—Deputy Minister Advanced Education and Career Development, Health, 1987–1998

Ron Hicks—Deputy Minister, Executive Council, 2004–2008

Oryssia J. Lennie—Deputy Minister, Federal and Intergovernmental Affairs, 1990–1997

Allister J. McPherson—Deputy Provincial Treasurer, 1984–1996

J. Peter Meekison—Deputy Minister, Federal and Intergovernmental Affairs, 1974–1984

Allison D. O'Brien—Deputy Provincial Treasurer, 1984–1999

Business Leaders

Robert J. Brawn—Oil executive

Doug Goss—Lawyer and businessman, Progressive Conservative Party, Finance

Marshall Williams—TransAlta Corporation, Chair, Financial Review Committee

Trade and Labour Associations

John McGowan—Alberta Urban Municipalities Association

Searching for Ropes and a Mast

How to Develop a Long-Term Plan for Alberta's Fiscal Future

Colin Busby

The Sirens were sea-nymphs who had the power of charming by
their song all who heard them, so that the unhappy mariners were
irresistibly impelled to cast themselves into the sea to their destruction. Circe directed Odysseus [Ulysses] to fill the ears of his seamen
with wax, so that they should not hear the strain; and to cause himself to be bound to the mast, and his people to be strictly enjoined,
whatever he might say or do, by no means to release him till they
should have passed the Sirens' island.

Odysseus obeyed these directions. He filled the ears of his
people with wax, and suffered them to bind him with cords firmly to
the mast. As they approached the Sirens' island, the sea was calm,
and over the waters came the notes of music so ravishing and attractive that Odysseus struggled to get loose, and by cries and signs to
his people begged to be released; but they, obedient to his previous
orders, sprang forward and bound him still faster. They held on
their course, and the music grew fainter till it ceased to be heard,

when with joy Odysseus gave his companions the signal to unseal their ears, and they relieved him from his bonds.

—Thomas Bulfinch,
The Age of Fable or Stories of Gods and Heroes

INTRODUCTION

Resource receipts can either be spent today or saved for the future. Fiscal decisions should therefore attempt to achieve a balance among current priorities, such as the delivery of public services, and long-term goals, such as ensuring the well-being of future generations. In practice, however, this balance is hard to achieve. The strategy of Odysseus, to plan ahead and have himself tied to the mast to stave off the threat of the Sirens, deserves the careful scrutiny of Alberta's fiscal policy makers, who face a difficult trade-off of using resource wealth for today's desires or for future benefits.

Saving, instead of spending resource revenues, is encouraged for a variety of reasons: to achieve better macroeconomic stability, to reduce revenue volatility for fiscal planning, to save for "rainy days," and to maintain the benefits of a finite resource bounty for future generations. This study focuses on the latter issue: fiscal planning to ensure intergeneration equity.

A long-term fiscal plan has yet to develop in Alberta for many possible reasons. One is a difference of public opinion on the need for saving resource revenues: many Albertans may prefer to save for the future privately, or may be planning to move to another jurisdiction in the future, thus dampening the motivation to save with the public purse. Complicating matters further is the fact that even if the need for public savings gathers support, a resource savings level, or a degree of fiscal restraint to make room for savings, will be difficult to agree upon.

Another potential reason for the lack of a savings plan is because key budget targets do not clearly communicate the impact of resources on the province's finances. As dependence upon larger resource receipts grows, the budget balance communicates less meaningful information to fiscal planners, underscoring the need for a revised bottom-line figure to focus attention on long-run budget issues.

Many commentators stress that the benefits of selling Alberta's limited resources today should be extended for future generations (FIPAC 2008; Wilson 2002; Roach 2007). In accordance with this principle, the government of Alberta mentioned in the 2010 Alberta Budget that "[the Alberta Government] has not, and will not, borrow from future generations to fund operations." In this chapter, I present a policy framework for fiscal saving decisions guided by an overarching principle that attempts to spread resource-wealth spending across each generation of Albertans. To do so, the province would need to calculate its expected resource wealth so that, were all resources sold and invested, only the annuity would be spent each year. It would put specific limits to annual resource spending targets, but revisions would be made to the calculation of resource spending every three years, thus adding flexibility as resource prices, estimates of reserves, etc., change and are better understood over time.

Were the government to pursue such a plan, it would need to devise strategies that make this proposal binding. A significant advantage of this plan is that it would prescribe stable and predictable annual revenues for general spending—a strength that should be exploited. The most promising options include linking the sacrifices from saving today to tangible future benefits, such as earmarking future spending to end-of-life health care services.

This chapter proceeds as follows. The first section examines the need for a long-term fiscal plan in Alberta and then discusses the necessary changes to fiscal reports to bring this about. The second section examines the foundation for achieving an intergenerationally equitable plan and then presents the basic assumptions to carry out such a plan. The third section presents the results and ways for the government to approach fiscal reforms. The final section presents options on how such a proposal can overcome the implementation challenges of this plan.

WHY A LONG-TERM FISCAL FOCUS?

The characteristics of resource revenues are different from revenues that are raised via other taxation sources. The main distinguishing feature is resources' finite quality: because non-renewable resources exist in fixed quantities, taking them out of the ground and selling them for cash represents a conversion of Alberta's physical wealth into financial wealth. Because non-renewable resources are assets that are the property of the province, arguably some of the benefits that stem from oil and gas exploitation should be preserved beyond its limited life. Households and individuals make plans to manage their assets in different ways than they manage their income—for example, to pay for education, large purchases, and perhaps retirement. In the same way, the province should treat natural resource revenues as assets to be managed and should not treat them as annual income. The strong link between resource revenues and government spending in Alberta suggests the province treats resource revenues the same as tax receipts from other, non-resource activities (Figure 9.1).

Another growing reason to make saving a priority is because as program expenses grow along with resource revenues, and the dependence on resource revenues entrenches, spending levels can become unsustainable. The trouble is that program spending is hard to scale back when revenues inevitably swing downward: when energy prices decline and revenues dry up, the costs of delivering public services often exceed budgetary resources, necessitating fiscal adjustments and committing Alberta to boom-and-bust cycles (Emery and Kneebone 2009). So a commitment to a savings plan would buffer the government's dependence and willingness to rely on resource revenues when energy prices rise, thus improving the stabilization role of fiscal policy. A final reason is the sheer accumulation of evidence on the need for a long-term plan with a saving focus (AFMC 2002; Wilson 2002; Roach 2007; FIPAC 2008).

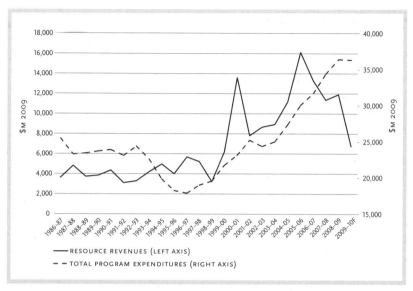

FIGURE 9.1 Resource Revenues Drive Program Spending, Millions (2009 dollars), 1986/87–2009/10

Source: Alberta Budget documents; Statistics Canada; author's calculations.

DEVELOPING A LONG-RUN FISCAL STANCE: THE IMPORTANCE OF THE PRIMARY NON-RESOURCE BALANCE

In Alberta, there is an important drawback from policy makers' emphasis on the annual budget balance: rapidly flowing resource revenues can mask the province's underlying fiscal position.[1] As expenditures grow with resource revenues, the province may be unprepared for when revenues dry up, or when resource production slows and one day expires.

Broadly speaking, Alberta's budgetary revenues, as currently reported in a given year, can be divided into three major revenue sources: resource revenues, RR_t, non-resource tax revenues, NRT_t, and interest income, INT_t. Expenditures can also be divided into program spending (spending on health, education, etc.), $PROGSP_t$, and debt service costs, DS_t.

The budget balance—the sum of all revenues minus all expenditures—is the traditional bottom-line figure in each budget (see equation (1) below). To get a clearer picture as to the revenue and spending decisions of governments over the course of a year, however, policy makers regularly remove net debt servicing and interest income from bottom-line results (see equation (2)). Another result emerges when focusing on non-resource revenues—revenues that come from income sources, not resource asset sales—within the budget. Each year, any shortfall between tax revenues from non-resource sources and what the government spends is naturally covered by resource revenues.[2] Alberta's "primary non-resource balance," represents non-resource revenues minus primary expenditures (see equation (3)).

Fiscal Equations:

1. *Budget Balance* = $(NRT_t + RR_t + INT_t) - (PROGSP_t + DS_t)$;
2. *Primary Balance* = $(NRT_t + RR_t) - (PROGSP_t)$, thus representing government net borrowing or lending without interest payments on government assets and liabilities;
3. *Primary Non-Resource Balance* = $NRT_t - PROGSP_t$, which in most cases will be in a deficit position.

A significant improvement to the financial reports of the province would highlight the primary non-resource balance, and as seen in Table 9.1, the balance can be easily extracted by transforming the information in current reports. The current methods for reporting Alberta's finances, shown in the left column of Table 9.1, lists all forms of revenues along with expenses, and then highlights the budget balance for a given year. The right column of Table 9.1 demonstrates how royalties and lease receipts—asset sale earnings—can be separated from all other forms of tax revenues. Then, primary expenses can be subtracted from this total, rendering the primary non-resource deficit (PNRD). From here, in any given year the government must use interest income, resource revenues, and/or debt to finance this deficit. If interest income and resource revenues in any year are greater than the PNRD, the traditional budget statements (column 1 of Table 9.1, and equation (1)) would be in a surplus position.

Alberta's Current Fiscal Summary		Proposed Fiscal Summary	
Revenues	**($millions)**	**Revenues**	**($millions)**
Personal income tax	8,648	*Resource Revenues*	7,315
Corporate income tax	3,113	*Non-Resource Revenues* **(A)**	
Education property tax	1,592	Total corporate, personal, other, etc.	24,702
Natural resource revenue*	7,315	*Interest Income* **(B)**	1,947
Investment income	1,947		
Other	4,059		
Federal transfers	5,090		
Total revenue (A)	**33,964**		

Expenditures (by function)		Expenditures (by function)	
Health	15,813	*Health, Education, Social Services, Other* **(C)**	38,376
Basic and advanced education	9,325	*Debt servicing costs* **(D)**	336
Social services	3,902	**Primary Non-Resource Deficit (A–C)**	**(13,674)**
Other	9,336		
Debt servicing costs	336		
Total expense (B)	**38,712**	Net Interest income **(B–D)**	1,611
		Resource Revenues	7,315
Surplus (Deficit) (A–B)	**(4,748)**	**Budget Balance for fiscal purposes (4,748)**	

*These revenues represent the annual receipts
from royalties and leases

Memo:
Market value of savings
*(Net financial assets including
pension obligations)* **13,347**

TABLE 9.1 Alberta's Budget Document Presentation, Current and
Proposed, 2010–11

Source: Alberta Budget 2010; author's calculations.

The first two fiscal indicators, the budget balance and the primary balance, are significantly affected by swings in oil and gas prices, and neither represents well the direction or stance of fiscal policy. To get a sense as to whether fiscal policy is expansive or contractionary, policy makers should look at Alberta's PNRD, shown as the dark, solid line in Figure 9.2 (Barnett and Ossowski 2003). A falling primary non-resource balance demonstrates either relative increases in resource-based spending or relatively low non-resource revenue collections. Large fluctuations over time represent an undisciplined approach to fiscal policy. Alberta's per capita PNRD fell in the 1980s with declining resource prices, and fell further after fiscal reforms in the 1990s only to have increased since.[3]

The PNRD is a key, internationally-recognized indicator of long-run fiscal sustainability for resource regions (Barnett and

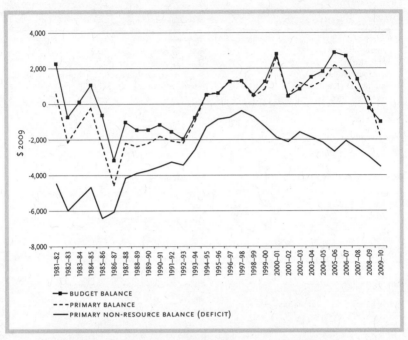

FIGURE 9.2 Alberta's Volatile Budget Balance and the Primary Non-Resource Balance, $2009 per capita, 1981/82–2009/10

Source: Alberta Budget documents; Statistics Canada; author's calculations.

Ossowski 2003).[4] Intuitively, the PNRD represents the level of resource-based spending that takes place in any given year, or the annual drawdown on resource wealth to bring the budget back to balance. The size of the PNRD, also understood as the level of resource-based spending, is an indicator of the province's current vulnerability to swings in the size and timing of resource royalties and associated revenues. On this score, Alberta is arguably as dependent on resource royalties and tax revenues in the early 2010s as it was in the late 1980s, meaning that shocks to the size of income from resource-related activities would have dramatic impacts on the province's bottom line.

A large PNRD should not necessarily be feared: its sustainability depends on how much resource wealth the Alberta government has saved and how much resource revenue it expects in the future. But as the value of annual receipts from resource activities grows, and as resource stocks approach physical or economic exhaustion, the budget balance can be a deceiving representation of the fiscal position. Because today's PNRD represents the hypothetical budget deficit were Alberta's resources to become unviable next year, the PNRD represents the long-term budgetary position of the province without a concerted effort to expand savings or increase taxes (Barnett and Ossowski 2003).

Focusing fiscal decisions on the PNRD does not mean that any particular year's resource revenues should not be spent, but rather that saving and spending decisions would be better made if they could be viewed separately from the annual inflow and timing of resource receipts. In contrast, the traditional budgetary balance measure provides little important information to a budget planner whose tax base has a high concentration of revenues—and particularly volatile ones—from a few core economic activities.

A FORWARD-LOOKING APPROACH TO RESOURCE WEALTH SPENDING DECISIONS

The PNRD would keep the focus of policy makers off annual fluctuations in resource revenues and would further allow for innovative approaches to guide resource-based spending and saving decisions. One simple approach to spending the earnings from resource-asset sales would aim to spread out the use of Alberta's resource bounty across current and future generations (see Shiell and Busby 2008).[5] Such a plan would attempt to reconcile the benefits of resource wealth for today's generation with future ones. To put it differently, much like individuals and households that take out mortgages and loans against estimates of future earnings power, today's resource spending decisions can be informed by a future outlook of resource production.

In other words, this plan is an empirical attempt to spend the annuity of Alberta's per capita resource wealth each year. Given estimates of population growth and resource wealth, budget planners would need to bring the per capita PNRD into line—by either adjusting spending or non-resource revenues—to ensure that the government does not spend too much, or too little, of today's generations' resource wealth entitlements.

Using the information available today, Albertans could annually target, and periodically revise, a desired PNRD that attempts to achieve an intergenerationally equitable outcome and provide each generation of Albertans the same amount of annual spending from resource wealth. This means negotiating the size of the PNRD—in other words, the appropriate drawdown from resource wealth—so that this fixed amount of spending from resource wealth can be maintained well into the future. Because the PNRD represents the province's long-term budgetary position, fiscal planners could set a constant per capita level for the primary non-resource gap so that enough savings, and the interest income from them, can be accumulated to bridge this gap when resources expire.

The main challenge with a fiscal plan that attempts to achieve an intergenerationally equitable level of resource-based spending is that the results, and the underlying principle, will lead to some controversy and debate. The downside of this proposal for an equal per capita level of resource-based spending is that it overlooks the fact that future generations of Albertans will be richer thanks to increasing productivity. Hence, it may be intergenerationally fair to spend more today than in the future—run a higher PNRD today, which declines over time—knowing that future generations would be naturally better off. In other words, the current proposal—that of a constant per capita PNRD—may be too generous to future generations and a declining level of resource-based spending, or a declining PNRD, over time would be better.

On the other hand, there is tremendous uncertainty surrounding the long-term economic viability of Alberta's non-renewable resources. Specifically, energy prices, reserves, and production are bound to evolve differently than expected, even by the most knowledgeable of forecasters. In order to hedge against that uncertainty, an intergenerationally equitable spending plan would therefore encourage less resource spending, and more savings, now, meaning the province incurs a much lower PNRD today.

I feel that the major forces described above, which push and pull the desirable per capita PNRD in different directions, generally offset. Therefore, I believe the notion of a constant per capita PNRD is both simple and balances key challenges from intergenerational equity principles. That said, I take up these challenges in a later section.

ASSUMPTIONS AND DATA

The desirable path of the PNRD depends mainly on two things: 1) the stock of financial savings today; and, 2) the estimated present value of future resource revenues.

Stock of Financial Wealth

Alberta produces different measures of total wealth. The standard budgetary measure for wealth is Alberta's net financial assets—which consists of all forms of traditional financial assets savings minus gross debt, liabilities for government-owned capital and enterprises and accounts payable (see FIPAC 2008). Yet this picture of total savings is far from comprehensive. Unfunded pension obligations—the estimated value of government workers' future pension benefits for which no provisions have been made—are a form of negative wealth (they are really loans to the governments from their employees that will have to be paid back upon employees' retirement); yet they do not always appear in Alberta's traditional "net financial asset" position.[6] These unfunded pension obligations are large, amounting to $9.5 billion in 2010, so that incorporating the costs of these agreements into savings measures for today would be more reflective of the province's financial position.[7] The majority of unfunded obligations, $7.4 billion in 2010, are for pre-1992 obligations to the Alberta Teachers' Pension Plan.[8]

For the purposes of this calculation, I use the measure of financial assets including future pension obligations, which amounts to roughly $13.4 billion in 2010.

Expectations of Alberta's Resource Future: Calculating Provincial Resource Wealth

The second part in estimating an intergenerationally equal PNRD depends upon future estimates of annual natural resource receipts and population growth. This requires assumptions for the following.

- *Prices*—For this I use the average of the reference- and low-case projections to 2035 in Energy Information Administration (EIA) (2010) and International Energy Agency (IEA) (2009), which results in the oil price gradually reaching $124 (in 2009 dollars) per barrel in 2035, and the price for natural gas rising to $6.7 per thousand cubic feet. The bitumen and synthetic oil price is converted from benchmark, sweet crude oil prices at a ratio of 0.45 according to the most recent four-year average ratio used in Alberta budget documents;
- *Reserves*—I use "remaining established reserves" for conventional oil, bitumen, and natural gas from Alberta Energy (2009) and the Canadian Association of Petroleum Producers (CAPP) (2010), which means 1.6 billion barrels of conventional oil, 160 billion barrels of non-conventional oil, and 40 trillion cubic feet of natural gas in 2009;
- *Production*—From 2010 to 2025, I use the projections in CAPP (2010) for conventional and non-conventional oil and for natural gas I use the projections in Alberta Energy (2009). For conventional oil and natural gas, annual production tapers off from 122 million barrels and 5.1 trillion cubic feet, respectively. After 2025, I assume a constant rate of production decline until exhaustion. For non-conventional oil production, I conjecture a continued rising level of production from 670 million barrels per year in 2010 to 2,250 million barrels in 2058, where the level of production shortly thereafter declines at a constant trend.
- *Real rate of return on savings*—I use 3.5% annually, which corresponds to a slightly conservative estimate of the real returns produced by a prudent portfolio over the last 40 years.

An asset mix of 60% equity and 40% bonds has produced an average real return of 4.3% from 1968 to 2008 (CIA 2009). I therefore choose a slightly lower estimate than the 40-year average given that returns have trended lower in the most recent decade.

- *Population growth*—The demographic forecast assumes that the population grows at 2007 fertility rates (1.90 births per woman), and the latest 10-year interprovincial and international migration averages. Annual population growth is projected to be, on average, 0.8% from 2010 to 2040, and 0.1% from 2040 to 2070, where it approaches zero thereafter.
- *Exchange rate*—I assume that the Canadian dollar remains near parity with the US dollar.

Under the assumptions above, I project that Alberta's known, extractable resources would reach exhaustion in the year 2107. To estimate future government resource revenues from the value of projected resource production, I simply take historical averages of royalty and lease revenues as a proportion of total sector revenues. From 1980 to 2005, royalty revenues have closely tracked 15% of total production revenues (Mansell and Schlenker 2006). I assume these rates continue; then, as conventional oil and gas reserves approach exhaustion, I assume that this average falls somewhat—to roughly 12%—as "low-quality production offsets" commence with the decline in quality of remaining reserves.

RESULTS

The calculation proceeds in two steps. First, all future resource revenues must be discounted back to today in present value, per capita terms. This must then be added to today's financial savings to get a measure of total wealth. From here, the annual per capita resource-based spending that could continue in perpetuity emerges as the level of interest income from savings, upon resource exhaustion, that is necessary to sustain a maximum PNRD in perpetuity.

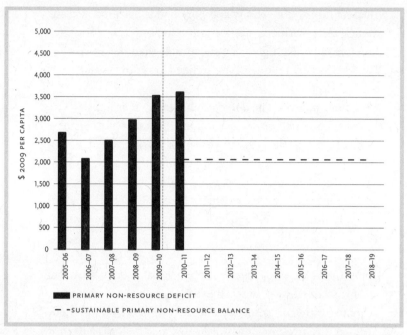

FIGURE 9.3 Alberta's Intergenerationally Sustainable Primary Non-Resource Deficit (Per Capita), 2005/06–2018/19

Source: Alberta Budget documents; author's calculations as described in text.

The results of this calculation show that Alberta could maintain a PNRD—a level of resource-based spending—of about $2,060 per capita each year into perpetuity (Figure 9.3). As long as this planned annual target for the PNRD is adhered to, excess revenues would be deposited into a savings fund so that the interest income from these financial assets will continue to provide revenues to future generations of Albertans. Today's per capita PNRD is, however, $1,540 higher than prescribed—about $5.7 billion in total—which means that spending would have to fall, or non-resource revenues would need to rise, by this amount to return the budget to a sustainable position.

The results further show that Alberta would need to build up total financial savings which, in nominal terms, must grow from $13 billion in 2010 to $45 billion in 2030, and further to $181 billion by 2050 as the production of non-conventional oil is projected to rise (Figure 9.4).

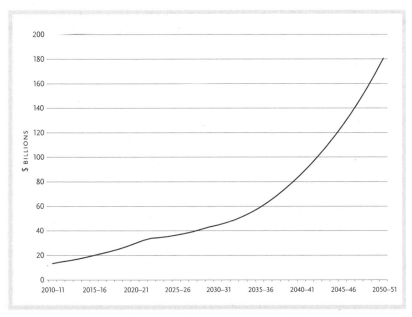

FIGURE 9.4 Total Financial Savings with an Intergenerationally Equitable
Fiscal Plan, $ Nominal, 2010/11–2050/51

Source: Author's calculations as described in text.

SENSITIVITY OF THE ASSUMPTIONS: EFFECTS OF DIFFERENT POPULATION, REAL RATES OF RETURN, AND PRICE PATHS ON THE CONSTANT PER CAPITA PNRD

Although I feel that the constant PNRD described above uses
assumptions that are both unbiased and reasonably conservative, for illustrative purposes I explore some important areas of
potential bias and possible disagreement in the assumptions.
Key sources of disagreement include assumptions concerning
the likely growth of the future population of Alberta, alternative
real rates of return, and different price futures for oil and gas.
To get a better sense as to how this intergenerationally equitable
fiscal plan would be affected, these differences in opinion can be
factored into the calculation of a constant, sustainable PNRD for

Outmigration Scenario	Per capita PNRD ($2009)	Difference from Baseline
Population rises, then falls to 2010 level	2,748	685

TABLE 9.2 Alternative Scenario for Population Growth

Source: Author's calculations as described in text.

Real Rate of Return	Per capita PNRD ($2009)	Difference from Baseline (3.5%) ($)
High (4.5%)	2,207	145
Low (2.5%)	1,830	(233)

TABLE 9.3 Alternative Real Rate of Return Scenarios

Source: Author's calculations as described in text.

the province, and what follows is a partial sensitivity analysis of these factors.

Population Growth Rates

A notable point of bias is, among others, the assumption that the provincial population is projected to grow consistently over the next 70 years. Many commentators have expressed concerns that much of the interprovincial migration to Alberta is perhaps transient (Berdahl 2008, Hirsch 2008). It has been further suggested that Alberta's low levels of resource savings stems from a limited attachment to permanent residence in the province. Were Alberta's total population to grow according to current 10-year trends until 2030, and then see outmigration, bringing the province's total population to 2010 levels by the year 2050, the level of allowable annual per capita spending today would rise, and the size of the fiscal gap would be reduced. In fact, the allowable per capita PNRD would grow to $2,750, roughly $685, or 30%, greater than the baseline scenario prescribes (Table 9.2). However, today's PNRD would still be about $850 per capita above the intergenerationally sustainable level.

Resource Prices	Per capita PNRD ($2009)	Difference from Baseline (EIA Baseline and Low Price Averages) ($)
High (EIA High Scenario)	3,845	1,781
Low (random walk; Oil = $78/barrel; Nat.Gas = $4/th.cub.feet, in $2009)	2,029	(34)

TABLE 9.4 Alternative Energy Price Scenarios

Source: Author's calculations as described in text.

Real Rates of Return

A major challenge to a future savings plan is the rate of return that future savings can earn through balanced risk portfolios. The last five decades have seen significant variation in real returns for an asset mix of 60% equity and 40% bonds, ranging from 3.8% from 1999–2008 to 6.2% from 1989–2008 (CIA 2009). Further, the preferences of Albertans to spend today as opposed to in the future could be reflected in a real rate of return that is too low—or in the opposite case, a real return that is too high. Were the real rate of return 1% higher or lower than the baseline scenario (3.5%), the results shown in Table 9.3 would emerge for the targeted PNRD.

Future Resource Prices

Empirically, the time paths of oil and gas prices appear to follow a random walk (Hamilton 2008)—meaning that because future prices are unpredictable, the best forecast for tomorrow's prices is today's price. On the other hand, there are also commentators who believe that the future price of oil and gas will reach extraordinary highs as the demand for energy from emerging countries increases and the supply becomes more and more expensive to extract (Rubin 2009). So, were the price of oil and gas to remain at today's levels, or, grow according to EIA's high price projections, which see oil prices rise to about $210 (2009 dollars) in the year 2035, the values for PNRD and differences from baseline shown in Table 9.4 would result.

Despite important changes to the PNRD when using alternative assumptions, in all but one alternative scenario—that of extremely high resource prices—Alberta's current PNRD is too large to maintain into the future.

GETTING ON TRACK: THE OUTLINE OF A
THREE- TO FIVE-YEAR BUDGET PLAN

My baseline estimates of future resource wealth show that expenditures must fall, or non-resource revenues must rise by $5.8 billion in order to get fiscal policy to approach a PNRD that can be sustained after non-renewable resources are physically exhausted. The results above suggest that Alberta's current per capita PNRD is higher than the intergenerationally equitable plan under most assumption scenarios. A plan to spread out government spending from Alberta's resource wealth over future generations would require some major changes in Alberta's present fiscal course: provincial expenditures would need to fall, or non-resource revenues would need to rise, by $5.8 billion to allow the benefits of Alberta's resource wealth to continue well into the future. The political reality is, however, that such an immediate adjustment to this path would likely be severe, disruptive, and have significant social and economic consequences. I therefore suggest the province look at a three- to five-year planning period to adjust expenditures and/or non-resource revenues to more sustainable levels. A transition plan would allow Alberta to set PNRD targets that approach a sustainable level, guiding the expenditure and/or non-resource taxation requirements of the province (Figure 9.5). But the longer the province takes to return to a PNRD guided by an equal per capita level, the smaller the benefit for future generations. The choices of revenue hikes or expenditure cutbacks to get to such a fiscal position, however, will not be easy.

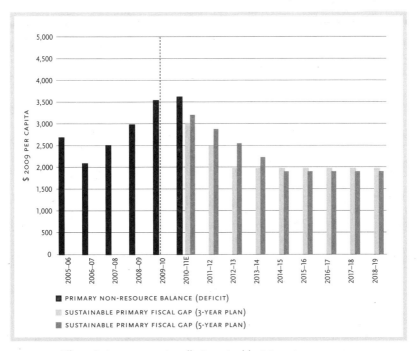

FIGURE 9.5 Alberta's Intergenerationally Sustainable Primary Non-Resource Deficit (Per Capita), Three- and Five-Year Adjustment Path, 2005/06–2018/19

Source: Alberta Budget 2010; author's calculations as described in text.

WHAT TO DO?

Advantages of Targeting a Constant Per capita PNRD

A major benefit of this plan is that it would allow for predictability of resource revenues for fiscal planning purposes, yet also provide some flexibility over time. Because under the proposed plan a predetermined amount of annual resource receipts will be available for next year's spending needs, this revenue stability should help eliminate any of the negative consequences of revenue volatility on government expenditures. Plus, revisiting the calculation every three years will allow some flexibility to government planners should the fiscal outlook change. As expectations of wealth are revised upwards or downwards, revisions to PNRD targets can be incorporated, allowing some room for adjustment to fiscal policy. As an example, many view Alberta's fiscal expansion since the mid-1990s the consequence of unconstrained spending. But to a limited extent, it makes sense that per capita government spending in Alberta has increased because in the early to mid-2000s much of the world began to officially recognize oilsands reserves as extractable, and technological advances made these unique resources more economical to extract.[9] Hence, the public wealth of the province rose as well. A principle-based rule, like the one proposed above, that solves for the province's total resource wealth each year would be able to adapt to such economic changes. Further, the plan detailed above does not necessarily preclude savings from occurring each year. For example, an unexpected downward shift in the future for global energy prices could be offset by an increase in the stock of extractable resource reserves. This might mean putting aside more resource wealth in the future when a resource stock is more likely to begin extraction.

Challenges

The above proposal is based on the principle that all generations of Albertans should be entitled to the same share of the province's resource wealth. In practice, achieving an intergenerationally equitable path for spending resource wealth is very difficult to accomplish. Public commitment to this plan, the rearrangement of budget documents away from the present form, and the assumptions of future expectations are all needed to make this plan actionable.

The main objection to the type of plan proposed in this chapter is that a savings framework needs be straightforward to gain public support, and a technical plan based on future wealth may be too complex to be operational. Yet, principle-based plans are clear in logic, with an overriding and simple goal: to ensure that each generation of Albertans is entitled to the same share of resource wealth. I contend that the main challenge for a government in imposing such a plan, like all savings plans, is the creation of a necessary, peer-driven enforcement mechanism. If Alberta's past holds any clues, the Klein reforms of the mid-1990s demonstrated that the government achieves difficult reforms when they clearly communicate the need for reform, and the reasons why, to the electorate—putting wax in peoples' ears, like Odysseus did, won't work (Cooper 1996). The ability of a fiscal rule to maintain public support over time—which translates into political will—is what truly matters (Drummond 2004).

Develop a Plan to Spread Out Resource Wealth: The Mast

With a revised budget presentation, policy makers can demonstrate to the public the revenues from non-resource economic activities, the annual saving from resource receipts, as well as the annual drawdown from resource wealth. Because energy revenues are placed directly into budgetary revenues, the electorate, not to mention fiscal planners, is deprived of a yardstick to distinguish what is being done with Alberta's resource bounty. The major benefit of this reform, besides improved transparency and a greater emphasis on future planning, would be to encourage a more informed public debate and understanding of the province's challenges in balancing today's needs with future ones. Without a clear separation and understanding of how resource receipts affect the province's finances, it will be difficult to build public support for a plan that aims to save resource wealth.

Alberta could benefit by adapting its fiscal summary statements with inspiration from other resource-based regions. The province should include a measure of its reliance on resource receipts, the PNRD, as part of its budget reports. From here, an intergenerationally equitable basis for reforms would need to be emphasized to the public and in government documents to ensure that the goals and operations of the plan can be clearly established.

Maintaining a Fiscal Plan: The Ropes

The trouble with applying the Odysseus–Sirens story to Alberta is that the leaders of the province are elected: when citizens don't like the directions of its leaders they can simply elect new ones. One element of a successful long-term fiscal plan is to ensure that the substance of a fiscal rule cannot be removed when there are short-run incentives to do so. Therefore, elements of a sustainable long-term plan must be integrated with the sphere of political influence.

What seems of critical importance is the need to tie the future benefits of a stricter savings plan to the immediate sacrifices that people make. As an example, Melville McMillan (2002) proposed that the province build savings through a provincial pension plan, with future benefit levels tied to length of residence. Another option, perhaps more applicable to the plan I propose, is to tie the payouts from the spending rules of this plan to program services that people enjoy now. The annual spending from resource wealth could be earmarked to spending priorities to bolster public support. For instance, three-quarters of the annual spending from resource wealth could be allocated to a health care fund, to be invested in important health care initiatives, such as bringing down wait times, whereas the final quarter could be earmarked to other expenses, such as education. This way, individuals can be assured that a reliable funding source would be available to cover significant portions of public service costs each year, buffering them from revenue volatility. The packaging of the plan could then include the financial stability it would provide for health care financing to boost its appeal.

CONCLUSION

"In the long run, we are all dead" is surely...a pervasive Siren theme. The contrary theme—that flexibility of choice is costly, and that the deliberate invention of inflexibility may be advantageous—is an ancient one, and deserves to be heard again....The Ulysses [Odysseus] myth reminds us that in both public and private choice, the selection of the rules to be applied to future plays of the game and devising the arrangements to enforce such rules are fundamental matters. (Brennan and Kliemt 1990, 127).

It remains a great challenge for the province of Alberta to develop a long-term fiscal plan. Were it to design a plan around the principle of intergenerational equity—which assumes that the province's finite resource base is an inheritance for all Albertans to enjoy—significant adjustments to the current stance of fiscal policy would need to take place. Steps to achieve this plan include better fiscal reporting on the impact of resources in fiscal policy decisions. The plan can then be enforced if, upon the delivery of annual spending from resource wealth, the benefits are carefully harnessed and tied to popular public services so that political forces that may move to counter the plan over time are better neutralized.

Fiscal reforms will either come by thoughtful, forward-looking planning, or they will be thrust on provincial taxpayers. Though there would be short-term pains, Albertans should not forget the main goals of reforms: to safeguard the delivery of government services in both good times and bad, and to ensure that Alberta remains an attractive place to live and invest for future generations.

Author's Note

The author would like to thank Ken Boessenkool, Bev Dhalby, Herb Emery, Lennie Kaplan, Stuart Landon, Alexandre Laurin, and Mel McMillan for comments on prior drafts. The author would also like to thank Leslie Shiell for his collaboration and insight on prior works. All errors are the responsibility of the author.

Notes

1. The extent to which the expansion or contraction of Alberta's financial position is thanks to resource revenues, or other forms of revenues, is difficult to determine. In the traditional sense, resource revenues appear in budget documents as revenues direct from royalties, leases, and fees. A broader definition of resource revenues would include the

personal, corporate, and other tax revenues earned from upstream and downstream industries that service the extraction sector, not to mention any additional spin-off effects. After all, these revenues are also volatile and linked to the time-limited nature of resource extraction; hence, the direct and indirect resource revenue distinction is an important one. Estimates of the economic activity of the oil and gas sector on provincial income and government revenues range from as much as 50% (Mansell and Schlenker 2006) to a low of 24% (Alberta 2007). Because there is a range of views on the size of indirect resource revenues (Alberta 2010), I use only royalties, leases, and fees for oil and gas exploration.

2. In case resource revenues in any given year are not sufficient to bring the budget back to balance, then resource assets must be drawn down or debt must be issued, in which case this acts as a reduction in resource wealth.

3. Budget 2008–09 removed a large source of non-resource revenues by cutting the $1 billion health premium, which further contributed to a widening primary non-resource gap.

4. What is termed the primary non-resource deficit here is often referred in the economic literature as the "primary fiscal gap" (Emery and Kneebone 2009; FIPAC 2008). Note that this differs from the use of the term "fiscal gap" in FIPAC (2008), however, in the sense that it does not include federal transfers.

5. Proposals for fiscal rules along these lines range from maintaining the total level of government spending of resource wealth over time to maintaining a constant ratio of resource-based spending to non-resource GDP.

6. See the Alberta Consolidated Financial Statements, Note 5, for an explanation of the breakdown of financial asset reporting in Alberta budget and financial statement documents. Alberta's Consolidated Financial Statements are published in the province's annual reports, which can be found at http://www.finance.alberta.ca/publications/annual_repts/govt/index.html.

7. See Schedule 11 of Alberta's Consolidated Financial Statements for a list of all the province's unfunded pension obligations.

8. In 2007–08, the government of Alberta assumed responsibility for the entire unfunded, predominantly employee share, portion of the Alberta Teachers' Pension Plan at an estimated cost of $2.3 billion at that time. One year later, in 2008–09, the government's actuarial evaluation of the pension plan liabilities concluded that the discount rate of future pension liabilities was much too high, and the downward revision raised total unfunded pension liabilities. This shows up on the balance sheet as a one-time incidence of dissaving, even though it could be argued that past pension liabilities should be revised downwards to take into account this realization as well. Nonetheless, the original cost of assuming the teachers' portion of the unfunded pension liability cost around $600 million more ($2.9 billion) than originally anticipated in 2007–08.

9. For instance, the *World Oil Magazine*, a widely circulated petroleum journal based in the Middle East, was the last major international petroleum publication to recognize the extraction viability of the oilsands in its annual 2007 reserves publication.

References

Alberta. 2010. "Energizing Investment: A Plan to Improve Alberta's Natural Gas and Conventional Oil Competitiveness." Project Committee Final Report to the Alberta Department of Energy.

Alberta, Department of Finance. 2007. "Energy and the Alberta Economy." Economic Spotlight. http://www.finance.alberta.ca/aboutalberta/ spotlights/2007_0918_energy_ and_ab_economy.pdf.

Alberta Energy. 2009. "Alberta's Energy Reserves 2008 and Supply/ Demand Outlook 2009–2018." Energy Resource Conservation Board, ST98-2009.

Alberta Financial Management Commission (AFMC). 2002. *Moving from Good to Great: Enhancing Alberta's Fiscal Framework*. Alberta Financial Management Commission Final Report.

Barnett, Steven, and Rolando Ossowski. 2003. "Operational Aspects of Fiscal Policy in Oil Producing Countries." In *Fiscal Policy Formulation and Implementation in Oil-Producing Countries*, edited by Jeffrey M. Davis, Rolando Ossowski, and Annalisa Fedelino, 45–81. International Monetary Fund.

Berdahl, Loleen. 2008. "Moving Forward: Western Canadian Attitudes about Mobility and Human Capital." Calgary: Canada West Foundation.

Brennan, Geoffrey, and Hartmut Kliemt. 1990. "Logo Logic." *Constitutional Political Economy* 1: 125–27.

Canadian Association of Petroleum Producers (CAPP). 2010. "Statistical Handbook." Calgary: Canadian Association of Petroleum Producers. http://www.capp.ca/library/statistics/handbook/Pages/default.aspx.

Canadian Institute of Actuaries (CIA). 2009. "Report on Canadian Economic Statistics 1924–2008." Canadian Institute of Actuaries.

Cooper, Barry. 1996. *The Klein Achievement*. Toronto: University of Toronto, Faculty of Management, Centre for Public Management.

Drummond, Don. 2004. "Do We Need Fiscal Rules?" In *Is the Debt War Over? Dispatches from Canada's Fiscal Frontline* edited by Christopher Ragan and William Watson, 313–28. Montreal: Institute for Research on Public Policy.

Emery, J.C. Herbert, and Ronald D. Kneebone. 2009. "Will it be Déjà vu All Over Again?" SPP Briefing Papers 2 (1). University of Calgary, School of Public Policy, April.

Energy Information Administration (EIA). 2009. "Annual Energy Outlook 2010: Early Release." US Department of Energy, December.

Financial Investment Planning and Advisory Commission (FIPAC).
2008. "Preserving Prosperity: Challenging Alberta to Save." Final
Report. Edmonton: Alberta Finance. http://www.finance.alberta.ca/
publications/other/2008-0131-fipac-final-report.pdf.

Hamilton, James D. 2008. "Understanding Crude Oil Prices." NBER
Working Paper 14492, November.

Hirsch, Todd. 2008. "Alberta's Artificially Robust Population Surge."
Edmonton Journal, June 28, A19.

International Energy Agency (IEA). 2009. "World Energy Outlook 2009."
International Energy Agency.

Kneebone, Ronald. 2006. "From Famine to Feast: The Evolution of
Budgeting Rules in Alberta." *Canadian Tax Journal* 54 (3): 657–73.

Mansell, Robert, and Ron Schlenker. 2006. "Energy and the Alberta
Economy: Past and Future Implications." Working Paper No. 1. Alberta
Energy Futures Project: University of Calgary, Institute for Sustainable
Energy, Environment, and Economy.

McMillan, Melville L. 2002. "Enhancing the Alberta Advantage: Achieving
Fiscal Stability via a Funded Alberta Pension Plan." In *Alberta's Volatile
Government Revenues: Policies for the Long Run*, edited by L.S. Wilson,
129–58. Edmonton: Institute for Public Economics, University of
Alberta.

Roach, Robert. 2007. "Save Your Money!" In *Alberta's Energy Legacy*, edited
by Robert Roach, 1–8. Calgary: Canada West Foundation.

Rubin, Jeff. 2009. *Why Your World is About to Get a Whole Lot Smaller*.
Toronto: Random House Canada.

Shiell, Leslie, and Colin Busby. 2008. "Greater Savings Required: How
Alberta Can Achieve Fiscal Sustainability from its Resource Rev-
enues." C.D. Howe Institute Commentary No. 263. Toronto: C.D. Howe
Institute.

Wilson, Leonard S., ed. 2002. *Alberta's Volatile Government Revenues:
Policies for the Long Run*. Edmonton: Institute for Public Economics,
University of Alberta.

Government Revenue Volatility in Alberta

Stuart Landon and Constance Smith

INTRODUCTION

Oil and natural gas prices often change rapidly, substantially, and unpredictably. The Alberta government is heavily exposed to energy price volatility as it relies to a large extent on revenue derived from the production of oil and natural gas. For Alberta, as with the governments of other oil producing jurisdictions, dealing with large revenue movements typically involves economic, social, and political costs. Rapid declines in energy revenues may lead to cuts in expenditures that are difficult to accomplish quickly and efficiently. Revenue volatility that drives government expenditures can also cause fiscal policy to be procyclical, thus magnifying movements in economic activity.

This chapter provides an analysis of the volatility of Alberta government revenues and, in so doing, considers the following questions. Is revenue volatility a problem? Are Alberta government revenues more volatile than the revenues of other provinces? What are the principal causes of Alberta government revenue volatility? Can revenue volatility be reduced through tax base diversification or hedging in futures and options markets? What impact do exchange rate movements have on revenue volatility? Could a revenue savings fund reduce volatility? These questions are addressed both in general terms and with explicit reference to the case of Alberta. Given the emphasis on revenue volatility, the important issues of expenditure volatility and intergenerational equity and fiscal sustainability are only addressed to the extent that they relate to revenue volatility.

We provide evidence that Alberta government revenues are considerably more volatile than the revenues of other provinces, but own-source revenues less royalty payments are of similar size and volatility as those of other provinces. One method proposed to reduce the volatility of revenues, tax base diversification (for example, use of a retail sales tax), is shown to have a relatively minor effect on overall revenue volatility since Alberta's royalty revenues are such a large share of own-source revenues. Revenue smoothing using futures and options markets can be expensive, is associated with significant political risks, and cannot eliminate all revenue volatility. As the Canadian dollar tends to appreciate when energy prices rise and depreciate when energy prices fall, exchange rate movements have smoothed Alberta government revenues, although not by a large amount. A simulation using Alberta data shows that a revenue savings fund could significantly reduce revenue volatility. This type of fund leads to greater revenue stability because the revenue it contributes to the budget in any particular year is based on revenues *averaged* over prior years and because a large proportion of the most volatile revenues, royalties, are deposited in the fund. Revenue uncertainty is also reduced with a savings fund since future revenue depends on known past contributions.

IS REVENUE VOLATILITY A PROBLEM?

Government revenue volatility may have important negative consequences. For example, revenue volatility increases uncertainty for both the public and private sectors. A government may wish to provide infrastructure and social services that reflect the long-run permanent component of income, but it is difficult to set the correct level of spending when it is not clear what part of volatile revenue changes is permanent and what part is temporary. The volatility of revenues also creates uncertainty for the private sector since it is more difficult to predict future government tax and spending policies, both of which may have important consequences for private sector profits and investment decisions. Using data for a wide variety of countries, government revenue and expenditure volatility has been shown to lead to slower economic growth (Barnett and Ossowski 2002; Afonso and Furceri 2008; Sturm, Gurtner, and Alegre 2009).

Another major consequence of revenue volatility is that, in many jurisdictions, volatile revenues induce volatile movements in government expenditures. When revenues expand during a boom, expenditures tend to grow rapidly, and, when revenues fall, expenditures are cut (although often more slowly than expenditures initially rose). That is, revenue volatility may cause governments to pursue stop-go procyclical fiscal policies (Sturm, Gurtner, and Alegre 2009). These procyclical policies accentuate the business cycle so that, rather than acting to reduce volatility, the government becomes a driving force magnifying economic fluctuations. The volatility of economic activity and the volatile provision of government services will reduce individual welfare if consumers are risk averse and, thereby, prefer less volatile income and consumption.[1] Further, given that there are real costs of moving resources between expanding and contracting sectors, it is especially important for government policy to help stabilize the economy, rather than to aggravate economic volatility.[2]

Government spending increases during revenue booms may increase the costs of goods purchased by the government. There is some indication that increases in government revenues are correlated with upward pressure on prices. In Alberta, the prices of current goods and services purchased by government rose at an average annual rate of 4.1% between 2002 and 2008, while they rose by only 2.6% in British Columbia and 3.3% in Ontario. During this same period, real per capita revenues were rising more than twice as fast in Alberta than in either Ontario or British Columbia.[3] Further, during booms, procyclical government spending competes with private sector spending, which can raise wages and other input costs, thereby increasing private sector costs.

Large increases in government revenues during booms may lead governments to spend on services and investment projects that have relatively low returns. The rapid expansion of programs and capital spending during revenue booms may also stretch the capacity of the government to provide services and monitor spending, leading to waste, inefficiency and the unproductive use of government funds (Barnett and Ossowski 2002). Further, during a revenue collapse, it is difficult to cut spending efficiently; that is, to first cut projects and services with the lowest return. Large spending cuts precipitated by a fall in revenues may also damage the morale and capacity of the public sector, leading to a more inefficient provision of public services.

To the extent that it is easier politically to raise government spending than to reduce spending, there may be a greater tendency to expand spending in revenue booms than to contract spending in busts. Thus, revenue volatility may result in an expansion of the size of government and, potentially, the implementation of an unsustainable fiscal plan that will necessitate even greater expenditure cuts in the future.

HOW VOLATILE ARE ALBERTA GOVERNMENT REVENUES?[4]

Alberta government own-source revenues are quite volatile relative to the revenues of the other provinces, as can be seen in Figures 10.1 and 10.2, where own-source revenue is defined as

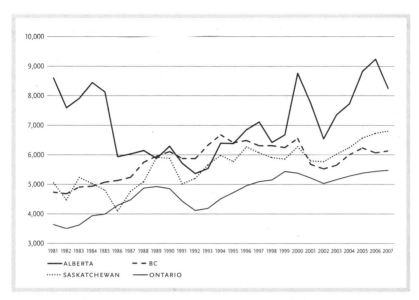

FIGURE 10.1 Real Per Capita Own-Source Revenues (2002 dollars)

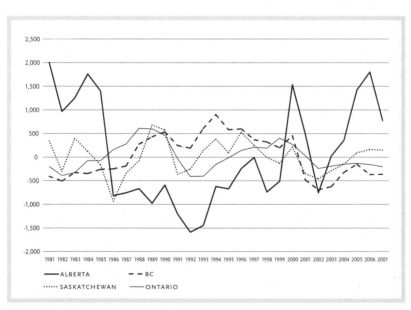

FIGURE 10.2 Real Per Capita Own-Source Revenue, Difference from Trend (2002 dollars)

	Alberta	Saskatchewan	British Columbia	Ontario
Real per capita revenue:				
Total revenue	8063	7327	6772	5508
Own-source revenue	7105	5639	5810	4707
Percentage share of total revenue	*88.1*	*77.0*	*85.8*	*85.5*
Own-source revenue minus royalties	4899	4817	5211	4684
Percentage share of total revenue	*60.8*	*65.7*	*76.9*	*85.0*
Coefficient of variation:*				
Total revenue	13.4	6.5	6.3	5.0
Own-source revenue	15.4	6.5	7.8	6.2
Own-source revenue minus royalties	6.7	9.2	8.1	6.2

TABLE 10.1 Average Real Per Capita Revenue and Volatility, 1981–2007

* The coefficient of variation is the ratio (multiplied by 100) of the standard deviation of the differences from an exponential trend to the average value of the series.
Source: Authors' calculations using Statistics Canada data. See the Data Appendix for more information.

total revenue less transfers from other levels of government.[5] Over the period 1982–2007, the year-to-year change in the real per capita own-source revenues of Alberta exceeded 10% nine times (that is, in 35% of the years). In comparison, this magnitude of a revenue change occurred on only six occasions in Saskatchewan, only once in British Columbia, and not at all in Ontario.

Another method of comparing the relative volatility of revenues is to examine the extent to which revenues deviate from trend. These deviations can be measured using the coefficient of variation—the normalized standard deviation.[6] This measure can be interpreted as the percentage of the average value of a variable—government revenues in this case—represented by one standard deviation of the differences of the variable from trend.[7] For 1981 to 2007, the coefficient of variation for Alberta

	Coefficient of Variation*
Real Per Capita Government Revenues:	
Total revenues	13.4
Own-source revenues	15.4
Own-source revenues minus royalties	6.7
Royalties	43.6
Direct taxes corporations	24.2
Interest and other investment income	14.9
Direct taxes persons	10.2
Retail sales tax†	12.0
Gaming profits†	6.3
Gasoline tax†	3.2
Real Per Capita Tax Base Variables:	
Corporation profits before taxes	36.0
Interest and miscellaneous investment income	21.4
Final demand	8.3
Wages, salaries, and supplementary labour income	8.2
Personal income	4.8
Expenditure on consumer goods	2.7
Real Energy Prices:	
West Texas Intermediate petroleum price, $US	46.9
West Texas Intermediate petroleum price, $C	39.4
Natural gas price, $US	46.3
Natural gas price, $C	42.0

TABLE 10.2 Volatility of Government Revenues and Selected Tax Bases in Alberta, 1981–2007

* The coefficient of variation is the ratio (multiplied by 100) of the standard deviation of the differences from an exponential trend to the average value of the series.
† Sample period is 1994–2007. This shorter sample is employed because the use of these taxes changed considerably in the late 1980s and early 1990s.
Source: Authors' calculations using Statistics Canada data. See the Data Appendix for more information.

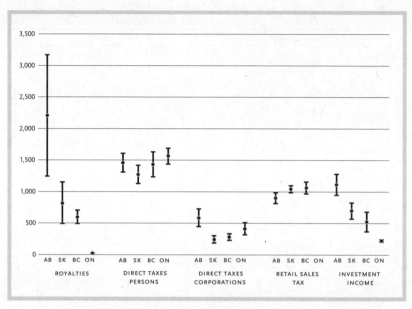

FIGURE 10.3 Average Real Per Capita Revenues and One Standard Deviation Band, 1981–2007 (2002 dollars)

government real per capita own-source revenues is 15.4. In other words, if the deviations of revenues from trend have a normal distribution, there is a 68% probability that revenues fall in a band around the average value of own-source revenues that is equivalent in magnitude to 30.8% of the average (while the probability that they fall outside this band is 32%). The coefficients of variation associated with the real per capita own-source revenues of British Columbia, Saskatchewan, and Ontario are 7.8, 6.5, and 6.2, respectively (Table 10.1).[8] Thus, Alberta's own-source revenues are more than twice as variable, relative to their average, as the revenues of the other three provinces.[9]

WHAT ARE THE CAUSES OF ALBERTA REVENUE VOLATILITY?

The greater variability of Alberta government revenues is driven principally by the highly volatile energy sector royalty component

	Alberta	Saskatchewan	British Columbia	Ontario
Own-source revenue minus royalties	0.75	0.86	0.92	1.0
Royalties	0.90	0.67	0.59	0.23
Direct taxes corporations	0.71	0.33	0.46	0.83
Direct taxes persons	0.42	0.20	0.66	0.74
Retail sales tax	—	0.53	0.49	0.75

TABLE 10.3 Correlation Coefficient between the Percentage Change in Total Own-Source Revenue and the Percentage Change in the Variable Indicated, 1982–2007

Source: Authors' calculations using Statistics Canada data. See the Data Appendix for more information.

of revenues as well as, to a much smaller extent, by the volatility of corporate profits (Figure 10.3 and Table 10.2).[10] Volatility in these revenue sources, in turn, is driven mainly by movements in energy prices.

The magnitude and volatility of royalty revenues in Alberta

As shown in Table 10.3, for Alberta, the simple correlation between the growth rate (percentage change) of real per capita total own-source revenues and the growth rate of royalty revenues is 0.90 over the period 1982–2007. The growth rate of corporate tax revenues had the next highest correlation with own-source revenues (0.71). In contrast, for personal income taxes, the second largest tax source in Alberta, the correlation coefficient with own-source revenues is only 0.42. In the other provinces, own-source revenues are less correlated with royalties and, in general, more correlated with personal income tax revenues.

The large impact of royalty volatility on own-source revenue volatility arises both because royalty revenues are volatile and because royalty revenues are the largest single component of own-source revenues in Alberta. On average, from 1981 to 2007, royalty revenues accounted for 31% of real per capita own-source revenues. The next largest revenue type, direct taxes on persons, accounted for only 20.5%. The share of royalty revenues in own-source revenues is large relative to other provinces (Table

	Alberta	Saskatchewan	British Columbia	Ontario
Royalties	31.1	14.6	10.3	0.5
Direct taxes persons	20.5	22.6	24.7	33.2
Retail sales tax*	2.0	16.0	18.0	22.6
Direct taxes corporations	8.3	4.4	4.9	8.8
Interest and other investment income	15.7	12.4	9.1	4.8
Contributions to social insurance and other transfers from persons	7.5	4.9	11.3	10.2

TABLE 10.4 Selected Revenue Types—Average Share of Real Per Capita Own-Source Revenues, 1981–2007 (in percent)

* Includes alcohol and tobacco taxes.
Source: Authors' calculations using Statistics Canada data. See the Data Appendix for more information.

10.4). Royalties made up only 14.6% of Saskatchewan government own-source revenues over the 1981–2007 period and were Saskatchewan's third largest revenue source (after direct taxes on persons and the retail sales tax). In British Columbia, royalties comprised only 10.3% of revenues (and were the fourth largest revenue type) while, in Ontario, royalties made up an insignificant component of revenues.

Not only are royalties by far the largest component of government revenues in Alberta, they are also the most variable. The coefficient of variation associated with royalty revenues in Alberta over the period 1981–2007 is 43.6 (Table 10.2).[11] A one standard deviation band around the average value of real per capita royalty revenues ranges from $1,245 to $3,169. The magnitude of this band, $1,924, is equivalent to 27% of average own-source revenues. In comparison, direct taxes on corporations, the second most variable component of revenues, with a coefficient of variation of 24.2, has a one standard deviation band of only $284.

The volatility of royalty revenues is due primarily to variation in energy prices, particularly the price of natural gas, as natural gas accounted for 45% of total royalty payments from 1981–2009 and 54% over the period 2004–05 through 2008–09 (Table 10.5). Over the 1982–2007 period, the simple correlation coefficients between the growth rate of real per capita royalty revenues

Fiscal Year	Natural Gas and By-products	Crude Oil Royalties	Bonuses for Sale of Crown Leases	Synthetic Crude Oil and Bitumen	Total Non-renewable Resource Revenue
1981–82	1768	1970	503	208	4669
1982–83	1453	1815	261	281	4005
1983–84	1210	2059	348	217	4029
1984–85	1359	2137	463	na*	4203
1985–86	1235	1888	495	na*	3841
1986–87	718	665	191	na*	1585
1987–88	638	858	480	na*	1970
1988–89	600	581	273	na*	1554
1989–90	548	642	222	16	1522
1990–91	576	707	222	21	1630
1991–92	420	520	131	16	1192
1992–93	513	485	80	31	1204
1993–94	651	354	331	30	1463
1994–95	562	491	437	93	1688
1995–96	444	466	255	138	1410
1996–97	559	596	399	220	1890
1997–98	680	368	439	79	1559
1998–99	581	178	184	23	931
1999–00	927	419	282	162	1777
2000–01	2583	538	416	255	3797
2001–02	1376	337	331	63	2126
2002–03	1638	376	181	58	2279
2003–04	1665	300	295	60	2346
2004–05	1875	371	365	209	2838
2005–06	2289	399	952	259	3915
2006–07	1525	356	627	614	3122
2007–08	1247	397	270	699	2644
2008–09	1303	402	248	664	2661

TABLE 10.5 Alberta Real Per Capita Natural Resource Revenues by Type (2002 dollars)

* Crude oil royalties for 1984/85–88/89 include synthetic crude products.
Source: Revenues are from various issues of the Government of Alberta, Department of
Energy, Annual Report. Data for population and the price index are from Statistics Canada
as described in the Data Appendix. These population and price data are annual, so data for the
calendar year in which the fiscal year begins are employed.

and the growth rates of the real Canadian dollar prices of natural gas and West Texas Intermediate (WTI) petroleum were 0.87 and 0.70, respectively (Table 10.6). Given the large share of royalties in revenues, changes in these prices drive changes in total real per capita own-source revenues—the correlations between the growth rates of real per capita own-source revenues and real Canadian dollar natural gas and petroleum prices are 0.68 and 0.72. In comparison, the correlations between changes in real per capita own-source revenues less royalty revenues and changes in real natural gas and petroleum prices are only 0.13 and 0.53, respectively.

As another indication of the importance of energy price variation to royalty revenue variation, the growth rate of real per capita royalties was regressed on the change in the real natural gas price, lagged royalties, and the lagged natural gas price. This regression explains 78% of the variation in the growth rate of royalties and all the coefficients in the regression are statistically significant. In contrast, a comparable regression explains only 17% of the variation in own-source revenues *less royalties*, and the two natural gas price variables in this regression are not statistically significant.

Given the close relationship between royalty revenues and energy prices, it is not surprising that royalty revenues are quite volatile since energy prices are also volatile (Table 10.2). The coefficients of variation over the period 1981–2007 of the real Canadian dollar prices of natural gas and WTI petroleum are 42.0 and 39.4, respectively. That is, the difference between the upper and lower bounds of a one standard deviation band around the averages of these prices is equivalent in magnitude to approximately 80% of the average price. These coefficients of variation are of similar magnitude to those of royalty revenues. The coefficients of variation of other tax bases tend to be much smaller. For example, the coefficient of variation of personal income, the tax base for the personal income tax, is just 4.8 (Table 10.2).

	Royalties	Natural gas price ($C)	WTI petroleum price ($C)
Real per capita Alberta government revenues:			
Total revenues	0.90	0.71	0.73
Own-source revenues	0.90	0.68	0.72
Own-source revenues minus royalties	0.42	0.13	0.53
Direct taxes persons	0.13	-0.08	0.28
Interest and other investment income	0.26	0.28	0.19
Direct taxes corporations	0.57	0.28	0.68
Royalties	—	0.87	0.70
Real per capita tax base variables, Alberta:			
Wages, salaries, and supplementary labour income	0.23	0.24	0.22
Personal income	0.20	0.14	0.20
Expenditure on consumer goods	0.16	0.07	0.25
Final demand	0.31	0.27	0.30
Interest and miscellaneous investment income	0.95	0.81	0.73
Corporation profits before taxes	0.83	0.70	0.71
Prices:			
Exchange rate (Canadian dollars per US dollar)	-0.13	-0.06	-0.31
Natural gas price, $US	0.86	0.98	0.52
Natural gas price, $C	0.87	—	0.49
West Texas Intermediate petroleum price, $US	0.66	0.46	0.98
West Texas Intermediate petroleum price, $C	0.70	0.49	—

TABLE 10.6 Correlation Coefficients between Percentage Changes, 1982–2007

Source: Authors' calculations using Statistics Canada data. See the Data Appendix for more information.

The volatility of non-royalty revenues

After royalties, corporate tax revenues are the most volatile revenue type in Alberta (Table 10.2). The coefficient of variation of real per capita Alberta corporate tax revenues for the period 1981–2007 is 24.2, which is similar to the volatility of corporate tax revenues in both Saskatchewan and Ontario. Although volatile, corporate tax revenues are not expected to be a large driver of overall revenue volatility because these revenues accounted for only 8.3% of own-source revenues during 1981–2007, one-quarter of the share of the more volatile royalty component of revenues. In fact, the real per capita dollar value of the one standard deviation band around average corporate tax revenues was almost identical to that for the much less volatile revenues from direct taxes on persons because personal income taxes contributed a much larger share of total revenues on average (20.5% of own-source revenues). Nevertheless, both royalty revenues and corporate tax revenues are more highly correlated with energy prices than are personal income tax revenues, and, thus, movements in energy prices may cause synchronized movements in both types of tax revenues, accentuating the volatility of total revenues (Table 10.6).

A comparison of the volatility of *non-royalty* own-source revenues in Alberta with the non-royalty own-source revenues in other provinces illustrates the importance of the role played by the volatility of royalty payments in generating Alberta government revenue volatility. While the coefficient of variation of Alberta's real per capita own-source revenues for the period 1981–2007 is 15.4, the coefficient of variation of own-source revenues less royalties is only 6.7 (Table 10.1). This is only slightly higher than the corresponding coefficient of variation for Ontario (6.2) and lower than the coefficients of variation for British Columbia (8.1) and Saskatchewan (9.2). As can be seen from Figure 10.4, the pattern of the differences of own-source revenues minus royalties from trend for Alberta is also similar to the pattern for the other three provinces.

Not only do Alberta non-royalty own-source revenues have a similar degree of volatility as those of Saskatchewan, British

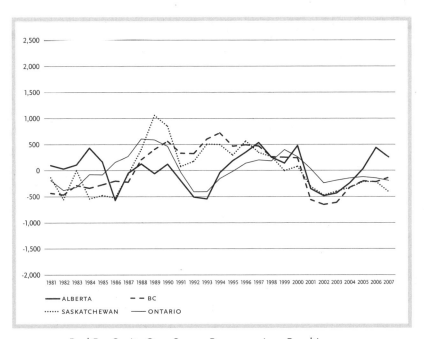

2,500
2,000
1,500
1,000
500
0
-500
-1,000
-1,500
-2,000

1981 1982 1983 1984 1985 1986 1987 1988 1989 1990 1991 1992 1993 1994 1995 1996 1997 1998 1999 2000 2001 2002 2003 2004 2005 2006 2007

—— ALBERTA   — — BC
······ SASKATCHEWAN   —— ONTARIO

FIGURE 10.4 Real Per Capita Own-Source Revenue minus Royalties, Difference from Trend (2002 dollars)

Columbia, and Ontario, they are also of a similar size in real per capita terms, as shown in Figure 10.5. Alberta's non-royalty real per capita own-source revenues averaged $4,899 over the 1981–2007 period, while the non-royalty own-source revenues of Saskatchewan, British Columbia, and Ontario averaged $4,817, $5,211, and $4,684, respectively (Table 10.1). Hence, Alberta's *non-royalty* own-source revenues are, on average, similar in terms of volatility and magnitude to the revenues of the other provinces.[12]

Alberta revenue volatility and the persistence of revenue changes

Alberta revenues have been volatile, and much of this volatility has been driven by persistent movements away from trend. As Figure 10.2 shows, real per capita own-source revenues were above trend from 1981 to 1985, below trend from 1986 through 1999, above trend in 2000 and 2001, below in 2002, and above

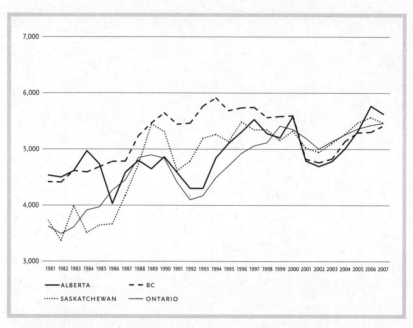

FIGURE 10.5 Real Per Capita Own-Source Revenue minus Royalties
(2002 dollars)

trend from 2003 through 2007. The longer-term movements in
revenues away from trend are driven by movements in royalties,
as own-source revenues minus royalties move above and below
trend twice as often as total own-source revenues (Figure 10.4).
The persistence of revenue movements above and below trend
are important because they imply that downturns in revenues
may not be short lived, while upturns may seem permanent and,
thereby, may induce too great an increase in spending.

Given the dependence of royalties on energy prices, the
long movements in own-source revenues away from trend
can be attributed to persistent movements in energy prices.
Considerable evidence suggests that oil prices follow a process similar to a random walk (Hamilton 2008).[13] This has two
important implications for the volatility of revenues. First, movements in revenues away from trend can be quite persistent as
there are no forces causing oil prices to return to some constant
equilibrium value. Second, if oil prices follow a random walk,

the best forecast of the oil price in *any* future period is the current oil price. Nevertheless, this forecast is likely to be a very poor forecast since it has a very high standard error due to the high variance of oil prices.[14] This means that royalty revenues, the component of revenues that is both most closely related to oil prices and the driver of the volatility in total revenues, will be extremely difficult to forecast and will have no tendency to converge quickly to some stable average value.

WHAT CAN BE DONE TO REDUCE REVENUE VOLATILITY?

Alberta government revenue volatility is primarily driven by royalty revenue volatility and this, in turn, is driven by energy price volatility. Energy prices are determined in world or North American markets and are effectively out of the control of the Alberta government. To reduce revenue volatility it is necessary to reduce the share of royalty revenues in overall revenues, say by tax base "diversification," or to reduce the volatility of royalty revenues, say by hedging or by smoothing royalty revenues through time.

Tax base diversification

Methods to reduce the share of revenues from the energy sector
One method to reduce revenue volatility is to decrease the dependence of revenues on the more volatile energy-related tax bases through tax base diversification. Tax base diversification is one motivation for suggestions that the government implement policies to diversify the economy away from energy-related activity. This method of tax base diversification has three significant shortcomings. First, this approach may take a long time to yield results and, second, is likely to be inefficient since it runs counter to Alberta's comparative advantage—the extraction of energy resources.[15] The third major shortcoming is that government-encouraged economic diversification relies on the government's ability to pick successful non-energy related industries, but there

is little evidence that governments can do this more effectively than the private sector.

Another way to reduce the dependence of total revenues on the energy sector is to collect less revenue from the more volatile energy-related tax bases—energy sector production (royalties) and corporate profits. For example, the Alberta government could have set royalty rates and corporate tax rates at levels that would have collected 25% less revenue than was actually collected from these sources over the 1981–2007 period. Assuming no change in other tax revenues, the lower tax rates would have caused own-source revenue volatility to be just 14% smaller—the coefficient of variation would decline from 15.4 to 13.2. On the other hand, average own-source revenues would fall by just under 10%. Thus, even with a significant revenue sacrifice, revenue volatility would remain high because royalties would continue to comprise a large proportion of total own-source revenues. More importantly, it may be undesirable to reduce royalties on the grounds of economic efficiency since, to the extent that royalties are taxes on rents, they are likely to be less distortionary than taxes on other tax bases. In addition, a cut in royalty rates would reduce the return to the owners of the resource, the residents of Alberta.

A sales tax

Another often-mentioned method of reducing revenue volatility through tax diversification is to place greater emphasis on the retail sales tax since this tax base has been relatively underexploited in Alberta (Table 10.4).[16] Including taxes on alcohol and tobacco, Saskatchewan collected $900 per capita in retail sales taxes on average from 1981 to 2007 (in constant 2002 dollars), Ontario collected $1,063, and British Columbia collected $1,043. In contrast, Alberta collected $141.[17] Thus, there seems ample opportunity for Alberta to significantly raise revenues through the imposition of a retail sales tax. Further, since the sales tax base tends to be relatively stable, greater reliance on a sales tax would reduce revenue volatility. For the 1981–2007 period, the coefficients of variation of two possible definitions of the retail sales tax base—real per capita expenditure on consumer goods and real per capita final demand—were just 2.7

	Alberta	Saskatchewan	British Columbia	Ontario
Total own-source revenue	15.4	6.5	7.8	6.2
Direct taxes persons	10.2	11.4	13.8	8.1
Direct taxes corporations	24.2	23.6	18.6	23.1
Interest and other investment income	14.8	18.3	29.9	8.9
Retail sales tax	—	9.5	5.4	8.8

TABLE 10.7 Coefficients of Variation for Selected Revenue Types, 1981–2007*

The coefficient of variation is the ratio (multiplied by 100) of the standard deviation of the differences from an exponential trend to the average value of the series.
Source: Authors' calculations using Statistics Canada data. See the Data Appendix for more information.

and 8.3, respectively. As shown in Table 10.2, these tax bases are much less volatile than energy prices. Sales tax revenues have also proved to be quite stable in other provinces. The coefficient of variation of real per capita sales tax revenue is only 5 for British Columbia, and approximately 9 for both Saskatchewan and Ontario
(Table 10.7).

A simple example illustrates the potential impact on Alberta revenue volatility of greater reliance on a sales tax. In this example, the change in revenue volatility is calculated when a volatile tax source—Alberta's corporate tax—is replaced with a more stable revenue source of almost equal magnitude—the real per capita retail sales tax revenues of British Columbia—for each year from 1981 to 2007.[18] Holding everything else constant, the adoption of a sales tax yielding per capita revenues identical to those collected by British Columbia, along with the elimination of the volatile corporate profits tax, causes the coefficient of variation of Alberta own-source revenues to fall by only 11.5% (from 15.4 to 13.6). Thus, even the complete replacement of volatile corporate tax revenues with much more stable sales tax revenues, yields a relatively small drop in the volatility of own-source revenues. The reason for this small change in volatility is that sales tax revenues are fairly small compared to royalties and, thus, the volatility of revenues would continue to be driven by royalties.

Other sources of revenue

Tax revenues could also be diversified by exploiting revenue sources other than the sales tax. Personal income tax revenues tend to be relatively stable and are only weakly correlated with royalties and energy prices (Tables 10.2 and 10.6).[19] On the other hand, in 2007, real per capita direct taxes on persons were already higher in Alberta than in British Columbia and Saskatchewan, although lower than in Ontario (and a similar comparison holds, on average, for the whole 1981–2007 period as shown in Figure 10.3). Thus, there may be little room to increase revenue from this source, particularly without significantly increasing the level of tax-induced distortions.

Income from interest and other investment income was, on average over the 1981–2007 period, the third largest component of Alberta own-source revenue. However, the real per capita contribution of this revenue source to total revenues has been falling over time, so these revenues are now a much less important component of total revenues than in the 1980s.[20] Further, given the current low level of real returns, it seems likely that this source of government income will continue to make a relatively small contribution to revenue. A significant advantage of revenue from interest and other investment income is that it is negatively correlated with both the level and growth rate of corporate tax revenue and is much less strongly correlated with royalties than is corporate tax revenue (Table 10.6). These revenues are also less volatile than either royalty revenues or corporate tax revenues (Table 10.2). Nevertheless, the potential for placing more emphasis on this type of revenue in the short run is limited because investment income depends on the level of past government saving.

Some of the smaller provincial tax bases are quite stable. For example, gasoline taxes have a coefficient of variation of only 3.2 over the 1994–2007 period, while the coefficient of variation for gambling revenues is 6.3. Payroll taxes have been a stable source of revenues in Ontario (with a coefficient of variation of only 2.1 over the 1992–2007 period),[21] and health care premiums were a stable source of revenues for Alberta. Nevertheless, greater use of these taxes to reduce overall revenue volatility is likely to have only a minor impact, and, in some cases, greater use of these taxes would have serious shortcomings. First, Alberta already exploits gambling revenues to a greater extent than the other provinces, so it is unclear whether there is much opportunity for further diversification into this tax base (particularly with competition from Internet gambling).[22] There may also be little room for further expansion of alcohol and tobacco taxes and greater reliance on property tax revenues could crowd out local government tax revenues. Second, while the gasoline tax base has been exploited less in Alberta than in other provinces—per capita real gasoline tax revenues in 2007 were $185 in Alberta, but were $350 in Saskatchewan, $215 in Ontario, and $250 in BC—the relatively small size of this revenue source in other provinces suggests that expansion is likely to be limited. Third, the introduction of a payroll tax (as used by Ontario) would raise the cost of labour and, potentially, have a negative impact on employment and other tax revenues. Finally, given the large share of royalty revenues in total revenues, and the magnitude of royalty volatility, none of the prospective tax bases are large enough and have enough room for further expansion to have an appreciable effect on overall revenue *volatility*. This is not to suggest that greater use of these tax bases would not have an impact on the *level* of revenues collected, just not on the *volatility* of revenues.

In summary, tax base diversification is likely to have a relatively minor effect on Alberta revenue volatility because royalty revenues are large and volatile relative to the alternatives. Tax base diversification can only reduce revenue volatility if the revenues collected from the unstable energy and corporate tax bases are significantly reduced as a proportion of total revenues. This would entail a significant increase in taxes from other sources and, thus, in the overall tax burden, or a significant decrease in the revenues collected from royalties and corporate taxes.

Revenue volatility and stabilization from exchange rate movements

Government expenditures (the wages of provincial government workers, for example) are mostly denominated in Canadian dollars, so the volatility of revenues in Canadian dollars is what matters to the government. The volatility of energy-related revenues in Canadian dollars depends on both the volatility of US dollar denominated energy prices and the volatility of the exchange rate. Given this link between exchange rate movements and revenue volatility, in order to understand revenue volatility, it is necessary to determine how exchange rate volatility affects the volatility of government revenues.

One way to assess the impact of the exchange rate on government revenues is to note that, since energy prices are denominated in US dollars, the Alberta government's royalty stream is similar to the returns from an investment in a US dollar denominated asset. For an investor in a foreign currency denominated asset, Campbell, Medeiros, and Viceira (2010) show that optimal investment risk management depends on the extent to which the exchange rate and the value of the foreign asset are correlated. As an example, they observe that the Canadian dollar tends to appreciate relative to the US dollar when the US stock market rises in value. This movement in the Canadian dollar when US equity prices change acts to smooth Canadian dollar denominated returns from US equity investments. Thus, there is less need for a Canadian investor holding US assets to hedge against currency risk. Indeed, full currency hedging would *increase* a Canadian investor's portfolio risk by eliminating the smoothing function of the exchange rate.

As in the US equity example of Campbell, Medeiros, and Viceira (2010), if the Canadian dollar rises (falls) in value with increases (decreases) in the US dollar price of oil, movements in the exchange rate would stabilize the Canadian dollar value of oil revenues. Evidence suggests that there exists this type of positive relationship between the Canadian dollar and energy prices, so the exchange rate works as a natural hedge with respect to oil price movements (Frankel 2010).[23] Bayoumi and Mühleisen (2006) find that the value of the Canadian dollar rises with energy prices and, commensurately, Taylor (2008) and Lipsky (2008) note that the value of the US dollar is negatively correlated with the oil price. Chen and Rogoff (2003) find positive co-variation between the exchange rate and the price of export commodities, such as oil, using data for Canada, Australia and

New Zealand, as do Chen, Rogoff, and Rossi (2008) who consider the same three countries plus Chile and South Africa. Further, evidence of such "commodity currencies" is presented by Cashin, Céspedes, and Sahay (2004) using a sample of 58 countries, including five industrial countries (Australia, Canada, Iceland, Norway, and New Zealand).

Another reason to expect the Canadian dollar to appreciate following a rise in the price of oil is the Bank of Canada's inflation targeting policy. Ragan (2005) argues that inflation targeting means that the Bank will tighten monetary policy following a rise in commodity prices, causing an appreciation of the Canadian dollar. As Ragan notes, in this way inflation targeting will tend to accentuate the positive oil price–Canadian dollar correlation, thus increasing the smoothing effect of exchange rate movements on Canadian dollar denominated energy revenues.[24]

The simple correlation coefficients reported in Table 10.6, which imply that a rise in energy prices leads to an appreciation of the Canadian dollar (a fall in the Canadian dollar price of a US dollar), are consistent with the evidence presented in the studies cited above. Therefore, movements in the Canadian dollar act to smooth movements in Canadian dollar denominated energy revenues. This is confirmed by the coefficients of variation presented in Table 10.2. These show that the real Canadian dollar prices of oil and natural gas are less variable than the US dollar prices (the coefficients of variation in Canadian dollars are smaller than those for the US dollar prices). This difference is greater for the price of oil, where the coefficient of variation for the real price of oil in US dollars is 46.9, while it is only 39.4 for the Canadian dollar price, a 16% difference.[25]

Although the coefficients of variation given in Table 10.2 indicate that exchange rate movements have reduced Canadian dollar oil and gas price volatility, the volatility of both prices in Canadian dollars is still quite high. Thus, the role of exchange rate movements in reducing revenue volatility is relatively small. Since the exchange rate moves for many reasons other than changes in energy prices, movements in the exchange rate only partly offset movements in US dollar denominated energy prices. This is confirmed by the estimates in Bayoumi and Mühleisen

(2006), obtained using quarterly data for the period 1972–2005, which indicate that a 1% increase in energy prices leads only to a contemporaneous 0.37% increase in the value of the Canadian dollar relative to the US dollar. In other words, the exchange rate does not move by enough to completely counteract the effect of US dollar denominated energy price movements on Canadian dollar denominated prices. This suggests that other methods of hedging may be necessary if revenue volatility is to be reduced.[26]

Smoothing with futures and options

Many different types of financial market instruments exist to reduce revenue uncertainty and volatility. Of these, the two most commonly used involve pre-selling commodities in futures markets and the purchase of put options—assets that give the option, but not the obligation, to sell a commodity at a stated price during a fixed period of time.[27] For example, in late 1990 and early 1991, the Mexican government purchased put options with a strike price of US$17 per barrel in order to protect its oil-related revenues from a price decline (Larson and Varangis 1996). Similarly, Texas set up a hedging program that operated on a regular basis from 1992 to 2000 to ensure that declines in oil prices did not lead to an overall budget deficit for the two-year duration of each budget period (Swidler, Buttimer, and Shaw 1999).

Futures markets
In Alberta, conventional crude oil royalties are paid in-kind.[28] By contracting to sell this oil at a fixed price on the date in the future when the in-kind royalty will be paid, it is possible to eliminate uncertainty with respect to the revenues that will be received from these royalty payments. For example, the revenues from the in-kind royalty payments to be received during a fiscal year could be made certain by selling 12 futures contracts at the beginning of the fiscal year equal to the quantities of oil that are expected to be delivered in each month of the year.

While futures markets can reduce revenue uncertainty, these markets have several shortcomings. The majority of transactions in futures markets involve relatively short-term contracts (one or two months), but to have a significant impact on uncertainty and the volatility of revenues, the government would need to enter into futures contracts that cover at least the current budget year. Futures markets may not be very liquid at longer maturities, which may make the sale of these contracts more difficult and more costly (Larson, Varangis, and Yabuki 1998; Domanski and Heath 2007; Borensztein, Jeanne, and Sandri 2009). Further, the price locked in by futures contracts will vary from year to year since the contracts are sold in different years. Thus, while futures contracts can make revenues more certain over short periods, they cannot *eliminate* the volatility of revenues over the long term. Nevertheless, the use of futures contracts may still *reduce* the level of volatility since futures prices appear to be less volatile than spot prices.[29]

A second problem is that exchange traded oil futures contracts are denominated in US dollars, so the sale of a futures contract would fix revenues in US dollars. To eliminate the uncertainty associated with the Canadian dollar value of these contracts, it would be necessary to enter a second contract to sell US dollars forward, thereby adding to hedging costs.

Futures contracts involve standardized commodities, such as WTI petroleum, but Alberta's oil is heavier and generally sells for less, with the differential between the WTI price and the price of Alberta oil varying over time.[30] This means that there is risk that the spread between the price of the WTI oil specified in the contract and the price of the oil produced in Alberta and delivered in-kind will change during the life of the contract, causing revenues to be different than expected.

A major shortcoming of the use of futures contracts to reduce Alberta government revenue volatility is that the sale of futures contracts is only practical for royalties that are received in-kind, a small part of total royalty revenues (Table 10.5).[31] The elimination of all variability in royalties from in-kind conventional oil payments would have little impact on overall royalty variability since conventional oil accounted for only 12.8% of total non-renewable resource revenues in 2005–2009, about 4% of total own-source revenues (Table 10.5).

The direct transactions cost associated with selling futures contracts is relatively small—Alaska (2002) estimates these costs to be about US$0.10 per barrel. On the other hand, it may be costly to allocate funds to the upfront margin payments required by the futures exchange. Daniel (2001) estimates that the required margins associated with futures sales are 5% to 10% of the value of the contract, so the cost in terms of the assets that must be committed to these margin payments could be substantial. Further, these payments can change significantly at short notice. Alaska (2002) estimates that a $5 per barrel rise in the oil price would have required it to increase its margin payment by US$950 million. Use of futures contracts by the Alberta government to reduce revenue volatility would require the government to commit a quantity of assets to margin payments and have sufficient liquid assets available to cover changes in the margin requirement.

Options markets

Another shortcoming of futures markets as a method to smooth revenues is that, while futures contracts remove downside price risk, they also eliminate the potential benefit of an energy price increase. Considerable public dissatisfaction is likely to ensue if revenues do not rise when energy prices rise. For this reason, a jurisdiction may prefer to purchase put option contracts—contracts which provide insurance against price declines by essentially giving the holder of the contract the *option*, but not the *obligation*, to sell a commodity at a stated price if the price falls below this "strike price." With this type of option, a government obtains the benefit of a price rise, if commodity prices rise rather than fall, but is protected against a price fall. Using data for 1990–2000, Daniel (2001) simulated a put option strategy and found that it raised the mean return (by eliminating two large price falls) and reduced volatility.

One of the benefits of options is that they do not restrict hedging to in-kind commodities only. For example, given the very high correlation between royalty revenues and energy prices, the Alberta government could insure itself against a royalty decline by purchasing an option to sell oil at a fixed price (the strike price) for a fixed period of time. If the price of oil fell, causing royalty payments to fall, the government would be able to counterbalance the fall in royalty revenues with the profits it would make by exercising the option (as long as the oil price fell below the strike price). The purchase of the put options would insure the government against a fall in its royalty revenues to the extent that oil prices and royalty revenues are correlated.

A number of oil exporting jurisdictions—Ecuador, Mexico, and Texas, for example—have used option contracts. In 2008, with the price of oil over US$100, Mexico hedged all of its oil sales for 2009 through the purchase of put options with a strike price of US$70 (Blas 2009). In December 2009, Mexico announced that it had hedged 230 million barrels of oil, a large proportion of its 2010 oil production, at a strike price of $57.[32] Despite the potential benefits of hedging, it is not common for energy exporting countries to hedge (Blas 2009; Borensztein, Jeanne, and Sandri 2009). Texas implemented a hedging program from 1992 to 2000, but other states—Alaska, New Mexico, Oklahoma, and Louisiana—have examined the costs and benefits of hedging and decided not to proceed in this direction. One reason jurisdictions have hesitated to use options markets to reduce the volatility of revenues may be political. Frankel (2010), Caballero and Cowan (2007), and Daniel (2001) note that the political costs of hedging can outweigh the benefits. In the case of a fall in the spot price, any financial gains from a hedging program may be seen as speculative returns. Further, if a government had not hedged, it would be easy to blame the international oil market for any budgetary problems. On the other hand, if the spot price remains above the strike price for the duration of the contract, the jurisdiction that purchased the put option would not reap an explicit benefit but would still bear the cost of purchasing the option. While this is a characteristic of every insurance contract, it may be difficult to explain to the public why the government committed significant resources to the purchase of options contracts that were worthless *ex post* (Caballero and Cowan 2007).[33] In Ecuador, this situation led to allegations of "corruption" (Daniel 2001). The asymmetric nature of the political risk associated with the purchase of options may be one reason why politicians have been very hesitant to commit resources to options programs.

Another major consideration with the use of put options to insure against a revenue fall is that these options are generally expensive. Using data for March 2, 2010, when the WTI spot price was US$80.53, a put option that expired in March 2011 with a strike price of US$80.5 would have cost $8.48 per barrel, making the cost of insuring $1 billion of oil approximately $105 million.[34] Given this price, the purchaser of the option would not receive any net benefit unless the spot price fell below US$72.02. Hedging with natural gas put options is even more expensive (most likely because the market is thinner). The cost of insuring $1 billion of gas for a year, with an at-the-money strike price was approximately US$165 million. If the price of the commodity remains above the strike price, the premium would be lost and government expenditures would have increased by the cost of the option. Using simulations, Swidler, Buttimer, and Shaw (1999) show that the purchase of put options leads to more frequent deficits than without hedging because the cost of the options increases expenditures. On the other hand, while deficits are more frequent, they are not as large as those that occur without hedging.

To hedge all its oil sales in 2009, Mexico paid $1.5 billion for put options with a strike price of $70 when the spot price was over $100 (Blas 2009).[35] In the end, Mexico netted $5 billion from this strategy (McCallion 2009), but if prices had not fallen below $70, the Mexican government would have spent an extra $1.5 billion without an explicit payoff. Simulations for the case of Texas in Swidler, Buttimer, and Shaw (1999) show that the ex post *net* insurance premium paid by Texas was equal, on average, to about 2.6% of oil revenues.[36] Alaska (2002) estimates that a three-year put option with a strike price $1 below the three-year futures price would have cost US$3 per barrel, or 11% of the spot price at the time (US$26). Mexico's 2010 hedge of 230 million barrels cost US$1.2 billion, a little over US$5 per barrel. When the hedge was announced in late 2009, the strike price of $57 was approximately $20 less than spot and futures prices.[37] In other words, Mexico paid US$5 per barrel to hedge for a relatively short period—a year—with a strike price far out-of-the-money. Given these costs, there may be a tendency to use hedging strategies only if spot prices appear to be far out of line. However, it is difficult to determine when prices are out of line and how long they will remain so, making this strategy speculative.

The cost of a put option depends on the time to expiration of the contract (shorter are cheaper), the extent to which the option is out-of-the-money (more out-of-the-money are cheaper) and the volatility of the price of the underlying commodity (less volatile are cheaper). One way to reduce the cost of the hedge is to purchase a shorter maturity option or one with a lower strike price. A three-month at-the-money put option is about half the price of a one-year option, while a one-year option that is 2.5% out-of-the-money is about 10% cheaper than an at-the-money option.[38] Of course, the level of insurance provided by the option would then be lower.

Another method of reducing the upfront cost of hedging is to *sell* an option to *buy* oil at a specific price (a call option) at the same time as the option to *sell* (the put option) is *purchased* (creating a no cost collar). The premium received for the option to buy would offset the premium paid for the option to sell. The problem with this procedure is that it puts an upper bound on the earnings from a price increase, and so eliminates some of the upside potential. Further, while it is costly, but riskless, to purchase any quantity of options to sell oil, selling call options (options to buy) in quantities that are greater than the quantity of in-kind oil royalty payments is risky. If the price of oil rises above the strike price, the government would be liable for a payment to the holders of the call options equal to the difference between the spot price and the strike price. If royalty payments have not also risen one-for-one with the price of oil, the obligation associated with the call option would exceed the royalty revenue increase, implying a net cost. Finally, unlike the purchase of a put option, the sale of a call would require the commitment of government resources to a margin payment.

There are several other shortcomings with the use of options as a method of smoothing revenues, most of which are similar to the shortcomings of futures contracts. Put options will only insure against a fall in prices during the length of the contract. Contract lengths are not indefinite, so full insurance cannot be obtained. Nevertheless, hedging may provide the government with time during which to plan adjustment. The purchase of longer contracts is likely to be more expensive as most of the liquidity in the options market is at very short horizons. Borensztein, Jeanne, and Sandri (2009) note that on NYMEX most hedging is for maturities of less than three months and the risk premium becomes very large for longer maturities.[39] It is possible to buy longer-term options in the over-the-counter market, but these contracts are illiquid and involve greater counterparty risk than options traded on an exchange. If a government follows a hedging program, particularly one using over-the-counter instruments, the government must possess sufficient expertise to run the hedging program, understand the risks, and monitor the activities of the hedging unit.[40] Hedging operations are often quite complex and Daniel (2001) argues that, without adequate institutional capacity, the use of these contracts can lead to less transparency and foster poor governance.

Revenue Volatility with a Savings Fund

The analysis above has made clear that revenue volatility in Alberta is driven by royalty volatility. On average over the 1981–2007 period, the magnitude and volatility of real per capita own-source revenues excluding royalties have been similar in Alberta, Saskatchewan, British Columbia, and Ontario. In the past, Alberta governments have created "saving," "stabilization," and "endowment" funds. However, the objective of these funds has not been the reduction of revenue volatility *per se*, and, in addition, there has been considerable discretion involved in the allocation of revenue into and out of these funds (Busby 2008).

It is straightforward to show that a savings fund could greatly reduce government revenue volatility. One form of this type of fund would, during each year, involve the commitment of a certain type or percentage of *current* revenues to the fund along with the withdrawal of a fixed percentage of the *total* assets or *long-term* earnings from the fund (or both). This type of savings fund would reduce revenue volatility because the revenue paid out by the fund in a particular year would be based on a *weighted average* of contributions from previous years. The ability of a savings fund to reduce volatility would be greater if most or all of the most volatile components of revenues (e.g., royalties) were deposited in the fund each year, leaving only the less volatile components of revenues, as well as withdrawals from the fund, to finance current spending. A savings fund would also reduce revenue uncertainty as current and future revenues would depend on past contributions to the fund. The government would, therefore, have more information on the future path of this component of revenues and could use this information to plan expenditures.

Using data on actual revenues over the past 30 years, a simple example shows the extent to which revenue smoothing with a savings fund can reduce revenue volatility.[41] Suppose the government of Alberta had committed 75% of royalty revenues to a savings fund from which each year it withdrew the real earnings of the fund (based on the average real interest rate over the previous 20 years) plus 5% of the total assets in the fund.[42] Since real interest rates vary considerably, greater smoothing is achieved with the use of the long-term average return. Under this scheme, average per capita own-source revenues available to the government (that is, net of contributions to and withdrawals from the savings fund) would have been only 4.5% lower than actual average real per capita own-source revenues for the 1981–2007 period. Further, real per capita own-source revenues, net of contributions to and withdrawals from the savings fund, would have still been 25% higher than the average for Saskatchewan, British Columbia, and Ontario. In addition, the total assets in the fund would have been close to $75 billion by 2007, and the coefficient of variation of own-source revenues (net of contributions to and withdrawals from the fund) would have fallen from 15.4 to just under 6, a decline in the volatility of own-source revenues of over 60%. As shown in Table 10.7, this coefficient of variation would have been lower than the coefficients of variation of British Columbia, Saskatchewan, and Ontario. Given this significant decline in revenue volatility, and the considerable costs associated with the rapid expansion and contraction of government programs, the budget revenue stabilization benefits of the fund could easily outweigh the 4.5% fall in available real per capita own-source revenues even without considering the $75 billion that would have been accumulated in the fund by 2007.

The specific example described above shows how a savings fund could significantly reduce the volatility of revenues. It does this in three ways. First, the most volatile component of revenues, royalties, are deposited in the fund. Second, revenue volatility is reduced through the use of a long-term *average* real interest rate (since returns vary considerably from year to year). Third, withdrawals each year are a *constant* fraction of the fund's stock of assets. This type of fund is not a stabilization fund or a "rainy day" fund, as extra funds are not withdrawn when there is a negative disturbance to revenues. It is a savings fund that can smooth revenues by weakening the link between current royalties and current budgetary revenues. A major advantage of a savings fund over a stabilization fund is that it does not require the government to identify the conditions under which contributions and withdrawals should be made. In addition, a savings fund may facilitate a process whereby government takes a long-term view of budgeting. Finally, the fund could be designed to be transparent and easily understood by the public.

The principal problem with the creation of a savings fund of this type is that, as the fund grows in size, pressure may mount for taxes to be cut or the proportion of assets withdrawn from the fund to be increased, particularly in times when revenues from other sources have fallen. As a consequence, it may be difficult to maintain contributions to the fund and prevent ad hoc withdrawals.[43]

CONCLUSION

Volatile revenues may lead to the inefficient provision of government services, stop-go procyclical fiscal policies, and, potentially, slower growth. Alberta's revenues are volatile relative to those of other provinces. This volatility is associated principally with the volatility of energy sector royalties. Own-source revenues less royalties are no more volatile than the corresponding revenues of other provinces. Further, the magnitude of Alberta's non-royalty own-source revenues is of similar size to those of other provinces.

The principal problem with revenue volatility is that it usually leads to volatile government expenditures. Revenue volatility would be much less of a problem if governments could maintain stable spending during revenue booms and busts. However, it is difficult to forecast the extent to which revenues are permanent when they depend heavily on energy price movements, and this makes it difficult to choose the correct balanced path for expenditures. History also shows that, across numerous countries and time periods, it is politically very difficult to control spending during revenue expansions, even if these are likely to be temporary.

Given the large contribution of the volatile royalty component to total government revenues, there are few practical methods available to stabilize revenues. The hedging of royalty revenues using futures and options markets is costly, cannot remove all volatility or uncertainty, and, given the experience of other jurisdictions, may have significant political risk.

On average, although not in every subperiod, movements in the exchange rate have tended to reduce the volatility of own-source revenues. While this smoothing effect has likely been increased by the Bank of Canada's policy of inflation targeting, exchange rate movements still act as only a partial hedge against energy price movements.

Tax base diversification, through the introduction of a sales tax, for example, is likely to have only a minor effect on revenue volatility. This follows because the more stable alternative tax bases have already been fully exploited or the maximum revenues that could be obtained from these tax bases are not likely to be large enough to have an appreciable effect on overall revenue volatility. The only way tax base diversification could have a large impact on revenue volatility is if there is a significant relative increase in taxes on non-energy-related tax bases, but this would imply a rise in the overall tax burden or a very large decrease in the revenues collected from royalties and corporate taxes.

The most promising approach to address revenue volatility is the creation of a savings fund into which the most volatile components of revenues are deposited. If withdrawals from the fund are a fixed proportion of the fund's total assets and are tied to the long-term earnings of the fund, there is a considerable reduction in the volatility of government budgetary revenues (net of contributions to and withdrawals from the fund). A fund of this type would also provide long-term revenue predictability.

Notes

1. The magnitude of the welfare loss associated with consumption volatility is the subject of much debate. For example, Borensztein, Jeanne, and Sandri (2009) suggest that the magnitude of the loss from this type of volatility may not be that large, while Morduch (1995) argues that it can be quite large.

2. These costs may explain why countries with highly volatile terms of trade, and, in particular, oil producers, tend to have slower growth rates (Blattman, Hwang, and Williamson 2007; van der Ploeg and Poelhekke 2009; Frankel 2010).

3. Using data for 1981 to 2007, the log of real per capita own-source revenues is found to be a significant determinant of the ratio of the government current expenditure price index to the CPI for both Alberta and British Columbia (although not for Saskatchewan or Ontario). This is another indication that revenue growth may increase the prices of government purchased goods.

4. Sources and definitions for the data used in the text, figures, and tables are given in the Data Appendix at the end of this chapter.

5. Revenue volatility depends on both movements in tax bases and changes in tax rates. Due to difficulties with obtaining data on different tax rates through time, for the most part, the analysis focuses on revenue volatility and does not distinguish whether this volatility is due to tax base or tax rate volatility.

6. To measure the volatility of revenues, the coefficient of variation is calculated using the following procedure. The natural log of revenues is regressed on a trend; the predicted values in levels are found by taking the exponential of the predicted values from this regression; a series of residuals is calculated by subtracting the predicted values in levels from the corresponding observation in the revenues data; and the coefficient

of variation is calculated as the ratio (multiplied by 100) of the standard deviation of these residuals to the average value of revenues. This method is similar to that used in Carroll (2009).

7. This means that the standard deviation is measured in the same units as revenues. For example, if the coefficient of variation is 10, and the average value of revenues is $1,000, the coefficient of variation implies that a one standard deviation band around the average ranges from $900 to $1,100. One shortcoming of this method is that two variables with the same coefficient of variation can represent one standard deviation bands that differ significantly in dollar terms if their mean values differ. Boresztein et al. (2009) use an alternative measure of volatility—the standard deviation of the residuals from a regression of the natural log of revenues on a trend. This is easier to compute and easier to compare across variables of different magnitudes because the average level and units of measurement are irrelevant. However, since this measure is the standard deviation of a log, it is difficult to relate to the units (dollars) in which revenues are measured. Nevertheless, here the two methods generate the same conclusions and relative comparisons.

8. Total real per capita revenues include transfers from other levels of government. Since the coefficients of variation are smaller for total revenues, relative to those for own-source revenues, federal transfers have, on average over the 1981–2007 period, reduced the volatility of revenues (although this has not been the case in every subperiod).

9. In real per capita dollar terms, the difference in volatility is even larger since Alberta's own-source revenues are at least 20% higher, on average, than the revenues of the other provinces. For example, the dollar equivalent of the one standard deviation band around average real per capita own-source revenues for Alberta is $2,188, while it is only $906 for British Columbia.

10. For royalty payments, we use Statistics Canada data on "royalties." These data include Crown lease payments but are distinct from the Statistics Canada data on "miscellaneous taxes on natural resources."

11. This level of variability is not unique to Alberta. Borensztein, Jeanne, and Sandri (2009) find that the standard deviation of de-trended commodity exports for 21 major petroleum exporters is 0.34, implying export revenue volatility of similar magnitude to the variability of Alberta's royalty revenues.

12. This comparison does not account for the different approaches used to levy education taxes in the four provinces.

13. The data used in this study are consistent with real oil and natural gas prices following a random walk. A regression of the log of the real Canadian dollar WTI petroleum price on its lag using data for 1982–2008 yields a coefficient of 0.8, while a similar regression for the real Canadian dollar natural gas price yields a coefficient on the lag of 0.91. Both coefficients are not significantly different from one, so a random walk with drift cannot be rejected.

14. Hamilton (2008) estimates that, with an oil price in 2008Q1 of US$115, the 95% confidence interval for 2008Q2 was $85–$156. However, as noted by Hamilton (2008), "To predict the price of oil one quarter, one year, or one decade ahead, it is not at all naive to offer as a forecast whatever the price currently happens to be." Engel and Valdes (2000) test a large number of models of oil price forecasts and find that a simple random walk, where the forecast of the future price is the current price, performs best.

15. These first two points are made by Arrau and Claessens (1992) in their study of methods of revenue stabilization for commodity exporters.

16. In a *Globe and Mail* column, DeCloet (2010) states that a provincial sales tax in Alberta would be "an economically-sensible idea."

17. US states also rely on the sales tax to a much greater extent than does Alberta. Median state sales tax revenue accounts for about 30% of total state revenues (Felix 2008).

18. To make the level of revenues similar in the two cases, British Columbia's actual real per capita retail sales tax revenues were used to replace Alberta's small real per capita retail sales tax revenues as well as its corporate tax revenues. Alberta's real per capita own-source revenues averaged $7,419 over the 1981–2007 period for the case incorporating the BC sales tax revenues as opposed to the actual value of $7,105.

19. If we regress the growth rate of real per capita wages and salaries and other labour income on the growth rate of the real Canadian dollar price of natural gas as well as the natural logs of the lagged values of wages and the natural gas price, the two natural gas price variables are insignificant and the R^2 is only 0.16. A similar result is found for real per capita personal income. In contrast, if a comparable equation is estimated with real per capita corporate profits as the dependent variable, the natural gas price variables are both significant and the R^2 is 0.51.

20. In 1981–1985, revenues from interest and other investment income accounted for 22.4% of own-source revenues, but this share had fallen to only 9.8%, on average, during 2003–2007.

21. Ontario collects approximately $300 per capita in payroll taxes (in 2002 constant dollars).

22. During 2007, in real per capita terms, Alberta collected $434 in gaming profits (in 2002 constant dollars) while British Columbia, Saskatchewan, and Ontario collected $223, $280, and $105, respectively.

23. The existence of this type of relationship seems reasonable since a rise in world demand for a major commodity export raises demand for the currency of the exporting country, causing the currency to appreciate in value.

24. An alternative monetary policy strategy, proposed by Frankel (2005), is for oil exporters to target the export price index (rather than CPI inflation). This policy would also cause a currency appreciation following an oil price rise.

25. The coefficient of variation for natural gas falls by only 9%. This smaller effect is not unexpected as the correlation between the

Canadian dollar and natural gas prices tends to be smaller than that between the dollar and oil prices.

26. The role of the exchange rate as a natural hedge appears to be misunderstood. Governments often point out that an appreciation of the Canadian dollar reduces Canadian dollar revenues, but rarely acknowledge the positive contribution to the smoothing of Canadian dollar denominated revenues from a depreciation of the currency when energy prices fall.

27. There are many other types of hedging contracts and hedging methods. One strategy is to invest in assets that have returns that are negatively correlated with energy prices. Caballero and Cowan (2007) suggest using options and futures markets to do this by shorting instruments such as the VIX or other assets whose returns are correlated with the demand for oil.

28. Alberta "accepts delivery of the Crown's royalty share of crude oil and sells it at current market value. Unlike other energy commodities, conventional crude oil royalties are paid with 'in-kind' product" (Alberta, Department of Energy, *Annual Report 2007–08*, 7).

29. Using data for 1990–2001, Daniel (2001) compares a strategy that would involve selling oil each month at the 12-month ahead futures price to a strategy that involves selling the same oil at the spot price when it is received in 12 months. He finds that the futures price is much less volatile than the spot price, but would also have resulted in a slightly lower average price over the sample. Domanski and Heath (2007) also find that futures energy prices may be less volatile than spot prices, at least for futures contracts that are far enough in the future, generally at least 12 months.

30. From 2004 to 2008, Alberta non-heavy oil sold in a range of 86% to 100% of the WTI price, while the range for heavy oil was 38% to 83% (http://www.energy.alberta.ca/1524.asp).

31. It is possible to hedge royalty payments, other than those paid in-kind, using futures contracts since movements in the price of oil and total royalty revenues are highly correlated. However, selling a quantity of futures contracts greater than the quantity of in-kind royalties would expose the province to a potentially large liability. For example, suppose the province sold a greater number of petroleum futures contracts than the quantity of its in-kind royalty payments and the price of petroleum rose relative to the price stipulated in the futures contracts. The province would then be responsible for making up the difference between the spot price and the contracted futures price without necessarily having a counterbalancing rise in its own revenues since energy prices and royalty revenues, although highly correlated, do not necessarily move one-for-one.

32. Mexico only appears to hedge periodically. For example, it did not hedge in 1998 when prices also fell.

33. A report by Alaska's revenue department warned, "If a program succeeded, it is unlikely the policy makers who took the initiative to create the program would be rewarded with public congratulations...."

On the other hand, if the state lost significant sums...the conventional wisdom is that public criticism would be harsh" (quoted in Blas 2009).

34. The purchase of the same quantity of contracts with a strike price of $78.50, $2 below the spot price, would have cost US$95 million. These calculations are based on NYMEX prior settlement prices as there were no actual trades.

35. The strike price of $70 was far below the spot price at the time, which was over $100. A minimum estimate of the per-barrel cost of this hedge is $1.60. This estimate assumes Mexico was producing 2.5 million barrels per day and that the options covered Mexico's entire production for the year.

36. Lower spot prices appear to be associated with much lower put option prices. Verleger (1993) gives the cost of Mexico's 1990–91 purchase of put options with a strike price of $17 as approximately $0.40 per barrel when spot prices were approximately $30. Lu and Neftci (2008) provide lower cost estimates for hedging using simulations (rather than actual market prices). They find that the cost of an at-the-money put option on oil was 4.1% for a one-year contract and 4.8% for three years. A 20% out of the money option on oil would cost 0.3% for a one-year contract and 1% for a three-year contract. That is, buying a three-year 20% out-of-the-money option for insuring an underlying portfolio of US$500 million of oil would cost $5 million.

37. This strike price is not that far below the US$61.69 WTI average price for 2009. It may have been less speculative to sell futures contracts for US$77, the reigning futures price in December 2009, but this would have eliminated the up-side potential.

38. These comparisons use NYMEX data from March 2, 2010.

39. It has been suggested that short-term contracts can simply be rolled over to facilitate longer maturity hedging (Verleger 1993; Borensztein, Jeanne, and Sandri 2009), but there is some debate about the risk associated with this procedure (Powell 1989; Larson and Varangis 1996).

40. As noted by Larson and Varangis, the "cases of Codelco (a copper producer in Chile), MG Corp. (a unit of Germany's Metallgesellschaft AG), Procter and Gamble Co., Orange County in California, Sumitomo, and Barings Bank have shown that the lack of internal controls and systems to monitor the exposure from using derivative markets can result in very serious losses" (1996, 28).

41. This example is intended for the purposes of illustration and does not adjust for the savings that were actually undertaken by the Alberta government during the sample period, such as saving through the Alberta Heritage Savings Trust Fund.

42. Frankel (2010) discusses funds with a similar cap on withdrawals.

43. Another budgeting method that has been used to reduce the risk of a revenue shortfall and the need to cut expenditures is to underestimate revenues. Tying expenditures to a downward-biased revenue forecast would not change the degree of revenue volatility, but would provide a

buffer against an unexpected fall in revenue. This type of policy could also be used as a backdoor method of creating a "rainy day" fund, if the "unexpected" surpluses are saved, but it is likely to be difficult to create a sizable fund in this way. A policy of this type also has two other shortcomings. First, the ex post budget surpluses that result on average can be easily identified and may induce demands for increased spending. Second, this type of policy will quickly make budget forecasts non-credible and could lead to a political backlash and calls for tax reductions, which would defeat the purpose of the buffer.

References

Afonso, Antonio, and Davide Furceri. 2008. "Government Size, Composition, Volatility and Economic Growth." ECB Working Paper 849, January.

Alaska. 2002. "Hedging Oil Revenue Summary." Alaska Department of Revenue, 21 October.

Arrau, Patricio, and Stijm Claessens. 1992. "Commodity Stabilization Funds." World Bank, International Economics Department Working Paper 835.

Ball, Laurence M. 2009. "Policy Responses to Exchange-Rate Movements." NBER Working Paper 15173. July.

Barnett, Steven, and Rolando Ossowski. 2002. "Operational Aspects of Fiscal Policy in Oil-Producing Countries." IMF Working Paper WP/02/177, October.

Bayoumi, Tamim, and Martin Mühleisen. 2006. "Energy, the Exchange Rate, and the Economy: Macroeconomic Benefits of Canada's Oil Sands Production." IMF Working Paper WP/06/70, March.

Bems, Rudolfs, and Irineu de Carvalho Filho. 2009. "Current Account and Precautionary Savings for Exporters of Exhaustible Resources." IMF Working Paper WP/09/33, February.

Blas, Javier. 2009. "Mexico's Big Gamble Pays Off," Financial Times, FT.com, 7 September.

Blattman, Christopher, Jason Hwang, and Jeffrey G. Williamson. 2007. "Winners and Losers in the Commodity Lottery: The Impact of Terms of Trade Growth and Volatility in the Periphery 1870–1939." Journal of Development Economics 82: 156–79.

Borensztein, Eduardo, Olivier Jeanne, and Damiano Sandri. 2009. "Macro-Hedging for Commodity Exporters." NBER Working Paper 15452, October.

Busby, Colin. 2008. "After the Oil Rush: A Blueprint for Alberta's Long-Term Happiness." E-brief, C.D. Howe Institute.

Caballero, Ricardo J., and Kevin Cowan. 2007. "Financial Integration without the Volatility," Massachusetts Institute of Technology, Department of Economics, Working Paper 08-04.

Campbell, John Y., Karine Serfaty-de Medeiros, and Luis M. Viceira. 2010. "Global Currency Hedging." *Journal of Finance* 65 (1): 87–121.

Carroll, Deborah A. 2009. "Diversifying Municipal Government Revenue Structures: Fiscal Illusion or Instability?" *Public Budgeting and Finance* 29 (1): 27–48.

Cashin, Paul, Luis F. Céspedes, and Ratna Sahay. 2004. "Commodity Currencies and the Real Exchange Rate." *Journal of Development Economics* 75: 239–68.

Chen, Yu-chin, and Kenneth Rogoff. 2003. "Commodity Currencies." *Journal of International Economics* 60: 133–60.

Chen, Yu-Chin, Kenneth Rogoff, and Barbara Rossi. 2008. "Can Exchange Rates Forecast Commodity Prices?" NBER Working Paper 13901, March.

Daniel, James A. 2001. "Hedging Government Oil Price Risk." IMF Working Paper WP/01/185, November.

DeCloet, Derek. 2010. "Truth, Lies and Alberta's Royalty Backtrack." *Globe and Mail*, 13 March.

Devlin, Julia, and Michael Lewin. 2004. "Managing Oil Booms and Busts in Developing Countries." Draft chapter for *Managing Volatility and Crises: A Practitioner's Guide*, March, World Bank.

Domanski, Dietrich, and Alexandra Heath. 2007. "Financial Investors and Commodity Markets." *BIS Quarterly Review* March, 53–67.

Engel, Eduardo, and Rodrigo Valdes. 2000. "Optimal Fiscal Strategy for Oil Exporting Countries." IMF Working Paper WP/00/118, June.

Felix, R. Alison. 2008. "The Growth and Volatility of State Tax Revenue Sources in the Tenth District." *Federal Reserve Bank of Kansas City Economic Review*, Third Quarter, 63–88.

Frankel, Jeffrey. 2005. "Peg the Export Price Index: A Proposed Monetary Regime for Small Countries." *Journal of Policy Modeling* 27: 495–508.

———. 2010. "The Natural Resource Curse: A Survey." Kennedy School Faculty Research Working Paper 10-005, Harvard University, February.

Hamilton, James D. 2008. "Understanding Crude Oil Prices." NBER Working Paper 14492, November.

Larson, Don, and Panos Varangis. 1996. "Dealing with Commodity Price Uncertainty." World Bank Policy Research Working Paper 1667, International Economics Department, Commodity Policy and Analysis Unit, October.

Larson, Don, Panos Varangis, and Nanae Yabuki. 1998. "Commodity Risk Management and Development." World Bank Policy Research Working Paper 1963, Development Research Group, August.

Lipsky, John P. 2008. "Commodity Prices and Global Inflation." Remarks by John Lipsky, First Deputy Managing Director, International Monetary Fund at the Council on Foreign Relations, New York City, May 8.

Lu, Yinqin, and Salih Neftci. 2008. "Financial Instruments to Hedge Commodity Price Risk for Developing Countries." IMF Working Paper WP/08/6, January.

McCallion, Pauline. 2009. "Mexico Hedges Oil Price at $57 in 2010." *Energy Risk* December 9.

Medas, Paulo, and Daria Zakharova. 2009. "A Primer on Fiscal Analysis in Oil-Producing Countries." IMF Working Paper WP/09/56, March.

Morduch, Jonathan. 1995. "Income Smoothing and Consumption Smoothing." *Journal of Economic Perspectives* 9 (3): 103–14.

Powell, Andrew. 1989. "The Management of Risk in Developing Country Finance." *Oxford Review of Economic Policy* 5 (4): 69–87.

Ragan, Christopher. 2005. "The Exchange Rate and Canadian Inflation Targeting." Bank of Canada Working Paper 2005-34.

Sturm, Michael, François Gurtner, and Juan Gonzalez Alegre. 2009. "Fiscal Policy Challenges in Oil-Exporting Countries: A Review of Key Issues." European Central Bank, Occasional paper series No. 104, June.

Swidler, Steve, Richard J. Buttimer, Jr., and Ron Shaw. 1999. "Government Hedging: Motivation, Implementation, and Evaluation." *Public Budgeting and Finance* 19 (4): 75–90.

Taylor, John B. 2008. "The Way Back to Stability and Growth in the Global Economy: The Mayekawa Lecture." Paper presented at the 2008 International Conference: Frontiers in Monetary Theory and Policy, The Institute for Monetary and Economic Studies, Bank of Japan, May 28.

van der Ploeg, Frederick, and Steven Poelhekke. 2009. "Volatility and the Natural Resource Curse." *Oxford Economic Papers* 61 (4): 727–60.

Verleger, Philip K. 1993. *Adjusting to Volatile Energy Prices*. Washington, DC: Institute for International Economics.

Data Appendix

All government revenue data are from the Statistics Canada CANSIM database, tables 3840004, 3840007, and 3840008. These are based on Provincial Economic Accounts. We chose to use Provincial Economic Accounts data rather than Statistics Canada's Financial Management System (FMS) data because the Provincial Economic Accounts begin in 1981, rather than 1988, and disaggregate royalty revenues from interest and other investment income revenues, which the FMS data do not do.

Data are converted to per capita terms using Statistics Canada population estimates for Alberta (V469503), British Columbia (V469818), Saskatchewan (V469188), and Ontario (V468558).

Values are converted to real terms using Statistics Canada price indices for net government current expenditure on goods and services for Alberta (V3840832), British Columbia (V3840036), Saskatchewan (V3840803), and Ontario (V3840745).

Tax base data for Alberta are in current dollars and are from the Statistics Canada CANSIM database:

- Wages and salaries and supplementary labour income (V687289),
- Corporation profits before taxes (V687290),
- Interest and miscellaneous investment income (V687291),
- Personal expenditures on consumer goods (V687648),
- Final domestic demand (V687680),

- Personal income (V691711).

Average annual exchange rate data (Canadian dollars per US dollar) are from the International Monetary Fund's International Financial Statistics database (identifier: 156. .RF.ZF...).

The West Texas Intermediate (WTI) petroleum price in US dollars is the period average from the International Monetary Fund's International Financial Statistics database (identifier: 11176AAZZFM17).

The Alberta natural gas price data were downloaded from the website of the Canadian Association of Petroleum Producers on February 10, 2010 (http://www.capp.ca/LIBRARY/STATISTICS/Pages/default. aspx#41uXUn7UFhok). These are annual averages in Canadian dollars.

Data on disaggregated natural resource revenues are from various issues of the *Annual Report* of the Alberta Government's Department of Energy.

Booms, Busts, and Gambling

Can Gaming Revenues Reduce Budget Volatility?

Brad R. Humphreys and Victor A. Matheson

INTRODUCTION

Legalized gambling provides a small but important contribution to state and provincial government finances. In 2006, state
lotteries provided $16.92 billion in net revenues to US states
while amusement taxes, which cover wagering at casinos, added
another $5.54 billion, and parimutuel taxes contributed just over
$300 million to state coffers. While this amount represented
only 2.36% of total state government general revenues in the US
in 2006 (excluding revenue transfers from the federal government), the combined $22.76 billion exceeds the revenue collected
at the state level from such common public finance mechanisms
as alcohol or tobacco excise taxes, sales of hunting, fishing, or
motor vehicle licences, estate and gift taxes, and severance taxes
(US Census Bureau 2009). Gambling revenues provide a similar
percentage of provincial revenues in Canada.

While government gaming revenues are modest in a relative sense, this chapter explores the question of whether gambling revenues can serve an important function in diversifying the tax "portfolio" utilized by state and provincial governments. In other words, can gaming revenues serve to cushion government budgets during economic downturns? The chapter begins with a brief history of legal gambling in the United States and Canada followed by an overview of the pros and cons associated with the use of legal gambling as a source of government tax revenue. The chapter then turns to an analysis of whether gaming revenues can indeed serve to reduce budget volatility and concludes with recommendations to policy makers.

HISTORICAL BACKGROUND

State and provincial lotteries have been a common form of public financing for much of the history of modern government in North America. As noted by Matheson and Grote (2008), early public works such Boston's Faneuil Hall as well as several of the first universities in the United States, including Harvard and Princeton, were financed, at least in part, by lotteries. In the United States, state sponsored lotteries remained popular until the early to mid-1800s, after which time a general public backlash against gambling, coupled with concerns about corruption in gambling, led to the demise of state authorized lotteries. By 1860 only Delaware, Missouri, and Kentucky still sponsored lotteries (Dunstan 1997). A generation later, the closure of the Louisiana Lottery in 1894 ushered in a 70-year period during which no US state operated a lottery game.

While other forms of legalized gambling existed in the United States in the first half of the twentieth century, notably charitable bingo, horse racing, and casino gambling in Nevada, state sponsored lotteries returned in 1964 with the introduction of the New Hampshire Lottery. New York became the second state to offer a state lottery in 1967 followed by New Jersey in 1970. By the end of the 1970s, 14 states offered lotteries, another 17 states plus the District of Columbia added games in the 1980s, and six more states instituted lotteries in both the 1990s and 2000s, bringing the total number of states with state sponsored lotteries to 43.

Government sponsored lotteries in Canada resumed in 1968 in Montreal with the introduction of the "voluntary tax," where players could "donate" money to the city government to pay for debts associated with the 1967 World's Fair in exchange for a chance to win prizes. While this "voluntary tax" was ultimately declared illegal by the courts, Canadian federal law was changed in 1969 to allow for state sponsored lotteries, and Quebec became the first province to offer such a game in 1970. The rest of the provinces followed suit between 1974 and 1976.

Casino gaming and parimutuel betting also have a long history in the United States and Canada that parallels that of state sponsored lotteries. Racetracks and gambling houses existed early in the colonial days. The first organized horse racetrack in the colonies was constructed on Long Island in 1665, while inns and roadhouses commonly had gaming rooms. As with lotteries, concerns about corruption and morality led to a decline in legalized gambling throughout the 1800s, although westward expansion provided opportunities for gambling to flourish in the lightly regulated saloons of the boom towns in the "wild west." By the early 1900s, casino gaming and parimutuel betting had been largely eliminated from the United States only to start to return during the Great Depression in the 1930s. Bingo was decriminalized in numerous states, beginning with Massachusetts in 1931 in order to provide opportunities for charities to raise much needed funds, and horse tracks were reestablished in 21 states by the end of the 1930s. By 2010, 41 states offered parimutuel betting at either horse or dog tracks.

Casinos were reintroduced into the United States when Nevada legalized essentially all forms of gambling in 1931, eventually leading to Las Vegas becoming the unofficial gambling capital of the country. Nevada maintained a virtual monopoly on casino gaming for over 40 years until 1976 when New Jersey became the second state to legalize casino gaming, and an Appellate Court ruling in Florida in 1979 gave Native American tribes in the US wide latitude to operate casinos on Indian reservations, a right that was solidified in 1988 with the passage of the Indian Gaming Regulatory Act. These pivotal decisions ushered in a tidal wave of casinos across the United States, so that by 2010, 42 states had casinos operating within their borders. Similarly, casino gambling in Canada has undergone significant increases over the past three decades. Casinos currently legally operate in all Canadian provinces.

ECONOMICS OF LOTTERIES AND GAMING TAXES

Typically, public finance economists examine a variety of factors in determining whether or not a specific tax is desirable. These factors include efficiency, vertical equity, horizontal equity, the user-pays principle, and others. Gambling revenues earn a decidedly mixed review when viewed in light of these criteria.

In terms of efficiency, gambling revenues clearly have plusses and minuses. Administrative costs are high, at least for operating state lotteries. Typically, administrative costs alone for state operated lotteries average in excess of 10% of the funds collected, and, in 2008, total operating costs for state-run lotteries in the United States averaged 13.1% of net revenue raised, excluding payments to retailers. Including payments to retailers, the administrative costs of state lotteries are closer to one-third of all revenues raised. On the other hand, the deadweight loss associated with lotteries is likely to be low, since consumers are relatively insensitive to the implicit "tax" rate imposed on gambling activities and since gambling is a voluntary activity. Given the fact that only those who choose to gamble are subject to this implicit tax, the presence of the lottery should be a welfare increasing activity rather than a welfare decreasing one.

It should also be noted that money spent by consumers on gambling and lottery tickets is money that is not available to be spent elsewhere in the economy. Since spending on other goods may be subject to sales tax or other revenue mechanisms, tax revenue generated by casinos and lotteries may simply substitute for tax reductions elsewhere in state government (Fink, Marco, and Rork 2004). This is not only true within states and provinces but also between states and provinces. As noted by Coughlin, Garrett, and Hernández-Murillo (2006), the presence of a neighbouring state with a lottery is a significant influence on whether a state itself adopts a lottery. The presence of casinos in nearby states is also frequently mentioned as a prime reason for a state to adopt casino gaming.

Vertical equity deals with the appropriate rate of taxation across income levels. It is here that proponents of legalized lotteries and gambling face their fiercest critics. By essentially any measure, lotteries are regressive in nature, with the poorest income groups spending a higher proportion of their income on these games than richer ones. In their examination of US lottery games, Clotfelter and Cook note that the "implicit tax [for lottery games] is regressive in virtually all cases" (1987, 533). Vaillancourt and Grignon (1988) come to a similar conclusion for Canadian lotteries. While they conclude that Canadian lotteries were somewhat less regressive than their American counterparts, they still conclude that lotteries are the most regressive form of taxation in Canada, with the exception of taxes on cigarettes. More recent literature, such as Price and Novak (1999; 2000) and Rubenstein and Scafidi (2002), comes to similar conclusions. Combs, Kim, and Spry (2008), for example, find that all seven lottery games they examine in Minnesota are highly regressive. Oster (2004) is notable for predicting that at certain jackpot levels the multistate Powerball lottery could actually become progressive, the only such instance documented in the academic literature, but even her results suggest that lotto jackpots would need to exceed $800 million before the implicit tax turns progressive, a level over twice that of any jackpot recorded in the United States.

The progressivity and regressivity of casino and parimutuel gambling taxes is subject to more question. In his seminal study, Suits (1977) concluded that casino gambling was an activity mostly engaged in by the rich, based on national survey data. Of course, at the time of that study, only Nevada offered casino gaming, so gambling required extensive travel on the part of participants. Borg, Mason, and Shapiro's (1991) follow-up study examined the gambling patterns of people who live in close proximity to casinos and found that when only local residents are considered, casino gambling is highly regressive. Considering the recent widespread expansion of casinos across the United States and Canada, is it likely that taxes collected on casino gaming have become significantly less progressive and more regressive over the past two decades.

A tax is horizontally equitable if the tax paid is similar for all individuals of the same income level. Obviously, the participation rates and levels for lotteries and gaming vary widely across populations. Given the voluntary nature of participation in gambling activities, however, most persons would not classify the lack of horizontal equity as a failing for lottery and gaming taxes.

The user-pays principle suggests that it is advantageous to design tax systems such that the users of particular government services pay for those services through taxes dedicated directly to individual government programs. For example, in the United States, road and highway construction and maintenance is funded through taxes on motor fuels. Those drivers using the most fuel, and theoretically using the most roads and highways, pay larger amounts into the highway fund. Lotteries and gaming taxes do not directly qualify as "user-pays" taxes, but the proceeds from many state lotteries are designated towards specific programs such as education, charitable organizations, or the environment. Of the 43 US states (plus the District of Columbia) that provide lottery games, over half earmark all lottery profits for a specific purpose, usually education, and another quarter reserve a portion of lottery revenues for a designated government program. Of course, the existence of a dedicated revenue source for, say, education, makes it easier for lawmakers to redirect other non-directed revenue sources away from education. In other words, tax dollars may be fungible.

The empirical evidence does, in fact, suggest that lottery revenues are quite fungible. For example, Garrett (2001) found that the presence of earmarked lottery funds in Ohio did not lead to a statistically significant increase in per-student expenditures on education. Similarly, Novarro (2005) analyzed panel data for all 50 US states and found that states with lottery proceeds dedicated to education increased spending on education by approximately 79 cents for every one dollar in lottery profits, while each dollar in non-earmarked lottery profits increased education spending by only 43 cents on average, suggesting partial but not complete fungibility of lottery revenues.

The last aspect of gaming revenue to be considered is its variability as a revenue source. Szakmary and Szakmary performed the most rigorous analysis of the variability of lottery revenues and their relationship to other revenue sources. In contrast to prior studies, they find that "lottery revenues do not destabilize total state revenues, because the low correlation of lottery revenues with revenues from other sources offsets the high stand-alone risk of lottery funding" (1995, 1181). Szakmary and Szakmary (1995) utilize portfolio theory to test the covariance between fluctuations in lottery revenue and fluctuations in other tax sources. A similar technique will be used in this chapter but extended to cover the 15 years since their work and extending the analysis to Canadian provinces.

DATA

Canadian data come from the Provincial and Territorial Government Revenue and Expenditures program operated by Statistics Canada. This annual census of provincial and territorial governments contains detailed data on revenues and expenditures based on the published financial reports of the various provincial governments. The data are consistent with the Financial Management System developed by Statistics Canada and are available over the period 1989–2008 as CANSIM Table 385-0002.

Our measure of total provincial revenue is "own-source revenue," an aggregate measure of provincial government revenues that includes income taxes, consumption taxes, property and related taxes, health and drug insurance premiums, contributions to social insurance plans, the sales of goods and services, and investment income. We subtract provincial revenues derived from health and drug insurance premiums and contributions to social insurance programs from own-source revenues in order to identify revenues generated from specific discretionary

Revenue Source	AB	BC	MB	NB	NL	NS	ON	PE	QC	SK
Personal Inc.	23.5%	26.0%	28.3%	26.6%	27.1%	33.8%	35.7%	25.9%	39.3%	22.3%
Corporate Inc.	8.8%	5.5%	4.3%	4.5%	4.2%	5.3%	9.6%	4.2%	5.2%	4.0%
General Sales	—	16.3%	17.0%	21.9%	25.6%	23.8%	21.9%	24.2%	15.6%	13.6%
Alcohol/Tobac.	2.4%	2.6%	2.5%	2.0%	5.3%	3.1%	2.5%	5.3%	1.9%	2.4%
Motor Fuels	3.2%	4.4%	4.0%	5.6%	5.5%	5.8%	4.9%	5.6%	3.8%	5.7%
Gaming	3.7%	2.3%	3.5%	2.4%	3.3%	3.1%	2.0%	2.0%	2.5%	3.0%
General Prop.	4.7%	6.6%	3.6%	7.6%	0.1%	—	0.1%	7.9%	0.0%	0.0%
Sale Gds/Serv.	3.5%	3.2%	3.3%	4.3%	5.8%	6.1%	3.8%	8.4%	4.2%	4.9%
Investment Inc	41.9%	21.9%	19.0%	16.8%	12.8%	9.6%	4.6%	9.7%	7.0%	27.2%

TABLE 11.1 Share of Total Provincial Revenues, Selected Sources, 1989–2009

provincial sources. Sales of goods and services include goods like water, land, and used structures; services sold include court and probate fees, tolls for transportation, admissions to public museums and recreational facilities, and educational services. Investment income includes natural resource royalties, interest income, and gains and losses on other securities. This revenue variable excludes transfers from other levels of government.

Table 11.1 summarizes the share of own-source revenues accounted for by a selected group of provincial government revenue sources. This is not a comprehensive list of revenue sources, so the shares do not sum to 100%. In Table 11.1 "—" indicates that the province does not collect taxes on this source; 0.0% means that the province collects a very small amount of revenue from this source. Personal income and general sales tax revenues are generally the two largest sources of provincial tax revenues. The exception to this is Alberta, which has no provincial sales tax and gets significant revenues from investment income, primarily from oil and gas royalties. Saskatchewan and British Columbia also derive significant revenues from investment income.

Remitted gaming profits make up a relatively small share of own-source revenues in Canadian provinces, between 2.2% and 3.7% on average. However, remitted gaming profits are a larger share of own-source revenues than alcohol and tobacco taxes in most provinces and are close to the share from motor fuel taxes in some provinces.

US data come from the State Tax Collections (STC) program operated by the Bureau of the Census. This program collects detailed sate tax revenue data for 25 categories of tax revenues; data are available back as far as 1950 and extend through 2006. Like the Canadian data, we include tax revenues from a number of important sources but do not analyze a comprehensive list of tax revenue sources.

The STC program does not include remitted gaming profits as a separate category of tax revenues, so we must construct a variable from other data sources. Gaming tax revenues appear in four distinct variables in the STC data: net lottery proceeds, parimutuel tax revenues, amusement tax revenues, and amusement licence revenues. Net lottery proceeds are funds returned to the state after prizes and administrative costs have been paid. Parimutuel taxes are collected on wagers on horse racing, dog racing, jai-alai, and other events and include "breakage" revenues from rounding on gambling payouts. Amusement taxes include taxes on casino gambling. Revenues for gaming licences issued to racetracks and casinos fall under amusement licences. The amusements category also contains licence revenue and taxes from non-gaming activities like movie theatres, athletic events, and video game machines, so some portion of these revenues are not related to gambling. Since casino and racetrack betting are not as common as lotteries, we use two gaming revenue variables: net lottery proceeds and gaming revenues, which we define as the sum of all three categories of gaming revenues.

Table 11.2 summarizes the share of own-source revenues accounted for by each revenue source in the US states that operated a lottery for at least 10 years. The "years" column shows the number of years over which these revenue shares were calculated. Nevada, which does not operate a state lottery but does allow casino gambling, has also been included in this table. Like the Canadian provinces, personal income taxes and general sales taxes account for the majority of tax revenues collected by US states. Five states (Florida, Nevada, South Dakota, Texas, and Washington) do not collect personal income taxes and four states (Delaware, Montana, New Hampshire, and Oregon) do not collect sales taxes.

State	Pers. Inc.	Corp. Inc.	Gen. Sales	Alc. & Tobac.	Motor Fuels	Gaming	Lottery	Prop	Gds. Serv.	Inv. Inc.	Years
AZ	20.0%	4.9%	36.5%	2.2%	6.1%	1.3%	1.2%	3.7%	1.1%	4.3%	25
CA	32.9%	8.0%	26.0%	1.3%	3.4%	1.4%	1.2%	3.8%	4.2%	3.8%	21
CO	3.2%	3.0%	19.7%	1.6%	6.4%	1.6%	1.1%	0.1%	0.6%	6.8%	24
CT	16.0%	8.1%	30.1%	3.1%	5.6%	4.3%	2.3%	—	1.5%	5.4%	34
DE	26.1%	6.2%	—	1.7%	3.8%	3.4%	3.2%	—	2.2%	8.7%	31
FL	—	4.2%	46.0%	3.9%	5.3%	3.7%	3.3%	2.1%	0.1%	4.0%	19
GA	35.7%	4.3%	27.8%	1.6%	4.0%	4.3%	4.3%	0.3%	0.1%	2.3%	13
IA	26.7%	3.2%	22.6%	1.9%	6.0%	2.2%	0.7%	0.0%	1.9%	3.9%	21
ID	27.8%	4.1%	25.4%	1.4%	6.8%	0.8%	0.8%	0.0%	2.4%	7.5%	17
IL	24.9%	6.7%	25.3%	2.6%	5.3%	3.6%	2.3%	0.9%	0.3%	5.1%	32
IN	26.5%	6.0%	26.3%	1.4%	5.3%	3.4%	1.4%	0.0%	0.0%	4.8%	17
KS	27.4%	4.7%	27.3%	2.6%	6.0%	0.9%	0.8%	0.8%	0.1%	3.8%	19
KY	24.5%	4.0%	20.9%	1.0%	4.8%	1.7%	1.5%	4.5%	0.0%	5.2%	18
LA	15.5%	3.0%	20.6%	1.5%	5.5%	3.7%	1.3%	0.4%	0.5%	9.8%	15
MA	38.7%	8.4%	15.4%	3.2%	4.0%	3.5%	3.0%	0.0%	0.7%	5.3%	34
MD	32.1%	3.7%	18.6%	1.9%	5.7%	3.8%	3.5%	2.3%	2.2%	4.2%	34
ME	23.5%	3.8%	25.4%	4.7%	6.4%	1.2%	1.0%	2.0%	4.0%	6.5%	33
MI	24.2%	9.9%	23.9%	3.1%	5.1%	2.7%	2.4%	3.6%	3.9%	4.0%	34
MN	33.1%	4.8%	22.7%	1.8%	4.1%	0.8%	0.5%	0.9%	0.0%	3.7%	17
MO	29.2%	3.2%	26.8%	1.5%	5.8%	2.4%	1.3%	0.2%	0.4%	6.2%	21
MT	22.8%	4.3%	—	2.0%	8.5%	2.3%	0.4%	9.3%	3.1%	12.5%	19
NE	26.5%	3.6%	26.1%	1.8%	7.1%	0.7%	0.5%	0.1%	0.6%	5.2%	13
NH	2.7%	12.1%	—	5.7%	8.5%	3.6%	1.9%	4.0%	23.3%	11.4%	34
NJ	20.2%	7.3%	22.7%	3.3%	3.9%	4.6%	2.9%	0.7%	6.0%	5.2%	34
NM	15.2%	3.1%	25.1%	1.1%	3.9%	0.8%	0.4%	0.7%	5.1%	13.0%	11
NV	—	—	39.9%	3.1%	6.3%	21.0%	—	2.9%	7.3%	5.1%	33
NY	40.3%	6.9%	17.1%	2.6%	2.1%	2.5%	2.0%	0.0%	17.2%	5.4%	34
OH	24.4%	4.7%	24.2%	2.8%	6.3%	2.9%	2.7%	0.7%	3.8%	3.2%	32
OR	43.4%	3.9%	—	2.3%	4.9%	2.6%	2.6%	0.1%	3.8%	10.2%	22
PA	20.6%	7.4%	23.5%	3.3%	5.2%	2.7%	2.6%	0.8%	4.8%	3.4%	34
RI	23.1%	4.4%	21.4%	3.3%	4.7%	3.5%	3.0%	0.5%	2.7%	10.8%	33
SD	—	3.2%	32.4%	2.4%	8.1%	5.7%	5.5%	—	0.3%	15.3%	19
TX	—	—	35.7%	3.0%	7.1%	2.9%	2.8%	—	0.2%	5.7%	14
VA	34.2%	2.7%	14.3%	0.9%	5.1%	2.0%	2.0%	0.1%	2.0%	5.2%	18
VT	21.7%	3.6%	12.0%	3.3%	4.6%	0.9%	0.9%	5.9%	3.6%	7.7%	29
WA	—	—	48.0%	3.0%	5.3%	1.0%	0.9%	11.9%	2.9%	3.0%	24
DC	22.8%	5.3%	15.2%	0.6%	0.9%	1.8%	1.8%	23.4%	3.7%	2.5%	20
WI	32.9%	4.4%	22.3%	2.0%	5.7%	1.1%	1.1%	0.6%	0.1%	4.9%	18
WV	19.6%	5.7%	22.4%	1.3%	6.0%	3.4%	3.1%	0.1%	1.6%	5.0%	21

TABLE 11.2 Share of Total US Revenues, Selected Sources and Years

Gaming revenues and net lottery proceeds do not account for a large share of own-source revenues, except in Nevada (21%), which has by far the loosest restrictions on gambling in the United States. Gambling revenues are more modest but relatively large in states such as New Jersey (4.6%) and South Dakota (5.7%) that have legalized casino gaming in specific cities in the state (Deadwood in South Dakota and Atlantic City in New Jersey), and gambling revenues are also high in states such as Connecticut (4.3%) that have major Native American casinos that have worked out revenue sharing agreements with the state. A few states (Georgia, Maryland, South Dakota, and West Virginia) get more than 3% of their own-source revenues from net lottery proceeds. Like Canadian provinces, many US states collect as much or more tax revenues from gambling as they do from alcohol and tobacco taxes.

EMPIRICAL MODEL AND RESULTS

This chapter borrows from the finance literature to estimate the relationship between gambling tax revenues and other revenues collected by state and provincial governments. In finance the *beta* (β) of a stock or portfolio is a number measuring its returns relative to those of an alternative portfolio, usually defined as the market as a whole. A beta of zero denotes no relationship between the idiosyncratic returns of a particular asset and the return earned by the overall market while a positive beta implies that an asset's value is likely to rise along with other assets in the market. A negative beta means that the asset generally decreases in value as the market as whole rises. Beta is calculated as

1. $$\beta = Cov\left(r_a, r_p\right) / Var\left(r_p\right)$$

where r_a measures the rate of return of the specific asset and r_p measures the rate of return of the portfolio. As noted previously, typically the portfolio used in most calculations of beta is the portfolio of all assets in the market as whole.

Beta can be estimated for any individual asset with regression analysis using the rate of return of the individual asset as the dependent variable and the rate of return for the market as a whole as the lone independent variable.

To assess the relationship between variation in specific sources of tax revenues and total own-source revenues, we estimate a "beta" for each of the revenue sources. In order to transform the statistic from finance to one that can be used in this application, we interpret the percentage change in own-source revenues as each province or state's market return and the percentage change in revenues from each revenue source as the return on specific "assets." Based on these assumptions, the beta for each revenue source, like the beta in finance, can be estimated from a linear regression

$$2. \qquad r_{s,t} = \alpha_s + \beta_s ros_t + e_{s,t}$$

where $r_{s,t}$ is the percentage change in annual tax revenues from source s in year t, ros_t is the percentage change in own-source revenues in year t, and $e_{s,t}$ is an unobservable equation error term. We assume that $e_{s,t}$ is distributed with mean zero and constant variance. β_s is the beta for revenue source s, and measures the sensitivity of variation in own-source revenues to variation in revenue source s over time.

Table 11.3 contains the beta estimates for each of the revenue sources in each Canadian province over the period 1989–2009. Each regression had 21 observations and the beta estimates were generally significantly different from zero at conventional levels. Recall that positive beta estimates identify revenue sources that vary directly with total own-source revenues and negative betas identify revenues sources that vary inversely with total own-source revenues. Put another way, revenue sources with positive betas increase the variation in own-source revenues over time and revenue sources with negative betas reduce the variation in own-source revenues over time.

The estimated betas from different revenue sources in Canadian provinces show wide variation with many positive and

	AB	BC	MB	NB	NL	NS	ON	PE	QC	SK
Personal Income	-0.22	1.31	1.54	1.22	0.51	1.59	0.96	1.61	1.20	0.01
Corporate Income	0.82	1.87	2.16	7.67	2.59	0.81	3.09	1.07	0.60	0.54
General Sales	—	0.68	0.09	0.83	0.74	0.66	0.57	0.30	1.11	0.14
Alcohol, Tobacco	-0.13	-0.29	-0.74	-0.59	0.27	2.67	-0.53	0.26	1.54	0.08
Motor Fuels	0.03	0.17	0.29	0.53	0.03	-0.15	-0.12	1.11	-0.43	-0.12
Gaming	0.18	-0.33	-0.32	-0.26	-0.64	-3.13	0.32	0.84	-0.15	5.96
General Property	1.47	0.31	-0.09	0.28	0.81	—	19.09	0.58	11.43	0.38
Sale Goods, Serv.	6.56	-0.47	0.23	0.37	0.30	1.25	2.20	2.10	-0.54	-0.09
Investment Inc.	1.86	1.59	1.50	0.73	4.09	1.30	-0.06	1.18	3.33	1.80

TABLE 11.3 Revenue Source Beta Estimates, Canadian Provinces, 1989–2009

negative betas. Corporate income taxes have the largest betas, indicating that this source of tax revenue has the largest variation over time. Garrett (2009) reported similar results for US states. In general, income taxes, general sales taxes, general property taxes, sales of goods and services, and investment income betas tend to be positive, indicating positive co-movement between these revenue sources and total own-source revenues. Income and general sales taxes contribute significantly to the variation in own-source revenues over time.

The negative betas are primarily in alcohol and tobacco taxes, motor fuel taxes, and remitted gaming profits. The beta for remitted gaming profits is negative in six of the ten provinces; the beta for alcohol and tobacco taxes is negative in five provinces. A negative beta indicates that revenues from this source increase when total own-source revenues decrease, contributing to stability in total own-source revenues over time. The betas in Table 11.3 indicate that variation in gaming revenue over time generally helps to reduce overall variation in provincial revenues; Szakmary and Szakmary (1995) reported a similar result for US states in the 1980s and 1990s. However, from Table 11.1, remitted gaming profits represent a relatively small fraction of own-source revenues, limiting the extent to which variation in gaming

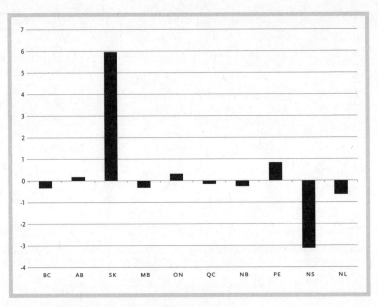

FIGURE 11.1 Provincial Gambling Revenue Betas

revenue can offset variation in own-source revenues over time in Canadian provinces.

Note that the betas for Alberta differ from many other provinces. In Alberta, the betas on property taxes, investment income, and the sale of goods and services are all relatively large. From Table 11.1, these revenue sources make up about 50% of provincial own-source revenues. This implies considerable variation in own-source revenues in Alberta over time, implying a relatively unstable provincial revenue stream.

Also note that the beta for gaming revenue for Saskatchewan is nearly six. This quite large and positive beta indicates substantial positive correlation between variation in gaming revenues and variation in own-source revenues in Saskatchewan. Figure 11.1 places this large beta for provincial gaming revenue in context by showing the relative sizes of the betas for gaming revenue in each province. The larger the beta, the stronger the correlation between gaming revenues and own-source revenues. From Figure 11.1, variation in gaming revenue contributes directly to variability of own-source revenues and hence to revenue

STATE	Pers. Inc.	Corp. Inc.	Gen. Sales	Alc. &. Tobac	Motor Fuels	Gaming	Lottery	Prop.	Gds. Serv.	Inv. Inc.
AZ	0.87	1.55	1.04	-0.08	0.80	0.48	0.38	0.46	0.02	4.15
CA	1.92	1.44	0.34	1.23	-0.34	-0.05	-0.07	0.86	0.46	0.90
CO	1.04	3.13	0.87	1.59	0.81	-0.43	-1.10	3.30	-1.16	1.45
CT	5.84	1.63	0.69	0.00	0.41	1.56	2.02	-1.13	3.46	0.21
DE	0.74	2.50	—	-0.17	-2.03	-0.31	0.92	—	4.89	0.70
FL	—	0.97	0.78	0.05	-0.77	6.15	10.37	2.67	-2.08	1.09
GA	1.29	2.28	0.75	0.64	0.57	2.16	2.16	0.09	4.54	0.96
IA	1.50	3.06	1.36	0.56	0.96	-0.80	2.65	—	-0.90	0.88
ID	1.37	3.03	0.66	0.74	0.07	-2.28	-2.39	-22.90	-0.17	0.33
IL	1.51	2.40	0.62	-0.25	1.50	0.48	0.57	25.44	4.85	2.06
IN	0.25	1.88	0.24	0.34	-0.10	-1.30	0.07	-0.75	1.88	0.80
KS	1.46	2.84	0.71	-0.29	0.44	3.55	2.74	-0.01	1.06	2.72
KY	1.88	3.91	0.79	3.09	-0.12	-1.26	-1.15	0.29	1.05	1.72
LA	1.00	2.05	0.53	-0.26	-0.11	-0.39	0.55	0.06	7.92	1.32
MA	1.23	1.40	1.23	-0.04	0.26	0.23	0.67	-53.64	5.23	1.69
MD	0.99	2.32	1.10	-0.06	0.52	2.85	5.45	1.13	0.71	3.69
ME	0.40	1.53	0.36	0.31	0.25	1.77	3.31	19.21	0.10	0.46
MI	1.76	3.07	1.02	0.42	0.52	0.52	0.79	1.11	0.11	0.67
MN	1.45	3.03	0.62	2.93	0.13	-3.02	-3.17	-154.75	0.13	3.74
MO	1.51	2.26	0.39	0.58	1.81	1.82	0.34	-0.02	9.15	2.50
MT	0.40	1.44	—	0.17	0.29	1.30	1.95	5.44	0.37	0.47
NE	0.61	1.64	1.46	1.14	0.12	-0.53	-0.89	-2.36	0.48	-0.36
NH	0.00	0.47	—	0.13	0.18	-0.03	0.48	782.26	0.42	0.30
NJ	9.00	1.69	0.28	0.12	-0.04	0.63	0.89	0.39	2.21	0.61
NM	-0.18	3.18	0.86	0.01	0.02	2.29	1.66	-0.56	3.37	1.37
NV	—	—	1.92	0.34	0.93	0.37	—	0.29	-0.83	1.53
NY	1.20	1.94	0.45	0.45	-0.06	0.80	2.34	-6.94	-0.87	1.71
OH	1.70	1.01	1.20	-1.35	0.44	1.47	1.98	-1.31	0.42	0.99
OR	1.43	1.31	—	0.28	0.90	1.77	1.51	133.43	-0.46	2.58
PA	1.37	1.99	0.26	0.04	-0.64	1.12	1.38	1.60	0.08	0.40
RI	1.34	1.63	0.46	-0.68	0.17	-1.06	-0.63	0.99	2.64	2.40
SD	—	1.11	0.96	0.43	-0.02	4.57	4.69	—	1.11	1.88
TX	—	—	0.73	0.35	0.02	-0.25	-0.25	—	4.26	3.05
VA	1.89	5.12	0.44	2.06	0.16	-1.47	-1.47	3.49	0.32	1.25
VT	0.60	0.77	0.57	-0.95	0.24	1.38	3.19	64.62	0.24	0.42
WA	—	—	1.06	0.21	0.87	1.81	1.80	0.87	0.07	3.08
DC	0.77	0.45	0.96	-0.50	-0.46	0.09	0.09	0.99	1.07	3.26
WI	1.86	1.09	0.30	0.28	0.72	-0.35	-0.39	1.06	-43.22	0.73
WV	1.07	1.51	2.12	0.13	0.79	0.31	1.72	-0.86	1.38	0.45

TABLE 11.4 Revenue Source Beta Estimates, US States

instability most in Saskatchewan, but in Alberta, Ontario, and Prince Edward Island, gaming revenue also contributes to revenue instability.

Table 11.4 contains the beta estimates for each of the revenue sources in each US state. The number of observations in each of these regressions is the number of years shown in Table 11.2, which represents the number of years that each state operated a lottery and reported net lottery revenues in the STC data. Generally, the beta estimates were significantly different from zero at conventional levels. An estimated beta of 0.00 in Table 11.4 means that the estimate was 0.004 or smaller.

The estimated betas for US states shown in Table 11.4 are similar to those for Canadian provinces. The betas for personal income taxes, corporate income taxes, and general sales taxes tend to be positive, indicating that variation in these revenues sources are positively correlated with variation in total own-source revenues and are more volatile than total own-source revenues. Alcohol and tobacco taxes, and motor fuel taxes do not have as many negative betas in US states as in Canadian provinces, suggesting that these revenue sources contribute more to total own-source revenue variation in the United States than in Canada.

As in Canadian provinces, the estimated betas for gaming revenues and lottery revenues contain many negative values. Fourteen of the gaming betas are negative, and ten of the lottery betas are negative in the 39 US states in the sample. However, the gaming and lottery betas are not uniformly negative in US states, and some are large and positive, like in Florida, South Dakota, and Maryland. In these states, variation in gaming and lottery revenue over time enhances the variability of state total own-source revenue over time. Variation in the gaming and lottery betas in US states, and Canadian provinces, is probably related to the specific mix of gaming and lottery products in place in each province or state. For example, the beta for gaming revenue in Indiana, a state with a number of riverboat casinos, is negative, while the beta on net lottery returns is positive. Net lottery revenues in Indiana rise and fall with total own-source revenues while revenues from the riverboat casinos do not.

CONCLUSION

The results presented here provide evidence that gaming revenues and revenues from lotteries reduce overall variability in state and provincial revenues over time. The estimated betas for gaming revenues are often negative, and the positive values tend to be smaller than the betas for commonly used alternative revenue sources such as sales or income taxes, suggesting that gaming revenues do not fall significantly in the face of declines in other revenue sources. Variation in gaming revenues tends to offset variation in other revenue sources in provinces and states. However, gaming and lottery revenues tend to be small relative to other revenue sources like sales and income taxes, limiting the ability of variation in gaming revenues that are negatively correlated with total own-source revenues to offset declines in total own-source revenues.

A majority of the revenue source betas in Tables 11.3 and 11.4 are positive, indicating significant positive correlation among revenue sources in provinces and states. This positive correlation means that total own-source revenue will vary substantially over time, potentially leading to severe budget shortfalls when these revenue sources all fall together. Unfortunately, unlike private investors who can construct portfolios of assets with both negative and positive betas to smooth out market variation, provinces and states must construct revenue streams with other properties in mind such as efficiency and equity. Revenues from many relatively equitable and efficient taxes appear to have significant positive correlation over time, placing provincial and state decision makers in a bind when attempting to smooth out variation in tax revenues over time. Gambling revenues can be an effective, albeit small, part of the solution to this problem.

Authors' Note

The Alberta Gaming Research Institute provided financial support for this research.

References

Borg, Mary O., Paul M. Mason, and Stephen L. Shapiro. 1991. "The Incidence of Taxes on Casino Gambling: Exploiting the Tired and Poor." *American Journal of Economics and Sociology* 50 (3): 323–32.

———. 1993. "The Cross Effects of Lottery Taxes on Alternative State Tax Revenue." *Public Finance Review* 21 (2): 123–40.

Clotfelter, Charles T., and Philip J. Cook. 1987. "Implicit Taxation in Lottery Finance." *National Tax Journal* 40 (4): 533–46.

Combs, Kathryn, Jaebeom Kim, and John Spry. 2008. "The Relative Regressivity of Seven Lottery Games." *Applied Economics* 40 (1–3): 35–39.

Coughlin, Cletus C., Thomas A. Garrett, and Rubén Hernández-Murillo. 2006. "The Geography, Economics, and Politics of Lottery Adoption." *Federal Reserve Bank of St. Louis Review* 88: 165–80.

Dunstan, Roger. 1997. "Gambling in California." Working Paper CRB-97-003, California Research Bureau.

Fink, Stephen C., Alan C. Marco, and Jonathan C. Rork. 2004. "Lotto Nothing? The Budgetary Impact of State Lotteries." *Applied Economics* 36: 2357–67.

Garrett, Thomas A. 2001. "Earmarking Lottery Revenues for Education: A New Test of Fungibility." *Journal of Education Finance* 26: 219–38.

———. 2009. "Evaluating State Tax Revenue Variability: A Portfolio Approach." *Applied Economics Letters*, 16: 243–246.

Matheson, Victor, and Kent Grote. 2008. "US Lotto Markets." In *Handbook of Sports and Lottery Markets*, edited by Donald B. Hausch and William T. Ziemba, 503–24. New York: North Holland.

Novarro, Neva. 2005. "Earmarked Lottery Profits: A Good Bet for Education Finance?" *Journal of Education Finance* 31: 23–44.

Oster, Emily. 2004. "Are All Lotteries Regressive? Evidence from the Powerball." *National Tax Journal* 57 (2): 179–87.

Price, D.I., and E.S. Novak. 1999. "The Tax Incidence of Three Texas Lottery Games: Regressivity, Race, and Education." *National Tax Journal* 52 (4): 741–51.

———. 2000. "The Income Redistribution Effects of Texas State Lottery Games." *Public Finance Review* 28 (1): 82–92.

Rubenstein, R., and B. Scafidi. 2002. "Who Pays and Who Benefits? Examining the Distributional Consequences of the Georgia Lottery for Education." *National Tax Journal* 55 (2): 223–38.

Suits, Daniel B. 1977. "Measurement of Tax Progressivity." *American Economic Review* 67 (4): 747–52.

Szakmary, Andrew, and Carol Matheny Szakmary. 1995. "State Lotteries as a Source of Revenue: A Re-Examination." *Southern Economic Journal* 61 (4): 1167–81.

US Census Bureau. 2009. Statistical Abstract of the United States: 2012 (128th Edition). Washington, DC.

Vaillancourt, F. and J. Grignon. 1988. "Canadian Lotteries as Taxes: Revenues and Incidence." Working Paper No. 8804, Université de Montréal, Département de sciences économiques.

Expenditure Management in Alberta

In Search of Stability

Al O'Brien

INTRODUCTION

Alberta has been seeking a fiscal policy framework to moderate the impact of volatile resource revenues on public spending levels and fiscal balances since at least the first global energy crisis in the mid-1970s. A variety of policy measures and fiscal frameworks have been adopted over the following three and a half decades, from savings rules and the establishment of the Heritage Savings Trust Fund in the 1970s, to legislated spending limits under the ill-fated Spending Control Act in 1992, to revenue budgeting, deficit, and debt repayment rules in the 1990s, and to the establishment of a stabilization fund, capital fund, and numerous research endowments in the 2000s. I would like to comment briefly on the success of these measures in stabilizing provincial spending, reflect on whether expenditure stabilization

is either feasible or desirable in the Alberta context, and offer a
few observations on current fiscal options for the province.

SPENDING VOLATILITY

The volatility of provincial expenditure in Alberta has been
well-documented. But, as both Boothe (1995) and Emery and
Kneebone (2009) have demonstrated, perhaps the major concern
is not the volatility of expenditure per se, but the asymmetric
form this volatility has taken. While spending has tended to track
revenue increases quite faithfully, it has been much slower to
adjust to revenue declines.

Economic and fiscal volatility has characterized the province since its formation in 1905, but I will restrict my review to
the last four decades, beginning with election of the Lougheed
administration in 1971. The first decade of the Lougheed administration saw a six fold increase in the provincial budget. Real per
capita spending doubled despite the province setting aside 30%
of resource revenues in the Alberta Heritage Savings Trust Fund
(AHSTF) beginning in 1976, building the AHSTF to $12 billion,
and net financial assets of the province to more than $8 billion
by March 31, 1982 (a level not seen again until 2003).

In the 11 years from 1982 to 1993, nominal revenues grew
by only 34%, while spending grew by 107%. The nine straight
annual deficits from 1985–86 through 1993–94 resulted in more
than a $20 billion deterioration in the consolidated financial
assets of the province.[1]

The four-year "Klein Revolution" initiated in 1993 saw continued modest growth of 17% in provincial revenue, but the 20%
reduction in spending during this period restored budget surpluses and began repair of the provincial balance sheet. The 11
years from 1997 through 2007 saw revenue growth of 129%, but
operating spending grew by 136% and capital spending grew by
750%. Nevertheless, accumulated surpluses during this period
resulted in the province building net financial assets of more
than $31 billion by March 31, 2008.

Resource receipts peaked in 2005–06, and by 2007–08 moderate growth of tax revenues was not sufficient to offset declines in resource receipts and investment income; revenue growth stalled, with total revenues increasing by only $152 million over the 2006–07 year. Financial year 2008–09 saw a $2.4 billion decline in overall revenue, followed by a further $2.3 billion decline in the next year. But mimicking the experience of the 1980s, operating spending continued to grow, by $3.9 billion in 2007–08, $3.2 billion in 2008–09, and a further $500 million in 2009–10. When capital spending and the growth of pension liabilities are added to the operating deficits, the province's financial assets are seen to have dropped by a third between March 31, 2007 and March 31, 2009, to $21 billion. As I write this chapter, the province's 2010 budget forecasts a modest increase of $400 million in revenue, but a further $1.5 billion increase in spending. If the budget estimates are realized, net financial assets will be down to $13.4 billion by March 31, 2011.[2]

STATUTORY MEASURES TO STABILIZE SPENDING

Over the past 40 years the province adopted a variety of statutory measures to stabilize its finances. These measures can broadly be categorized as "savings rules," "budgeting rules," "capital funds," and in one brief experiment in 1992, direct "spending rules."

Arguably the most successful of these measures were the "savings rules," represented by the creation of the Alberta Heritage Savings Trust Fund in 1976, which called for 30% of non-renewable resource revenues to be "saved" for future generations (though 20% of that amount could be invested in the Capital Projects Division, which included such public works as provincial parks); and the requirements of the 1995 Balanced Budget and Debt Retirement Act (BBDRA), which called for elimination of the $8.3 billion net debt of the province over 25 years.

Another approach was that of mandated budgeting rules, represented by the Deficit Elimination Act of 1993 (DEA) and the Financial Responsibility Act of 1999 (FRA). The DEA required not only that the province meet certain prescribed fiscal balances over the four-year timeframe of the deficit elimination plan followed by a prohibition on planned deficits, but prescribed a five-year averaging rule for estimating non-renewable resource revenues to be included in the fiscal plan. Of particular relevance to expenditure management, the DEA required that any revenues in excess of the budget estimates be applied to reduce the deficit or repay debt, i.e., unbudgeted revenue could not be used to fund additional expenditure.[3]

The initial 1999 version of the FRA replaced the DEA requirement to utilize a five-year average of actual non-resource revenue for fiscal planning (which had been amended by the BBDRA to require the lesser of the five-year average or 90% of the forecast for the coming year) with a requirement to provide for an "economic cushion" of not less than 3.5% of total revenues. It softened the DEA prohibition on unbudgeted spending to permit spending of 25% of the economic cushion, as well as 25% of revenues in excess of the budget estimates.

The FRA also established a new 25-year plan to eliminate the province's $13.5 billion remaining "accumulated debt" following the achievement of the BBDRA goal to eliminate "net debt," which was forecast to be achieved by March 31, 2000. This renewed debt retirement plan was to be funded by 75% of the annual "economic cushions," plus 75% of any surplus revenues.

The province has also experimented throughout the past 40 years with various approaches to capital funding, starting with the aforementioned Capital Projects Division in the AHSTF, then the 1986 Capital Fund, which funded a variety of health, post-secondary, and water resources projects until it was consolidated into the general revenue fund in 1994, and most recently the 2003 Capital Account, which focused largely on mitigating the impacts of annual capital appropriations on capital planning until its elimination in 2009.

Finally, in 1992 the province experimented with direct statutory limits on aggregate spending, in the form of the Spending Control Act, which prescribed aggregate limits on spending growth of 2.5% for 1992–93, 2.25% for 1993–94, and 2.0% for 1994–95. As a practical matter however, the act only prevented approval of Special Warrants that would exceed the spending limit, and in the spring of 1993 the legislature simply authorized supplementary estimates "notwithstanding the Spending Control Act." The act was repealed later that spring with the passage of the Deficit Elimination Act.

BUDGET PROCESS MEASURES

The province has also experimented with a variety of planning and budgeting processes over the past four decades. A key focus of innovations in the province's budgeting processes over the years has been to avoid "incrementalism" in budgeting, and to focus decision making and accountability on results and effectiveness, rather than inputs; but stabilization and/or restraint of spending was frequently a secondary objective.

The introduction of program budgeting in the mid-1970s was in many ways the most ambitious of these experiments (see Alberta Treasury 1976, 1). The stated goals of the move to program budgeting were "to achieve a more effective presentation of Government activities and to obtain more comprehensive information for setting priorities and approving budgets (Alberta Treasury 1974, 1). The introduction of program budgeting in 1976 was accompanied by the elimination of the capital account in the general revenue fund, with capital expenditures being treated simply as an object of expenditure. The previous votes for capital and operating expenditures by department were restructured to provide combined appropriations by program. The new program budget structure was clearly successful in providing more meaningful information on government activities, but when the revenue reversals of the 1980s arrived, it did not provide a sufficiently robust decision-making framework to support the difficult priority setting and resource allocation decisions required by the new fiscal realities in the province.

In an attempt to adjust budget decision making to meet these new realities, the Treasury Board adopted an "A-B-X" budgeting model in which spending allocations were analyzed in terms of base spending (the A budget), proposals for new or enhanced programs (B budgets), and opportunities for eliminating or reducing program spending (x budgets). As we have seen, while real per capita spending growth was stabilized after 1986, in nominal terms spending grew by more than triple the rate of revenue growth between 1982 and 1993.

Undoubtedly the most successful budgeting innovations adopted by the province over the past 40 years were the four-year spending targets established in 1993 and the three-year business plans of 1994–95. The spending targets were achieved or exceeded by virtually all ministries except health. Similarly, the program adjustments and performance goals included in the 1994–95 three-year business plans were generally achieved by 1996–97. Moreover, these new processes were successful, for at least a few years, in focusing meaningful attention on results achieved in the delivery of public services rather than the costs and inputs used in providing those services.

Many might argue that this could not have been achieved without the legislated deficit targets of the DEA. Boessenkool (2010), for example, has argued that "the lessons from history are clear: Budgets in Alberta are much more likely to meet their objectives when paired with clear fiscal rules—especially legislated fiscal rules." In my view, the achievements during the first term of the Klein government show that political leadership, effective communication with the electorate and stakeholders, and budget and financial management processes that maximize managerial flexibility and accountability are the keys to achieving administrative and fiscal reform in government.

I would argue that the fiscal rules legislated by the Klein government under the Deficit Elimination Act, Balanced Budget and Debt Retirement Act, and the Financial Responsibility Act were principally important as vehicles to communicate the government's commitment to its fiscal goals, rather than providing the immoveable "bulwarks" to ensure responsible and accountable fiscal decision making in the province for which many hoped.

Another innovation of the early Klein years was net budgeting. Net budgeting permits departments to apply revenues received through the sale of goods and services against the cost of delivering those goods and services without annual appropriation of the gross expenditure. This approach had been used historically in limited circumstances through the use of statutory "revolving funds." A typical example was the School Book Branch revolving fund in the Education Ministry, which allowed the branch to net revenues from the sale of books to school boards against the cost of acquisition. In 1994, however, the government implemented a much more generalized policy that sought to decentralize and simplify budget decision making by authorizing net budgeting in all instances "where the user-pay principle is appropriate and where the level of expenditure and revenue is related to the program's volume of activity" (Alberta Treasury 1994, 131). Significant examples of this approach were the netting of health care and Blue Cross premiums in the health ministry and of fuel taxes and revenues from driver and motor vehicle licensing in the transportation and utilities ministry. The introduction of net budgeting was heavily influenced by the notions of Osborne and Gaebler (1992). It was seen as a vehicle to encourage creativity and innovation, as well as simplify resource allocation by allowing the "market" to allocate resources in areas where the government was in effect selling goods and services.

However, Treasury Board ministers soon became alarmed that the use of net budgeting was encouraging ministers and officials to escalate user fees excessively, and, while in many cases appropriations continued to be netted by associated revenues, strong central control over fee setting removed the entrepreneurial incentives that had been seen as the original attraction of the net budgeting approach.

The final budget process issue that should be examined is that of capital budgeting. I distinguish between capital budgeting and the statutory capital funds discussed above. The latter involve specific statutory entities with dedicated funding, whereas by capital budgeting, I am referring simply to the practice of segregating the acquisition of fixed assets from operating expense. As noted above, until 1976 the province maintained separate operating and capital accounts, although the definition of capital revenues and expenditures was quite arbitrary, and depreciation was not charged to operating expense. In 1993, the province reinstated a distinction between operating expense and capital expenditures in the budget but continued to expense capital expenditure for balance sheet purposes and did not charge amortization to operating expense. It also replaced the 1976 practice of voting funds for each program within a ministry with three single votes for operating, capital, and non-budgetary expenditures.

From 1994 through 2003, the province capitalized fixed assets in departmental statements and included amortization in operating votes and financial statements. The consolidated fiscal plan, however, removed amortization from operating expense and added capital expenditures to determine the surplus or deficit, in conformity with the "net debt" model of government accounting which remained the generally accepted accounting standard recommended by the Public Sector Accounting Board.

In 2004, the province went to a full "accrual" model of accounting, in accordance with new accounting standards approved by the Public Sector Accounting Board. The annual surplus or deficit was based on operating expenditures only, with fixed assets recorded on the balance sheet and forming part of the "net assets" of the province. The 2004 changes to the treatment of capital investment in the consolidated fiscal plan of the province followed closely on the amendments to the FRA in 2003 which established the Alberta Sustainability Fund, the Capital Account, and the requirement for a consolidated capital plan. These innovations in capital funding and planning certainly coincided with a dramatic rise in infrastructure investment in the province: "capital plan" expenditures grew from $1.7 billion in 2003–04 to $7.6 billion in 2008–09, before abating to $6.8 billion in 2009–10 and an estimated $7.2 billion in the 2010–11 fiscal year.

It is very difficult to assess the impact of any of these alternative approaches to capital budgeting. From 1976 to 1993, no consolidated summary of capital spending within the general revenue fund is available, while the existence of the capital projects division in the AHSTF and the Capital Fund from 1986 to 1994 make it difficult in any event to differentiate the effect of the two capital funds from the treatment of capital spending in the province's general budgetary account. In the case of the re-establishment of separate capital votes and accounting in 1994, the fact that capital spending was still expensed in terms of debt and deficit calculations would be expected to mute any impact on overall expenditure management and stabilization.

The 2003 and 2004 changes could be expected to initiate a more significant response in terms of budgetary decisions and priorities, but, unfortunately, the fact that the most significant capital investments by the province—those for health and education infrastructure—continued to be recorded as operating grants, minimizes the potential impact of the budgeting and accounting change on capital expenditure stabilization. Only the province's direct capital expenditures, $2.8 billion of the $7.2 billion included in the 2010 capital plan, are in fact capitalized and then amortized over their useful life. In the case of the much more significant capital assets financed by the province in the SUCH (schools, universities, colleges, and hospitals) sector, the province has accounted for these entities on an equity basis, meaning that only the net surplus or deficit of schools, universities, colleges, and hospitals is included in the province's operating results, and even that net number is excluded from the operating results "for fiscal plan purposes." Provincial grants to finance capital projects in the SUCH sector are included in both operating expense and the "capital plan."

The 2003 introduction of a three-year consolidated capital plan has no doubt contributed to improved stability in capital planning and decision making, but the overall impact of the 2003 measures has not improved the simplicity and clarity of the province's expenditure management. The elimination of the "capital account" in 2009 was a positive step in this regard, but the announcement in the 2010 budget—that while the province's financial statements will conform with new accounting standards requiring full consolidation of the SUCH sector, the province's budgets will continue to exclude the sector—will lead to further complexity in understanding provincial expenditure, and in comparing planned to actual spending.

DO FISCAL RULES WORK? DOES IT MATTER?

The Heritage Savings Trust Fund savings "rule" seemed to work initially, but was abandoned under the spending and revenue challenges of the 1980s. The deficit and debt retirement targets of the 1990s were achieved, but the planning and accountability processes which were to ensure prudent fiscal management after the health of the province's balance sheet was restored seemed feeble in the face of large unexpected surpluses. The pace of spending growth particularly since 2004, and it's "stickiness" since the revenue peak of 2006, seem to affirm Emery and Kneebone's (2009) view that it is indeed "déjà vu all over again." And despite a variety of capital funding and budgeting approaches, the most important determinant of capital spending appears to remain the availability of funds.

In short, I would conclude that the most important "rule" governing the province's spending patterns remains that "revenue creates spending." This is consistent with Boothe (1995, 112) who found that the "tax price of government services" is a significant determinant of spending, but works much more quickly to increase spending when non-tax revenues grow than it does to reduce spending when non-tax revenues decline. I do not think one should take this experience as a sign of despair; the province did improve its net financial position by $44 billion between 1993 and 2008. But I think it does show that legislated fiscal rules are no panacea for addressing the fiscal challenges inherent in a resource-dependent economy, and, in the end, both political leadership and public consensus are critical to success in meeting these challenges.

I think we should also be careful in assuming that volatility in public expenditure is always and everywhere a bad thing. Clearly there are negatives associated with "booms" in public spending: public sector wages and particularly capital costs become inflated, economic cycles are exacerbated, and the secular level of public expenditure may be raised through the asymmetric response of spending to revenue volatility. But I think the Alberta experience also suggests that both "booms" and "busts" in public expenditure levels contribute to creativity and innovation in the public sector. Most available performance measures suggest that the quality of public services in the province is equal to or better than national norms, although I recognize that Duckett, Kramer, and Sarnecki (2013) conclude that in the case of health care, costs in Alberta are higher than the national average while outcomes are poorer than those in other provinces. It is interesting that these mediocre health outcomes have been accompanied by less "volatility" than other areas of provincial spending. On balance, I would argue that one should not preclude the possibility of a public sector analogy to the "creative destruction" in the private sector that Schumpeter associated with business cycles.

CONCLUSION

While a long-term sustainable fiscal policy that recognizes the finite nature of our resource wealth is critical to the province's future economic and social well-being, the primary components of such a policy should be a stable and sustainable tax structure and greater stability in our capital planning and investment. I believe that some degree of responsiveness in our spending base to fluctuations in revenue is both inevitable given public expectations in a democracy and desirable to support a realistic long-term fiscal plan. However, it would clearly be preferable to relate such expenditure adjustments to variations in the level of general tax revenues, rather than predominantly to variations in non-renewable resource receipts.

The achievement of a sustainable fiscal policy is not a simple matter of passing legislation to enforce savings or budgeting rules. Fiscal policy, whether enshrined in legislation or simply endorsed through the usual mechanisms of the Westminster parliamentary model, must enjoy the understanding and support of the public and key stakeholders. Surely this is a key lesson from the "Klein Revolution." And a second lesson from that experience is that simple and open communication of public policy issues and options is critical to public support. The treasurer of that day kept reminding us in the Treasury that "there's no problem we can't make bigger." Regrettably, during the course of the 1980s, provincial budgets and financial reporting had become increasingly opaque, seriously diminishing the credibility of the government on fiscal issues. A critical element in the success of the 1990s reforms was moving to consolidated budgets, quarterly financial reporting, understandable deficit and debt targets, and clear business plans accompanied by meaningful measurement of results.

The introduction of a three-year capital plan with the 2003 budget was a positive step in improving the clarity and transparency of the provincial fiscal plan. But continuing efforts to "manage the surplus" over the last decade through such vehicles as the sustainability fund, capital account, and an array of new endowment funds have left the keenest students of provincial fiscal policy at least somewhat bewildered regarding the state of the province's finances. While the elimination of the capital fund and consolidation of research endowments in 2009–10 should reduce this complexity, the decision discussed above regarding the divergence of budgeting and reporting with respect to the SUCH sector, as well as the exclusion of "Alberta Innovates" corporations from the budget accounts, is not encouraging.[4]

I think it is essential that the province move its budgetary fiscal plan to full accrual in the SUCH sector, in line with reporting in the province's audited financial statements. Consistent treatment of capital spending, depreciation, and operating surpluses or deficits in the province's budgets and financial reports would make a significant contribution to the simplicity and transparency of provincial fiscal planning and expenditure management. This would still leave some ambiguity in the treatment of capital support for municipal infrastructure, which is not included in the provincial reporting entity, but it would meet the basic test of ensuring that provincial financial statements report results against the province's budget plan. Capitalization of the approximately $2 billion of annual grants to the SUCH sector for capital purposes will have a significant impact on the province's reported operating balance, and the resulting difference in this critical fiscal measure between the budget and the consolidated statements will engender substantial ambiguity regarding the state of the province's finances.

Secondly, I think it is important to focus on two key provincial fiscal measures: the annual operating surplus or deficit, and the province's net financial assets. In the interests of simplicity, clarity, and common sense, these measures should be consistent in the fiscal plan and the consolidated financial statements of the province. It is time to eliminate the distinction between "revenues for fiscal plan purposes" and "revenues for financial statement purposes," between "liabilities for fiscal planning purposes" and liabilities. The exclusion of large pension liabilities from "net financial assets," for example, has long since served its purpose, and now simply adds complexity without clarity to understanding the province's finances and its expenditure plan.[5] The distinction between financial assets, which can be used to repay debt or to fund future operating expense, and capital assets, which will be used in the delivery of future services but in the public sector do not normally provide a source of future income, should be clear.

Apart from simplifying and clarifying the province's "bottom line," however, I believe the single greatest challenge in developing and gaining necessary public support for sustainable long-term fiscal policies is to seek better ways to communicate the reality of non-renewable resource receipts in the province's fiscal framework. The report of the Alberta Financial Investment and Planning Advisory Commission (FIPAC) (2008) addressed the issue through its analysis of the "fiscal gap" between program spending and tax revenue and also recommended simplification of the structure of provincial savings funds, but I do not believe the FIPAC recommendations go far enough in simplifying the presentation of the province's fiscal plan.

The critical requirement to improve public understanding of provincial finances should be to change the language we use to describe resource receipts.[6] I would like to see the term "natural resource revenue" in the province's fiscal summaries relabelled, "receipts from the sale of Crown-owned resources"[7] and a subtotal shown for "operating revenue," which would exclude these receipts.[8] I would then term the total of operating revenue and resource receipts "total receipts" or some similar term, to recognize that the proceeds of the sale of an asset are not "revenue."

In an ideal world, the province would record the value of its Crown resources on the statement of financial position and exclude receipts from resource sales from the operating statement completely, but both measurement challenges and the impact on the reported "surplus/deficit" may preclude this approach, at least in the medium term.[9] It would, however, be feasible and desirable to include a schedule in the financial statements and the budget that would highlight the estimated value of Crown-owned resource assets, the depletion of those assets through annual production, and the proportion of the proceeds of the sale of Crown resources utilized to fund operating expense, capital investments, and the purchase of financial assets.

In closing, I cannot help but make two final observations. The first is that sustainable and effective expenditure management in the province is unlikely to be achieved unless we are successful in addressing the health spending issues, an issue that is addressed by Duckett, Kramer, and Sarnecki in the following chapter. The second is that it is unlikely that we can achieve a sustainable fiscal structure in Alberta without reducing our dependence on the sale of non-renewable natural resources to fund the delivery of current public services.

Notes

1. Financial assets are net of provincial pension liabilities.
2. This figure is net of pension liabilities but excludes the SUCH sector (schools, universities, colleges, and hospitals) and, in 2010, Alberta Innovates corporations.
3. An exception was permitted where "in the opinion of the Provincial Treasurer, the money is urgently required because of an emergency or a disaster" (DEA).
4. For example, significant Alberta Health Services deficits will be reported as incurred in the financial statements, but only recorded in the fiscal plan when they are funded through grants, making it difficult to compare budgeted to audited health spending. We have already seen

the confusion that this treatment created in the 2010 budget. The most important variance, however, will come through the capitalization and amortization of capital investments in the financial statements, while the budget will expense these amounts as grants.

5. Pension liabilities were originally excluded on grounds that they were subject to a 50-year "debt repayment plan," distinct from the 25-year plan to eliminate the province's other "net debt." Neither plan now exists.

6. I have referred to "resource receipts" throughout this chapter rather than resource revenues, although in a concession to historic terminology, I have included these receipts in referring to total provincial "revenue."

7. I recognize that technically these receipts should be termed, "sale of Crown-owned resources and exploration/development rights."

8. The historical fiscal summaries included in the provincial budget include a subtotal for "total own-source revenue," but it excludes federal transfers, not resource revenues. See Alberta Finance and Enterprise, 2010, 89.

9. Note that under contemporary accounting standards, changes to the market valuation of Crown-owned resources arising from changes in valuation or in estimated reserves would presumably be recorded in the annual operating results of the province. Given the magnitude of these assets, this treatment could make the historic volatility in Alberta's recorded revenues look benign.

References

Alberta Finance and Enterprise. 2010. "2010–13 Fiscal Plan."
Alberta Financial Investment and Planning Commission. 2008. "Preserving Prosperity: Challenging Alberta to Save." Alberta Finance and Enterprise, January.
Alberta Treasury. 1974. "Illustration of a Program Budget, Industry and Commerce." Supplement to the 1974 Budget Address.
———. 1976. "Estimates of Expenditure, 1976–77."
———. 1994. "Budget 94."
Boessenkool, Ken. 2010. "Alberta Budget: The Other Story." *Edmonton Journal*, 18 February.
Boothe, Paul. 1995. "The Growth of Government Spending in Alberta." Canadian Tax Paper No. 100, Canadian Tax Foundation.
Duckett, Stephen J., Gordon Kramer, and Liesje Sarnecki. 2013. "Alberta's Health Spending Challenge: Inter and Intraprovincial Differences in Health Expenditure." In this volume.
Emery, J.C. Herbert, and Ronald D. Kneebone. 2009. "Will it be Déjà vu All Over Again?" spp Briefing Papers 2 (1). University of Calgary, School of Public Policy, April.

Osborne, David, and Ted Gaebler. 1992. *Reinventing Government: How the Entrepreneurial Spirit is Transforming the Public Sector.* Reading, MA: Addison-Wesley.

Alberta's Health Spending Challenge

Inter and Intraprovincial Differences in Health Expenditure

Stephen Duckett, Gordon Kramer, and Liesje Sarnecki

INTRODUCTION

In 2008, Alberta's provincial government health expenditure was $3,741 per capita. This contrasted with an average of $3,262 per head of population for the other Canadian provinces, a difference of almost $500. In 2008, amongst the Canadian provinces, only Newfoundland and Labrador spent more per head on health care than Alberta. But just over ten years previously, Alberta's per capita spend was roughly the same as the rest of Canada, in fact almost $200 less. This timeframe coincides with what Hickey (2006) refers to as the period of "renewed expenditure" following periods of "escalating costs" (1975–1990) and "spending restraints" (1990–1996); Boychuk (2002) adopts similar terms referring both to the "restraint" of the early-to-mid 1990s and that the "recent pattern of expenditure increase is likely a response to pent up demand (from) the mid-1990s."

In this chapter we review the trends in provincial government health expenditure (hereafter "health expenditure") that have led to these differences in per capita spending between Alberta and the other provinces. The review is policy-oriented, highlighting the apparent choices that contributed to Alberta's higher level of spending.

There is an extensive literature that analyzes *international* differences in health expenditure. An important finding from these studies is that wealthier countries tend to spend more on health as a proportion of GDP (Anderson and Hussey 2001, Reinhardt, Hussey, and Anderson 2002). Three further conclusions from the literature on cross-national studies of health expenditure are noteworthy. First, health expenditure tends to increase faster than GDP (Pfaff 1990; Gerdtham et al. 1992; McGuire et al. 1993). Second, increased use of technologies is associated with higher total health spending (Reinhardt, Hussey, and Anderson 2002). Unlike the situation in many other industries, new technologies in health care thus appear to be additive rather than reduce costs through productivity improvement. A similar conclusion has been found in a study looking at differences between states in the United States (Baker et al. 2003). Differences in use of technologies between countries appear to be greater in diagnostic technologies (e.g., CT scanners, MRI) rather than therapeutic technology (Slade and Anderson 2001). Finally, there does not appear to be a relationship between health expenditure and health status (McGuire et al. 1993), possibly because of the number of intervening variables, for example whether provided services are effective (Filmer and Pritchett 1999).

There have also been a number of Canadian studies that examine *interprovincial* differences in health expenditure adopting similar methods and yielding similar results to the international studies (Di Matteo and Di Matteo 1998; Landon et al. 2006; Di Matteo 2009).

Two "grey literature" studies adopt a policy-oriented focus similar to ours. Shanahan and Gousseau (1997) used a cross-sectional approach to study differences between Manitoba and other provinces. They acknowledged the deficiency of cross-sectional studies but were limited by the data available at the time. More recently, Hickey (2006) analyzed health spending in Saskatchewan, which involved a comparison of interprovincial trends. Although Hickey's report identified some factors that contributed to Saskatchewan's health expenditure trends (e.g., fee increases for physicians), this was not its main focus.

Two recent papers have examined Alberta's health spending, addressing whether or not it is "sustainable." Building on their previous work, Di Matteo and Di Matteo (2009) examine trends in Alberta's health expenditure, both in total and by type of expenditure, to estimate future spending under a variety of assumptions. They question whether past trends are sustainable without changes in policy settings on either the expenditure or revenue side.

McMillan (2009) incorporates a brief review of health expenditure in a canter across a number of areas of provincial government expenditure. His analysis of interprovincial comparisons of expenditure does not appear to adjust for the age-gender composition of the population and so his conclusion that "relatively speaking, health spending in Alberta does not seem to be excessive" ignores a significant exogenous driver of differences in health expenditure (2009, 3).

The studies in the economics literature focus on explaining differences in health expenditure between countries or provinces, and thus include in their models factors that could be regarded as endogenous, that is, within the control of decision makers, with the number of physicians per thousand population being the most notable example. In contrast, we adopt a decision or policy-oriented approach and hence take a more limited view of what factors are exogenous, focusing only on demographic and general economic factors.

Our approach is thus based on the assumption that expenditure growth is the result of explicit or implicit policy choices to spend (or not spend) on health care. In that sense we take a broad view of power and policy, incorporating decisions and non-decisions, and the framing of choices about what can be considered on the policy agenda or radar (Lukes 1974). These choices were made explicitly or by default, by politicians or provincial officials, and/or by decision makers in health authorities overspending their legislatively endorsed budget, being funded for that, and thus establishing a new higher base. Thus we refute Hickey's conclusion that

> the debate is further complicated by the fact that due to the nature and structure of our existing system, we do not collectively and deliberately choose our consumption level of health care—in many ways and instances, it merely occurs. Thus, from a larger public policy perspective, the implications of and alternatives to increased health spending are not well defined or widely understood, and the opportunity for public discussion limited. (2006, 1)

In this chapter, we first standardize for exogenous factors and then examine trends in health expenditure, activity, and unit costs in five specific areas that together account for 83% of Alberta's total health expenditure: hospitals (41% of total health expenditure); other institutions (6%); capital expenditures (7%); physician expenditure (18%), and public health expenditure (11%). We then analyze whether Alberta's increased spending leads to increased access or quality of care. Intraprovincial comparisons are then made to identify specific implications and policy choices for Alberta as a result of the interprovincial comparisons.

PROVINCIAL GOVERNMENT HEALTH EXPENDITURE

Table 13.1 shows trends in health expenditure from 1996 to 2008 comparing Alberta with all other Canadian provinces on four metrics. It can be seen that health expenditure has been increasing in all provinces over the last decade. In Table 13.1 Alberta is compared with other provinces rather than the rest of Canada, as expenditure in the territories is quite different from expenditure in other provinces, partly because of the different geography (very small populations, very large areas), partly different demography (younger populations, greater proportion of Aboriginal populations), and partly that the small size of the populations leads to lack of scale economies and volatility in expenditure patterns.

Jurisdiction	1996	1997	1998	1999	2000	2001	2002	2003	2004	2005	2006	2007	2008
Expenditure per Unadjusted Capita, Current Dollars*													
Alberta	1,474	1,600	1,689	1,910	2,069	2,300	2,471	2,603	2,812	3,070	3,278	3,520	3,741
Other Provinces	1,673	1,718	1,811	1,913	2,068	2,193	2,322	2,487	2,620	2,782	2,933	3,109	3,262
Difference	-198	-118	-122	-3	1	107	150	117	192	288	345	411	479
Expenditure per Unadjusted Capita, Constant Dollars (2002, Adjusted with Canada CPI)†													
Alberta	1,658	1,770	1,850	2,057	2,168	2,352	2,471	2,532	2,686	2,869	3,005	3,157	3,279
Other Provinces	1,882	1,900	1,984	2,059	2,168	2,242	2,322	2,419	2,503	2,600	2,689	2,789	2,859
Difference	-223	-130	-134	-3	1	110	150	113	184	269	316	368	420
Expenditure per Adjusted Capita (Adjusted for Age and Gender), Constant Dollars (2002, Adjusted with Canada CPI)† ‡													
Alberta	1,855	1,969	2,051	2,261	2,360	2,534	2,640	2,677	2,812	2,979	3,099	3,235	3,338
Other Provinces	1,877	1,882	1,948	2,003	2,086	2,135	2,185	2,249	2,299	2,357	2,400	2,455	2,485
Difference	-23	87	103	258	274	399	455	428	513	622	699	780	854
Expenditure per Adjusted Capita (Adjusted for Age and Gender), Constant Dollars (2002, Adjusted with Alberta and Canada CPI)† ‡													
Alberta	1,908	2,020	2,099	2,298	2,382	2,563	2,640	2,636	2,780	2,949	3,011	3,059	3,132
Other Provinces	1,877	1,882	1,948	2,003	2,086	2,135	2,185	2,249	2,299	2,357	2,400	2,455	2,485
Difference	31	138	151	295	297	428	455	387	481	591	611	604	648

TABLE 13.1 Indication of Trends in Provincial Government Health Expenditure Per Capita by Jurisdiction, 1996–2008

* *Source of expenditure data: Canadian Institute for Health Information, National Health Expenditure Trends, 1975–2008 (Ottawa: CIHI, 2008).*
† *Source of consumer price index values: Statistics Canada, CANSIM, Table 326-0021 and Catalogue nos. 62-001-x and 62-010-x.*
‡ *Adjusted population is weighted by all-sector expenditure by age and gender (2007/08 Population-Based Funding Weights for Alberta). Alberta's weights were applied across all provinces.*

As Table 13.1 shows, in 1996 Alberta spent about $198 in current dollars less per head of population than the rest of Canada. By 2008, however, Alberta was spending $479 more per head of population than other provinces: in just over a decade per capita expenditure increased $677 more per head in Alberta compared to other provinces. By 2008, Alberta had moved from spending slightly less per head of population to spending about 13% more. Health expenditure in current dollars in Alberta increased

154% over the period compared to a 95% increase in the rest of Canada.

Standardizing into constant 2002 dollars marginally reduces the apparent magnitude of Alberta's faster spending growth, with Alberta's spend in constant dollars increasing $640 per head of population more than other provinces.

Health service utilization is greater amongst older people than younger and so an important exogenous factor that would account for higher levels of health expenditures is the age distribution of the population (Di Matteo and Di Matteo 1998; Canadian Institute for Health Information 2005). Women also tend to consume more health services than men. However, Alberta has a younger population than the other provinces and is not aging as rapidly: when one adjusts for the age and gender distribution of the population, Alberta would be expected to have lower levels of expenditure than other provinces. But standardization for the age and gender distribution of the population causes Alberta's expenditure growth to diverge further from that of other provinces. On an age-gender standardized basis, Alberta spent $23 per head less than other provinces in 1996, but by 2008 spent $854 more per head. Alberta's increase in age-gender adjusted per capita spend is thus $876 per head greater than other provinces.

A further exogenous factor is that Alberta, in the last few years, has experienced higher levels of inflation relative to other provinces. Standardizing Alberta's health spend by taking into account the general inflation in the Alberta economy (with expenditure in other provinces standardized at the general Canadian inflation rate) reduces the difference in per capita spend to $648 per head of population in 2008 compared to $31 in 1996, a $617 difference in the increase in per capita expenditure.

Taking all the exogenous factors into account, Alberta in 2008 was the highest spending province, exceeding the next highest spender, Newfoundland, by $92 per capita or 3% (adjusting for age, gender, and inflation).

As noted above, international comparisons identify that income or wealth of a society impacts on the level of health spending. Health care, at the national level, is in that sense, a "luxury good," that is, as countries increase in wealth, they are likely to spend a higher proportion of their available resources on health care. The same factors apply, although not to the same extent, when one examines interprovincial comparisons of health care (Di Matteo and Di Matteo 1998; Ariste and Carr 2003; Di Matteo 2003; 2004; 2009; Bilgel 2004).

But as indicated earlier, the approach adopted in this analysis is a policy-oriented one, focused on the decisions that have led to these differences in provincial spending. We therefore do not treat provincial income as an exogenous variable driving and determining health expenditure; rather, Alberta's relative wealth has meant that the resources were available to fund certain health policy choices, such as investment decisions in capital. That being the case, no adjustment is made in subsequent analyses for provincial wealth.

COMPOSITION OF HEALTH EXPENDITURE

Trends in provincial spending over the period 1996–2008 by type of expenditure show significant differences in how the components of health expenditure have increased over the last decade (see Table 13.2). Taking hospitals and other institutions together (accounting for 34% of Alberta's excess spend over other provinces; other institutions being nursing homes, designated assisted living, and other specialist health services such as rehabilitation hospitals or mental health institutions), expenditure across Canada has increased in real terms over the period. But spending patterns in this area, as in others, have diverged. In 1996 Alberta spent about $23 more per age-gender adjusted head of population on hospitals and other institutions compared to other provinces, but by 2008 the spending in Alberta was more than $200 greater than in other provinces. Alberta's rate of growth in real spending was 37% compared to 19% growth in other provinces.

Hospitals and other institutions are to some extent substitutes; that is, if there is inadequate supply of other institutions, patients may backup in hospitals as "alternate level of care"

Jurisdiction	1996	1997	1998	1999	2000	2001	2002	2003	2004	2005	2006	2007	2008
Hospitals													
Alberta	848	905	925	980	1,025	1,098	1,129	1,118	1,206	1,254	1,265	1,260	1,281
Other Provinces	862	805	819	818	846	852	872	892	916	920	937	944	954
Difference	-13	99	105	162	180	247	257	226	290	334	328	316	327
Other Institutions													
Alberta	229	228	214	211	202	205	180	168	181	179	177	183	193
Other Provinces	193	238	260	265	275	283	289	293	299	303	305	303	303
Difference	36	-10	-45	-55	-73	-78	-109	-125	-118	-124	-128	-120	-110
Subtotal Hospitals and Other Institutions													
Alberta	1,078	1,133	1,139	1,190	1,227	1,303	1,308	1,286	1,388	1,433	1,443	1,443	1,474
Other Provinces	1,055	1,043	1,079	1,083	1,121	1,135	1,161	1,185	1,216	1,223	1,243	1,248	1,257
Difference	23	89	60	107	106	169	147	101	172	210	200	196	217
Capital													
Alberta	50	49	52	117	129	162	186	182	179	204	223	227	209
Other Provinces	61	63	65	83	95	96	97	105	108	121	115	120	116
Difference	-11	-15	-13	34	34	66	88	78	71	82	109	107	94
Physicians													
Alberta	361	355	369	379	383	413	454	473	476	501	520	564	576
Other Provinces	405	414	419	424	429	438	443	453	463	473	486	501	506
Difference	-43	-59	-50	-44	-46	-25	11	21	13	28	34	64	70
Public Health													
Alberta	110	147	177	235	239	254	243	237	265	335	346	345	343
Other Provinces	93	91	101	112	122	134	134	151	145	160	164	182	191
Difference	18	56	76	123	117	120	109	85	120	176	183	163	152
All Other Health Expenditure													
Alberta	309	337	361	376	404	431	450	457	472	476	478	479	529
Other Provinces	265	271	284	301	319	332	349	355	368	381	392	404	414
Difference	44	67	77	75	85	99	100	102	104	95	86	76	115
Total Provincial Government Health Expenditure													
Alberta	1,908	2,020	2,099	2,298	2,382	2,563	2,640	2,636	2,780	2,949	3,011	3,059	3,132
Other Provinces	1,877	1,882	1,948	2,003	2,086	2,135	2,185	2,249	2,299	2,357	2,400	2,455	2,485
Difference	31	138	151	295	297	428	455	387	481	591	611	604	648

TABLE 13.2 Trends in Provincial Government Health Expenditure*
in Constant (2002) Dollars†, per Adjusted Capita‡ by Category of
Expenditure and Jurisdiction, 1996–2008 (*opposite*)

* *Source of expenditure data: Canadian Institute for Health Information, National Health
Expenditure Trends, 1975–2008 (Ottawa: CIHI, 2008).*
† *Source of consumer price index values: Statistics Canada, CANSIM, Table 326-0021 and
Catalogue nos. 62-001-x and 62-010-x. Alberta expenditures were adjusted with Alberta-Specific
CPI. Other province expenditures were adjusted with Canadian CPI.*
‡ *Adjusted population is weighted by all-sector expenditure by age and gender (2007/08
Population-Based Funding Weights for Alberta). Alberta's weights were applied across all
provinces.*

patients (patients who no longer need acute care but have no
appropriate accommodation into which to be discharged). The
difference in the pattern of investment between Alberta and
other provinces comparing hospitals and other institutions is
stark. Over the study period, Alberta increased its investment by
50% in real terms on a per capita basis in hospitals but decreased
its investment in other institutions by about 16%. The other
provinces had a quite different pattern of investment choices:
hospital investment in the other provinces increased by about
11% compared to other institutions increasing by 57%. In per
capita terms, Alberta spent about $13 less per head on hospitals
in 1996 than other provinces but $327 more per head in 2008.
But for other institutions, Alberta spent $36 more per head in
1996 but its spending lagged $110 per head in 2008. This pat-
tern of investment was relatively constant over the period with
Alberta continuing to increase its hospital investment (and its
excess spend compared to other provinces) over the period and
pursue an apparent strategy of relative disinvestment in other
institutions. The consequence of this pattern of investment will
be discussed later in terms of the patterns of utilization.

The hospital investment strategy is reflected in the difference
in capital spend. Over the period 1996–2008, Alberta's spending
on capital (accounting for 15% of Alberta's excess spend compared to other provinces) increased more than fourfold (319%),
from spending around $50 per head to spending more than
$200 per head in real terms. In contrast, other provinces' capital

Agreement	Period
AHW–AMA Agreement	1995/96–1997/98
AHW–AMA Agreement	1998/99–2000/01
AHW–AMA Agreement	2001/02–2002/03
Master Agreement #1	2003/04–2005/06
Master Agreement #2	2006/07–2007/08
Master Agreement #3	2008/09–2010/11

TABLE 13.3 Alberta Government and Alberta Medical Association Agreements, 1996–2011

investment almost doubled from around $60 per head to around $115 per head. In the first three years of the period (1996–2008) Alberta's capital spending was less than the other provinces, but for the last years of the period (2006–2008), coinciding with an economic boom for the province, Alberta was spending about $100 more per head every year than the other provinces.

The trend in physician spending (accounting for 11% of the difference in Alberta's spend compared to other provinces) is in part influenced by the choices and compromises made by government and the Alberta Medical Association in negotiating the various agreements that govern physician fee-for-service payments and other remuneration to physicians. Table 13.3 shows the relevant agreement phases. It can be seen (Table 13.2) that Alberta's physician expenditure started to diverge from other provinces toward the end of the 2001/02–2002/03 agreement.

Investment in public health (Table 13.2) also shows stark differences in spending. Differences in public health spending account for almost a quarter (23%) of the difference in Alberta's spend compared to other provinces. Over the period 1996–2008 Alberta has more than tripled its expenditure on public health (211% increase), whereas spending in other provinces has doubled (107% increase). Alberta's spending on public health doubled in the period 1996–1999 and increased steadily through to 2004 and then jumped by about $70 per capita over the period 2004–05 and continued at that higher level over the remaining period.

IMPACT ON ACTIVITY AND UNIT COSTS

Higher relative expenditure could be caused by a higher volume of services, or higher unit costs, or both. In this section we review activity and price data to disentangle these effects. Unfortunately, different data sources need to be used for these analyses and so consistent time trends for the full period of the preceding analysis are not available.

Hospitals

The additional investment in hospitals means that Alberta now has relatively greater capacity to provide hospital care as compared with both the past and other provinces. It is over 50 years since Milton Roemer reported a study of hospital activity that led to a critical insight in hospital planning, now known as Roemer's Law: that a built bed tends to become a filled bed (Roemer 1961).

As Table 13.4 shows, over the period 2003–2007, Alberta provided more days of hospital care and admitted its residents at a substantially higher rate, than other provinces. In 2003, Alberta's bed day rate of 710 bed days per age-gender adjusted head of population was 26% above that of other provinces. Over the period 2003–2007, bed day provision declined in other provinces by about 7% whereas Alberta's provision was essentially stable, so by 2007 Alberta provided 35% more bed days than other provinces.

In 2007 (the latest year for which data are available), Alberta admitted just over 100 patients per thousand population (adjusted for age and gender) relative to the 60 per thousand admission rate in other provinces. (Standard reporting of hospital activity is based on people discharged from hospital; the technical term is "separations" as it also includes deaths and transfers.) Across the country, the rate of hospital admission has been declining over the reporting period but Alberta's decline (about a 10% reduction in the number of admissions per head) is occurring at a slightly slower pace compared to the other provinces, where the decline in admissions over the same period is 13%.

A consequence of this higher level of provision is that cases that might otherwise be treated in community settings are

Jurisdiction	2001	2002	2003	2004	2005	2006	2007
Bed Days per Adjusted Capita (All cases)* †							
Alberta	—	—	710	710	717	712	708
Other Provinces	—	—	565	571	566	534	526
Difference	—	—	145	140	151	178	182
Separations per Adjusted Capita*							
Alberta	115	114	114	112	110	106	104
Other Provinces	70	67	66	67	65	62	61
Difference	45	47	48	45	44	44	43
Average Resource Intensity Weights (Typical Cases)*							
Alberta	—	—	0.91	0.91	0.92	0.94	0.94
Other Provinces	—	—	0.97	0.98	1.00	1.01	1.02
Difference	—	—	-0.06	-0.07	-0.08	-0.07	-0.08
Ratio of LOS to ELOS (Typical Cases)*							
Alberta	—	—	1.04	1.05	1.04	1.03	1.01
Ontario	—	—	0.99	0.98	0.97	0.95	0.94
British Columbia	—	—	0.99	0.97	0.97	0.96	0.96
Other Provinces	—	—	1.12	1.10	1.10	1.07	1.05
Hospital Expenditure per Resource Intensity Weight (Typical Cases)* ‡							
Alberta	—	—	13,137	14,355	15,101	15,425	15,714
Other Provinces	—	—	13,106	12,685	12,732	13,451	13,703
Difference	—	—	31	1,669	2,370	1,974	2,011
Hospital Expenditure per Resource Intensity Weight (All Cases)* ‡							
Alberta	—	—	7,686	8,433	8,801	8,921	8,847
Other Provinces	—	—	8,359	8,058	8,135	8,427	8,522
Difference	—	—	-673	375	666	494	326
Total Nurses per 100,000 Adjusted Capita in any Workplace§ **							
Alberta	1,025	987	994	1,027	1,025	984	—
Other Provinces	957	891	914	906	903	895	—
Difference	69	96	80	121	122	89	—
Total FTE Nurses Employed in Hospitals per 100,000 Adjusted Capita †† ‡‡**							
Alberta	—	—	—	—	623	646	658
Other Provinces	—	—	—	—	480	478	499
Difference	—	—	—	—	143	168	159

Jurisdiction	2001	2002	2003	2004	2005	2006	2007
Average Hourly Compensation to FTE Nurses Employed in Hospitals†† ‡‡							
Alberta	—	—	—	—	30.08	29.64	31.02
Other Provinces	—	—	—	—	30.72	28.29	30.69
Difference	—	—	—	—	-0.64	1.34	0.33
Total FTE Nurses Employed in Hospitals per 1,000 Inpatient Separations* †† ‡‡							
Alberta	—	—	—	—	56.87	61.01	63.47
Other Provinces	—	—	—	—	54.10	56.67	60.57
Difference	—	—	—	—	2.77	4.34	2.90
Total FTE Nurses Employed in Hospitals per 1,000 Resource Intensity Weight (RIW)* †† ‡‡							
Alberta	—	—	—	—	43.74	45.51	46.19
Other Provinces	—	—	—	—	41.33	41.89	43.94
Difference	—	—	—	—	2.41	3.62	2.25

TABLE 13.4 Selected Measures of Hospital Activity, Employment and Unit Cost by Jurisdiction, 2001–2007

* *Source: CIHI Portal, extracted November 3, 2009. Parts of this material are based on data and information provided by the Canadian Institute for Health Information (CIHI). However, the analyses, conclusions, opinions, and statements expressed herein are those of the authors, and not necessarily those of the Canadian Institute for Health Information.*
† *Adjusted for difference in age and gender using the direct method of adjustment.*
‡ *Source of expenditure data: Canadian Institute for Health Information, National Health Expenditure Trends, 1975–2008 (Ottawa: CIHI, 2008).*
§ *Source: Canadian Institute for Health Information, Health Care Providers, 1997 to 2006, A Reference Guide (Ottawa: CIHI, 2008).*
** *Unless otherwise stated, adjusted population is weighted by all-sector expenditure by age and gender (2007/08 Population-Based Funding Weights for Alberta). Alberta's weights were applied across all provinces.*
†† *Source: Canadian Institute for Health Information, MIS Costing Database, provided by Greg Zinck.*
‡‡ *2006 Values exclude Prince Edward Island as nursing data was not provided in this year.*

admitted and treated in hospitals in Alberta. As a result, the average intensity or complexity of the patients treated in Alberta is
8% lower compared to other provinces (the measure in Table 13.4
is the "average resource intensity weight," a measure derived by
standardizing the typical case using the Canadian Case
Mix Groups).

Another way excess bed provision can play out is in terms
of more patients staying relatively longer in hospital than is
the norm in other provinces. Despite evidence in the literature
that richer nurse staffing is associated with shorter length of
stay (Lang et al. 2004, Kane et al. 2007), this is not supported
by an interprovincial comparison of Alberta with other provinces. There is a substantial difference in length of stay (LOS)
patterns across Canada, with Ontario and British Columbia, in
particular, having a tight approach to length of stay. The typical patient in those provinces (taking into account the patient's
diagnoses and the procedures performed on the patient) has an
average 5% shorter length of stay than would be expected if the
Canadian norms apply. Length of stay in other provinces (other
than Alberta, British Columbia, and Ontario) is marginally above
the Canadian average, with Alberta's hospitals also keeping their
patients slightly longer.

Cost per inpatient treated increased significantly over the
period 2003–2007. Using the measure of cost per complexity-
adjusted patient treated for all cases, for example, Alberta's costs
increased around 15% over this period compared to a 2% increase
in other provinces. As a result Alberta moved from a position of
complexity-adjusted patients costing around 10% less than other
provinces to one where patients cost around 4% more.

Part of the reason for this higher cost is because of the
number of staff employed in hospitals. Using nursing staff as
an example, Alberta's hospitals employ about 30% more nursing
staff per head of adjusted population than the other provinces.
A similar pattern can be seen in terms of full-time equivalent
nurses per separation and per complexity-weighted separation,
with Alberta employing about 5% more nurses in 2007 on these
metrics than other provinces. There is no clear comparative trend
in these metrics. In addition to this volume effect, the average

hourly nursing compensation for nurses employed in hospitals is marginally higher in Alberta compared to other provinces.

Health Professionals

Physicians

In 2008, Alberta had about 20% more physicians per 100,000 age-gender adjusted population compared to other provinces (about 24% more family physicians, about 13% more specialists). In 1997, there was roughly the same number of family physicians and specialists per head of population in Alberta and the other provinces. Over the period 1997–2008, the number of physicians per head of population (both family physicians and specialists) declined in the other provinces by about 7%, but increased by around 12% in Alberta (15% for family physicians and 9% for specialists).

Not only are there more physicians per head of population in Alberta relative to other provinces, but Alberta's physicians get paid on average more per head than other provinces (for specialists $362,761 versus $311,097; for family physicians $267,060 versus $236,342, in 2005).

Nurses

For the last decade, Alberta has consistently had more total nurses per age-gender adjusted population. In 2006, for example, Alberta had 984 nurses per 100,000 adjusted population, about 10% more than the 895 nurses per capita in other provinces. Alberta's relativities were slightly different for registered nurses and licensed practical nurses. Alberta had about 10% fewer licensed practical nurses compared to other provinces, offset by about 12% more registered nurses compared to other provinces.

Other Professions

The relatively greater provision for physicians and nurses is also seen in a range of other health professions. For example, Alberta has about 11% more dental practitioners (dentists and dental hygienists) relative to other provinces, about a third more pharmacists and occupational therapists, and about 40% more physiotherapists than other provinces. In terms of technologists, in 2006, Alberta had about 26% more medical laboratory technologists, 16% more medical radiation technologists, and almost 50% more respiratory therapists than other provinces.

Equipment

High technology equipment is substantially more prevalent in Alberta. For example, Alberta has about 50% more magnetic resonance imaging machines per 100,000 population (adjusted for age and gender; 0.78 in Alberta versus 0.52 in other provinces).

Public Health

The "public health" category of health expenditure is relatively heterogeneous, and, although there have been enhancements in the reporting of this expenditure line in recent years (Hicks, Ballinger, and Campbell 2002), the development of robust measures of ambulatory care, and public health generally, is still a work in progress.

Unfortunately, the absence of metrics in public health precludes decomposition into price and volume effects. This very lack of metrics may have been a contributor to the relatively rapid growth in spending in this area. In the absence of clear metrics to describe either outputs or outcomes, incremental investments are based on persuasion and negotiation rather than evidence-based criteria. The relatively faster growth of public health expenditure, compared to hospital expenditure, for example, may be a special case of the "Baumol effect," named after Nobel Laureate, William Baumol. The relevant aspect of Baumol's work attempted to explain why expenditure growth in service industries, such as health care and the arts, occurs faster than traditional industries such as manufacturing (Baumol 1993; 1967). Baumol's thesis is essentially that there are two sectors of the economy: progressive (characterized by where there are increases in labour productivity) and non-progressive (where the inherent nature of the service means that the opportunity for productivity increases is limited). Baumol cites a number of examples but a characteristic of these "non-progressive" industries is that "the human touch is crucial," that the service provided is inherently personal and labour intensive so that a metric of output might be hours of care delivered.

Although Baumol developed and characterized his model as a dichotomy, it is also possible to think of progressive to non-progressive industries as being a continuum, and within the health sector there might be differential characteristics in different parts of the sector. Public health and primary care, for example, are characterized by lower capital intensity than hospitals, and thus hospitals may have greater opportunities for productivity growth than primary care or public health.

Baumol's work should not be stigmatized as suggesting that societies should not invest in non-progressive industries; in fact, Baumol himself noted that "contrary to appearances, we can afford ever more ample medical care, ever more abundant education, evermore adequate support of the indigent...it is only an illusion that we cannot do so, and the main step needed to deal effectively with our fiscal problems is to overcome that illusion" (Baumol 1993, 21).

Although there have been productivity increases affecting the non-progressive sectors (improvements in travel time, for example), further productivity improvements can be achieved in this area by, for example, harnessing new technologies (e.g., devices to allow home monitoring, telehealth technologies) and to structure payments for primary care and public health to encourage innovation and workforce optimization.

	1994	1995	1996	1997	1998	1999	2000	2001
Percentage of people who waited longer than 3 months for non-emergency surgery*								
Alberta								14.8%†
Canada								19.2%
Physician's experience of waiting time for patients‡								
Alberta Actual	5.5	6.9	7.3	7.0	7.8	8.7	9.0	8.2
Alberta Reasonable	5.0	5.4	5.3	4.6	4.3	4.9	4.8	4.7
Canada Actual	5.8	5.7	6.2	6.8	7.3	8.2	9.0	9.2
Canada Reasonable	5.2	5.4	5.4	4.2	4.3	4.5	4.7	4.7
Proportion of emergency hip fracture surgery undertaken on same or next day§								
Alberta								
Canada								

TABLE 13.5 Selected Satisfaction and Access Measures, Alberta vs. Canada/Other Provinces

Source: Statistics Canada, Canadian Community Health Survey.
† *2001 is estimate with high standard of error.*
‡ *Source: The Fraser Institute's national waiting list surveys, 1995–2009.*
§ *Source: Canadian Institute for Health Information, Health Indicators, 2008 (Ottawa: CIHI, 2008); Canadian Institute for Health Information, Health Indicators, 2009 (Ottawa: CIHI, 2009). Does not include Quebec.*

SUMMARY: EXPENDITURE TRENDS

The overall patterns revealed by this analysis are that, compared to other provinces, Alberta:

- placed a relatively greater emphasis on hospital-based development, with a resulting impact on higher utilization;
- invested heavily in "public health." Lack of performance metrics means that it is not possible to identify resulting benefits in terms of outputs, or decompose into price and volume effects;
- employs more nurses to staff hospitals and pays more to physicians and nurses; and
- has a higher unit cost of hospital care.

	2002	2003	2004	2005	2006	2007	2008	2009
Percentage of people who waited longer than 3 months for non-emergency surgery*								
Alberta	13.0%	19.5%	17.5%					
Canada	17.4%	19.0%	18.3%					
Physician's experience of waiting time for patients‡								
Alberta Actual		8.5	8.3	8.6	7.8	8.9	9.4	9.6
Alberta Reasonable		4.7	5.0	4.9	4.9	5.6	5.9	5.8
Canada Actual		9.5	9.5	9.4	9.0	9.1	8.7	8.0
Canada Reasonable		4.8	5.2	5.2	5.5	5.8	6.0	5.8
Proportion of emergency hip fracture surgery undertaken on same or next day§								
Alberta					66.8%	61.5%	61.9%	
Canada					65.2%	63.3%	62.5%	

IMPACT ON ACCESS AND QUALITY

Alberta's higher spending could be justified if it were associated with commensurate improvements in health care process or outcomes of care. However, the impact of Alberta's different patterns of expenditure on access and quality is quite mixed.

Access

There are two main data sources for information on waiting times: patients and providers. The Canadian Community Health Survey provides information from consumers every second year about their experience with waiting for non-emergency services. Table 13.5 shows that the proportion of Albertan patients who reported waiting more than three months for non-emergency surgery deteriorated over the survey periods from 2001 to

2007. In the first two surveys, Albertans reported shorter waiting times than the rest of Canada, but this advantage had been eliminated by the latter two surveys, with Alberta's performance being almost the same (marginally above or below) the Canadian average.

The Fraser Institute surveys physicians to ask about the experience of their patients (Esmail 2009). As Zeithaml, Parasuraman, and Berry (1990) have pointed out, customer satisfaction depends on both the perceived service received (in this case the actual waiting time) and the expected service (a surrogate is the Fraser Institute survey on the physician's perception of "reasonable wait"). Table 13.5 shows both actual and reasonable waits for Alberta and all of Canada (Canadian data include Alberta). There appears to be slight tendency of Alberta physicians, especially in recent years, to have tighter expectations of what might be regarded as "reasonable waits." Actual waits appear to be little different between Alberta and the Canada average: to the extent there is a difference, it does not reflect an Alberta advantage.

There is relatively little difference between the Fraser Institute data and the Canadian Community Health Survey data. Although different methods are adopted, and as a result there are marginal differences between the two measures, there is no evidence to suggest that Alberta's higher level of hospital provision has led to any advantage in waiting times for Alberta compared to other provinces.

Another measure of waiting times is for emergency access. The Canadian Institute for Health Information provides information on wait times for urgent hip fracture surgery, measured as the risk-adjusted proportion of people with a hip fracture who have surgery on the same or next day. Again there appears to be little or no difference between Alberta and the Canadian average on this measure; to the extent differences are apparent, more recent years suggest Alberta performs worse than the Canadian average.

Thus, in terms of hospital access, at least, there does not appear to be any difference between Alberta and other provinces.

	1996	1997	1998	1999	2000	2001	2002	2003	2004	2005	2006
Average life expectancy at birth*											
Alberta	78.5	78.9	79.1	79.2	79.5	79.7	79.7	79.9	80.2	80.3	80.5
Other Provinces	78.4	78.6	78.8	79.0	79.4	79.7	79.8	80.0	80.3	80.5	80.8
Neonatal mortality rate (deaths < 28 days per 1,000 pop)† ‡											
Alberta	1.2	0.7	0.6	0.9	0.6	0.6	0.7	0.9	0.5	0.7	0.6
Canada	1.0	0.9	1.0	0.8	0.7	0.8	0.8	0.7	0.7	0.7	0.5
Perinatal mortality rate (deaths < 7 days per 1,000 pop)§ **											
Alberta	7.0	6.2	4.7	6.7	6.7	6.5	7.3	7.0	7.3	7.1	6.3
Canada	6.7	6.6	6.2	6.2	6.1	6.3	6.3	6.3	6.2	6.3	6.1

TABLE 13.6 Selected Outcome Measures, Alberta vs. Canada/Other Provinces

* Source: Statistics Canada, Table 13.102-0511, Life expectancy, abridged life table, at birth and at age 65, by sex, Canada, provinces and territories, annual, CANSIM.
† Includes age at time of death between one and six days.
‡ Source: Statistics Canada, Table 13.102-0507, Infant mortality, by age group, Canada, provinces and territories, annual (table), CANSIM.
§ Perinatal death is the death of a child under one week of age (zero to six days) or a stillbirth of 28 or more weeks of gestation. Source: Statistics Canada, Table 13.102-0507, Infant mortality, by age group.
** Source: Statistics Canada, Table 13.102-0508, Perinatal mortality and components, Canada, provinces and territories, annual, CANSIM.

Quality

Summary measures of overall health status do not reveal an unequivocal Alberta advantage. In 1996, Albertans enjoyed a marginal advantage in terms of average life expectancy at birth (see Table 13.6). Although over the ensuing decade life expectancy in Alberta and other provinces improved, the rate of improvement in Alberta was slower than in other provinces, and by 2006 Alberta's comparative advantage in life expectancy had evaporated. Measures of neonatal and perinatal mortality show a mixed picture. While there have been improvements in neonatal mortality rate in both Alberta and Canada over the decade 1996–2006, the rates for Alberta and Canada are essentially equivalent. There has been a marginal improvement in perinatal mortality across Canada, but the pattern in Alberta has been

Jurisdiction	Type of Cancer			
	Prostate	Breast	Colorectal	Lung
Alberta	91	88	60	12
Canada	94	87	62	15

TABLE 13.7 Cancer: Relative Survival Ratios, Alberta and Canada, Five-Year Relative Age Standardized Survival Ratio (%), Cancers Diagnosed 2002–2004

Source: Canadian Cancer Registry database at Statistics Canada

slightly different. Although small numbers yield some volatility in the rates, it appears that Alberta's perinatal mortality rate is somewhat higher than the rest of Canada.

Table 13.7 shows data on comparative survival rates for four key types of cancer. Albertan survival rates are marginally below Canadian averages for three of the four major cancers.

A critical overall summary measure of outcomes is the health-adjusted life expectancy, combining both the length of life and the extent to which life is lived with a disability or health impairment. In 2001 (latest year), Alberta's health-adjusted life expectancy at birth was below that for all of Canada for both males (67.6 years versus 68.3) and females (69.7 years versus 70.8). In the case of females, there is almost a one-year gap in health-adjusted life expectancy at birth. There is a similar pattern for health-adjusted life expectancy at age 65. Albertan males and females can look forward to a marginally shorter period of healthy life compared to the all of Canada figures (males: 12.6 in Alberta versus 12.7 for Canada; females 14.0 versus 14.4).

Another measure of quality is patient satisfaction. The Canadian Community Health Survey provides information on the proportion of the population who rate quality of care on two different scales: quality of care received and the extent to which they are satisfied with health care services received. Table 13.8 shows that on both measures, the satisfaction of Albertans is marginally below that of residents of other provinces.

A further measure of quality is readmission rates to hospital care (see Table 13.9). Here there is incomplete information for other provinces, but on three of the four measures for which

Jurisdiction	2000	2003	2005
Quality of health care services received rated as excellent or good*			
Alberta	83.6%	85.7%	85.9%
Other Provinces‡	84.4%	86.8%	85.2%
Very or somewhat satisfied with health care services received*			
Alberta	82.1%	83.5%	84.1%
Other Provinces‡	84.6%	85.3%	85.0%
Quality of hospital care received rated as excellent or good†			
Alberta	79.6%	81.3%	82.9%
Other Provinces‡	80.2%	83.9%	82.0%
Very or somewhat satisfied with hospital care received†			
Alberta	80.3%	79.8%	81.8%
Other Provinces‡	79.5%	82.3%	80.8%

TABLE 13.8 Canadian Community Health Survey Patient Satisfaction Ratings

* Source: Table 13.105-0280, Patient satisfaction with any health care services received in the past 12 months, by age group and sex, household population aged 15 and over, Canadian Community Health Survey (CCHS 1.1, 2.1 and 3.1), Canada, provinces and territories, occasional.
† Source: Table 13.105-0281, Patient satisfaction with most recent hospital care received in the past 12 months, by age group and sex, household population aged 15 and over, Canadian Community Health Survey (CCHS 1.1, 2.1 and 3.1), Canada, provinces and territories, occasional.
‡ Includes the Territories.

Jurisdiction	Acute Myocardial Infarction (AMI)	Asthma	Prostatectomy	Hysterectomy
Alberta	4.2	4.0	2.1	1.3
Ontario	5.4	5.0	2.7	1.1
British Columbia	5.6	5.5	2.3	1.1
Canada†	5.6	4.8	2.5	1.2

TABLE 13.9 Readmission Rates (2005/06–2007/08)*

* Source: Canadian Institute for Health Information, Health Indicators, 2009 (Ottawa: CIHI, 2009).
† Includes the Territories.

Peer Group	Planning Zone	1996	1997	1998	1999	2000	2001
Metro	Calgary Metro	670.7	649.1	686.5	741.1	698.1	718.1
Metro	Edmonton Metro	664.9	698.6	786.3	851.0	839.3	846.7
Metro Bedroom	Calgary Bedroom	671.4	677.0	683.5	712.1	700.9	700.4
Metro Bedroom	Edmonton Bedroom	657.5	655.9	693.2	711.4	687.6	682.1
Regional	Lethbridge	711.4	836.3	845.4	860.3	902.0	809.3
Regional	Medicine Hat	1,086.9	1,009.0	1,042.7	928.9	952.0	940.9
Regional	Red Deer	949.3	1,075.5	1,066.9	1,053.3	1,073.8	1,106.4
Regional	Grande Prairie	891.3	868.7	1,020.8	984.6	915.3	878.7
Regional	Fort McMurray	1,184.5	1,246.2	1,257.9	1,262.9	1,397.1	1,436.0
Rural	Rural South	924.2	974.4	1,013.2	1,014.9	979.0	941.8
Rural	Rural Central	1,033.8	1,046.7	1,054.5	1,109.1	1,062.3	1,043.9
Rural	Rural North	1,047.8	1,079.0	1,078.1	1,031.1	982.4	1,003.8
Remote	Remote North	1,412.2	1,544.0	1,429.1	1,461.9	1,234.0	1,129.9
	Calgary	670.3	651.1	686.0	737.7	697.9	716.0
	Edmonton	654.2	678.7	756.5	811.7	797.3	801.7
	Alberta	783.8	799.5	838.4	869.6	842.1	841.8

TABLE 13.10 Age Adjusted Inpatient Day Rates per 1,000 by Resident Planning Zone and Fiscal Year (All Institutions)

information is available Alberta performs better than the all-Canada measure and also compared with Ontario and British Columbia. Alberta's readmission rate for acute myocardial infarction, asthma, and prostatectomy is below the comparators, but its readmission rate for hysterectomy is above the comparators.

In summary, Alberta's higher levels of spending on health care do not yield an unequivocal benefit in terms of faster access, higher levels of satisfaction with processes of care, or better health care outcomes.

INTRAPROVINCIAL COMPARISONS

These interprovincial comparisons have a parallel in terms of differences within Alberta. Any policy response to the differences revealed between Alberta and other provinces must

Peer Group	Planning Zone	2002	2003	2004	2005	2006	2007	2008
Metro	Calgary Metro	717.5	710.4	704.8	723.2	712.5	712.7	720.6
Metro	Edmonton Metro	876.3	877.5	874.3	880.8	903.4	883.4	901.8
Metro Bedroom	Calgary Bedroom	689.8	664.7	681.3	688.2	611.1	628.5	663.3
Metro Bedroom	Edmonton Bedroom	721.0	679.3	713.3	720.5	695.1	716.0	696.7
Regional	Lethbridge	834.6	771.9	789.5	741.6	782.0	757.3	789.9
Regional	Medicine Hat	970.5	984.4	902.1	878.9	877.9	841.3	837.5
Regional	Red Deer	1,040.9	1,036.8	1,048.5	1,071.6	1,016.8	945.9	955.9
Regional	Grande Prairie	842.5	934.3	930.7	881.1	715.9	855.2	719.4
Regional	Fort McMurray	1,195.5	1,028.4	1,088.8	1,453.2	1,261.3	1,049.4	930.8
Rural	Rural South	874.6	859.1	810.8	797.5	782.3	802.3	821.0
Rural	Rural Central	1,048.3	1,047.2	1,015.6	1,031.2	1,013.6	975.9	914.8
Rural	Rural North	1,005.5	973.2	968.5	966.6	904.3	935.5	934.1
Remote	Remote North	1,185.1	1,101.4	1,032.9	1,077.8	1,095.4	1,323.3	1,119.1
	Calgary	714.4	704.9	701.1	718.7	700.1	702.0	712.7
	Edmonton	832.1	823.8	829.6	835.3	844.0	834.5	842.7
	Alberta	845.1	834.0	826.2	831.8	816.3	811.3	811.0

recognize intraprovincial differences that create different patterns of care in different parts of the province.

Table 13.10 provides information on age-gender adjusted bed day rates for hospital care, while Table 13.11 provides age-gender adjusted separation rates for hospital care. These tables provide information on the major metropolitan areas (Edmonton and Calgary), bedroom communities around those two centres, the major regional cities, rural centres, and the remote north of the province.

It can be seen that residents of Edmonton had a higher utilization rate than residents of Calgary over the period. In 2008, for example, Edmonton residents were admitted to hospital at approximately a 6% higher rate than residents of Calgary (on an age-gender standardized bases). The difference in bed utilization was even greater: Edmontonians consumed 25% more bed days than Calgarians.

All of the regional centres have a slightly higher admission rate than the metropolitan centres, but there are also differences between these regional centres. Residents of Medicine Hat, for

Peer Group	Planning Zone	1996	1997	1998	1999	2000	2001
Metro	Calgary Metro	99.3	98.4	96.5	94.6	91.4	89.3
Metro	Edmonton Metro	91.3	90.9	94.5	95.0	93.5	91.2
Metro Bedroom	Calgary Bedroom	113.8	113.0	116.2	118.8	116.4	111.1
Metro Bedroom	Edmonton Bedroom	107.2	103.4	106.6	105.3	102.4	101.7
Regional	Lethbridge	120.7	121.6	119.8	117.6	121.6	105.5
Regional	Medicine Hat	150.8	158.9	153.8	151.2	152.3	143.7
Regional	Red Deer	146.9	150.7	151.7	141.0	146.2	143.2
Regional	Grande Prairie	137.9	137.7	145.2	143.0	135.7	137.7
Regional	Fort McMurray	165.7	157.3	156.3	162.5	151.9	146.6
Rural	Rural South	168.1	166.7	166.2	166.4	159.5	153.3
Rural	Rural Central	172.0	169.7	169.3	171.5	163.3	160.1
Rural	Rural North	192.9	188.3	189.6	183.7	179.4	169.3
Remote	Remote North	262.0	255.2	250.1	223.2	224.6	213.9
	Calgary	100.5	99.6	98.2	96.8	93.7	91.4
	Edmonton	94.3	93.1	96.8	97.0	95.3	93.5
	Alberta	123.5	122.1	122.5	121.0	117.9	114.1

TABLE 13.11 Age Adjusted Separation Rates per 1,000 by Resident Planning Zone and Fiscal Year (All Institutions)

example, had a hospital admission rate in 2008 of 130 per thousand population, almost 25% higher than the 106 per thousand population rate of Lethbridge residents. The difference between the two cities was much less in terms of bed days (6%), suggesting the admission rate difference was driven by low acuity, low length of stay admissions.

Rural Alberta has a slightly higher separation rate than the regional centres, but there are also differences between the rural north and other parts of rural Alberta. The remote north also has higher utilization rates than all other parts of Alberta. There is no evidence of differences in health status (either better or worse) to explain these differences in hospital utilization rates, so the most likely explanation is different practice patterns, possibly an example of Roemer's Law.

Table 13.12 provides information about total utilization and costs for all health care use including family practice, emergency departments, and hospitals. This table uses a measure known as clinical risk groups (CRGS) that groups patients by the nature

Peer Group	Planning Zone	2002	2003	2004	2005	2006	2007	2008
Metro	Calgary Metro	90.6	91.8	91.4	92.9	90.8	88.1	85.1
Metro	Edmonton Metro	92.9	94.5	93.4	94.4	96.6	91.8	90.1
Metro Bedroom	Calgary Bedroom	109.6	109.3	105.6	106.4	101.9	97.8	96.5
Metro Bedroom	Edmonton Bedroom	103.2	101.8	102.7	103.6	98.0	95.6	91.4
Regional	Lethbridge	109.7	108.9	107.6	105.7	111.3	108.0	105.7
Regional	Medicine Hat	140.0	137.5	137.8	139.2	132.0	134.6	131.3
Regional	Red Deer	140.8	134.6	136.8	132.3	131.3	121.6	119.3
Regional	Grande Prairie	132.8	140.8	137.2	135.3			
Regional	Fort McMurray	151.0	143.2	132.8	133.8	124.4	113.1	107.3
Rural	Rural South	147.2	146.2	138.8	139.6	136.1	131.9	128.5
Rural	Rural Central	159.9	157.2	154.6	154.7	147.3	138.3	124.8
Rural	Rural North	169.6	166.5	166.1	164.0	149.2	147.1	141.8
Remote	Remote North	222.7	195.1	183.9	187.1	189.2	192.8	171.6
	Calgary	92.6	93.6	92.9	94.4	92.0	89.2	86.5
	Edmonton	95.2	96.1	95.5	96.6	96.6	92.5	90.1
	Alberta	114.4	113.9	112.6	112.9	109.1	105.3	101.2

of their health care problems over the year (Hughes et al. 2004). This allows healthy people to be separated from all other clusters. On this measure there is no evidence that Albertans are becoming healthier. Over the period 2001/02–2006/07 for example, the Albertan population increased from about 2.9 million to 3.2 million, an average annual growth rate of 1.7%. The healthy population, that is, those without either acute or chronic illnesses in any year, increased at a lower rate, 1.3%. Those with major illnesses, malignancies, and major chronic illnesses increased over twice the rate of the population as a whole. This suggests that the Albertan population is getting sicker over this period rather than healthier.

Table 13.12 also shows the direct costs associated with population in each of the health states as measured by clinical risk group. It can be seen that about 70% of the population are either healthy or had a significant acute illness in 2006–2007. However, this group of the population only accounted for around 37% of total health care costs. The remaining 30% or so of the

Health State	Calgary	Edmonton	Total	Population Proportion 2006/07	Cost Proportion 2006/07	Population Growth Rate 2001/02—2006/07
Healthy	$354	$386	$388	62.5%	30.3%	1.3%
Significant Acute	$602	$651	$660	7.6%	6.2%	0.4%
Single Minor Chronic	$807	$921	$885	10.8%	12.0%	2.3%
Multiple Minor Chronic	$1,499	$1,576	$1,595	1.6%	3.3%	2.0%
Single Dominant or Moderate Chronic	$1,395	$1,512	$1,515	13.2%	25.0%	3.3%
Pairs—Multiple Dominant and/or Moderate Chronic	$3,669	$3,832	$3,863	3.7%	17.7%	4.3%
Triples—Multiple Dominant Chronic	$10,081	$11,560	$10,518	0.2%	2.9%	4.6%
Malignancies—Metastatic, Complicated or Dominant	$4,725	$5,268	$5,293	0.2%	1.4%	5.1%
Catastrophic	$11,312	$8,959	$9,551	0.1%	1.4%	4.9%
Total	$711	$828	$802	100%	100%	1.7%

TABLE 13.12 Expenditure per Person, Alberta, by Health Utilization Cluster (Clinical Risk Groups), 2006–07

population consumed 70% of the costs, with particular concentration of costs in some groups; for example, the 3.7% of the population with "multiple dominant and/or moderate chronic illnesses" consumed almost 18% of the total costs. This confirms the Pareto 80:20 rule, which suggests that a small proportion of the population consumes a very large proportion of the costs. This analysis suggests that management of chronic disease will become increasingly important in responding to health care challenges in the future.

CONCLUSION

In summary, compared to other provinces Alberta spends more per head (after adjusting for age and gender) in terms of government expenditure on health both in total and in most areas of spending. As a result of this increased spending, more health services are provided and there is a consequent greater utilization of health care by Albertans compared to residents of other provinces. But volume effects are not the only differences: health services in Alberta are more expensive than in other provinces, in part, because of greater employment of skilled personnel and, in part, because those skilled personnel are paid more.

However, this higher level of investment does not guarantee quicker access to care, and there are only marginal differences in health outcomes between Alberta and Canada as a whole. To the extent there are differences, Albertans health outcomes are poorer than those in other provinces.

Developing a response to this pattern of higher expenditure for marginal returns is quite complex. However, it is clear that Alberta should continue to embrace strategies that directly improve health outcomes and directly contribute to improved longevity. This would be supported by reviewing the existing levels of public health expenditure to identify those areas where there may be a greater benefit in terms of outcomes for the funding invested and a greater emphasis on evaluating health care investments generally. Investing in prevention or primary care to reduce demand for hospitalization also seems warranted.

The higher level of provision of hospital care has not led to better access in terms of waiting times. This suggests a need for further review of the way in which hospitals are working, possibly through patient flow initiatives, so that the "trapped value" that must exist within hospitals can be released to improve access for Albertans. Contemporary approaches to waiting time management (central intake, common prioritization) should also be explored.

None of these initiatives though are likely to generate quick returns. Thus, just as Alberta's divergence from the rest of Canada in terms of spending occurred over a decade, strategies to position the Albertan health care system differently—so that it diverges in a positive way in terms of improved healthy life expectancy and improved access—are also likely to take some time to show appreciable benefits.

AUGUST 2011, BY STEPHEN DUCKETT

The stimulus for the analysis in this chapter was a request by the Board of Alberta Health Services for advice on Alberta's relative health spending position compared to the rest of Canada. The context of the request was the significant shift in the budget parameters imposed by the government of Alberta in 2009.

The presentation made at the 2010 "Boom and Bust Again" conference (http://www.uofaweb.ualberta.ca/ipe/pdfs/ Healthcare-Expenditures-ipe-70510.pdf) was almost identical to that presented to the board. I made the same presentation to about 20 internal and external audiences over the ensuing six months, as part an attempt to educate people about the performance reality and the need for health system change.

The analysis in this chapter shows that Alberta's performance in terms of health and health care had declined over the previous decade on almost every dimension: cost, waiting times, outcomes. This reality was very different to the public perception, which was that performance of the health system was relatively good.

Within a year of the creation of Alberta Health Services, the short-term economic environment in Alberta changed with the collapse of oil and gas prices. Prior to Alberta Health Services' creation, public health spending had grown at almost 10% per annum: these historic patterns of runaway health spending growth were seen as no longer sustainable. In addition to imposing a lower spending target (6% growth), the government indicated it expected Alberta Health Services to live within the government-determined budget.

Given that the budget parameters only became known early in that financial year, with staffing at an all-time high and generous wage increases to be absorbed, the turnaround required was great, involving savings of around $1 billion to be achieved within 12 months. The government budget announcement did not make clear to the public the extent of savings required in the health sector, undermining Alberta Health Services' legitimacy in pursuing budget reductions.

This chapter was written when I was president and chief executive officer of Alberta Health Services, so the conclusions and policy implications had to be phrased circumspectly. No longer in that position, I can now be more direct in my conclusions about appropriate policy choices.

First, the province needs to end its obsession with hospitals. The other provinces have recognized that, and their spending priorities reflect contemporary best practice in health policy: that systems need to give priority to primary care in spending and service development choices. More and more Albertans are living with chronic diseases, and the best way to respond to this is to encourage self-management and community support, which in turn needs to be supported by an enhanced primary care system.

Second, and related to the first point, is a need to invest in community care and seniors' accommodation. Over the last decade, in contrast to Alberta's priorities, other provinces invested in these areas. The result of Alberta's underinvestment is that hospital beds are occupied by people who don't need or want to be there ("alternate level of care patients"). Alberta currently has the equivalent of a whole hospital occupied by such patients, adding to the inefficiency of the system.

Third is the need for constraint in collective agreement negotiations. There have been very generous agreement settlements in the past, which contribute to the high costs of care in the province (and contribute to bidding up wage rates nationally) but don't yield commensurate dividends in recruitment, retention, or improved services for Albertans.

Finally, the incentive structures in the health system need to change, so that the pursuit of efficiency is part of the ethos of the system, alongside a concern for equity and provision of high quality care. The best way to start to introduce efficiency incentives is through activity-based funding, where the budget of a service or hospital is based on the negotiated activity expected to be performed (e.g., days of care for nursing home residents of a particular dependency level, or the number of patients treated in a hospital, adjusted for their diagnoses), paid for at a benchmark price.

The reality is that health sector performance in Alberta is poor on practically every dimension. The trajectory Alberta has been following is downward, with funding largesse in the boom times being used to paper-over poor system performance. The presentation at the "Boom and Bust Again" conference and this chapter used data from the period before the creation of Alberta Health Services to demonstrate that reality. Acknowledging the challenge before us is necessary before it can be addressed. It is my hope that Albertans will acknowledge the need for change and will accept the need to pursue all three system objectives of equity, quality, and efficiency, simultaneously.

References

Anderson, Gerard, and Peter S. Hussey. 2001. "Comparing Health System Performance in OECD Countries." *Health Affairs* 20 (3): 219–32.

Ariste, Ruolz, and Jeff Carr. 2003. "New Considerations on the Empirical Analysis of Health Expenditures in Canada: 1966–1998." Health Canada.

Baker, Lawrence, Howard Birnbaum, Jeffrey Geppert, David Mishol, and Erick Moyneur. 2003. "The Relationship between Technology Availability and Health Care Spending." *Health Affairs*, November. http://content.healthaffairs.org/cgi/content/full/hlthaff.w3.537v1/DC2.

Baumol, William J. 1967. "Macroeconomics of Unbalanced Growth: The Anatomy of Urban Crisis." *American Economic Review* 57 (3): 415–26.

———. 1993. "Health Care, Education and the Cost Disease: A Looming Crisis for Public Choice." *Public Choice* 77 (1): 17–28.

Bilgel, Firat. 2004. "The Determinants of Canadian Provincial Health Expenditures: Evidence from Dynamic Panel." In *Canadian Economics Association, 38th Annual meetings*. Ryerson University, Toronto. http://economics.ca/2004/papers/0088.pdf.

Boychuk, Gerard.W. 2002. "The Changing Political and Economic Environment of Health Care in Canada." Discussion Paper. Commission on the Future of Health Care in Canada.

Canadian Institute for Health Information. 2005. "Provincial and Territorial Government Expenditure by Age Group, Sex and Major Category: Recent and Future Growth Rates." Ottawa: CIHI.

Di Matteo, Livio. 2003. "The Income Elasticity of Health Care Spending." *The European Journal of Health Economics* 4 (1): 20–29.

———. 2004. "What Drives Provincial Health Expenditure?" *Canadian Tax Journal* 52 (4): 1102–20.

Di Matteo, Livio, and Rosanna Di Matteo. 1998. "Evidence on the Determinants of Canadian Provincial Government Health Expenditures: 1965–1991." *Journal of Health Economics* 17: 211–28.

————. 2009."The Fiscal Sustainability of Alberta's Public Health Care System." SPP Research Papers: The Health Series 2 (2). University of Calgary, School of Public Policy, April.

Esmail, Nadeem. 2009. "Waiting Your Turn: Hospital Waiting Lists in Canada." *Studies in Health Care Policy.* Vancouver: Fraser Institute.

Filmer, Deon, and Lant Pritchett. 1999. "The Impact of Public Spending on Health: Does Money Matter?" *Social Science and Medicine* 49: 1309–23.

Gerdtham, Ulf-G., and Bengt Jönsson. 2000. "International Comparisons of Health Expenditure: Theory, Data and Econometric Analysis." In *Handbook of Health Economics,* vol. 1a, edited by A.J. Culyer and J.P. Newhouse, 11–53. Amsterdam: Elsevier.

Gerdtham, U.G. et al. 1992. "An Econometric Analysis of Health Care Expenditure: A Cross-section Study of the OECD Countries." *Journal of Health Economics* 11: 63–84.

Hickey, Daniel. 2006. "Health Spending in Saskatchewan: Recent Trends, Future Options." Saskatchewan Institute of Public Policy, Scholar Series.

Hicks, Vern, Geoff Ballinger, and Terry Campbell. 2002. "Public Health and Administration in National Health Expenditures: Feasibility Study." In *National Health Expenditure Database.* Canadian Institute for Health Information.

Hughes, John S., Richard F. Averill, Jon Eisenhandler, Norbert I. Goldfield, John Muldoon, John M. Neff, and James C. Gay. 2004. "Clinical Risk Groups (CRGS): A Classification System for Risk-Adjusted Capitation-Based Payment and Health Care Management." *Medical Care* 42 (1): 81–90.

Kane, R., T. Shamliyan, C. Mueller, S. Duval, and T. Wilt. 2007. "The Association of Registered Nurse Staffing Levels and Patient Outcomes: Systematic Review and Meta-Analysis." *Medical Care* 45 (12): 1195–204.

Landon, Stuart, Melville L. McMillan, Vijay Muralidharan, and Mark Parsons. 2006. "Does Health-Care Spending Crowd out Other Provincial Government Expenditures?" *Canadian Public Policy* 32 (2): 121–41.

Lang, Thomas, Margaret Hodge, Valerie Olson, Patrick Romano, and Richard Kravitz. 2004. "Nurse–Patient Ratios: A Systematic Review on the Effects of Nurse Staffing on Patient, Nurse Employee, and Hospital Outcomes." *Journal of Nursing Administration* 34 (7–8): 326–37.

Lukes, Steven. 1974. *Power: A Radical View.* London: Macmillan Press.

McGuire, Alistair, David Parkin, David Hughes, and Karen Gerard. 1993. "Econometric Analyses of National Health Expenditures: Can Positive Economics Help to Answer Normative Questions?" *Health Economics* 2 (2): 113–26.

McMillan, Melville L. 2009. "Breaking the Myth: Alberta's Spending Is Mediocre at Best." Edmonton: Parkland Institute, University of Alberta.

Pfaff, Martin. 1990. "Differences in Health Care Spending across Countries: Statistical Evidence." *Journal of Health Politics, Policy and Law* 15 (1): 1–24.

Reinhardt, Uwe E., Peter S. Hussey, and Gerard F. Anderson. 2002. "Cross-National Comparisons of Health Systems Using OECD Data, 1999." *Health Affairs* 21 (3): 169–81.

Roemer, Milton. 1961. "Bed Supply and Hospital Utilization: A Natural Experiment." *Hospitals: Journal of the American Hospitals Association* 35: 36–42.

Shanahan, Marian, and Cecile Gousseau. 1997. "Interprovincial Comparisons of Health Care Expenditures." Manitoba Centre for Health Policy.

Slade, Eric P., and Gerard F. Anderson. 2001. "The Relationship between Per Capita Income and Diffusion of Medical Technologies." *Health Policy* 58: 1–14.

Zeithaml, Valarie A., A. Parasuraman, and Leonard L. Berry. 1990. *Delivery Quality Service: Balancing Customer Perceptions and Expectations.* New York: The Free Press.

Bradford Reid's Mission

*The Practice and
Promotion of Evidence-Based
Decision Making*

Alice O. Nakamura

INTRODUCTION

Bradford (Brad) Reid was an economist who believed in evidence-based decision making. In his own research he was not satisfied with just proffering economic theory and other conceptual arguments; he sought to provide empirical evidence based on the outcomes of real-life natural experiments. He also believed that having empirical evidence for Canada matters.

Brad would have appreciated the collection of papers that were presented at the conference held in his memory and subsequently collected here. Each paper advances evidence-based decision making in one or both of two ways: (1) as additions to the policy-relevant empirical economics literature for Canada, or (2) as helpful contributions to the cause of improving the data available for policy-relevant research and decision making in Canada.

The preceding chapters of this volume call attention to the many challenges that Alberta, in common with many other commodity-based economies, now faces. One of these challenges is the economy's dependence on the natural resource sector. A second is the continuing volatility of natural resource prices, especially including the prices of oil and gas. A third is the challenge of ensuring that taxpayers get good value for their tax dollars, which will make it easier to hold the line on spending increases. A fourth is the issue of how to respond to mounting concerns about global warming in a largely resource-based economy. And a fifth challenge concerns saving resource revenues. We begin by providing a brief overview of how the papers collected here contribute to these themes. The sheer breadth of these challenges, and the need to address them, leads us next to ask a fundamental question that was raised explicitly or implicitly in a number of these contributions: Why does evidence-based decision making *not* seem to be more the norm in Canadian public affairs?

While an answer to this question is elusive, and might justify an entire research agenda on its own, the question itself leads quite naturally to consideration of a related issue not dealt with in this collection because it erupted after the conference was held: the summer of 2010 Statistics Canada disaster. This development, considered in the context of the preceding chapters, and developments in the European Union, points toward urgently needed reforms to protect the information that Canadians in all walks of life need in order to be able to practice evidence-based decision making. Protecting Canada's data sources is an important component of helping to ensure a bright future for evidence-based decision making in Canada.

CHALLENGES FACING ALBERTA

In his contribution, John Murray, deputy governor of the Bank of Canada, explains some of the reasons why it is important for Canada to have economists, like Brad, who work (worked) on Canadian problems. Canada is different. For example, primary commodities account for about 10% of Canada's GDP, 5% of Canada's total employment, and 45% of Canada's export sales. In contrast, the United States is a large net importer of primary commodities. In this respect, the United States is similar to most other advanced economies, whereas Canada, Australia, and Norway are different. Further, within Canada, Alberta is different from most other provinces, with resources accounting for roughly 32% of Alberta's GDP in 2006. Alberta needs economic analysis and plans that take account of the special features of its economy.

Jason Brisbois, Ted Chambers, and Nicholas Emter fill in the Canadian economic and policy context using the example of Alberta. In their study, Alberta's economic performance is measured by employment variability and productivity growth across selected periods. They find mixed evidence on diversification in Alberta and conclude that, to secure further diversification, the private sector does not need government direction, but it does need the "right" set of incentives, including the absence of a sustained fossil fuel price bubble. Bev Dahlby, Mel McMillan, and Kathleen Macaspac also focus on economic diversification, which they note has long been considered a route to more stable economic performance for an economy. Their chapter compares the economic stability of Alberta with Ontario, a province considered to be better diversified than Alberta. Yet, they conclude that the degree of instability of the Alberta economy has diminished over the past 15 to 20 years, both in absolute terms and, especially, relative to Ontario. It appears that Ontario's industrial mix has not or does not provide as much protection against economic instability as it once did, while the economic instability associated with the more natural resource-based economy of Alberta has diminished since the 1970s and early 1980s.

Energy prices change substantially and unpredictably, causing large and uncertain movements in revenues from oil and gas. Hence, Alberta government revenues are considerably more volatile than the revenues of other provinces, although Alberta's own-source revenues (excluding royalty payments) are similar in volatility to those of the other provinces. Brad Humphreys and Victor Matheson explore the idea of using increased gambling revenues to reduce overall revenue volatility. They note that in many of the provinces and states where studies have been done, the variation in gambling revenue was found to have a negative correlation with variation in own-source revenues, and hence gambling revenue variation served to reduce the variation in total government revenue over time. The authors note, however, that gambling revenues tend to be small relative to other revenue sources like income taxes, which limits the capacity of variation in gambling revenues to offset downturns in total own-source revenues.

In a far-ranging empirical study, Stuart Landon and Constance Smith consider other more conventional methods to reduce the volatility of Alberta's revenues. They show that tax base diversification (via, for example, use of a retail sales tax) would be an ineffective option because Alberta's royalty revenues are too large a share of total own-source revenues. They also demonstrate that revenue smoothing using futures and options markets would probably be an overly expensive remedy and could carry significant political risks. It is often noted that the Canadian dollar tends to appreciate (depreciate) when energy prices rise (fall) and that this serves to smooth out some of the exchange rate induced movements in Alberta government revenues. However, Landon and Smith show that the effects of this remedy are too small to meet Alberta's revenue smoothing needs.

However, Landon and Smith show that a revenue savings fund *could* significantly reduce the volatility of the revenue available to pay for public services. They explain that with this type of fund, the revenue the fund contributes to the budget in any particular year would be based on revenues averaged over prior years, leading to considerably greater stability in the revenues used for paying for public programs. Thus, Landon and Smith argue for a savings fund into which the most volatile components of Alberta revenues would be directly deposited. If withdrawals from the fund were set as a fixed proportion of total fund assets and tied to the long-term earnings of the fund, there would be a considerable reduction in the volatility of government budgetary revenues. Of course, for Alberta to save more, the province must also spend less.

Increasing public demands for more health services may make it hard for Alberta to save more. Stephen Duckett, Gordon Kramer, and Liesje Sarnecki report that, in 2008, Alberta's provincial government health expenditures were more than 15% above the average per head of the other Canadian provinces. In contrast, just over ten years previously, Alberta's per capita spending on health was somewhat less than the per head average in the rest of Canada. These authors find that Alberta's currently higher level of spending is associated with higher utilization, higher unit prices, and higher factor prices. They note that, for the last decade, Alberta has consistently had more physicians and nurses and also more other health professions such as dental practitioners. Nevertheless, they do not find that Albertans have had quicker access to care, at least in the areas they considered. They also report that there are only marginal differences in health outcomes between Alberta and Canada as a whole. Moreover, to the extent there are health outcome differences, Duckett, Kramer, and Sarnecki find that the Alberta outcomes have been poorer than those in other provinces. They claim that the extensive literature that analyzes international differences in health expenditure also fails to find a relationship between health expenditure and health outcomes. Their implication seems to be that spending more on health services, by itself, in no way assures better outcomes. Their chapter points to the need for ongoing data collection, monitoring, and empirical research about the outcomes of health services expenditures in Canada. Studies of this sort would be far more powerful, of course, if researchers could access comparable data over time for each of the provinces.

In a somewhat different vein, Roger Gibbins considers the significant challenge to Alberta's economy posed by global warming. He notes that, over the long run, policy evolution will encourage an economy that uses less carbon, or at least that emits less of the by-products of using carbon. Nevertheless, he recommends that Alberta should continue to build the province's conventional resource industries. More specifically, he argues for continuing with conventional resource extraction, but in a manner that meets policy expectations in a carbon-concerned world. The strategy would be based on cleaner production of coal, gas and oil, including from the oilsands. If successful, Gibbins argues that Alberta's new technological expertise could find global markets.

Turning to the challenge of saving, Colin Busby argues that because non-renewable resources exist in fixed quantities, taking them out of the ground and selling them for cash represents a conversion of Alberta's physical wealth into financial wealth. He points out that non-renewable resources are assets that are the property of the province and argues it is in the interest of all Albertans to ensure that economic prosperity from oil and gas exploitation continues well beyond the limited life of these deposits. To this end, he argues for reforms to Alberta's fiscal framework that are designed to improve fiscal transparency and the feasibility of a long-term savings plan. He claims that, at present, the total amount of government savings is almost entirely unknown to the average Albertan, with one cause of this being the complexity of Alberta's financial accounts. Busby argues furthermore for the application of full accrual accounting measures of savings, including the value of government-owned capital assets, the main goal of which is to safeguard the delivery of government services in both good times and bad and to ensure that Alberta remains an attractive place to live and invest for future generations.

Al O'Brien observes that Alberta has been seeking a fiscal policy framework to moderate the impact of volatile resource revenues on public spending levels since at least the first global energy crisis in the mid-1970s. He argues that it is not the volatility of provincial expenditure in Alberta that is most worrisome, but rather the asymmetric form this volatility has been taking. More specifically, he is concerned that while spending has tended to track revenue increases, it has been much slower to adjust to revenue declines. Based on this, O'Brien argues that the single greatest challenge in developing and gaining necessary public support for sustainable long-term fiscal policies is to find better ways to communicate the reality of non-renewable resource receipts in the province's fiscal framework. He argues that consistent treatment of capital spending, depreciation, and operating surpluses or deficits in the province's budgets and financial reports would make a significant contribution to the simplicity and transparency of provincial fiscal planning and expenditure management.

Almost as a way of summing up a number of these saving-related issues, Robert Ascah asks why it is that we don't save more. He traces out a detailed history of Alberta's efforts to boost savings and considers the extent to which this appeared to be a government priority in different eras. As a contrast to this pre-dominately statistical analysis, Ascah turns to a more qualitative analysis of these issues based on findings from interviews and a survey of individuals who were involved directly or indirectly in decision making in Alberta, or who had a financial interest in the policy decisions around taxation, regulation, investment and spending. These shed some interesting light on the trade-offs and considerations that underlie many of the decisions and non-decisions that were made at different times. Based on his analysis, the author makes several recommendations that include placing limitations on the capacity of elected officials to enact short-term, expedient fiscal policies that are likely to have long-term, and likely undesirable, consequences for the Alberta economy.

It is interesting that many of the revenue and expenditure issues mentioned in the chapters in this volume also touch on the question of the appropriate division of revenue-generation and expenditure responsibilities between the provincial and federal levels of government, a topic that especially interested Brad.

A 2005 paper co-authored by Brad and Stuart Landon focuses on empirically determining the effect of the centralization/decentralization of government activity on economic growth, regional inequality, and household inequality. The authors note that the empirical literature that examines the relationship between decentralization and growth is tiny, especially in comparison with the importance of research of this sort.

Landon and Reid (2005) explain that the main economic argument advanced in favour of decentralized government activity has been that this can enhance the efficiency of government activity by providing market-type competition pressure on governments if voters and taxpayers can and do move in response to differences in tax levels and the provision of public goods and services by local governments. They note, however, that it is also possible that decentralized systems will be less efficient since the provision of some public goods and services is believed to be subject to economies of scale. Also, less wealthy regions will have, by definition, a poorer tax base with which to finance the provision of public goods and services as well as transfers designed to redress individual and family level inequality. Thus, the "right" degree of decentralization for government activities cannot be determined purely by theory. Lacking the sorts of data needed to investigate these issues directly for Canada, Landon and Reid use data over time for thirteen OECD countries.

THE QUESTION OF WHY EVIDENCE-BASED DECISION MAKING SEEMS NOT TO BE THE RULE

In their contribution to this volume, Herbert Emery and Ronald Kneebone note that economists have been persistent in their attempts to enlighten governments about the sorts of policy choices that are consistent with better outcomes over time given the inevitability that resource sector booms will be followed by busts. They lament that this advice has not been heeded.

According to *Wikipedia*, "Decision making can be regarded as an outcome of mental (cognitive) processes leading to the selection of a course of action among several alternatives."[1] We all see examples around us of many sorts of decision making including:

- Flipping a coin or taking a random draw,
- Prayer or astrology,
- Taking advice from someone in authority, though they have no special expertise regarding the decision to be made,
- Taking advice from an acknowledged expert,
- Accepting the first option that the available information suggests is likely to lead to the desired result,
- Choosing the option with the highest probability of success,

- Choosing the option with the highest expected monetary payoff,
- Listing and weighing all of the main advantages and disadvantages.

Only the last five of the above listed types of decision making usually are thought of as evidence-based.

It would be interesting to know if the prevalence of evidence-based decision making differs across the Canadian provinces. It would also be interesting to know if the prevalence of this sort of informed decision making has changed over recent decades in Canada. A related question that might be easier to answer empirically is whether the use of official statistics measures like the inflation rate in wage agreements and contracts and programs, differs across the provinces or has changed over time.

It would be desirable to know far more about both the prevalence and the factors that encourage evidence-based decision making. We suspect that one important factor is the availability of suitable statistical evidence. As explained in the following section, Canada has just embarked on a reduction in the availability of high quality statistical information that could prove useful as a natural experiment for investigating how data quality and availability affect evidence-based decision making and the empirical research on which that sort of decision making tends to depend.

A POST-CONFERENCE STEP BACKWARD

The chapters in this collection make the point, repeatedly, that evidence-based decision making is hampered when there is a lack of relevant and reliable information. The census of population is one of the few sources of data in Canada that provides information on local jurisdictions. These data have been of special value for understanding the economic conditions in different parts of a large and highly varied province like Alberta.

One of the regular duties of Statistics Canada has been to carry out population censuses. Since Confederation, Canada has had a mandatory census with questions on religion, ethnic background, occupation, school attendance, literacy, infirmities, and much else (Dillon 2010; Veall 2010). Many of these questions were on the long-form census that, since 1971, had gone to 20% of households. The remaining 80% of the households received the short-form census, which has just basic questions on age, sex, marital status, family relationships, and mother tongue.

However, in June of 2010, six weeks before the forms were to go to the printer, the Harper government announced—without public consultation—that in 2011 the census would consist of only the short form, which would go to all households. The previously mandatory long form would be eliminated and replaced by the voluntary National Household Survey (NHS). The government has argued that the data will continue to be of high quality with less state coercion. Yet, this is not what experience to date leads experts to expect. When this decision was taken, Canada's Chief Statistician Munir Sheikh scarified his career and resigned. The previous chief statistician Ivan Fellegi informed Canadians, "The change means we will spend upwards of $100 million to gather unusable data."[2]

As David A. Green and Kevin Milligan (2010) explain, the long-form census plays a vital role in the Canadian statistical system. Take the example of the Labour Force Survey (LFS). The LFS is a monthly survey used to obtain key information for constructing unemployment, employment, and participation rates. It is the basis for all the unemployment rate statistics reported by Statistics Canada, which makes it the basis for many policy considerations. For example, the unemployment rates constructed from it are also used at the regional level as part of calculating eligibility for Employment Insurance. Beyond its direct uses, the LFS is made even more important because it is used as a starting point for a large proportion of voluntary surveys conducted by Statistics Canada.

The creation of the LFS sample starts with choosing a sampling frame. A stratified sampling design is used, which means that the survey designers first cut up Canada into strata or geographically and demographically defined groups. Clusters within each stratum are then chosen, and random dwellings within these chosen clusters are contacted. Both the definition of the strata and clusters and the sampling rates within clusters are determined using data from the most recent census. Beyond the stratification, once survey responses are collected, a further correction for non-response bias is made. Households are effectively sorted into groups by certain demographic characteristics. The proportion of responders in these groups is compared to a benchmark, and corrections are calculated so that the responses from the survey can reflect the whole population.

Without the census, both the stratification and weighting stages of all other household surveys will be affected. For the LFS this will mean inferior statistics on unemployment and employment. Privately collected (e.g., by polling firms) surveys must also be compared to some standard to ensure they are providing unbiased statistics. To ensure the quality of these surveys, the mandatory census short and long forms are important. Thus, tampering with the census has impacts on a long list of other data in Canada. It will have negative impacts on the many economic decisions based on statistics (e.g., whether and where to establish a new store).

In an open letter in September 2010, Mel Cappe (clerk of Privy Council, 1999–2002), David Dodge (governor of the Bank of Canada, 2001–2008), Ivan Fellegi (chief statistician, 1985–2008), and Alex Himelfarb (clerk of Privy Council, 2002–2006) called for a reaffirmation of the UN Fundamental Principles of Official Statistics, including the principle that the chief statistician is responsible for issues of methodology and technique of data collection and production.[3]

Two issues are raised. One is that ordering the chief statistician to make this change when his disagreement is clear now (given his resignation) contravenes the UN Fundamental Principles of Official Statistics, including the principle that the chief statistician is responsible for issues of methodology and technique of data collection and production. A second is that there are multiple important reasons why the census long form is an essential part of how Statistics Canada has been producing high quality official statistics, and there is no credible plan (yet, at least) for how an acceptable level of quality can be maintained without a mandatory long-form census being reinstated.

Statistics Canada was previously internationally recognized as one of the best statistical agencies in the world in part because of its former de facto arm's length independence from the sorts of political influence that destroy the credibility of official statistics whether or not actual tampering with the data occurs. According to the UN Statistical Commission (2004), as paraphrased by Thompson (2010),

> Objective, reliable and accessible official statistics give people and organizations, nationally and internationally, confidence in the integrity of government and public decision making on the economic, social and environmental situation within a country....Compilation and release of data should be free from political interference, so as to ensure impartiality of the national statistical office.

Canada once met those standards, but no longer does.

Canada and the European Union (EU) have moved in opposite directions where official statistics are concerned. In 2000, the EU launched its famous Lisbon Strategy, with the stated goal of catching up with the United States and other global competitors. In order to monitor the progress of the Lisbon Strategy, a new working methodology was developed—the so-called Open Method of Coordination (OMC). As part of the OMC initiative, the EU countries agreed on new, higher standards of independence and professional conduct for their national statistics institutes, and for Eurostat, which is the overarching official statistics organization for the EU. A main element in the OMC is to learn from best and worst practices.

CONCLUSION

Brad Reid practiced and promoted evidence-based decision making, and his published papers continue to help others make choices based on careful empirical evidence and continue to inspire other researchers and students to produce more research of this sort.[4] He would have been delighted by the papers in the "Boom and Bust Again" conference and this volume. The contributions practice the tough love ways of evidence-based decision making. These are also works that could not exist without authors who believe passionately that Canada matters, and who devoted their careers to learning about Canada.

And Brad would surely have been saddened by the fate that has befallen Statistics Canada since the "Boom and Bust Again" conference was held. Hopefully, however, others will soon find ways to right this situation. Hopefully, Statistics Canada's present problems will prove to be a short-run aberration, and high quality official statistics and evidence-based decision making will turn out to be Canada's long-run destiny.

Author's Note

This paper was inspired and informed by presentations at the conference titled "Boom and Bust Again: Policy Challenges for a Commodity-Based Economy" that was held in honour of Bradford G. Reid on May 6–7, 2010 in Edmonton, Alberta, Canada. References are to chapters that appear in this volume. Big thanks are due to David Ryan for his insightful and very helpful input on this chapter, on the volume, and on the conference. David's efforts were a tremendous tribute to Brad. Actions will always speak loader than words, and especially so with Brad, since he was an action sort of person.

Notes

1. *Wikipedia*, s.v. "Decision making," accessed January 21, 2011, http://en.wikipedia.org/wiki/Decision_making.
2. This was one of five ill effects of the change described by Fellegi in a CBC Radio interview on July 14, 2010. For details, see http://contrarian.ca/2010/07/15/harpers-reformers-vandalize-the-census/ and http://www.cbc.ca/thecurrent/2010/07/july-14-2010.html.
3. The full letter, dated September 9, 2010, which includes excerpts from the *United Nations Fundamental Principles of Official Statistics* can be found at http://www.savestatcan.ca/pdf/Letter%20to%20the%20Prime%20Minister%20from%20Cappe,Dodge,Fellegi,Himelfarb.pdf.
4. See the detailed listing of Brad's publications in Chapter 2 of this volume.

References

Dillon, Lisa. 2010. "The Value of the Long Form Canadian Census for Long Term National and International Research." *Canadian Public Policy* 36 (3): 389–93.

Green, David A., and Kevin Milligan. 2010. "The Importance of the Long Form Census to Canada." *Canadian Public Policy* 36 (3): 383–88.

Landon, Stuart, and Bradford G. Reid. 2005. "The Impact of the Centralization of Revenues and Expenditures on Growth, Regional Inequality and Inequality." Working Paper 2005(4), Institute of Intergovernmental Relations, Queen's University.

Thompson, Debra. 2010. "The Politics of the Census: Lessons from Abroad." *Canadian Public Policy* 36 (3): 377–82.

United Nations, Economic and Social Council, Statistical Commission. 2004. "Implementation of the Fundamental Principles of Official Statistics." Report of the Secretary-General, 35th session, 2–5 March. Accessed 28 October 2012. http://unstats.un.org/unsd/statcom/doc04/2004-21e.pdf.

Veall, Michael R. 2010. "2B or not 2B? What Should Have Happened with the Canadian Long Form Census? What Should Happen Now?" *Canadian Public Policy* 36 (3): 395–99.

Contributors

Robert L. Ascah holds degrees in commerce and public administration (MA) from Carleton University. He completed his doctorate in political science at the University of Alberta in 1984. Before his appointment as director of the Institute for Public Economics, he worked for the Alberta public service, and, in 1996, he joined Alberta Treasury Branches. In 1999, Ascah's PHD dissertation *Politics and Public Debt: The Dominion, the Banks and Alberta's Social Credit* was published.

Jason Brisbois (MBA, Memorial University, Newfoundland) is director of the Western Centre for Economic Research (WCER), University of Alberta. He had a 26-year career in public sector finance and economics, with positions in several provinces. Prior to joining the WCER, he was chief economist of Western Economic Diversification, Canada where he commissioned and conducted research on the western Canadian economy.

Colin Busby is a senior policy analyst with the C.D. Howe Institute in Toronto. While writing broadly on economic issues, his emphasis is on fiscal and social policy with a concentration on demographic and labour market concerns. Colin holds a BCOMM from the University of Alberta and an MA in economics from the University of Ottawa.

Edward J. (Ted) Chambers (PHD Economics, University of Nebraska) was dean of the University of Alberta Faculty of Business from 1969 to 1976, then director of the Western Centre for Economic Research from 1989 to 2001. He has published extensively in the fields of business fluctuations and regional economics. His present research interests are primarily in western Canada's economic position in the international economy and the role of small business in western Canada.

Bev Dahlby is the distinguished fellow in tax and economic growth at the School of Public Policy and professor of economics at the University of Calgary. He has published extensively on tax policy and fiscal federalism and has served as a policy advisor to the federal and provincial governments, the IMF, and the World Bank. In 2010–2011, he was a member of the Jenkins Panel on federal support for research and development.

Stephen Duckett is a professor in the School of Public Health at the University of Alberta and director of the Health Program at the Grattan Institute in Melbourne, Australia. During 2009–2010, he was the foundation president and chief executive officer of Alberta Health Services, Canada's largest provider of health care. Professor Duckett is an economist with a master's and PHD in health administration from the University of New South Wales. He is a fellow of the Academy of the Social Sciences in Australia.

J.C. Herbert Emery has a PHD in economics from the University of British Columbia and is a professor in the Department of Economics at the University of Calgary. He has published work on the long-run development of Canada, Alberta, and Saskatchewan with a focus on the role of natural resource exports.

Nicholas Emter (BA Honours Economics, University of Alberta) is a research assistant at the Western Centre for Economic Research. Currently studying law, he has undertaken many projects on the western Canadian economy and Alberta exports.

Roger Gibbins was president and CEO of the Canada West Foundation from 1998 until his retirement in May 2012. He is professor emeritus of political science at the University of Calgary, where he started his academic career in 1973. Roger has authored, co-authored, or edited 22 books and more than 140 articles and book chapters, most dealing with western Canadian themes and issues. In 1998, he was elected a fellow of the Royal Society of Canada. In 2007, he was awarded the Alberta Lieutenant Governor's Award for Exceptional Achievement, Distinctive Leadership and Outstanding Contribution to Public Administration, and, in 2010, he received an honorary doctorate from the University of Northern British Columbia. He currently lives in Calgary where he remains actively involved in Canadian public policy debates.

Brad R. Humphreys is a professor in the Department of Economics at the University of Alberta where he holds the chair in the economics of gambling and serves as associate chair (graduate program). Before joining the University of Alberta in 2007, he was on the faculty at the University of Illinois at Urbana–Champaign. He holds a PHD in economics from the Johns Hopkins University. His research on the economics of participation in physical activity and exercise, the gambling, economics, and financing of professional sports, and the economics of higher education has been published in various academic journals. In July 2011, he became editor-in-chief of *Contemporary Economic Policy*.

Ronald Kneebone is a professor of economics and director of economic and social policy in the School of Public Policy, both at the University of Calgary. His published research has dealt with issues pertaining to the political economy of government deficit and debt reduction, the history of government fiscal and monetary relations in Canada, and the characteristics of Canadian federal, provincial, and municipal fiscal policy choices.

Gordon Kramer is the executive director of patient/care-based funding for Alberta Health Services, the sole public health care region in Alberta, Canada. With a master's degree in health services administration, he has held a number of positions dealing with quality assurance, utilization analysis, and funding allocation in Alberta. He currently leads a team of economists and data analysts who are developing funding allocation methodologies and forecasting models for the province.

Stuart Landon is professor of economics at the University of Alberta. His current research interests are in the areas of fiscal rules, interest rate determination, and macroeconomic policy. He has published academic papers in Canadian, US, European, and Australian economics journals on a wide variety of topics and received the 2006 John Vanderkamp prize (along with three co-authors) for a paper on health spending in *Canadian Public Policy*.

Kathleen Macaspac is an economist with the health economics and forecasting group at Alberta Health. Prior to joining the department in 2010, Kathleen worked as an economist in Alberta Finance where she prepared economic analyses and macroeconomic forecasts for the provincial budget. Kathleen holds an MA in economics from the University of Alberta and BSC in applied economics from De La Salle University in Manila, Philippines. She lives in Edmonton with her husband and daughter.

Victor A. Matheson is an associate professor in the Department of Economics at the College of the Holy Cross in Worcester, Massachusetts. He earned his PHD in economics from the University of Minnesota. He is the author of over a dozen journal articles or book chapters focusing on the economics of lotteries and gaming and has testified before the Illinois State Legislature regarding the government revenue impact of riverboat casinos. He would not be opposed to winning Canada's Lotto Max.

Melville McMillan is professor emeritus in the Department of Economics at the University of Alberta where he has been a faculty member since 1975. His BA and MSC are from the University of Alberta and his PHD (1973) is from Cornell University. He remains active academically with a post-retirement appointment in the department and as a member of the Institute for Public Economics.

John D. Murray was appointed deputy governor of the Bank of Canada in January 2008. In this capacity, he is one of two deputy governors responsible for overseeing the Bank's analysis of domestic and international economic developments in support of monetary policy decisions. As a member of the Governing Council, he shares responsibility for decisions with respect to monetary policy and financial system stability and for setting the strategic direction of the Bank.

Alice O. Nakamura is a professor with the University of Alberta School of Business. She holds a PHD in economics from the Johns Hopkins University and a BS in economics from the University of Wisconsin at Madison. She has also received an honorary doctorate of law from the University of Western Ontario. She has published extensively in the areas of price and productivity measurement, labour economics, econometric methodology, and social policy, and she has served on many federal government advisory committees in Canada. She has been an external researcher with the Philadelphia Federal Reserve Bank since 2005 and on the board of the International Association of Research on Income and Wealth since 2009.

Al O'Brien retired as deputy provincial treasurer of the Province of Alberta in May 1999 after a 35-year career in the Alberta Public Service. He received his honours degree in economics from the University of Alberta in 1964, his master's degree in 1969, and an honorary LLD in 2007. Al is a fellow of the Institute for Public Economics, a senior fellow of the C.D. Howe Institute, and a member of the Order of Canada. He chaired the expert panel on equalization and territorial formula financing, which reported to the federal minister of finance in June 2006.

David L. Ryan is a professor in the Department of Economics at the University of Alberta, where he specializes in applied econometrics. He joined the university after completing a PHD in economics at the University of British Columbia in 1983, following previous degrees in economics at Monash University in Australia. From 2002 to 2012 he was also the director of CBEEDAC, the Canadian Building Energy End-Use Data and Analysis Centre in Edmonton. His recent research interests, which are predominantly quantitative in nature, focus on issues concerning energy economics.

Liesje Sarnecki currently specializes in analyzing health care expenditure, utilization, and methods of performance measurement in her work as a senior analyst with Alberta Health Services, an organization responsible for the delivery of health services to people living in Alberta. Liesje is a master's student at the University of Alberta, Department of Economics. In her spare time, she enjoys exploring her creative side through photography and graphic art.

Constance Smith is a professor in the Department of Economics at the University of Alberta. Previous appointments include economist in the Research Department at the Bank of Canada, visiting fellow at the Australian National University, visiting scholar at the Victoria University of Wellington, and acting director of the Institute for United States Policy Studies at the University of Alberta.

Institute for Public Economics

The Institute for Public Economics (IPE) was formed in the fall of 1996 to promote research and teaching in public economics—the study of the public sector and its influence on the economy and society. The goal of the institute is to enhance understanding of public policy issues by conducting and disseminating research results through publications, conferences, and teaching. The institute supports research in all areas of public economics including theory, applied, and policy research. Institute-sponsored research is critical, unbiased, openly disseminated, and independent of outside influences.

The IPE is housed in the Department of Economics at the University of Alberta, which contains Canada's largest group of active researchers in the field of public economics. Most IPE fellows are members of the Department of Economics, but some fellows are members of other universities, in government, or with international agencies.

Many IPE fellows enjoy international reputations and regularly provide policy advice to municipal, provincial, and federal governments, as well as international agencies such as the IMF and the World Bank.

Index

Aalborg, Anders, 193n10
Alberta
  changes to industrial mix in,
    88–96
  economic instability of, 72–82,
    97–98, 337
  evidence of boom-and-bust
    cycles in, 228–33, 238–41
  and global warming, 133–34,
    137–38, 148n1
  manufacturing in, 122, 124, 146
  portfolio analysis of
    employment stability in,
    121–29
  productivity in, 128–29, 208
  renewable resource potential of,
    136–37
  sources of output instability in,
    82–88

strategic economic options for,
    138–48.
  See also boom-and-bust cycles;
    natural resource revenues
Alberta, Government of
  attempts to ameliorate boom-
    and-bust cycles by, 285,
    287–95
  budget process measures,
    289–93
  expenditures during boom-and-
    bust cycles, 41–42, 48–49,
    106, 176, 181, 185, 286–87,
    310, 340–41
  and intergovernmental relations,
    164, 181–82, 189, 194n17
  investment in knowledge-based
    economy, 139–40
  investment in technology, 141,
    146–47

obstacles to saving resource revenue by, 184–88, 189–90, 341
pension fund costs, 209
policies of diversification of,
107–13, 130
policy recommendations for
curbing spending, 190–92,
194n22
reasons for lack of saving plan
by, 200–01
recommendations for long-term
fiscal budgeting, 295–98
record of expenditures by, 51–54,
152–78
record of saving by, 55–56,
152–56
revenue from royalties, 49–51,
57n5
savings initiatives presented to,
195n28, 195n33, 196n39
statutes to stabilize spending by,
287–89
suggested changes to fiscal
reports, 203–07
suggested long-term fiscal plan
for, 202, 207–21
and term limits, 190–91
use of savings fund to offset
boom-and-bust cycles,
254–57, 258
view of tax revenue, 162, 173, 187,
190.
See also Alberta Heritage
Savings Trust Fund (AHSTF);
health care; natural resource
revenues; and under specific
premiers' names
Alberta Cancer Prevention Legacy
Fund, 177
Alberta Economic Development
Authority (AEDA), 110–11
Alberta Energy Company, 166
Alberta Heritage Foundation for
Medical Research, 141
Alberta Heritage Savings Trust
Fund (AHSTF)
and Capital Projects Division,
169, 287, 288

cutting back on, 182–84, 193n6
Getty government management
of, 55, 170–71, 194n23
and intergovernmental
relations, 181–82, 194n17
Klein government management
of, 157, 174–75, 176, 177
Lougheed government
management of, 55, 163–69,
188–89, 194n15, 286
quote from the Alberta Heritage
Savings Trust Fund Act,
151–52
symbolism of, 188–89
value of, 55–56, 58n9
Alberta Housing Corporation, 170
alternative energy, 130–31, 136–37
Asia, 36, 117–19, 143–44

Balanced Budget and Debt
Retirement Act (BBDRA), 287
Bank of Canada commodity price
index (BCPI), 37
Baumol, William, 316–17
boom-and-bust cycles
Alberta government attempts to
ameliorate, 285, 287–93
in Australia, 114, 116–17
Canada's reaction to, 31–33,
34–35
cause of, in Alberta, 232–37
comparison of Alberta savings
and expenditures in, 152–56
comparison of Alberta with
other provinces, 125, 228–32,
337
consequences of, 27–31, 227–28
diversification as offset for,
105–07, 241–42, 245, 257–58,
338
effect on private sector, 33, 107,
185, 227, 228
experience of, 1–2
evidence of, in Alberta, 228–33,
238–41
forecast of future, 35–37
long-term fiscal plan as buffer
to, 202

methods to offset impact of, 226, 241–58, 262n43
of 1980s, 2, 41–42
persistence and unpredictability of, 239–41
positive results from, 294–95
relation to economic growth, 43–49, 57n1
and royalties, 40, 43, 49, 232–37, 242
and spending resource revenues, 41–42, 48–49, 106, 176, 181, 185, 286–87, 310, 340–41
of 2008, 39, 42
use of gambling revenue to offset, 268, 270–72, 283, 337–38
use of savings fund to offset, 254–57, 258
British Columbia, 145

Canada, Government of
and commodity boom of 1970s, 31–32, 337
and equalization, 182
and Alberta Heritage Savings Trust Fund, 164, 181–82
investment in technology, 141
and National Policy, 134–35, 148n3
reaction to boom-and-bust cycles, 31–33, 34–35, 337
and Statistics Canada controversy, 336, 343–46, 347
and tax structure, 163
and 2008 financial collapse, 34–35
Canada West Foundation, 195n33
capital budgeting, 181, 291–93. See also infrastructure spending
Capital Projects Division (CPD), 169, 287, 288
Cappe, Mel, 345
Chambers, Edward J., 40, 43–46, 67
climate change, 131. See also global warming

Collins, A.F., 187, 194n15
commodity-based economies
and attraction of diversification, 105–06
and Australia's diversification policy, 114–17
curse of, 25–27
effect of booms on, 31–32
effect of price volatility on, 27–31
future of, in Canada, 135–36
and Malaysia's diversification policy, 117–19
passive responses to global warming, 137–38
strategic future options for, 138–48. See also Alberta, Government of
commodity curse, 25–27
Crown corporations, 164–69, 170

debt
Alberta statutes passed to eliminate, 287–88
Klein government and, 173–74, 175, 176, 177, 185
Lougheed government and, 169
public support for paying off, 186, 194n25
Social Credit attitude towards, 162
Stelmach government and, 177, 179
decentralization, 341–42
Decore, Laurence, 172
Deficit Elimination Act (DEA), 287–88, 290
Dinning, Jim, 175
diversification
Alberta government's policy history of, 107–13, 130
as alternative to boom-and-bust cycles, 105–07, 241–42, 245, 257–58, 338
analysis of economic instability in Alberta/Ontario, 72–82, 97–98, 337
Australia's attempt at, 114–17

and changes to industrial mix in
    Alberta/Ontario, 88–96
and global warming, 134
link to stability, 60–61, 62–63
Malaysia's policy of, 117–19
and portfolio analysis of
    employment in Alberta,
    121–25
and portfolio variance approach,
    65–72
private sector role in, 108–09,
    110, 112, 129–31
pros and cons of, 59–60
relation to economic growth,
    126–29, 337
shortcomings of studies on,
    119–21
and sources of output instability
    in Alberta/Ontario, 82–88
strategic options for, 138–48
through gambling revenue, 244,
    245
Dodge, David, 345
Dutch Disease, 62

economic growth
    and decentralization, 341–42
    and diversification, 62–63
    relation to employment growth,
        126–29, 337
    and resource booms, 43–49,
        57n1
    and specialization, 60–62
economic stability/instability
    analysis of Alberta/Ontario,
        72–82, 97–98, 337
    changes to industrial mix in
        Alberta and Ontario, 88–96
    link to diversification, 60–61,
        62–63
    of manufacturing sector,
        67–69, 82–83
    measures of, 63–65
    of oil and gas sector, 82–83, 89,
        92, 94, 95, 97, 98
    portfolio analysis of, 121–29
    and portfolio variance approach,
        65–72

sources of, 82–88
Ecuador, 251
education, 139, 177
emergency spending, 176, 184
emerging market economies
    (EMES), 36
employment, 66–67, 74–75, 114,
    121–29, 337
equalization, 182
European Union (EU), 346
evidence-based decision making,
    335, 341–47
exchange rate movements, 245–48,
    257, 261n26, 338

Fellegi, Ivan, 344, 345
financial collapse (2008), 34–35, 135
Financial Management
    Commission, 176
Financial Responsibility Act (FRA),
    287, 288
Florida, Richard, 138–40
futures curves, 35–36
futures markets, 248–50, 261n29

gambling
    and diversification of revenue,
        244, 245
    economics of taxes on, 270–73
    history of, 268–70
    to offset boom-and-bust cycles,
        268, 270–72, 283, 337–38
    profits from, 260n22, 273–77
    relation to other revenue,
        277–82
    US take from, 267, 275–77,
        281–82
gasoline taxes, 244, 245
Gateway pipeline, 143
Gerhart, Clarence, 158–60, 193n11
Getty government, 109, 170–72,
    194n22, 286
global warming
    as challenge to Alberta
        economy, 131, 133–34, 137–38,
        148n1
    future strategies for, 138–48,
        339–40

Gordon, Donald F., 40, 43–46

Harcourt, Vernon, 159
Harper government, 344
Hartwick Rule, 46
health care
  access to and quality of, 295,
    319–24, 329, 339
  Alberta spending compared to
    other provinces, 301, 304–07,
    328–29, 339
  breakdown of spending on,
    307–10
  intraprovincial comparisons of,
    324–28
  studies on, 302–03
  suggestions for improvement to,
    220, 328–32
  trends in unit costs of, 310–19
hedging programs, 248–54, 257,
  261n27, 261n31, 262n40,
  262n43
Himelfarb, Alex, 345
Hinman, E.W., 159, 161, 162
Hyndman, Lou, 167–68

inflation, 31–32, 34–35, 175, 228, 247
infrastructure spending
  and capital budgeting, 181,
    291–93
  Capital Projects Division, 169,
    287, 288
  on health care, 309–10
  and Alberta Heritage Savings
    Trust Fund, 169, 288
  Klein government and, 176, 177,
    184, 195n28
  Lougheed government and,
    187–88, 193n9
interprovincial trade barriers, 33
investment income, 53, 167, 183,
  244, 260n20
Investment Operations Committee,
  175

Kessler, Gordon, 181
Klein government
  diversification policies of, 110–11

management of natural resource
  revenue, 157, 172–78, 184, 185,
  194n25, 195n28, 286–87
  and public spending, 42, 52,
    53–54, 189, 194n24, 196n41,
    290
knowledge-based economies,
  138–40

long-form census dispute, 336,
  343–45, 347
Lottery Fund, 194n21
Lougheed government
  and diversification policy,
    107–09
  and Alberta Heritage Savings
    Trust Fund, 55, 163–69,
    188–89, 194n15, 286
  and infrastructure spending,
    187–88, 193n9
  and intergovernmental
    relations, 164, 181–82, 189
  management of natural
    resources revenue, 163–69,
    286

Malaysia, 117–19
Manning government, 157–62,
  193n10
manufacturing sector
  in Alberta diversification, 122,
    124, 146
  difficult times for, 135–36
  instability of, 67–69, 82–83
  and National Policy, 134–35
  output shares of, 91, 92–94
  and overseas diversification,
    114–18
  variance effect of, 94–98
McClellan, Shirley, 177
Mexico, 251, 252–53
Miller, Fank, 189

nanotechnology, 141
National Policy, 134–35, 148n3
natural resource revenues
  Canada's reliance on, 24–25
  depletion of, 20, 180–81

long-term fiscal plan for, 202,
207–21, 340
makeup of, 221n1
management under Getty,
170–72, 286
management under Klein, 157,
172–78, 184, 185, 194n25,
195n28, 286–87
management under Lougheed,
55, 163–69, 188–89, 286
management under Manning,
156–62
management under Stelmach,
179, 287
obstacles to saving, 184–88,
189–90, 341
and persistance of boom-and-
bust cycles, 239–41
public consultation on, 180, 186,
195n35
saving of, 147, 152–56, 185–86,
191–92, 195n28, 262n43
as source of boom-and-bust
cycles in Alberta, 232–37
spending during boom-and-bust
cycles, 41–42, 48–49, 106,
176, 181, 185, 286–87, 310,
341–42
and suggested changes to fiscal
reports, 203–07, 340
used to close budget gap, 52–54.
See also Alberta, Government of;
and *under specific premiers'
names*
net budgeting, 290–91
Nicol, Ken, 195n28
non-renewable resources, 133–34,
140–47, 148n2
Northern Gateway pipeline, 143

oil and gas sector
and economic instability, 82–83,
89, 92, 94, 95, 97, 98
role in diversification, 129–31
oilsands, 180–81, 218
Ontario
and Alberta oil, 42

analysis of economic instability
of, 72–82, 97–98, 337
changes to industrial mix in,
88–96
and Alberta Heritage Savings
Trust Fund, 194n17
sources of output instability in,
82–88

payroll taxes, 244, 245, 260n21
pension plans, 209, 220, 222n8
portfolio variance framework,
65–72, 82–88, 121–25
private sector
and Alberta government
diversification policy,
108–09, 110, 112, 130
effect of boom-and-bust cycles
on, 33, 107, 185, 227, 228
and Klein spending cuts, 173
and Lougheed government
policy, 187
and Social Credit, 161–62, 187
view of spending resource revenue, 181
and volatility of corporate tax
revenue, 238–39, 242, 243
privatization, 115, 171
productivity, 128–29, 208
program budgeting, 289–90
public consultation
on Alberta government
diversification policy, 109,
110–11
and approval of long-term fiscal
plan, 218–19, 220, 295
and disposal of natural resource
revenue, 180, 186, 195n35
on government saving, 184, 186,
200
Klein government and, 174,
194n25, 290
and referenda on fiscal savings,
191–92
put options, 248, 250–54, 261n33

Redford government, 189
Reform Party, 172

Reid, Bradford
background of, 3, 15–17
decentralization study of,
341–42
and evidence-based decision
making, 335, 346–47
publications of, 17–19, 21–22
range of economic interests of,
19–21
renewable energy, 130–31, 136–37
resource rents, 40, 43, 49, 57n4,
157–58, 181. *See also* royalties
resource revenues. *See* natural
resource revenues
retail sales tax, 242–43, 257–58, 338
Roemer, Milton, 311
royalties
Alberta government's record on,
49–51, 57n5
and boom-and-bust cycles, 40,
43, 49, 232–37, 242.
See also resource rents

sales taxes, 242–43, 257–58, 338
Saskatchewan, 69, 142, 280
savings
comparison to expenditures
in boom-and-bust cycles,
152–56
initiatives on, presented to
Alberta Government,
195n28, 195n33, 196n39
of natural resource revenue,
147, 152–56, 185–86, 191–92,
195n28, 262n43
obstacles to, for Government of
Alberta, 184–88, 189–90, 341
public consultation on, 184, 186,
191–92, 200
reasons for lack of, by
Government of Alberta,
200–01
record of, by Government of
Alberta, 55–56, 152–56
use of to offset boom-and-bust
cycles, 254–57, 258

savings funds, 254–56, 338. *See also*
Alberta Heritage Savings
Trust Fund (AHSTF)
Sheikh, Munir, 344
specialization, 60–62, 63
Spending Control Act, 194n22, 285,
288–89
Statistics Canada, 336, 343–46, 347
Stelmach government
diversification policies of, 111–12
management of natural resource
revenue, 177, 179, 287
and public spending, 42, 189,
201
Sustainability Fund, 176
Syncrude, 148n2, 166

Taft, Kevin, 195n35, 196n39
taxes/tax revenues
Alberta government view of,
162, 173, 187, 190
corporate, 163, 238–39, 242, 243
definition of tax revenue, 57n6
economics of gambling taxes,
270–73
gasoline, 244, 245
payroll, 244, 245, 260n21
sales taxes, 242–43, 257–58, 338
used to cover spending, 51, 54
used to lessen boom-and-bust
cycles, 242–45
volatility of, 233, 238–39
trade liberalization, 33, 96, 115–16
Tuer, David, 176
2008 financial collapse, 34–35, 135

United States, 143, 267, 268–70,
275–77, 281–82

value-added exports, 142–43, 144
Vencap Equities, 168

Western Canada Concept, 181
Williams Report, 172

Will the Real Alberta Please Stand Up?
Geo Takach
456 pages | 20 B&W photographs, map, notes,
selected bibliography
978-0-88864-543-2 | $34.95 (T) paper
Alberta/History/Cultural Studies

Retiring the Crow Rate
A Narrative of Political Management
Arthur Kroeger
John Fraser, Afterword
280 pages • 20 B&W photographs, map, charts,
notes, bibliography, index
978-0-88864-513-5 | $34.95 (T) paper
Political Science/Agriculture/Memoir

Politics and Public Debt
*The Dominion, the Banks and
Alberta's Social Credit*
Robert Ascah
216 pages • appendices, notes, bibliography,
index
978-0-88864-306-3 | $29.95 (T) paper
Politics/Debt